POLAND'S CONSTITUTIONAL BREAKDOWN

OXFORD COMPARATIVE CONSTITUTIONALISM

Series Editors
Richard Albert, William Stamps Farish Professor of Law,
The University of Texas at Austin School of Law
Robert Schütze, Professor of European and Global Law,
Durham University and College of Europe

Comparative constitutional law has a long and distinguished history in intellectual
thought and in the construction of public law. As political actors and the people
who create or modify their constitutional orders, they often wish to learn from the
experience and learning of others. This cross-fertilization and mutual interaction
has only accelerated with the onset of globalization, which has transformed the
world into an interconnected web that facilitates dialogue and linkages across
international and regional structures. Oxford Comparative Constitutionalism
seeks to publish scholarship of the highest quality in constitutional law that deepens
our knowledge of local, national, regional, and global phenomena through the lens
of comparative public law.

Advisory Board
Denis Baranger, Professor of Public Law, Université Paris II Panthéon-Assas
Wen-Chen Chang, Professor of Law, National Taiwan University
Roberto Gargarella, Professor of Law, Universidad Torcuato di Tella
Vicki C. Jackson, Thurgood Marshall Professor of Constitutional Law,
Harvard Law School
Christoph Möllers, Professor of Public Law and Jurisprudence,
Humboldt-Universität zu Berlin
Cheryl Saunders A.O., Laureate Professor Emeritus, Melbourne Law School

Poland's Constitutional Breakdown

WOJCIECH SADURSKI

OXFORD
UNIVERSITY PRESS

OXFORD

UNIVERSITY PRESS

Great Clarendon Street, Oxford, OX2 6DP,
United Kingdom

Oxford University Press is a department of the University of Oxford.
It furthers the University's objective of excellence in research, scholarship,
and education by publishing worldwide. Oxford is a registered trade mark of
Oxford University Press in the UK and in certain other countries

First Edition published in 2019

Impression: 2

Published in the United States of America by Oxford University Press
198 Madison Avenue, New York, NY 10016, United States of America

British Library Cataloguing in Publication Data
Data available

Library of Congress Control Number: 2018967781

ISBN 978-0-19-884050-3

Printed and bound by
CPI Group (UK) Ltd, Croydon, CR0 4YY

Preface

In March 2018 an Irish court handed down a judgment in a case which, on the face of it, was simple, easy, and routine: a suspected drug trafficker, a national of another European Union (EU) country, was sought by his country of citizenship under the European Arrest Warrant (EAW) system. All procedures had been correctly followed: the identity of Mr Artur Celmer was confirmed, no less than three arrest warrants were properly filed, and there were no objections to the surrender based, for instance, on the severity of possible punishment in the country that sought to bring Mr Celmer to justice—Poland. All—well, *almost* all—conditions for the surrender under the EAW were met.

And yet, Justice Aileen Donnelly refused to authorize the extradition of Mr Celmer and instead made a request to the Court of Justice of European Union for a preliminary ruling. The main reason for this was that because of recent legislative changes in Poland, there was a strong suspicion that the rule of law there was systematically damaged, and this undermined the mutual trust that underpinned the EAW process.

The twenty-three-page judgment[1] makes fascinating legal reading. It refers to a lot of extrinsic material—to the opinions of the Venice Commission (the European Commission for Democracy Through Law) and to the European Commission's (EC's) Reasoned Proposal on the use of sanctions (Art. 7 procedure) against Poland. The accuracy of these documents, Justice Aileen Donnelly said, was not in question because they 'amount to specific, updated, objective and reliable information as to the situation regarding the threat to the rule of law in Poland'.[2] And the conclusion must be that the EC's Reasoned Proposal

> is, by any measure, a shocking indictment of the status of the rule of law in a European country in the second decade of the 21st Century. It sets out in stark terms what appears to be a deliberate, calculated and provocative legislative dismantling by Poland of the independence of the judiciary, a key component of the rule of law.[3]

And if that was not enough, '[e]ven "the constitutionality of Polish laws can no longer be effectively guaranteed" because the independence and legitimacy of the Constitutional Tribunal are seriously undermined'.[4]

---

[1] Minister for Justice and Equality v. Celmer [2018] IEHC 119.
[2] Ibid., para. 122.
[3] Ibid., para. 123.
[4] Ibid., para. 123, quoting Reasoned Proposal in accordance with Art. 7(1) of the Treaty on European Union regarding the rule of law in Poland, 20 December 2017, para. 180(1).

Deliberate, calculated, and provocative. How could that have happened, especially in a country that was only a few years earlier widely, and justifiably, applauded for its achievements in democratic consolidation, human rights, and judicial independence? Or perhaps, as a bewildered Polish government immediately retorted, the Irish judge was badly mistaken, misled, and ignorant of the real situation in Poland? Polish deputy minister of justice Michał Warchoł expressed his incredulity that 'general, abstract deliberations, projections and speculations' could become the basis for a judgment, and suggested that the Irish court simply did not understand his government's reforms.[5]

If only this were true. This book provides an account of what happened, why it happened, and how it happened, with the consequence that this Irish court's judgment was not only possible, but also eminently justified.

I begin in Chapter 1 with an outline of the general characteristics of the Poland's constitutional transformation since 2015, and then an explanation of why the concept of 'anti-constitutional populist backsliding' is the most appropriate way of describing it. It is *anti-constitutional* because it proceeds through statutory 'amendments' and outright breaches of the Constitution; it is *populist* because the ruling elite, while dismantling checks and balances, is actively fomenting societal support and mobilization; and it is *backsliding* because it should be seen against the baseline of high democratic standards achieved in the recent past. Chapter 2 provides an outline of constitutional history in post-communist Poland after 1989, emphasizing the sources and contours of a constitutional consensus which had been dominant in Poland for much of that period, as encapsulated in the Constitution of 1997 (still in force) that provides an important insight into the background of the anti-constitutional transformation of post-2015. In the chapters that follow, I provide a detailed account of how comprehensive and momentous the legal changes are, some going so far as to dismantle institutional checks on the government, including the paralysis of the Constitutional Tribunal (CT), and then its conversion into an active supporter of the government (Chapter 3). Chapter 4 examines how the changes capture the regular courts and law enforcement institutions, while Chapters 5 and 6 study the impact on the entire state apparatus and erosion of a number of individual and political rights, such as the right to assembly, freedom of speech, and privacy. Chapter 7 then offers some explanations of the sources of *Prawo i Sprawiedliwość* (Law and Justice (PiS) party) electoral success and then of its huge popularity in society. In Chapter 8 I reflect upon whether the European context may offer some remedies or solutions to the Polish crisis, and argue that the EU must (both for practical and principled reasons) intervene decisively in the case of Poland's breach of Article 2 of Treaty on European Union (TEU) values, that

---

[5] See Christian Davies, 'Ireland refuses extradition over concern at Polish justice reforms', *Guardian* (London, 14 March 2018) online edition, https://www.theguardian.com/world/2018/mar/13/ireland-refuses-artur-celmer-extradition-poland-justice-reforms-ecj (accessed 20 October 2018).

is, those of democracy, the rule of law, and individual rights. In Chapter 9, I take a step back from this detailed account to offer more general observations on what the Polish case can teach us about the vexed question, hotly debated in political science and constitutional theory these days, namely whether a 'populist democracy' or 'illiberal democracy' is still a democracy *tout court*. In the Afterword, I look into the future.

A final caveat needs to be made. The emphasis on backsliding in this book implies that the construction of authoritarian populism in Poland is very much a work in progress. It is dynamic, moving along a trajectory the subsequent stages of which are uncertain. Kaczyński's Poland is not Erdoğan's Turkey; we can roughly discern its directions, but we do not know the endpoints. Hence, any descriptive characterization of the emerging regime must come with a proviso that it is tentative, and that the only thing that is certain is that there are no certainties about further developments. All formulae adopted to describe the system must be preceded by 'quasi' or 'semi'; contradictory trends and forces are simultaneously present and pull the state in opposite directions. It is not a plateau but movement, and even if the populist-authoritarian forces seem today dominant, their triumph is by no means a fait accompli.

The frantic pace of Polish backsliding also means that the account provided here will likely no longer reflect the ever-changing situation when this book reaches its first readers. This means that the value of this account will be largely historical—which is not to downplay it, but to qualify it in an important way. The legal status quo described here is valid as of 1 October 2018.

A personal disclosure: for me, Poland is not just a case study to be examined as a specimen of a crisis of democracy and constitutionalism. To me Poland is *my* country, which I love, and so there are occasions in the book when I abandon a dispassionate and detached style, and let my emotions speak. I feel that I need not apologize for that, but I should place it as a warning at the outset. I believe that this book is accurate, but neutral it is not.

Acknowledgements

This book was quick in the making, but I managed to incur huge debts to a large number of people. My special thanks go to Bojan Bugarič, Adam Czarnota, Martin Krygier, Laurent Pech, and Mirosław Wyrzykowski who read large parts of the manuscript, providing me with very helpful suggestions and advice. Of course, I do not want to entangle any of them in endorsement for my substantive propositions and assessments.

I was unusually lucky in being able to rely on the work and assistance of some extremely talented young scholars who agreed to act as my researchers: Kirsten Gan, Mateusz Grochowski, Mariana Olaizola Rosenblat, and especially Michał Marek Ziółkowski. Whatever is good in this book is owed largely to them.

There are several other colleagues and friends with whom I discussed various issues related to the subject of this book before and during its completion, and to whom I am very grateful: Bruce Ackerman, Susan Rose Ackerman, Richard Albert, Leszek Balcerowicz, Jack Balkin, Stanisław Biernat, Paul Blokker, Adam Bodnar (who planted in my mind the idea of writing this book), Tom Gerald Daly, Andrzej Drzemczewski, Moshe Cohen-Eliya, Rosalind Dixon, Grzegorz Ekiert, Monika Florczak-Wątor, Lech Garlicki, Tom Ginsburg, Aleksandra Gliszczyńska-Grabias, Mark Graber, Jan T. Gross, Gabor Halmai, Samuel Issacharoff, Vicki Jackson, Ronald Janse, Dimitry Kochenov, Tomasz Tadeusz Koncewicz, Ewa Łętowska, Marcin Matczak, Jan-Werner Müller, Gerald Neuman, Phillip Pettit, Robert Post, Rick Pildes, Jiri Priban, Adam Przeworski, Michel Rosenfeld, Andrzej Rzepliński, Kim Lane Scheppele, Robert Schuetze, Eugeniusz Smolar, Gila Stopler, Anna Śledzińska-Simon, Joseph Weiler (who insisted that the book should be very short—advice I tried to heed) and Jan Zielonka.

Special, everyday support was given to me by Anna, Alan and (in his own, inimitable way) Pikuś—and I am very grateful to them, too.

An early version of a part of Chapter 3 was published by the *Hague Journal on the Rule of Law* in 2018, DOI: 10.1007/s40803-018-0078-1—and I am grateful to the Editor, Professor Ronald Janse and Publisher, T.M.C. Asser Press, The Hague, for their kind permission to include a rewritten and updated version here. Earlier versions of some observations and accounts of developments scattered throughout this book were included in my chapter in Mark A. Graber, Sanford Levinson, and Mark Tushnet's (eds), *Constitutional Democracy in Crisis?* (OUP 2018), and I am also very grateful to the editors of that volume and to the publisher for their permission to use some of that material.

***

Czesław Miłosz wrote, addressing himself to the rulers:

> Do not feel safe. The poet remembers.
> You can kill one, but another is born.
> The words are written down, the deed, the date.[6]

Many professional lawyers and legal scholars, in Poland and elsewhere, are doing the poet's work today. Some of the most formidable activists are in the teams named 'Wolne sądy' (Free Courts) and 'Archiwum Wiktora Osiatyńskiego' (Wiktor Osiatyński Archive). They make sure that everything is 'written down, the deed, the date'. I dedicate this book to them.

---

[6] Translated by Richard Lourie. Excerpt from 'You Who Wronged' from The Collected Poems 1931–1987 by Czeslaw Milosz. Copyright © 1988 by Czeslaw Milosz Royalties, Inc. Reprinted by permission of HarperCollins Publishers.

Contents

List of Abbreviations   xiii

1. Anti-constitutional Populist Backsliding   1
2. Before the Breakdown: 1989–2015   35
3. Dismantling Checks and Balances (I): The Remaking of
   the Constitutional Tribunal   58
4. Dismantling Checks and Balances (II): Judges and Prosecutors   96
5. Undoing the Institutions of the Democratic State   132
6. An Assault on Individual Rights   150
7. Why Did It Happen?   162
8. Europe to the Rescue   192
9. Illiberal Democracy or Populist Authoritarianism?   242
   Afterword   267

Bibliography   273
Index   281

List of Abbreviations

ABW	*Agencja Bezpieczeństwa Wewnętrznego* (Internal Security Agency)
CBA	*Centralne Biuro Antykorupcyjne* (Central Anti-corruption Bureau
CCJE	Consultative Council of European Judges
CEE	Central and Eastern Europe
CJEU	Court of Justice of the European Union (also: ECJ: European Court of Justice)
CoE	Council of Europe
CT	Constitutional Tribunal
DD	delegative democracy
EAW	European Arrest Warrant
ECHR	European Convention on Human Rights
ECtHR	European Court of Human Rights
EEC	European Economic Community
ENCJ	European Network of Councils for the Judiciary
EU	European Union
IPN	*Instytut Pamięci Narodowej* (Institute of National Remembrance)
KOD	*Komitet Obrony Demokracji* (Committee of Defense of Democracy)
KPN	*Konfederacja Polski Niepodległej* (Confederation of Independent Poland)
KRRiTV	*Krajowa Rada Radiofonii i Telewizji* (National Council of Radio and TV Broadcasting)
KRS	*Krajowa Rada Sądownictwa* (National Council of the Judiciary)
LPR	*Liga Polskich Rodzin* (League of Polish Families)
MJ	minister of justice
NATO	North Atlantic Treaty Organization
NGO	non-governmental organization
ONR	*Obóz Narodowo-Radykalny* (National-Radical Front)
OSCE	Organization for Security and Co-operation in Europe
PACE	Parliamentary Assembly of CoE
PG	prosecutor general
PiS	*Prawo i Sprawiedliwość* (Law and Justice) party
PKW	*Państwowa Komisja Wyborcza* (National Electoral Commission)
PO	*Platforma Obywatelska* (Civic Platform)
PRL	*Polska Rzeczpospolita Ludowa* (Polish People's Republic
PSL	*Polskie Stronnictwo Ludowe* (Polish Peasants' Party)
PZPR	*Polska Zjednoczona Parta Robotnicza* (Polish United Workers' Party)
RT	Round Table
SAC	Supreme Administrative Court

SC	Supreme Court
SLD	*Sojusz Lewicy Demokratycznej* (Democratic Left Alliance)
TEU	Treaty on European Union
TFEU	Treaty on the Functioning of the European Union
UP	*Unia Pracy* (Labour Union)
UW	*Unia Wolności* (Freedom Union)
VC	Venice Commission (The European Commission for Democracy through Law)
ZUS	*Zakład Ubezpieczeń Społecznych* (Social Insurance Institution)

1

Anti-constitutional Populist Backsliding

A dramatic change in Polish politics occurred after 2015, not as a result of a coup, but through a takeover by democratically elected politicians by and large playing by the democratic rules of the game. It started with two national elections. The first was the presidential election on 10 and 24 May 2015 that was won marginally (51.55 to 48.45 per cent) and unexpectedly by the Law and Justice (*Prawo i Sprawiedliwość* (PiS)) party candidate Andrzej Duda—a young and largely unknown political newcomer. The only pre-presidential public offices held by Duda were as member of the European Parliament, deputy minister of justice, and minister for legal issues in the office of President Lech Kaczyński. He was hand-picked by PiS leader Jarosław Kaczyński who, according to all accounts, did not want to run because most people expected a solid victory by the incumbent, Bronisław Komorowski, supported by the Civic Platform (*Platforma Obywatelska* (PO)) party, but who had run an apathetic, chaos-ridden campaign. The second step occurred soon after: in the parliamentary elections of 27 October 2015, with just 37.5 per cent of the vote (and 18 per cent of all those eligible to vote, with a voter turnout of only 50.9 per cent), PiS won with an absolute majority of five seats, giving it the authority to govern single-handedly. It ended the two-term, eight-year domination by the centrist-liberal PO, ruling in coalition with the politically moderate Polish Peasants' Party (*Polskie Stronnictwo Ludowe* (PSL)).

Victorious populism in Poland is part of a broader surge of populism worldwide, and more specifically in Europe, with populism being in turn a species of a broader phenomenon of general global discontent with liberal democracy in recent years. From 2000 until 2017, the number of populist parties in Europe almost doubled, from thirty-three to sixty-three, and the share of the vote for populist parties reached 24.1 per cent (or 17.7 per cent if one considers right-wing populism only) while in 2000 it was only 8.5 per cent. This trend has been particularly pronounced in Central and Eastern Europe (CEE) where, between 2000 and 2017, populists' vote share tripled, reaching more than 31 per cent in 2017, with five of every six populist votes going to the far right. The populist impact has been registered not only in the populist parties entering into ruling coalitions as junior partners (as in Austria and Switzerland), but also, as in the Netherlands, in the influence of their programme upon mainstream parties that, in order to compete for the vote, have gravitated towards populist agendas, such as anti-immigration policies and the protection of cultural or religious purity. In countries traditionally

Poland's Constitutional Breakdown. © Wojciech Sadurski 2019. Published 2019 by Oxford University Press.

considered liberal and tolerant, populist parties have succeeded in becoming the country's second largest (as in Denmark) or third largest (as in Sweden).

But the Polish and Hungarian cases are different. Nowhere else in Europe did populist parties manage to dismantle the institutional system of checks and balances. In some countries (such as the UK Independence Party in the United Kingdom or the Freedom Party in Austria), populists did not even display any particular illiberalism when it came to the constitutional structure of government. The Hungarian-Polish assault upon constitutional checks and balances is special, and more specifically, Poland is unique in its ostentatious disregard for its own formal constitutional rules.

The Dimensions of Polish Constitutional Breakdown

The scope of the change after the twin 2015 victories in Poland was as huge as it was unexpected. In an article published at the beginning of 2016, and so written in 2015, two British scholars opined that 'Hungary's slide toward semi-authoritarianism is arguably an exceptional case reflecting a specific combination of a restrictive conservative-nationalist right wing, strongly majoritarian institutions, and economic recession.'[1] The failure to include Poland into the 'to watch' list was understandable. No economic or political crisis of major proportions preceded the populist takeover: to the contrary, after the fall of communism, Poland had enjoyed a six-fold increase in gross domestic product, and was the only country in the European Union (EU) that did not experience negative growth as a result of the global recession of 2008. The country's longing for embeddedness in supranational structures was met by membership in the Council of Europe, the EU, and the North Atlantic Treaty Organization (NATO), and the government changed hands six times since 1990, thus showing the exemplary characteristics of democratic alternation of power.

PiS had already experienced a previous episode of rule, in 2005–7, which to some extent prefigured the current regime (see Chapter 2). There were, however, three major differences that characterized the 2005–7 episode compared to that commencing in 2015. First, as the dates indicate, it was very short and, at the time, PiS clearly lacked any earlier experience of government—an experience that would teach PiS a lesson, which it clearly relied upon in 2015, that once you come to power, you need to introduce all the radical projects right at the start of the term. Second, PiS in 2005–7 did not have an independent majority, and was constrained in its rule by coalition partners, such as the Self-Defence (*Samoobrona*) and the League of Polish Families (*Liga Polskich Rodzin* (LPR))—a factor that exerted a gravitational pull upon PiS towards the centre of the political spectrum. Both Samoobrona and the LPR were parties of the populist right, so in order to distinguish itself PiS naturally gravitated towards the centre. By contrast, today there are no serious PiS rivals on the right, so there are no strategic disincentives for PiS to adopting radical right-wing positions. The third difference has to do with personalities. Lech Kaczyński, Jarosław Kaczyński's twin brother, was president at the time, and had a clearly moderating effect upon Jarosław. But for all these differences, the 2005–7 episode foreshadowed what was to happen with the next victory of PiS.

No time was wasted in 2015. The end of the year witnessed the beginning of a fundamental authoritarian transformation: the abandonment of dogmas of liberal democracy, constitutionalism, and the rule of law that had been so far taken for granted. And even if, as is usually the case, the practice of implementing these principles was far from perfect before the PiS victory, there had at least been a widespread consensus that these values were standards to be pursued. With the suffocating command of Jarosław Kaczyński over all centres of political power, these principles were abandoned in 2015, ostensibly in the name of a purely majoritarian democracy, and of the 'sovereign' people having a right to rule as it wishes. The use of the 'sovereign' as a legitimating factor became widespread, often reaching almost grotesque forms. In a newspaper interview, when asked about whether he liked PiS's changes to the constitutional court, the Constitutional Tribunal (CT), Mr Maciej Mitera, one of the judge-candidates to the 'new' National Council of the Judiciary (*Krajowa Rada Sądownictwa* (KRS)) and later its spokesperson, answered: 'If the representatives of the sovereign decided so, I submit myself to it.'[2] The 'will of the sovereign', expressed allegedly through an electoral choice ('winner takes all'), was declared a fundamental legitimation for a general transformation of the state (even if many of its aspects had not been announced in the electoral campaign) and as a reason to downplay checks and controls upon the executive and legislative branches. PiS's campaigns against first the CT and later the regular courts have rested upon the idea that any restraints upon the political majority are by their nature anti-democratic.

Victor Orbán's Hungary was declared the model to emulate, with Kaczyński promising 'Budapest in Warsaw' as its goal,[3] and the copycat effect should not be underestimated. It is fair to describe PiS rule so far as 'an accelerated and condensed version of what the ruling Fidesz party has accomplished in Hungary since 2010, when Viktor Orbán began his second stint as prime minister'.[4] Indeed, the trajectory of Fidesz and PiS have followed a similar pattern. Both began as reasonably mainstream parties regarding themselves initially as moderate parties of the establishment, only later embarking upon radical shifts towards right-wing, conservative, and nationalistic populism, emphasizing sovereignty of the nation especially against larger EU structures and, at the same time, the exclusion of migrants. The sequence of the main 'reforms' in Poland in many respects closely parallels that in Hungary a few years earlier:

- fast-tracking of radical legislative changes; attacks on non-governmental organizations (NGOs)

- new media legislation
- disempowering and capturing the Constitutional Court; removal of the 'old' judges (of ordinary courts) by lowering the retirement age
- specific attacks on the chief justices of the respective Supreme Courts
- restructuring of the KRS through the politicization of its selection; altering the membership rules of the electoral commission with the effect of giving the ruling party control of the commission
- identifying the EU as a foreign, hostile entity which illegitimately interferes in the internal affairs of its member states.

In late 2017 a leading Polish journalist assessed the situation:

Orbán's state is Kaczyński's Poland as it will be in 5 years' time, because he ruled Hungary that much longer than PiS. In this period Orbán captured the supreme court and ordinary courts, got rid of the National Council for the Judiciary, set up an Office of National Media, and devoted [state] budget money to finance propagandist public TV. The last five independent newspapers were taken over by the Prime Minister's people in August 2017. Advertising campaigns targeting political rivals are financed from public money. NGOs have fallen under state control, and electoral rules have been changed.... And the society? Over 40 percent still support Orbán. The Prime Minister has effectively scared the Hungarians by an alleged threat of invasion by immigrants ...[5]

Still, there are important differences between the two cases. Most important, thanks to Fidesz winning a constitutional majority, there was formal constitutional change in Hungary, which made it possible 'to transform the constitutional order and slide into some form of authoritarianism entirely through legal means,'[6] with no such change or amendment available to Kaczyński. The new Hungarian Constitution—adopted in great haste and protected by a requisite two-thirds majority for changes—is deeply ideological, emphasizing conservative and Christian values, and is meant to constitute a quasi-sacred charter[7] of Orbán's self-avowed illiberal democracy: a symbolic and political asset that Kaczyński in Poland lacks. There are also other differences:

- political power in Hungary is much more embedded in the economic power of ultra-rich oligarchs than in Poland (leading to the label of Hungary as a 'mafia state')[8]
- Orbán is pro-Russian while PiS is ostentatiously anti-Russian; Orbán (whose party is a member of the European People's Party in the European Parliament, while PiS is in the European Conservatives and Reformists group) acts more pragmatically in EU fora than PiS

- Polish centrist opposition is much stronger than the Hungarian opposition, and in Poland there is no strong party alternative any further to the right (like Jobbik in Hungary) that exerts right-wing pressure on the ruling party
- the Church is dominant and has a strong political influence in Poland, but not in Hungary
- commercial independent media are strong in Poland but weak in Hungary.

While individual aspects of Polish backsliding may have their counterpart in this or that democratic state, what makes Poland such a troublesome case is *the comprehensiveness and the cumulative effect* of the ways in which liberal democracy is being undone. Rather than carefully sequencing the changes and applying them seriatim, thus giving the system an opportunity to neutralize their effects, 'reforms' have been enacted more or less simultaneously, or at least through incremental changes where the timing of one change overlapped with another, and yet another. A question (articulated by a legal scholar with regard to a different constitutional system) could have been raised: 'Could steady pressure against all these institutions, all at once, cause them to crumble because they cannot rely on one another for support?'[9] In the case of Poland post-2015, the answer was, unfortunately, affirmative. A virus in a sick body reinforces pathologies in other parts of the body, while a virus in a healthy body is likely to be disabled from having a detrimental effect. A single illiberal change does not provoke a major breakdown if it takes place in the environment of a general liberal constitutional context. In Poland, however, it is a populist offensive *tous azimuts*: an all-out assault on liberal constitutionalism. And it is systemic: individual elements are functionally connected with the others. For instance, the paralysis of the CT was a prerequisite for the adoption of illiberal laws made immune from effective constitutional scrutiny. These illiberal laws, for example, on the right to assembly, make it more difficult to protest against capture of the CT. In this way, the sum is more than its parts. There is analogy here to Mark Tushnet's description of Singapore's authoritarian constitutionalism. He constructs the useful figure of 'a fallacy of decomposition' where 'the components *lack* a property but the aggregate might have it'; he also uses the concepts of 'a "slice and dice" or disaggregated approach' which, with regard to the analysis of Singapore's authoritarianism, 'is almost certainly inappropriate'.[10] The same can be said about Poland. At the same time, the fact that some individual legal provisions may exist in isolation from other problematic arrangements and practices in some unimpeachably democratic states is a powerful rhetorical instrument for regimes such as in Poland, and also imposes constraints upon critics, including those abroad. Foreign political actors may be loath to condemn democratic backsliding 'if such practices enforce laws that exist in their own legal systems, lest they be criticized as hypocritical'.[11]

The change can also be *incremental* even if it occurs quickly. So it is often difficult to identify a precise tipping point: no single new law, decision, or transformation seems sufficient to cry wolf. Only after the fact do we realize that the line dividing a liberal democracy from a fake one has been crossed: threshold moments are not seen as such when we live in them. As Aziz Huq and Tom Ginsburg note: 'The precise point ... at which the volume of democratic and constitutional backsliding amounts to constitutional retrogression will be unclear—both ex ante and contemporaneously'.[12] They add, using a grim metaphor: 'Like the proverbial boiling frog, a democratic society in the midst of erosion may not realize its predicament until matters are already beyond redress.'[13] And then it is beyond redress. This, as Huq and Ginsburg further observe, also makes any opposition to democratic backsliding less effective because there is usually no single event or governmental conduct that could mobilize the resistance by sending a clear signal 'that democratic norms are imperilled'.[14] In Poland warnings about the fall of democracy have often been received with incredulity, or with objections of being hysterical or paranoiac. The language of democratic collapse has been seen by some as inflated, disproportionate, and counterproductively eroding the emotional content, which may be warranted in some unspecified future. As Nancy Bermeo puts it: 'slow slides towards authoritarianism often lack both the bright spark that ignites an effective call to action and the opposition and movement leaders who can voice that clarion call'.[15] But the effect of these multiple 'slow slides', rather than a clarion call, might render an obituary in order.

Many democratic backslides occur *without a formal change* of institutions and procedures, so they are invisible to a purely legal account. As Gábor Attila Tóth remarks: 'many such regimes ostensibly behave as if they were constitutional democracies, but, in fact, they are majoritarian rather than consensual, populist instead of elitist; nationalist as opposed to cosmopolitan; or religious rather than secular'.[16] Institutions and procedures remain the same but their substance is radically changed by practice. For instance, parliamentary legislative procedures remain, formally, the same as before, but by adopting a scheme whereby all important governmental initiatives are proposed as private members' bills, the requirements of consultations, expert opinions, and impact audits are dispensed with. There *is* a discussion in the parliamentary legislative committee, but with PiS having an absolute majority, and the opposition MPs being given, for example, one[17] or two[18] minutes for their speeches, the discussion is turned into a sham. In this way, the intended meaning of many procedures and institutions is eroded, and they are converted into façades. Institutions become hollow.[19] *Toutes proportions gardées*, it is like in the state of the 'people's democracy': there were 'elections', but without competition and choice; a 'parliament', but no opposition and no open debate; a 'president', but supreme power was elsewhere. There was even (in Poland after 1985) a CT, but it would not invalidate any laws that were important to the ruling elite. As a result, for an external observer the radical shift in the meaning of institutions, procedures, and roles may be invisible because they often remain, *legally speaking*, the same as before. As Martin Krygier observes, 'One striking novelty of these new populisms is that, while like most populists they undermine constitutionalism, they do so with often striking attention to the forms of law'.[20] But these 'forms of law' are used, in practice, to undermine the underlying values of the rule of law, which are to constrain arbitrary use of unlimited power. Kaczyński is no Leninist: just like Orbán, he knows and skilfully uses the legitimating value of formal legality—except when the political costs of legality are found by him and his advisers to be too high.

This may be translated into a 'Martian's test': would an intelligent and otherwise well-informed Martian, having for herself all the information culled only from the formal structures of government, and knowing none of the practice, discern the non-democratic character of the regime? Probably not; she would see all the institutions and procedures she knows from the democratic toolbox available to her. Ozan Varol uses the concept of 'stealth authoritarianism', that is, a genre of authoritarianism that faithfully uses various democratic structures for non-democratic purposes: 'Stealth authoritarianism refers to the use of legal mechanisms that exist in regimes with favorable democratic credentials for anti-democratic ends'.[21] For instance, representatives of stealth authoritarianism 'employ seemingly legitimate and neutral electoral laws, frequently enacted for the purported purpose of eliminating electoral fraud or promoting political stability, to create systemic advantages for themselves and raise the costs to the opposition of dethroning them'.[22] Another example applicable to the Polish case is that stealth authoritarians 'rely on judicial review, not as a check on their power, but to consolidate power'.[23] As I show in Chapter 3, this is precisely the use of judicial review that the PiS regime conferred upon the CT: rather than acting as a constraint upon the government, the tribunal has become a constraint upon the opposition and an active helper of the government. But, formally speaking, judicial review *is there*, and unless one ascertains the actual substance and arguments of the decisions taken, as our Martian is unlikely to do, one will not see a difference between democracy and stealth authoritarianism, even though there was no stealth, naturally, in the ways the CT was taken over. As Varol puts it, '[s]tealth authoritarianism creates a significant discordance between appearance and reality by concealing anti-democratic practices under the mask of law'[24]—and this discordance is a predicament suffered both by our Martian and, more often in the real world, by well-meaning foreigners, often not knowing the language, the context, and the actual substance of practices they observe from the outside.

This immediately indicates why even those genuinely committed to democracy and acting in good faith may be sincerely confused about what is going on in countries captured by stealth authoritarians: there are no tanks on the streets, political opponents are not tortured or imprisoned, and there is no prior restraint on the media. The institutions seem to function as before, and the Constitution is not necessarily voided. To ascertain the reality one must inquire into the *meanings* of public actions, into the pedigree and character of actual persons who occupy key positions, and into how they are dependent upon a hierarchy of authority, at the apex of which there is a leader unconstrained by constitutional rules. 'Elected autocrats maintain a veneer of democracy while eviscerating its substance.'[25] Understanding this substance takes time, effort, and requires certain skills, including knowing context, path dependence, and language.

Backsliding is all the more difficult to discern since many reforms are presented as a *defence* of democracy rather than a subversion. By returning obsessively to the figure of the sovereign who has elected a party to a parliamentary majority, the rulers claim a democratic legitimacy for dismantling the counter-majoritarian checks and balances in the system. By subjecting the election of judges to parlia- mentary control, PiS alleges that it is actually introducing *more democratic* mech- anisms than those that were in place so far. By electing CT judges known for their pro-PiS political views, PiS alleges that it is imbuing the tribunal with better repre- sentation of actual societal preferences.

The institutional changes discussed in this book are a part of a broader popu- list syndrome in which a key role is played by a catastrophic *drop in the norms of civility* of discourse, with an accompanying loss of trust. When government's opponents are treated as traitors and haters of their own nation, they feel that they have no choice but to respond in kind, and reciprocate with accusations of similar intensity. As a result, there are no shreds of mutual respect, or of the rec- ognition that, while the government and the opposition differ in their interpret- ation of the public good, they are equally sincere in the quest for common interest. What is missing is mutual self-restraint, in which (in the words of János Kis in the Hungarian context):

> the party in opposition can safely expect the party in government to refrain from
> taking advantage of its majority in order to permanently exclude its rival from
> power, while the party in government can safely expect the party in opposition
> not to strive toward debilitating day-to-day governance.[26]

No such mutual expectations, which are a key to democratic governance, exist in Poland now. Both sides deny legitimacy to each other: the opposition is seen by PiS as treacherous and non-patriotic and hence undeserving of ever returning to power, while PiS is viewed by its opponents as having transgressed the minimal conditions of democratic legitimacy. Jack Balkin's words written about the United States under President Donald Trump also apply to Poland: 'People not only lose trust in government but also in other people who disagree with them. Political opponents appear less as fellow citizens devoted to the common good and more like internal threats to the nation.'[27] Polish politics is polarized along lines so fun- damental that loyal cooperation between the main parties for a higher good is unthinkable these days. Supporting a party has become more a matter of essen- tial identity than of policy preferences. As political scientists know all too well, a low level of interpersonal trust is a favourable background for antidemocratic backsliding.[28]

This mutual distrust between the parties and the electorates radiates upon (and is partly reflective of) a more general societal distrust in politics and public institutions. Poland has one of the lowest levels of party membership in Europe (approximately 1 per cent of the adult population, compared to 2.3 per cent in Germany and 3.8 per cent in Sweden). Voters' party loyalties are extremely shallow and devoid of strong commitments: for instance, 18 per cent of those who voted in 2011 for the Democratic Left Alliance transferred their votes in 2015 to the vehemently anti-communist right-wing PiS. The dominant form of societal mobilization in recent years was single-issue protests, which were often episodic and non-institutionalized (e.g. about Anti-Counterfeiting Trade Agreement, an anti-abortion legislative initiative). Moreover, those protests did not translate into increased support for opposition parties. In the words of the sociologist Maciej Gdula, 'It is as if the opposition parties and society did not interact with each other. ... It is as if the enthusiasm and energy of the protests did not match the actions and words of the politicians.'[29] Such strong rejection of institutional politics creates a favourable social ground for anti-constitutional populism: when institutions matter so little, it is no wonder that the institutions that *are* there turn out not to be resilient in the face of a resolute and energetic assault.

The level of political distrust in Poland is catastrophic—distrust in politicians, parties, institutions, and other fellow citizens (paraphrasing a line in *The Economist* after the 2016 US election, one could say that 'Half of Poland can scarcely believe that the other half has chosen PiS').[30] Whatever the roots of this distrust, it has been used largely by PiS as a political-sociotechnical device aimed at returning to power. After the air crash of 2010 (discussed in Chapter 7) that killed a number of Poland's most prominent political figures, PiS provoked mass hysteria by pointing fingers at leading politicians of the time as guilty of a conspiracy, as well as warning that they would be prosecuted after the political changeover. The party's allegations without any evidence that the outcomes of elections had been systematically rigged served to magnify cases of corruption out of proportion to further undermine trust in the government, and they did. The generalized distrust towards politics gave rise to an attitude of 'symmetrism' (this is what the West used to call, before the fall of communism, moral equivalence): PiS may be bad, but its predecessors in power were not much better, so why bother fighting for the replacement of one with the other? This is yet another powerful, if only negative, source of PiS's persistently good rankings in opinion polls, and the unlikelihood of a 'Polish Macron' (an idealized figure standing for a genuine pro-European, liberal-democratic saviour against illiberal, populist and nationalistic forces) emerging in the foreseeable future.

This deep distrust is partly driven by the continued mass deception propagated by ruling party politicians. Prime Minister Mateusz Morawiecki, in office since late 2017, excelled at telling regular lies, and the fact-checking media have had a field day. Some examples of overt lies publicly uttered by Morawiecki are:

- that he had been personally responsible for negotiations on Poland's accession to the EU (in fact, he was just a low-ranking member of a large team in charge of accession negotiations at the time)
- that when he was the CEO of a bank, that bank never granted loans in Swiss Francs (in fact, it did; the matter is highly sensitive in Poland)
- that 80 per cent of the Polish media belongs the government's enemies (a number never explained, and wildly implausible)
- that he reduced central government bureaucracy (not true: his government had a record number of secretaries and under-secretaries of state, but some of them were transferred to the fictional position of 'councillor' in order to make the statistics look better), and so on.

Similarly, among other examples, in December 2017, President Duda announced that the work of the CT was now 'back to normal' (not true; as shown in Chapter 3, the number of judgments are much fewer than under the previous presidency of the CT).[31]

The other dimension of Poland's post-2015 transformation is the active, deliberate, ideological, and cultural 'counter-revolution' that is displayed not only in official declarations but also in actual governmental acts.[32] While it does not amount to any comprehensive ideological platform for PiS rule, it is nevertheless quite clear that the elected authoritarians have an agenda that is anti-modernist, anti-progressivist, and anti-liberal. A number of offices and programmes to combat discrimination were discontinued as soon as PiS came to power. For instance, in June 2016, just over six months after its electoral victory, PiS extinguished the governmental Council for Counteracting Racial Discrimination, Xenophobia and Intolerance. Significantly, this happened at a time when there had been a clear rise in acts of violence—verbal and physical—against non-whites in Poland. Public schools ceased to accept visitors from NGOs running workshops against intolerance and xenophobia while also opening their doors to radical nationalistic groups such as the neo-Nazi National-Radical Front (*Obóz Narodowo-Radykalny* (ONR)). The government stopped subsidies for civil society activities such as the so-called Blue Line, a phone-in for young persons in desperate psychological situations, often on the verge of committing suicide. In turn, governmental subsidies were generously conferred upon religious and right-wing groups, such as the network of organizations connected with Catholic-fundamentalist Radio Maryja. In their public, official statements, leading PiS politicians appealed to traditional and conservative values while distancing themselves from liberal and progressive ideologies.

This was grotesquely articulated by Witold Waszczykowski, minister for foreign affairs until early 2018, who ridiculed 'a Marxist pattern' according to which the world is supposed to move towards 'a new mix of cultures and races, a world of bicyclists and vegetarians'.[33] Somewhat less comically, during a March 2016 state visit to Hungary, President Duda deplored the crisis 'of the values on which European civilisation was built ... that has Latin roots and is based on the stem of Christianity... All these ideals in today's Europe are being lost, are being forgotten and trampled on by other ideologies that in fact distort the essence of humankind and humanity'.[34] Similarly, in one of his first TV interviews after elevation to the office, Prime Minister Morawiecki asserted that Poland has a mission of 're-Christianising Europe'.[35] All these manifestations of cultural counter-revolution have been enthusiastically promoted in public education, public media, and the pro-PiS commercial media.

The cultural counter-revolution led by PiS is connected with a significant re-orientation of Polish foreign policy. In general, foreign policy is much more at the mercy of domestic policy than it was before; as some experts in the field noted, '[u]nlike any other post-1989 government, the PiS administration treats foreign policy as secondary to domestic objectives'.[36] Re-orientation has affected official arguments about the strong alignment of Poland with the West. Since the 1989 transition, all governments and also all parties in power have emphasized an unconditional 'return to Europe' as the strategic trajectory of an independent and democratic Poland, accompanied by a strong hostility towards placing Poland in a sort of 'twilight zone' between East and West, with uncertain security commitments from foreign powers. But this rhetoric was embedded within a broader package of ideological commitment to liberal, constitutional democracy, to universal human rights, and generally, to the ideal of an 'open society'. Now that these fundamental ideological commitments have been challenged and largely rejected by the ruling elite, Poland's pro-Western orientation has also been put into question. As a report by an influential think-tank observes:

> For the first time since 1989 the government and party in power are not only making use of or emphasising the language of national egoism, but also anti-Western rhetoric (occasionally strongly so). It is aimed squarely at those values and principles which were meant to be the anchor of Poland's presence in the EU according to the philosophy of its integration, beginning in the '90s.[37]

This anti-Western orientation is undergirded by the ruling elite's condemnation, supported by a large part of the population and in particular by the Catholic Church, of Western 'decadence' in its respect for procreative rights (defined by the traditionalist right in Poland as manifesting the 'civilization of death'), and toleration of same-sex unions.[38] The fact that many Poles, especially those who are pro-PiS, are at the same time strongly anti-Russian prevents these attitudes from pushing Poland into alliance with Putin's Russia, but nevertheless they erect important obstacles to strongly and unconditionally aligning Poland with 'the West', unless 'the West' is identified with Donald Trump and parties belonging to the European Conservatives and Reformists group in the European Parliament (of which PiS is a member). At the same time, the rejection by visionaries such as former Prime Minister Tadeusz Mazowiecki or former Foreign Minister Bronisław Geremek of a Poland placed somewhere in a twilight zone between West and East has given way to the fanciful idea of an Intermarium (*Trójmorze*). This is the idea of an alliance between a number of states in CEE with Poland taking a leading role, which stems from equal suspicion of Russia and Germany, both of which, according to PiS strategists, have equally domineering intentions for Poland. (Kaczyński, in his more fantastic rhetoric, even used to call Poland under the PO, the previous ruling party, a Polish-Russian 'condominium'). This worldview was presented as an alternative to the PO's vision of Poland being a co-equal partner in a 'Weimar Triangle' with Germany and France. Suspicion against Germany, often escalating into hatred, is frequently used for domestic purposes, with Germany being presented as a country that owes Poland allegedly unpaid reparations for the Second World War, or as unwilling to accept its responsibility for the crimes of Holocaust. In this way, foreign policy is viewed by PiS and its leader primarily as a tool of domestic policy imperatives—often with disastrous consequences for the position of Poland in Europe and its relationship with its closest allies and supporters.

This vision is primarily based on a suspicion of the outside world, and on the celebration of national sovereignty as the supreme value in a nation's policy, which needs to be forever defended and strengthened. The outside world is represented as constantly trying to interfere in Polish affairs, partly for its own self-interest and partly out of instinctive 'anti-polonism' (a new term, coined by Jarosław Kaczyński), and often using internal political opposition (and also the media, NGOs, and judges) as its willing or unwitting agents of influence. The only exception to this dislike of universal, supranational or foreign powers is the Holy See.

What's in a Name?

There are different characterizations in contemporary constitutional theory and political science aimed at grasping the essence of developments similar to those described in this book. Each of them captures an important aspect of Polish backsliding—though not necessarily its most significant characteristic. Some scholars talk about 'constitutional rot' (Jack Balkin)[39] or 'democratic decay' (Tom Daly).[40] The former has been used to describe the United States, the latter aims to include Poland and also Hungary as its manifestations. Both 'rot' and 'decay' connote a degradation that is slow and almost impersonal, occurring without a plan—a suggestion that does not do justice to the energy, enthusiasm, and designs that PiS has for Poland. In turn, the concept of democratic 'backlash'[41] unhelpfully suggests revenge or a reaction against some excesses on the part of that against which the backlash occurs.

The label 'illiberal democracy', made famous by Fareed Zakaria[42] and used by many more recent writers, to describe (among other things) Poland under PiS,[43] is perhaps too charitable. It pre-empts that which needs to be shown, namely that illiberal backsliding maintains its essentially democratic character, and ignores the possibility that 'illiberal democracy' is an oxymoron. After all, it may be claimed that 'illiberal democracy' is, by its nature, only a temporary phenomenon and must either evolve towards liberal democracy or degenerate into illiberal authoritarianism: the illiberal factors in democracy, including the displacement of individual rights, must erode democracy at its core—the fairness of electoral process. (This is one of the propositions advanced in Chapter 9 of this book.)

Some writers emphasize the authoritarian character of the developments, and talk about 'new authoritarianism'.[44] The use of the concept of 'authoritarianism' *may* imply the insensitivity of rulers to the need for social support and their reliance on brute force. And yet, populists such as Kaczyński or Orbán certainly care a great deal about social legitimacy, in the sense of actual popular support for their rule, and the label 'authoritarianism' fails to distinguish between populist power and a regime predominantly based on naked coercion and political violence. Repression against opponents in Poland is a relatively minor phenomenon, and while it does happen (the treatment of demonstrators participating in anti-government rallies; harassment of judges defined by the rulers as enemies), it is far from being the main pillar of government. In contrast, the label 'populism' captures the fact that the regime is sensitive to public opinion; that it follows public opinion surveys with interest and concern; and that it occasionally changes some of its policies or withdraws policy initiatives if they turn out to be unpopular and the benefits of pursuing those policies do not compensate for the government's loss of popularity.

David Landau's concept of 'abusive constitutionalism'[45] is not adequate for Poland because it only takes account of those reductions in democratic qualities brought about by changes in the constitutional order (by constitutional amendments and replacements, as in Colombia, Venezuela, and Hungary); while in Poland an important fraction of the changes were achieved by extra- and unconstitutional measures. Some political scientists use the awkward concept of 'democratic deconsolidation' and explicitly apply this concept to Poland under PiS.[46] But there are problems with this, too. First, it may seem fanciful to some to imply that before PiS's ascent to power, Poland was a 'consolidated' democracy: consolidation by its very nature takes time. Second, while, for the democratic deconsolidation authors, its main indicators are found in low and shallow support in public opinion for democratic rule,[47] the emphasis in this book is on the structural institutional transformation away from democracy.

The notion of a 'hybrid regime'[48] lacks any substantive informative value: it says that there is a mixture but does not tell us of what. Finally, the concept of a 'constitutional coup d'état'[49] or merely 'a constitutional coup'[50] may be helpful in conveying the sense of outrage at the displacement of a constitutional frame of political change, but is not accurate to describe Polish developments because a coup d'état is normally launched by one group against a *different* group currently in power rather than consolidating (through anti-constitutional means) its own power. In the phenomena described here, the incumbent *stays in power*, though with greatly increased capacities of political action, and under different rules of the game. The continuity of the identity of the rulers both before and after the radical transformation of the regime renders the language of a coup misleading.[51] It unhelpfully merges together two distinct models of democratic reversal: a coup and an incumbent takeover in which a democratically elected leadership undermines key tenets of democracy.[52]

My own formula lacks the crisp elegance of some of these labels but it better expresses, in my view, the essence of the developments in Poland after the 2015 elections. I call it 'anti-constitutional populist backsliding', and all three ingredients are equally important. They will now be discussed in turn.

'Anti-constitutional'

The anti-constitutional character of the current regime has many facets. First of all, the real centre of power is elsewhere than constitutionally decreed. It is centred in one person, Jarosław Kaczyński, who is commanding the country without constitutional responsibility and accountability (his only state function is being a member of parliament) which makes it a significantly different case from that of Orbán's Hungary. The constitutionally described central institutions of executive power are the president and prime minister who wield negligible power, except for that which is delegated to them by Kaczyński, and which can be withdrawn at any time. Occasional manifestations of a very limited 'independence' of the president are generally considered by acolytes of Kaczyński as breaches of an unwritten compact and as irritating cases of disloyalty.

This situation was prefigured in the writings by Stanisław Ehrlich, an important legal theorist in communist Poland, initially a devout Stalinist who became in his late years a disillusioned Marxist and self-avowed reformist, and who coined (without any negative or critical intentions) the concept of a 'centre for political direction' (*centralny ośrodek dyspozycji politycznej*) which is a de facto ruling entity—not to be confused with any formal institutions designed by the Constitution—issuing strategic directives for all state institutions. Ehrlich was Jarosław Kaczyński's professor and doctoral supervisor, and both Kaczyński brothers participated in a *privatissimo* seminar of Ehrlich in the early and mid-1970s.[53] The irony of Kaczyński replicating such a pattern of power was not lost on some observers: 'notwithstanding the anticommunist rhetoric of prominent members of the ruling Law and Justice party in Poland, this structure of power closely resembles that which was characteristic of the former, communist system, where the secretary of the communist party had the greatest power and prerogatives'.[54]

The everyday politics of PiS Poland provides constant, multiple proofs as to who wields the real power. When President Duda vetoed two of three laws on the judiciary by the government in July 2017 (see Chapter 4),[55] to the surprise and irritation of Kaczyński, this mini-crisis within the ruling elite was followed by a series of face-to-face meetings between Kaczyński and Duda, aimed at forging a 'compromise'. In these meetings, neither the prime minister nor the minister of justice, who nominally drafted the laws, took part. In another striking episode, when the newly formed Council of National Media tried to fire the chairman of public TV, Jacek Kurski (whose rivalry with the head of the council Krzysztof Czabański is well known), all three PiS members on the council were urgently summoned to see Kaczyński and then immediately, and humiliatingly, they cancelled the decision dismissing Kurski, who remains the chairman of public TV up to now.

This pattern has settled for good: *Nowogrodzka* (the Warsaw street address of the PiS headquarters, where Kaczyński has his office) has become synonymous with the true locus of power. When ministers need a strategic decision to guide their action, they 'go to Nowogrodzka Street'. When they want to inform journalists that Kaczyński has not yet decided about this or that important issue within their portfolio, they use a proxy: 'a political decision has not yet been made'. A decision by the leader conclusively ends any controversy and becomes official policy: *Nowogrodzka locuta, causa finita*. Occasional speeches by or interviews with Kaczyński (invariably, to the 'friendly media' who never ask embarrassing or difficult questions) are treated as programmatic guidelines for state policies. All major reforms (including those discussed in this book) are initially foreshadowed by Kaczyński in his public statements. Ministers obediently consider their role as that of turning Kaczyński's announcements into policies within their portfolio, and if they publicly come up with their own initiative, it is only if Kaczyński has decided to leave them a specified scope of discretion in a given sphere. The paramount role of Kaczyński in the Polish political system, though totally invisible to the constitutional design, has also been accepted and recognized as such by foreign journalists or politicians who seek meetings with him in precedence to meeting the prime minister or the president, knowing that this is where the true power resides. It is also general knowledge that in all politically sensitive issues, the captured institutions, such as the CT or the Council of National Media, decide exactly as the political leadership wishes.

The second dimension of the anti-constitutional character of PiS power is governance through multiple breaches of the Constitution. As will be evidenced in this book, the Constitution has been routinely violated in a number of ways. The takeover of the CT is one, though not the only, arena in which breaches of the Constitution have been committed: the parliamentary resolution of 25 November 2015 (with a PiS majority, of course) on the removal of 'legal effects' of the election of judges at the end of the previous parliamentary term violates the Constitution because the Constitution provides for an exhaustive number of instances in which a term of a judge can be extinguished, and the Parliament has no such power. The refusal by the president to swear in correctly elected judges violates the Constitution, which does not give the president any such role in designing the composition of the CT. It also unilaterally (by the president) changes the constitutional system for the appointment of judges of the CT because it assumes that the president has the prerogative of refusing to swear in some judges, hence to veto the election by the Parliament—a prerogative unknown to the Constitution. The governmental refusal to publish some of the CT judgments is another usurpation by the government of powers that it does not hold. These are just a few examples related to the dismantling of the CT, with many more discussed in Chapter 3. Put together, they confirm Mark Tushnet's observation (based on other cases, not Poland) that an authoritarian regime 'faces no constraints on abandoning law, courts, and constitutionalism when doing what would serve the regime's interests – or, perhaps more interestingly, when law, courts, and constitutionalism appear to be interfering with the regime's (other) goals'.[56] That is precisely what has been going on in Poland. The regime's use of the Constitution is highly selective, and coloured by its general distaste for the liberal checks and balances the Constitution enshrines. It is not that the Constitution carries no weight; rather, it could be easily trumped by whatever was considered an important regime goal.

The third dimension of the anti-constitutional character of PiS rule is the series of de facto 'amendments' to the Constitution via statutes that significantly alter constitutional dispensations. As former CT judge Mirosław Wyrzykowski wrote about one particular example of such an amendment (namely that of the law on the CT of 22 December 2015):[57] 'For the first time in the thirty-year history of Polish constitutional judiciary, the [Constitutional] Tribunal was confronted with a statutory regulation which changed the constitutional order of the state'.[58] The distinction between this and outright breaches of the Constitution is of course blurred: 'changing' the constitution through statutory means is in itself a breach of the Constitution. But I am separating this category from the previous one in order to focus on those statutory actions that were meant to circumvent the Constitution, and to highlight an important characteristic of the PiS regime, namely that it has engineered fundamental 'constitutional changes' without having an electoral mandate to do so. In the absence of the super-majority necessary for a constitutional change, it proceeded by adopting statutes that in fact contravened constitutional provisions. The setting-up, by statute, of the Council of National Media, was a way of disempowering a constitutional body, the National BroadcastingCouncil, by endowing the former with many of the tasks of the latter (mainly, with regard to supervision of public media, a task transferred fully to the new council).[59] Several statutory provisions concerning the CT were meant to circumvent other constitutional provisions. For instance, in order to silence Professor Stanisław Biernat, then vice-president of the CT (a constitutionally designated office), a statute of 13 December 2015[60] invented the position of acting president who performed the actions normally falling upon the vice-president, with the difference that they fully met the expectations of PiS. To give another example: the statute on the KRS[61] introduced a number of uncon-stitutional provisions fundamentally changing the composition and structure of that body compared to its constitutional design: it extinguished the constitution-ally settled terms of office of the KRS judges-members and introduced, contrary to the Constitution, a system of electing KRS judges-members by Parliament rather than by their peers.[62] In a similar way, a statute on the Supreme Court (SC) extin-guished the explicit constitutional term of office of the chief justice of the SC by lowering the retirement age of SC judges from seventy to sixty-five, which affected Chief Justice Małgorzata Gersdorf, notwithstanding that her term of six years is conferred by the Constitution and only ends in April 2020.

The process of amending the Constitution by statute marks the main difference between Orbán's Hungary and Kaczyński's Poland: what Kaczyński occasioned by statutes, Orbán had brought about by a brand new Constitution followed by a number of constitutional amendments. For instance, the fundamental change of the composition of the Constitutional Court in Hungary by increasing the number of judges from eleven to fifteen and then prolonging the terms of office of already sitting judges from nine to twelve years was achieved solely by constitutional changes. This immediately allowed the ruling coalition to reach a target of eight out of fifteen judges appointed by it. The removal of the compulsory retirement age for Constitutional Court judges entrenched the domination of Fidesz-appointed judges into the future. As Grażyna Skąpska puts it: 'The Hungarian case presents an example of an intelligent play with constitutional system as an instrument of political majority, and a hypocritical conformity with the requirements of consti-tutional democracy and civil rights protection – expressed in the constitution, but changed in the amendments to the constitution'.[63]

One may ponder over which of these two situations is worse: worse, that is, from the point of view of the standards of liberal constitutionalism. On the one hand, one may claim that the Hungarian style of illiberalism via constitutional changes is more damaging in the long term, because illiberal changes are being entrenched well into the future: a future non-Fidesz government may lack a constitutional majority and be straitjacketed in its conduct by the illiberal Fundamental Law. By changing not only the Constitution but also, for instance, the electoral law, Fidesz managed to lock in its advantage. The entrenchment also applies to a number of officials appointed for very long terms of office, and who are likely to maintain their offices even under a non-Fidesz government: for instance, members of the Council of National Media are appointed for nine years, as is the chief prosecutor (previously, six years). On the other hand, however, one may speculate that constitutional amendments via statutes along with simple breaches of the Constitution, Polish-style, are more destructive of the principles of constitutionalism and the rule of law. In Hungary, the disempowerment of the Constitutional Court was done *lege artis*; in Poland, it was more a demolition job than the restructuring of an institution, in full disregard of the constitutional provisions.

In any event, there is no doubt that for the Kaczyński regime, the absence of a capacity to introduce formal constitutional amendments, or even bring about a new constitution, is seen as a burden and liability; something to overcome in the next elections. Having formal constitutional tools at its disposal is important for populist and authoritarian leaders. As David Landau shows, constitutional change often works in tandem with packing institutions such as the courts: formal constitutional amendments make changes in personnel and policies more durable, and render populist incumbents more difficult to dislodge.[64] Venezuela and Hungary provide two examples used by Landau to make this point, while Poland is an example of a country where 'governing populists have not yet carried out changes at this level',[65] that is, at the level of formal constitutional change.

Constitutional texts serve many other functions useful to authoritarians and populists, beyond entrenching them in power well into the future. These other functions may also be sought after by the PiS regime, and may add to the attractiveness of pursuing a constitutional majority. The first is of a purely *symbolic* nature: to manifest the break with the bad old days (liberal, cosmopolitan, elitist, etc.), and the genuine commitment of the rulers to traditional, national, and religious values. Hungary's new Constitution contains a large number of such feel-good patriotic-nationalistic messages, mainly in its Preamble, and they constitute a sort of constitutional 'cheap talk':[66] they are a low-cost investment in generating loyalty by citizens to the new order. Second, new constitutional texts also provide *guidelines* to the lower ranks of the party and electorate at large, which may be unaware of all the policy intricacies, and yet who may need to master the arguments in discussions and polemics with opponents.[67] Third, constitutional texts provide *signposts* as to the desired trajectory even beyond the political life of the present leader; better than party programmes, with their inevitable sectarianism, new constitutions outline the perspectives for the regime to evolve towards. This signposting is an important tool for the *mobilization* of supporters, and at the same time (often) shaming the opponents who may be unable to counter with equally impressive sounding signposts. Fourth, and probably most importantly, new constitutions may *facilitate political action*, which under the old constitution is more costly and burdensome. By reducing political costs (both domestic and international) consequent upon the breaches of the old constitution, or having to find ways of subterfuge without openly violating its text, a new constitution may be better adapted to the preferences of populist leaders regarding the most effective procedures, mechanisms and institutions in the state they govern.[68]

The functions of constitutions in a populist environment—entrenching personnel and policies into the future, symbolism, guidelines, signposting, mobilizing supporters while demoralizing opponents, and the facilitation of political action by lowering political transaction costs—make constitutional change a desirable action to pursue, but one which, these days at least, is unavailable to Jarosław Kaczyński in Poland. But it may be stated with almost complete certainty that each populist leader, knowing of the aforementioned repertoire of benefits of a new constitution, will aim at achieving constitutional change. Hence, the trajectory of populist systems lacking a new constitution will likely be along the lines of finding ways to equip itself with a brand new constitutional text, or at least (as second best) with deep constitutional amendments. This may explain why, in 2017, President Duda proposed to hold a referendum on a new constitution, preceded by a long period of public debate. The initiative was eventually crushed by his own party in 2018, for fear of the political fallout if the referendum turned out to be a fiasco, which would have been very likely.

Finally, and to state the obvious, perhaps the most striking aspect of the unconstitutional character of the post-2015 developments in Poland is the fact that changes have been preceded and facilitated by the incapacitation of the main device of constitutional maintenance in Poland after the fall of communism: the CT. As David Law and Mila Versteeg note in their pioneering work on 'sham constitutions', 'abusive governments can be expected to combine sham constitutions with sham judicial reviews. Government disrespect for a right will therefore translate into cramped judicial interpretation or enforcement of the right'.[69] Disabling the CT from being an effective and robust interpreter and enforcer of the Constitution must be seen as an *instrumental* step towards a situation in which the Constitution, while formally valid, does not matter when it conflicts with the government's designs for rearranging the boundary between its own targets and the sphere protected by constitutional principles and rights as interpreted so far. Sham judicial reviews support the government in emasculating constitutional constraints upon its actions. As a consequence, the Constitution stops being 'self-executing' because it lacks an internal legal instrument of assuring its self-binding character; its domination is eliminated by a politically dominant force.

When PiS violates the Constitution, it does so not on behalf of some revolutionary goals that would trump constitutional provisions, but rather by claiming that it does so on the basis of *its own* interpretation of the Constitution, an interpretation that is as good as, indeed better than, that of the SC, the Ombudsman, numerous scholars and law faculties, or the Venice Commission. The public understanding of the transformation by PiS is largely legalistic;[70] legal provisions are strictly adhered to even if they are depleted of canonical, traditional or even plausible interpretations of their meanings. By doing so, PiS has undermined the conditions for a rough consensus regarding constitutional meanings, which is a prerequisite of the subjection of politics to the Constitution, and hence of constitutionalism itself. There are no longer solid definitions within the political class about what counts as a constitutional violation—and this is perhaps the main significance of the unconstitutional character of PiS rule in Poland post-2015.

'Populist'

Populism is a vague and contested concept but, however understood, it is an important qualifier to my description of Polish anti-democratic backsliding. The notion of populism emphasizes that what is going on in Poland is not authoritarianism simpliciter, but that it is an illiberal condition whereby the rulers *care* about popular support. The notion of authoritarianism per se may apply to regimes that are totally insensitive to the level of societal support of their rule, and govern through considerable use of violence, but this is not the case of Poland post-2015. We need a language to distinguish between, on the one hand, authoritarianisms that rule by resorting to bare force and where a degree of societal support for the rule is not important for the rulers because they know that they can, and they do, rely on oppression and coercion; and, on the other hand, illiberal regimes that want to be liked or even loved, at least by a significant segment of the electorate. This does not necessarily render them democratic (once they begin dismantling separation of powers, constitutional checks, and democratic rights, they undermine democracy itself) but it makes them qualitatively different from the regimes that are authoritarian, and where public opinion does not count. In contrast, populists care a great deal about societal support, obsessively follow opinion polls to check their popularity rankings, and have a special weakness for mass rallies as a method of mobilizing 'the people'.[71]

The manifestations of populism, so understood, are manifold in Poland. Firstly, the government has been actively seeking popular approval, aiming to increase its support base of eligible voters beyond the 18 per cent it obtained in the 2015 elections, in particular by setting in place various welfare policies, such as a spectacularly popular programme '500+' consisting of monthly payments of PLN 500 (EUR 120) for child after the first—a programme that has benefited over two million families, poor and wealthy alike. This amounts to mass clientelism: 'the exchange of material and immaterial favors by elites for mass political support'.[72] And this clientelism is, in a typically populist vein, underwritten by moralized rationales, about the need to recognize those decent but poor, hard-working and long-suffering people, whose dignity has been, so far, violated by the insensitive elites.

Secondly, using the scholarly definitions of 'populism' as anti-pluralism, governmental propaganda has consistently applauded 'unity' and 'community' as paramount social values, and at the same time depicted the opposition as the enemy, as evil, and illegitimate. Anti-elite and anti-establishment sentiments were skilfully deployed against minorities and the opposition. Ironically, even the most excluded and disadvantaged of all groups, that is asylum-seekers and refugees, have been depicted as part of a plan designed by the European and Polish elites to threaten the whole population of Poland, which has let virtually none of them into the country. To make the paradox even more telling, the PiS elite, controlling all levers of power, still exploits its allegedly outsider status. A sense of being an embattled, continuously endangered group fighting the vicious establishment has become so much a part of PiS's identity and self-perception that even when in power it often presents itself (and is presented by pro-PiS media) as an outsider in opposition to the establishment.

Thirdly, political change has been managed through public propaganda campaigns aimed at winning the support of 'ordinary people'. The 'elites' have been represented as the sole beneficiaries of the post-1989 transition, while the 'ordinary people' were allegedly excluded from the resultant benefits. The usual sequence in this management of change has followed a similar script. First, a campaign of hate against a particular target group (judges, journalists, civil servants appointed by the former government, ex-communists) is launched, usually by governmental media; then some selectively chosen defects and pathologies taken from different eras (often, long overcome) are presented in a *pars pro toto* manner; the promise of a large-scale 'replacement of elites' and a 'redistribution of prestige' is made by the rulers; mass mobilization of public resentment is then organized, followed by actual legal changes.[73] This is why capturing the media (to start with, the public broadcasting media, having the largest coverage and impact) was the first and essential step in managing public sentiments, and in particular negative emotions of hatred, disaffection, and resentment. Just to give the reader an idea of the content of Polish public media propaganda, a typical news service on TVP (this stands for TV Poland, but its critics expand the initialism to TVPiS) these days is built on three elements, usually in this order: (1) the government and in particular the leader have had great successes and fulfil their promise to care for ordinary people; (2) the opposition is ignorant and treacherous, as well as divided by personal ambitions but, above all, it has no programme other than a return to the despicable status quo ante; and (3) 'Europe' is decadent and arrogant, and suicidal in allowing Islam to take over (and that is why many reasonable people abroad praise Poland so much).

The populist characteristics of the rhetoric employed by the ruling elite correspond to what many scholars, and in particular Jan-Werner Müller, describe as its fundamentally anti-pluralist character, and a usurpation of the role of true representative of the real identity of the people. As Müller observed, 'The claim to *exclusive* moral representation of the real or authentic people is at the core of populism.'[74] Kaczyński and his closest collaborators and propagandists have occasionally used this claim, in particular when denouncing the opposition and anti-governmental demonstrators. A favourite rhetorical tool has been to represent critics as foreign agents, even if unknowingly, and as those who simply dislike Poland—hence, have no claim to speak for Polish interests. The ruling elite does not often appeal to the

Stalinist-sounding concept of 'enemies of the people' but characterizations of the government's critics come close to such invective.

The argument here has so far proceeded as if the concept of 'populism' were clear, uncontested, and consensually adopted. Of course, it is not. There are many understandings of 'populism', some of which simply identify it with 'popular' governmental initiatives; others, with state interventionism in the economy,[75] or with a focus on a closeness to working people, 'blue-collar workers', farmers, and other lower or lower middle classes;[76] or still others with an ideology that opposes bad elites to good people, and celebrates the 'general will' as the basis for policy-making.[77] In recent years the most influential understanding is offered by Jan-Werner Müller who identifies populism with anti-pluralism, and more specifically, to repeat a quotation just used, with making the 'claim to *exclusive* moral represen-tation of the real or authentic people'.[78] As Müller explains, not all anti-pluralists are necessarily populist, but all populists make such a claim to exclusive repre-sentation. Populists, Müller adds, attempt 'to speak in the name of the people as a whole' and 'to morally de-legitimate all those who in turn contest that claim (which is to say: those who contest their involuntary inclusion in a "We the People"; such resisters to populism are effectively saying: "not in our name")'.[79]

While Müller is certainly correct that this type of rhetoric can often be found in populist manifestos and public statements, I doubt whether Müller's criterion of populism is sufficiently stable and determinate to distinguish populist from non-populist politicians and governments: it focuses too much on what populists *say* as opposed to what they *do*. This is even more explicit in the claim by another emi-nent student of populism, Cristóbal Rovira Kaltwasser, that 'populism is conceived of as *a moral discourse*, which by pitting "the pure people" against "the corrupt elite" defends the idea that popular sovereignty should be respected by all means.'[80] Similarly, for Bart Bonikowski populism is 'a form of political discourse' which can be best 'measure[d] … at the level of political speeches, or even speech elements'.[81] I do not deny the importance of a specific *discourse* for populist politics. It matters a great deal, and it carries distinctive characteristics, with its own style of dema-goguery, easy simplifications, enemy targeting, and unattainable promises, in add-ition to those features briskly encapsulated in the quote from Kaltwasser. But to hinge a characterization fully on either rhetoric, narrative or discourse is always risky: politicians often use their speech in a strategic or deceptive way, and in par-ticular do not always reveal the deep understandings (such as that about exclusive representation of real people) that motivate them to action.

As a result, this definition is both over-inclusive and under-inclusive. It is, on the one hand, *over-inclusive*: Müller's criterion is unlikely to provide a good distinc-tion between populists and perfectly unimpeachable democrats who, in a pluralist democracy, often (though not always) claim that they have actually better grasped the *true* common interest than their opponents; they claim to find a better amal-gamation between different ingredients of public good and more rational trade-offs between incompatible preferences than their opponents. Such a claim is a common staple of democratic politics, and making it does not taint a politician or a party as 'populist'. Especially in a democracy in which ideologically determinate political parties decline in importance, as is the case today, politicians will increasingly appeal to a broadly understood public good rather than to the sectoral interests of this or that constituency. As Stefan Rummens observes:

> Since well-established ideological divisions have lost much of their appeal, it has thereby become almost unavoidable for politicians to claim to represent 'the people' (rather than some subsection of society) and to tell a story about the collective identity of the community they believe significant parts of the electorate night identify with.[82]

This does not necessarily render them 'populist'; at most, it makes them appear to pursue popularity, which is a basic job requirement for all politicians. On the other hand, the definition is under-inclusive: populists such as Kaczyński or Orbàn do not necessarily say, 'We and only we are the people',[83] and that those who disagree with them are beyond the pale of the nation, that they are not 'real' Poles, Hungarians etc. Rather, they may characterize, and try to delegitimize, their opponents by presenting them as corrupt, mistaken, treacherous, serving foreign powers etc. To hinge an understanding of populism on making anti-pluralist *claims*, as Müller urges, is to hook our understanding of populism to the shifting sands of public rhetoric.

My understanding of populism identifies it with *actions*, which usually speak louder than words: in this sense, it is different from Müller's view because it sees populism not as an ideology but rather a form of political organization. But it overlaps with Müller's understanding in that it is, inter alia, connected with anti-pluralism or, more specifically, hostility to *institutional* pluralism. Populists typically try to build bridges to the 'real' people above the heads of intermediary institutions that in a constitutional democracy mediate between the people and the exercise of power. They dislike and disparage these institutions even if, as Kaczyński does, they pay lip service to them, but in the process, erode them of the reasons that underlie the creation of these institutions in the first place. Their political action is usually of a plebiscitary character, aimed at translating the will of the mythical, pre-political people into political action; they 'bypass all forms of intermediation' and 'rely on unmediated, quasi-direct appeals'.[84] Society, as a complex web of diverse preferences, interests, and identities, which triggers a pluralistic structure aimed at aggregating those diversities in a compromise-based polity, is displaced by a homogenous entity, the interests of which are best grasped by the populists, that is, the ultimate leader. *The people* are one, and those who reject us are not the people; and *we* are *their* representatives, so no intermediation between or interference with our pure representation of them can be countenanced. This, admittedly vague and under-theorized, understanding of populism will be adopted in this book.

It is also clear that when I speak of populism, I have in mind only its right-wing variant. According to some, 'left-wing populism' does not exist because left-wing parties do not appeal to the measures characteristic of populism, such as the style of politics that feeds on over-simplification and demagoguery. According to those critics, left-wing populism would be self-defeating because it would contradict what grassroots left-wing movements ultimately want, namely an expanded and inclusive public sphere with an active and critical role in checking government policies.[85] I will not adopt such a restrictive definition, which excludes the very possibility of left-wing populism, but it is irrelevant for our discussion, focused as it is on Poland. In Poland, as virtually everywhere else in the post-communist world (as opposed to Western and in particular Southern Europe), left-wing populism has been almost non-existent. Some consider the movement *Samoobrona*, which was a coalition partner of PiS in 2005–7, to be left-wing (by its pro-redistributive slogans), and certainly in its political style, demagoguery, and violently 'anti-elite' approach it *can* be characterized as populist. But it was short lived, and made only an ephemeral impact on the Polish political system. Elsewhere in the region, during some of its various iterations, the Slovak party Smer (Direction) could have been viewed as left-wing populist movement, as in Lithuania, with the agrarian-populist Peasant and Greens Union as part of the governing coalition. Overall, however, the right-wing variety clearly dominates in the landscape of populism in CEE. This is explained well by Ben Stanley:

> The relative absence of left-wing populism [in the CEE region] reflected the compatibility of nationalist, traditionalist, and authoritarian attitudes with anti-market economy stances. Right-wing populists were able to articulate this combination of ideological views without difficulty, whereas populists who laid claim to a left-wing identity had to be more careful in associating themselves with non-progressive political currents.[86]

Perhaps the main difference between left-wing populist movements (e.g. the Syriza in Greece and Spain's Podemos) and right-wing populists is that, for the former, the targeting of an outsider as someone to be warned against is irrelevant or is of only small significance, while in the case of right-wing populists it is usually one of the essential elements of their programme. As John Judis puts it, '[l]eftwing populists champion the people against an elite or an establishment', while right-wing populism is 'triadic' in that adherents 'champion the people against an elite that they accuse of coddling a third group, which can consist, for instance, of immigrants, Islamists, or African American militants'.[87] For those of a left-wing sensitivity, targeting the 'other', who are usually the weakest and the most vulnerable, would be against the most fundamental progressive values. In this way, left-wing populism is neither necessarily exclusionary nor inegalitarian; left-wing populists generally 'accept political liberalism's commitment to equality'.[88]

In any event, a clear characterization of PiS as right-wing as opposed to left-wing is difficult because, while some traits of its programme are typically right-wing (nationalism, ostentatious religiosity, celebration of hierarchical authority and tradition), others may be seen as more of a left-wing variety (massive economic transfers towards the worse-off). This uncertainty of characterization is related to the fact that, as with any populism, and in particular any populism in power, PiS's populism is only very thinly ideological. The general trend in Europe is for populist parties to combine redistributive policy and opposition to austerity measures with strong anti-immigration and anti-minorities impulses. In pursuit of vote maximization, which is its main aim, PiS explicitly uses appeals to the strongly ideological items of its programme only occasionally, whenever it needs to win (or win back) its most radical base, without however alienating the more moderate supporters. In this respect, Kaczyński is in line with other populist leaders who 'put vote maximization ahead of ideological purity'.[89] That is why Kaczyński himself is vague about his comprehensive vision of a society, except for some banalities about dignity or traditional values. Since today's PiS is a new iteration of a centrist, mainstream party, no one expects him to enunciate such a vision.

In principle, it may be thought that the very idea of populism need not put it necessarily on a collision course with democracy and compel it to pursue authoritarian solutions. Some versions and manifestations dubbed as 'populist' do not imply authoritarianism. For instance, the campaign for Brexit was generally viewed as a strong manifestation of populism, and indeed carried certain features associated with populism: dislike of the existing political establishment, and in particular of mainstream political parties; fear of or hatred towards the 'others', in particular migrants and refugees; strong economic and political nationalism, associated with the dislike of globalization, European supranationalism, etc. The UK Independence Party's populist appeal was based first and foremost on its anti-EU and anti-immigrant sentiments (two issues that were easily merged into one in the mouth of skillful demagogues),[90] but there was very little about the pro-Brexit movement to suggest that its proponents were hostile to the idea of political democracy, to pluralism, and to the principles of political representation, even though the very idea of a referendum on Brexit was clearly a choice of a plebiscitary mode of politics.[91] But the use of plebiscitary politics within a broader framework of parliamentary democracy is not, per se, evidence of a dangerous or invidious pluralism. Similarly, it is not clear whether left-wing populists in Greece or Spain are hostile to democratic processes (both parties took part in the parliamentary elections in their respective countries, and never questioned the outcomes, with Syriza even winning the general election in January 2015)[92] even if they occasionally criticize specific democratic processes in their countries—something that is a legitimate matter for any democratic party or movement to pursue.

But populism, Polish or Hungarian style, *is* anti-democratic and authoritarian, because it connects the usual populist repertoire (nationalism, plebiscitary style of politics, xenophobia, and fear of others) with dismantlement of the institutional mechanisms that are essential to political democracy. As is documented in detail in this book, and in particular in Chapters 3–5, both these instances of populists in power manifest, in addition to populism-defining characteristics, clear authoritarian traits: the dismantlement of institutional constraints on political power (especially, but not limited to, courts of various sorts), restrictions on political rights (including freedom of the media), and manipulation of electoral law in order to favour the incumbents and, above all, to concentrate virtually all of the political power in the hands of the leader of the electorally victorious party. Insofar as some of these assaults on the conditions of democracy are still in early gestation in Poland (especially as far as restrictions of political rights and freedoms are concerned), we may speak of a movement *towards* authoritarianism rather than a fully fledged authoritarian regime. As Bojan Bugarič says, 'authoritarian populists in Hungary and Poland have successfully institutionalized, through legal reforms, a new version of semi-authoritarian regime, which is halfway between "diminished democracy" and "competitive authoritarianism".'[93] And if we adopt the realistic view that a characterization of 'authoritarianism' allows for judgments of degree, rather than being black-and-white, whether we define the Polish case as semi-authoritarianism or as a system on the road towards authoritarianism or as authoritarianism at an early phase of maturation, is a pedantic question. The choice of terminology may have a pragmatic use in expressing one's degree of reprobation, but as an analytical matter it is of no import. What matters is that these authoritarian movements are, in Poland as in Hungary, part of a broader package that includes typically populist ideology and instruments. Whether populism is intrinsically related to authoritarianism of the sort that Orbán and Kaczyński espouse is something that is beyond the goals of this chapter to reflect upon, but such a discussion is offered in Chapter 9 of this book.

Bugarič, when reviewing contemporary studies about how populists in power undermine democracy, concludes that there are four symptoms of such a democratic degradation.[94] All these four symptoms are present, to different degrees, in Poland and Hungary. The first is attacks upon the essential checks and balances of the executive and legislative branch. In Poland it was reflected mainly in the paralysis of the CT and in turning it into an aide to the government. Similarly, in Hungary the capture of the Constitutional Court proceeded through changing the rules for nomination of judges, then by restricting the court's jurisdiction, and finally by court-packing, which included an increase in the number of judges, thus producing a safe Fidesz majority on the court. In both countries, an assault on regular courts proceeded along very similar lines, including the restructuring of the SC and the lowering of the retirement age for judges to get rid of possibly recalcitrant judges and create vacancies for loyalists. The second symptom is an attack on free media. In Poland, this was reflected in the full colonization of public media, but is also at an early stage insofar as the commercial media is concerned. In contrast, in Hungary, almost all the main commercial media (including the second-largest private TV channel) found themselves in the hands of the government's allies. In both countries, the regulatory institutional system of media was changed to suit the needs of the executive branch. The third aspect is a populist attack on civil rights and liberties. In Poland such assaults are visible in the changes in the law of assemblies, with some assemblies being 'more equal than others, in freedom of speech (the law on the Holocaust), and the rights of NGOs. Finally, the fourth aspect is the degradation of the quality of elections. In Poland, it is reflected in a systemic change to the institutional system of the electoral process, with all central and local institutions of elections 'dejudicialized' and staffed by persons dependent upon the executive. In Hungary, changes in the electoral system were effected by a combination of gerrymandering, reductions in the parliamentary seats, and the capture of the Elections Commission. As one can see, the general observations regarding populism's assault on democracy around the world have been reproduced in Poland and Hungary.

'Backsliding'

The concept of 'backsliding' is also central to the characterization of Polish developments in recent years because its dynamism and path-dependence is essential. In Poland, just as in Hungary, in contrast say to Russia or Belarus, we deal with instances of significant deterioration in democratic qualities already attained. In fact, it had been generally acknowledged that both Hungary and Poland were among the most successful post-transitional democracies in CEE, and indeed achieved the greatest successes of their entire respective histories: never before had either of these countries attained a combination of democratic governance generated by free and fair elections, rapid growth in standards of living, and safe international environments secured by membership both in the EU and NATO. In an article back in 2002, a prominent US political scientist listed Poland and Hungary in the category of 'the leaders of the group' of countries that were 'en route to becoming successful, well-functioning democracies' within a broader 'transitional' category.[95] Without any exaggeration, one may say that both countries have never had it so good in their past, all the more in their recent past.

This fact is significant to understand the specificities of the situation, because the trajectory of backsliding has to be distinguished from the absence of democratic progress in countries that have not achieved a satisfactory level of democracy in the first place,[96] or where the current status quo has emerged as a result of the relative democratization or liberalization of an oppressive regime. Path dependence matters a great deal and we need a language to distinguish cases such as Poland and Hungary (with recent high, though not yet strongly, consolidated democratic achievement fresh in its collective memory and in institutional legacies) from states that are 'stuck somewhere on the assumed democratization sequence, usually at the start of the consolidation phase'.[97] The trajectory in the form of a bell curve that Poland has traversed is completely different from a static plateau of Belarus, Moldova or Russia, and these differences produce salient political and constitutional consequences/effects. The states that have backslided from a superior position are held to higher standards by their citizens and by the outside word, because these higher standards had once been achieved or approximated. There are institutional legacies, such as constitutional interpretations in the case law or practices of good conduct by authorities, which exert normative pressure upon the current authorities. The coexistence and interactions of authoritarian leaders with the democratic institutions that evoke fully democratic standards latent in the collective memory of the society yield distinctive patterns of political behaviour and legal actions not found in the authoritarian states without such a past.

The use of the notion of backsliding emphasizes a temporal dimension, and highlights a retrogression that is not visible in a time-slice account. As Renata Uitz observed acutely (with regard to Orbán's Hungary), '[r]eflecting on the changes introduced by the new constitutional rules (rather than simply taking a snapshot of these rules) and accounting for the practical consequences of these changes, have revealed a pattern of elimination of constitutional constraints on the exercise of political powers and the resulting instances of self-perpetuation through constitution-making'.[98] This reference to a 'snapshot' is important because a system, if not viewed in a diachronic way, may bear a resemblance to some similar systems in perfectly democratic countries. What is missing in a snapshot account is that the removal (or hollowing-out) of certain institutions in comparison to the previous status quo erodes the system of safeguards, while in a different system that may bear superficial resemblances to a country that slid back, the role of such safeguards is played by different mechanisms or by legal and political culture. This is, for instance, the case of constitutional review which, when emasculated in Poland or Hungary, leaves a gap because the system had used such review to provide crucial protections that elsewhere (e.g. in legal systems lacking a constitutional court) has been provided by other institutions.

The word 'backsliding' accurately describes *the process of reversal*, and the fact that there is no rapid, immediate rupture, as in a coup. It also emphasizes a *process* as opposed to a state of affairs. As Ellen Lust and David Waldner describe it: 'Backsliding occurs through a series of discrete changes in the rules and informal procedures that shape elections, rights and accountability. These take place over time, separated by months or even years'.[99] But at the same time, one should be warned that the use of the word 'backsliding' should not connote (as the word *may* suggest to some) something impersonal, purposeless, almost haphazard.[100]

There is energy, restlessness, zeal, and purposefulness in Poland after 2015—as is evidenced in the rest of this book.

It is also important to resist a possible, but potentially misleading, implication of the concept 'backsliding' that it is some form of reversal to the *ancien regime*, or at least that 'backsliding can be directly traced back to the survival of structures, mentalities, and habits of [*sic*] rooted in communism'.[101] This idea may be one among many possible characterizations of the populist breakdown of constitutionalism in Poland or Hungary, particularly salient for the purpose of political rhetoric and polemics, but any analogy with the communist or immediate post-communist structures is a non-starter. Both supranational and domestic institutional structures are completely different, and if the notion of backsliding may be seen as a reversal of democratic practices and achievements, it is not in the direction of state socialism or communism. It does not follow that one should abstain from analyses of sources of the backsliding as being connected, inter alia, with value formations, which have their sources in the pre-1989 period: both in the sphere of 'demand' for policies and 'supply' of political programmes, the attitudes and expectations of political actors and their constituencies are shaped, constrained, and affected, among other things, by attitudes formed under communism.[102] But today's backsliding is not along a road back to communism.

Notes

1. James Dawson and Seán Hanley, 'The Fading Mirage of the "Liberal Consensus"' (2016) 27/1 *Journal of Democracy* 20, 20.
2. Agata Łukaszewicz, 'Dobra muzyka … zawsze się obroni', *Rzeczpospolita* (Warsaw, 22 February 2018) 15.
3. 'Przyjdzie dzień, że w Warszawie będzie Budapeszt', <https://www.tvn24.pl/wiadomosci-z-kraju,3/przyjdzie-dzien-ze-w-warszawie-bedzie-budapeszt,186922.html> (accessed 2 August 2018).
4. Arch Puddington and Tyler Roylance, 'The Dual Threat of Populists and Autocrats' (2017) 28/2 *Journal of Democracy* 105, 112.
5. Jerzy Baczyński, 'Niewygodne przesłanie', *Polityka* 7 (Warsaw, 7 November 2017) online edition.
6. Grażyna Skąpska, 'The Decline of Liberal Constitutionalism in East Central Europe' in Peeter Vihalemm, Anu Masso, and Signe Opermann (eds), *The Routledge International Handbook of European Social Transformations* (Routledge 2017) 130, 134.
7. See Bogdan Góralczyk, 'Axiological Disintegration of the EU? The Case of Hungary' (2015) 18 *Yearbook of Polish European Studies* 81, 87.
8. Balint Magyar, *Post-Communist Mafia State: The Case of Hungary* (CEU Press 2016).
9. Eric A. Posner, 'The Dictator's Handbook, US Edition' in Cass R. Sunstein (ed.), *Can It Happen Here? Authoritarianism in America* (HarperCollins 2018) 1, 16. Posner raises this question with regard to a hypothetical he formulated regarding President Trump's assault on institutions.

10. Mark Tushnet, 'Authoritarian Constitutionalism' (2015) 100 *Cornell Law Review* 391, 409–10 and 410, footnote 101.
11. Ozan O. Varol, 'Stealth Authoritarianism' (2015) 100 *Iowa Law Review* 1673, 1734.
12. Aziz Huq and Tom Ginsburg, 'How to Lose a Constitutional Democracy' (2018) 65 *UCLA Law Review* 78, 118, footnote omitted.
13. Ibid. 119.
14. Ibid. 119, footnote omitted.
15. Nancy Bermeo, 'On Democratic Backsliding' (2016) 27/1 *Journal of Democracy* 5, 14.
16. Gábor Attila Tóth, 'The Authoritarian's New Clothes: Tendencies Away from Constitutional Democracy', *Policy Brief* (The Foundation for Law, Justice and Society 2017) 2.
17. The parliamentary discussion on the Supreme Court Act on 19 July 2017, <http://orka.sejm.gov.pl/Zapisy8.nsf/0/FD57E6B95B10AB16C125816F003ACDF4/$file/0215108.pdf> (accessed 25 April 2018).
18. The parliamentary discussion on the Constitutional Tribunal Act on 21 December 2015, <http://orka.sejm.gov.pl/Zapisy8.nsf/0/CBCDE2C33B340E53C1257F37004B0580/$file/0011008.pdf> (accessed 25 April 2018).
19. For the concept of hollow institutions, see Dawson and Hanley (n. 1) 23.
20. Martin Krygier, 'Institutionalisation and Its Discontents: Constitutionalism versus (Anti-) Constitutional Populism in East Central Europe', Democratic Politics in Global Crisis? Challenges, Approaches, Resistances, lecture delivered to Transnational Legal Institute, King's College London, Signature Lecture Series, 17 November 2017; on file with the author, 4.
21. Varol (n. 11) 1684.
22. Ibid. 1679.
23. Ibid.
24. Ibid. 1685.
25. Steven Levitsky and Daniel Ziblatt, *How Democracies Die* (Crown Publishing 2018) 5.
26. János Kis, 'Introduction: From the 1989 Constitution to the 2011 Fundamental Law' in Gábor Attila Tóth (ed.), *Constitution for a Disunited Nation: On Hungary's 2011 Fundamental Law* (CEU Press 2012) 1, 15.
27. Jack M. Balkin, 'Constitutional Rot' in Cass Sunstein (ed.), *Can It Happen Here? Authoritarianism in America* (HarpersCollins 2018) 19, 26–27.
28. See Ellen Lust and David Waldner, 'Unwelcome Change: Understanding, Evaluating and Extending Theories of Democratic Backsliding' (USAID, 2015) [PDF] <http://pdf.usaid.gov/pdf_docs/PBAAD635.pdf> 21–22 (accessed 9 November 2017).
29. Maciej Gdula, *Nowy Autorytaryzm* (*New Authoritarianism*) (Wydawnictwo Krytyki Politycznej 2018) 10–11.
30. 'Election 2016: How it Happened', *The Economist* (London, 12 November 2016) ('Half of America can scarcely believe the other half has chosen Mr. Trump').
31. For these, and many other examples of lies, deceptions, and manipulations, see Dominik Uhlig, 'Pinokiowie', *Czarna Księga, Gazeta Wyborcza* (Warsaw, 17 October 2018) 10–11.
32. I am grateful to Mr Eugeniusz Smolar for pointing my attention to the facts and statements referred to in this paragraph, personal communication, 4 March 2018.

33. See 'Poland's New Government Dislikes Critical Media, Vegetarians and Cyclists', *The Economist* (London, 4 January 2016), online edition, <https://www.economist.com/europe/2016/01/04/polands-new-government-dislikes-critical-media-vegetarians-and-cyclists> (accessed 4 July 2018).

34. 'Poles and Hungarians have preserved good values', speech by Andrzej Duda (19 March 2016) <http://www.president.pl/en/news/art,126,poles-and-hungarians-have-preserved-good-values.html> (accessed 4 July 2018).

35. As reported in 'Poland's New Prime Minister: Return to Christian Roots Only Way to Stop Europe's Decline' (*LifeSiteNews*, 14 December 2017) <https://jtcontracelsum.blogspot.com/2017/12/polands-new-prime-minister.html> (accessed 4 July 2018).

36. Andrzej Balcer, Piotr Buras, Grzegorz Gromadzki, and Eugeniusz Smolar, *Change in Poland, but what change? Assumptions of Law and Justice Party Foreign Policy* (Stefan Batory Foundation 2016) 2.

37. Ibid. 14, emphases omitted.

38. As recently as 2016, over 60 per cent of Poles were against same-sex partnerships, while over 25 per cent were in favour, ibid. 11.

39. Balkin (n. 27).

40. Tom Gerald Daly, in a number of I-CONNECT blog posts and columns, including 'Enough Complacency: Fighting Democratic Decay in 2017' (*I-CONNECT*, 11 January 2017) <http://bit.ly/2uuLGXe> (accessed 9 January 2018).

41. See Jacques Rupnik, 'Is East-Central Europe Backsliding? From Democracy Fatigue to Populist Backlash' (2007) 18/4 *Journal of Democracy* 17.

42. Fareed Zakaria, 'The Rise of Illiberal Democracy', *Foreign Affairs* (November/December 1997) 22.

43. Bojan Bugarič and Tom Ginsburg, 'Assault on Postcommunist Courts' (2016) 27/3 *Journal of Democracy* 69, 73–75.

44. Tóth (n. 16).

45. David Landau, 'Abusive Constitutionalism' (2013) 47 *UC Davis Law Review* 189.

46. Roberto Stefan Foa and Yascha Mounk, 'The Signs of Deconsolidation' (2017) 28/1 *Journal of Democracy* 5, 11–12.

47. Ibid. 5–8.

48. See Larry Diamond, 'Thinking about Hybrid Regimes' (2002) 13/2 *Journal of Democracy* 21.

49. With respect to Hungary, see Magyar (n. 8) 113.

50. See e.g. Kim Lane Scheppele, 'Constitutional Coups and Judicial Review: How Transnational Institutions Can Strengthen Peak Courts at Times of Crisis (with Special Reference to Hungary' (2014) 23 *Transnational Law & Contemporary Problems* 51.

51. But see Scheppele: she defends using the word 'coup' because 'the end result turns the prior constitutional order on its head without a legitimating process to confirm the changes', ibid. 51–2.

52. For insistence on the need to distinguish between coups and 'endogenous termination' where democratically elected leaders end the democratic process themselves, see Ko Maeda, 'Two Modes of Democratic Breakdown: A Competing Risks Analysis of Democratic Durability' (2010) 72 *Journal of Politics* 1129.

53. Personal disclosure: so did I.

54. Skąpska (n. 6) 140.

55. For more about the veto, see Marcin Matczak, 'Is Poland's President Duda on the Road to Damascus?' (*VerfBlog*, 26 July 2017) <http://verfassungsblog.de/is-polands-president-duda-on-the-road-to-damascus> (accessed 9 January 2018).

56. Mark Tushnet, 'Authoritarian Constitutionalism: Some Conceptual Issues' in Tom Ginsburg and Alberto Simpser (eds), *Constitutions in Authoritarian Regimes* (CUP 2014) 36–40.

57. Act of the 22 December 2015 amending the Act on the Constitutional Tribunal.

58. Mirosław Wyrzykowski, 'Antigone in Warsaw' in Marek Zubik (ed.), *Human Rights in Contemporary World: Essays in Honour of Professor Leszek Garlicki* (Wydawnictwo Sejmowe 2017) 370, 380.

59. Act of 22 June 2016 on the Council of National Media. The council is charged with the control of national broadcasters (Polish Television, Polish Radio, and Polish Press Agency) having the competence to appoint or dismiss presidents, members of supervisory boards, and management boards as well as other members of public broadcaster's statutory bodies.

60. Provisions on Introduction of the Act on the Organisation and Proceedings before the Constitutional Tribunal and the Judges of the Constitutional Tribunal Status Act. (After Sejm had passed the statute and the Senate had not submitted amendments, the President signed the statute on 19 December 2016.)

61. Act of 8 December 2017 on the amendment of the Act on the National Council of the Judiciary and some other acts.

62. See more: Marcin Matczak, 'President Duda is Destroying the Rule of Law instead of Fixing it' (*VerfBlog*, 26 September 2017) <http://verfassungsblog.de/president-duda-is-destroying-the-rule-of-law-instead-of-fixing-it> (accessed 9 January 2018); Wojciech Sadurski, 'Judicial "Reform" in Poland: The President's Bills Are as Unconstitutional as the Ones He Vetoed' (*VerfBlog*, 28 November 2017) <http://verfassungsblog.de/judicial-reform-in-poland-the-presidents-bills-are-as-unconstitutional-as-the-ones-he-vetoed> (accessed 9 January 2018).

63. Skąpska (n. 6) 134.

64. David Landau, 'Populist Constitutions' (2018) 85 *University of Chicago Law Review* 521, 532–37.

65. Ibid. 536.

66. On constitutional cheap talk, see Tom Ginsburg and Alberto Simpser, 'Introduction: Constitutions in Authoritarian Regimes' in Tom Ginsburg and Alberto Simpser (eds), *Constitutions in Authoritarian Regimes* (CUP 2014) 1, 7.

67. This function corresponds, roughly, to what Ginsburg and Simpser describe as 'set[ting] up institutions to control lower-level agents', ibid. 4.

68. This corresponds roughly to the 'operating manual' function of constitutions, ibid. 6.

69. David S. Law and Mila Versteeg, 'Sham Constitutions' (2013) 101 *California Law Review* 863, 877.

70. In public discourse, though, there were exceptions. At the beginning of the constitutional crisis in Poland, in November and December 2015, some MPs referred to the theory of the Sejm's (Parliament's) supremacy over the tribunal and other constitutional bodies. Their justifications were based directly on the concept of the primacy of the nation's will over the law, see e.g. Konrad Morawiecki, in *Sprawozdanie Stenograficzne z 2. posiedzenia*

Sejmu Rzeczypospolitej Polskiej w dniu 25 listopada 2015 r. (Minutes of the Meeting of Sejm of the Republic of Poland on 25 November 2015) 78; Marek Ast, in *Sprawozdanie Stenograficzne z 3. posiedzenia Sejmu Rzeczypospolitej Polskiej w dniu 2 grudnia 2015 r.* (Minutes of the Meeting of Sejm of the Republic of Poland on 2 December 2015) 14–15.

71. See Kurt Weyland, 'Populism: A Political-Strategic Approach, in Cristóbal Rovira Kaltwasser' in Paul Taggart, Paulina Ochoa-Espejo, and Pierre Ostiguy (eds), *The Oxford Handbook of Populism* (OUP 2017) 48, 56–8.

72. Jan-Werner Müller, 'Populism and Constitutionalism' in Cristóbal Rovira Kaltwasser, Paul Taggart, Paulina Ochoa-Espejo, and Pierre Ostiguy (eds), *The Oxford Handbook of Populism* (OUP 2017) 590, 596.

73. For repeatability of this sequence, see Ewa Łętowska, 'Zmierzch liberalnego państwa prawa w Polsce' (2017, no. 1–2) *Kwartalnik o prawach człowieka* 5, 11.

74. Müller (n. 72) 593, emphasis in original.

75. See e.g. Ross Douthat, 'The Pull of Populism' *New York Times* (New York, 14 February 2018), online edition (accessed 16 February 2018). The *New York Times* columnist writes about 'a nationalism-infused deficit financed populism' as a strand in current American conservatism, opposed to libertarianism; its programmatic claims are promises of 'infrastructure spending, universal health care, protectionism, middle-class tax cuts—a right-wing Keynesianism for the common man'.

76. In his monumental biography of Stalin, Stephen Kotkin notes that 'Stalin had never been a worker himself, had clashed bitterly with the one genuine worker in the politburo (Tomsky), and rarely visited factories. But he nurtured a deep populist streak'; Kotkin goes on to describe Stalin's writing a preface to a female textile worker pamphlet on socialist competition. This subsection of the chapter in Kotkin's book is entitled 'Populism', Stephen Kotkin, *Stalin*, vol. 2 (Allen Lane 2017) 18.

77. Cas Mudde, 'Populism: An Ideational Approach' in Cristóbal Rovira Kaltwasser, Paul Taggart, Paulina Ochoa-Espejo, and Pierre Ostiguy (eds), *The Oxford Handbook of Populism* (OUP 2017) 27–47.

78. Müller (n. 72) 593, emphasis in original.

79. Ibid. 601.

80. Cristóbal Rovira Kaltwasser, 'Populism and the Question of How to Respond to It' in Cristóbal Rovira Kaltwasser, Paul Taggart, Paulina Ochoa-Espejo, and Pierre Ostiguy (eds), *The Oxford Handbook of Populism* (OUP 2017) 489, 490, emphasis added.

81. Bart Bonikowski, 'Ethno-nationalist populism and the mobilization of collective resentment' (2017) 68 (Suppl. 1) *British Journal of Sociology* S181, S186.

82. Stefan Rummens, 'Populism as a Threat to Liberal Democracy' in Cristóbal Rovira Kaltwasser, Paul Taggart, Paulina Ochoa-Espejo, and Pierre Ostiguy (eds), *The Oxford Handbook of Populism* (OUP 2017) 554, 560.

83. Müller (n. 72) 601.

84. Weyland (n. 71) 58.

85. Albert Ogien and Sandra Laugier, *Antidémocratie* (La Découverte 2017) 73–4.

86. Ben Stanley, 'Populism in Central and Eastern Europe' in Cristóbal Rovira Kaltwasser, Paul Taggart, Paulina Ochoa-Espejo, and Pierre Ostiguy (eds), *The Oxford Handbook of Populism* (OUP 2017) 140, 147.

87. John B. Judis, *The Populist Explosion* (Columbia Global Reports 2016) 15.

88. Mark Tushnet, 'Comparing Right-Wing and Left-Wing Populism' in Mark A. Graber, Sanford Levinson, and Mark Tushnet (eds), *Constitutional Democracy in Crisis?* (OUP 2018) 639, 645.
89. Weyland (n. 71) 50.
90. See Judis (n. 87) 140.
91. See Gráinne de Búrca, 'How British was the Brexit Vote?' in Benjamin Martill and Uta Staiger (eds), *Brexit and Beyond: Rethinking the Futures of Europe* (UCL Press 2018) 46.
92. Judis (n. 87) 114–30.
93. Bojan Bugarič, Central Europe's Descent into Autocracy: On Authoritarian Populism, 2018–2019 CES Harvard Open Forum Paper Series 5, footnote omitted.
94. Ibid. 12–14.
95. Thomas Carothers, 'The End of the Transition Paradigm' (2002) 13/1 *Journal of Democracy* 5, 9.
96. See Steven Levitsky and Lucan Way, 'The Myth of Democratic Recession' (2015) 26/1 *Journal of Democracy* 45, 53–4.
97. Carothers (n. 95) 10.
98. Renáta Uitz, 'Can You Tell when an Illiberal Democracy is in the Making? An Appeal to Comparative Constitutional Scholarship from Hungary' (2015) 13 *International Journal of Constitutional Law* 279, 296.
99. Lust and Waldner (n. 28) 7.
100. I owe this observation to Martin Krygier.
101. Zsolt Enyedi, 'Populist Polarization and Party System Institutionalization: The Role of Party Politics in De-Democratization' (2016) 63 *Problems of Post-Communism* 210, 216.
102. See similarly ibid. 216.

2

Before the Breakdown: 1989–2015

Poland entered an era of deep democratic transformation on the eve of the last decade of the twentieth century, equipped with a constitution written during the darkest years of Stalinist repression in the early 1950s, as approved by Stalin himself, who had personally introduced a number of corrections to it.[1] The Constitution of the Polish People's Republic of 1952—like other constitutions of 'really existing socialism' or 'popular democracies' in the region, modelled as they were on the Soviet (Stalinist) Constitution—was strong on declaratory articulations of rights, but weak on their enforcement, accentuated citizens' duties accompanying their rights, and emphatically rejected the idea of separation of powers, favouring instead the idea of the 'unity of power'. After all, the sovereign—i.e. the 'working people in the towns and countryside'—would not allow its powers to be fragmented or constrained in any way.

Even in official legal doctrine, not to mention in reality, the Constitution was not self-executing or directly applicable, but rather operated via parliamentary legislation. In the words of the Polish Supreme Court in its judgment of 1955: 'Constitutional norms ... [are] unsuitable for direct practical application in everyday life of the society without being expanded in ordinary statutes and other normative acts'.[2] It was less a legal document, more an ideological signpost. This is not to say that there were no positive constitutional developments prior to the fall of communism. In the last years of the regime especially, the establishment of the Supreme Administrative Court (1980), the Ombudsman's office (1987), and the Constitutional Tribunal (CT) (1992 and 1995) were significant steps towards placing at least some limits on arbitrary power, but these developments were in spite of, rather than on the basis of, the original constitutional text.

The Constitution provided for intricate relationships between the Parliament (Sejm), the Council of Ministers, and the Council of State (the 'collective head of state')—as if these were real seats of power. It did not mention, however, the *Polska Zjednoczona Parta Robotnicza* (PZPR) (Polish United Workers Party,[3] where all the actual decisions were made within its Political Bureau, with the constitutionally designed bodies acting as mere rubber-stamps and executors of decisions taken elsewhere. As the (bad) old joke went, the Constitution was so valuable because it was hardly used.

Perhaps the best characterization of the Constitution was offered not by a constitutional scholar, but by a political scientist, Adam Przeworski:

Poland's Constitutional Breakdown. © Wojciech Sadurski 2019. Published 2019 by Oxford University Press.

> What the Polish Communists did in 1952 was to write an operating manual, but not for the car they were to drive. As long as the car functioned, powered by the force of the Soviet Army, no manual was needed. But when it started breaking down, no one knew how to fix it.... By the time it occurred to the rulers to constitutionalize their rule, it was too late.[4]

If the 1952 Constitution was never in touch with the political realities of a non-sovereign, party-governed Poland, it was all the more out of place in 1989. With the Constitution so obviously obsolete and inconsistent with the principles of liberal democracy which Poland now proclaimed, one might imagine that one of the first and most urgent tasks for politicians of the transitional era would be to write and enact a brand new, comprehensive Basic Law as quickly as possible. To do so would have been immeasurably easier than transforming the economy from centrally planned to market-based, or to rebuild its political culture from authoritarian to democratic. And yet, the opposite happened. Poland, being the first to overturn the old system, was the last (not counting Hungary where the first comprehensive constitution after the fall of communism was enacted in 2011) of all Central and Eastern Europe (CEE) post-communist states to adopt a fully fledged, new constitution.

There were many reasons for this, most of them having to do with strong party fragmentation in the post-1989 political landscape, and also the church's unwillingness to endorse the secular constitution on which the left insisted. But the main reason, strange though it may sound, was that a new constitution was not *all that* necessary. Despite calls to take advantage of the window of opportunity created by a 'constitutional moment',[5] the political system in the early and mid-1990s did reasonably well without a comprehensive new constitution. This was because the gap was being quite satisfactorily filled by what were, jointly, good proxies for a new constitution: the Round Table (RT) agreements, the 'Small Constitution' of 1992, and the case law of the invigorated CT. These three elements combined created a workable living constitution for the transitional era, and greatly reduced the incentives that politicians had for hastily working on a new constitution. They will now be briefly discussed in turn.

The Round Table's Constitutional Dimension

The true constitutional basis for the Polish transition to democracy was the April 1989 agreement of the RT. The agreement was in fact a pact, a compromise and thus possessed both immense benefits and costs. It was a way out of the deadlock that Poland found itself in by the end of 1980s. Neither the governing elite had sufficient will or resources to rule in the absence of even minimal legitimacy, nor did the opposition, i.e. mainly the Solidarność movement, have the power or intention to forcibly overthrow these rulers. The contract was between the 'governmental side' (the government, the Communist Party, two satellite parties, and pro-government trade unions) and the opposition (i.e. the Solidarność trade union—at the time, still formally delegalized—and its experts). The constitutional system of government that emerged from two months of negotiations had all the traits of a bargain, based on the initial understanding that the communists would share rather than surrender power, and that the main point of the first democratic election was not so much to build a perfect democracy, but rather to restrict the authoritarianism of the *ancien régime* by allowing some space for the opposition and liberalizing its practices. The communists were still strong enough (or so the rest of the society thought) to paralyse the transition, while the opposition was still too weak (or so its dominant factions thought) to govern. The common denominator was provided by a joint realization that things must change, and that the use of violence, by either side, was not an attractive option.

The details of the RT agreement supplied specific mechanisms for this compromise. The central element was a new electoral system that would allow the opposition, and in particular the newly re-legalized Solidarność, to take part in elections to be held in June of that year, after an almost immediate dissolution of the current Sejm; however, Solidarność was only permitted to contest 35 per cent of the seats in the Sejm, but otherwise all seats in the Senate. The Senate's power of veto of the Sejm's statutes (though capable of being overridden by a two-thirds vote in the Sejm) was an institutional expression of the mild (non-final) political veto by Solidarność of the PZPR controlling the majority of the Sejm. The 'governmental side' later agreed to the proposal by Solidarność to open up a quota of seats for democratic election in exchange for guaranteeing the maintenance of the *ancien régime*'s overall stronghold on the system, i.e. the powerful presidency, with the assurance that this position would be held by the martial law enforcer General Wojciech Jaruzelski, with the power to declare a state of emergency in order to restore law and order if necessary. To the PZPR, this was meant to ensure that the regime would be maintained, even if it was softened and liberalized.

A newly established president to replace the rubber-stamping Council of State was to be elected for six years by the combined chambers of the Sejm and Senate, which would only give the communists a marginal majority. The president acquired relatively broad but largely unspecified competences in the fields of defence, internal security and foreign affairs, and also in appointing the prime minister in case of a vote of no confidence by the Sejm to the government. In addition, the president would have the power of legislative initiative and veto (though capable of being overridden by the Sejm with a two-thirds majority), of dissolution of the parliament (in case of non-adoption of the budget or of an encroachment upon presidential constitutional prerogatives), and as already mentioned, of declaring martial law. The latter was seen as the ultimate guarantee for the maintenance of the position of the communists. The main restriction on presidentialism was the fact that it provided for parliamentary, rather than direct, election of the president.

From the very beginning, the Jaruzelski presidency was doomed to insignificance. Jaruzelski agreed to stand for election only after much procrastination, and only after his proposal to nominate his Minister of Interior General Czesław Kiszczak was resoundingly rejected by Jaruzelski's own party—which had already coloured the office as rather marginal. Jaruzelski was then elected thanks to silent 'complicity' by the Solidarność deputies who deliberately abstained from voting, and the vote was calibrated by Solidarność strategists (in particular, by Professor Bronisław Geremek) with the utmost precision so that Jaruzelski was in fact only elected with a majority of one vote, to the ultimate humiliation of the general. In these circumstances, Jaruzelski adopted an approach of self-restraint and did not take advantage of all the powers that he could constitutionally have enjoyed. All this meant that strong presidentialism did not take root in Poland at the outset of the transformation. One may of course speculate about the possible turn of events if Lech Wałęsa had taken the top office immediately after the RT rather than, as turned out to be the case, one and a half years later—but the political conditions (consider that Poland was at the time surrounded by 'people's democracies' and 'hosted' some sixty thousand Soviet troops on its soil) did not exist for such a radical move. Nevertheless, the vicissitudes of politics in 1989 shaped an ambiguity in the office of president that was to mark the constitutional system of Poland in the following decades.

The constitutional amendments passed in April 1989 by the old, Communist-dominated Sejm swiftly and with no objections (which suggests to Bruce Ackerman, correctly, that it was the RT that has become the country's legitimate constitutional authority),[6] were a direct implementation of the RT agreements and paved the way to a peaceful transition, but also prefigured some important characteristics of the Polish constitutional system for years to come. These amendments were not part of a comprehensive democratic blueprint, but rather a practical and context-sensitive expression of very specific and pragmatic concerns responding to contingencies of the time. On the one hand, there were the concerns of the opposition aiming to acquire a broad representation in the Senate (which had been specially established for this purpose) and a narrower, but still significant, representation in the Sejm. On the other hand, it was the governmental side's concern to secure its interests through the newly restored position of president. Polish bicameralism and semi-presidentialism have their roots in this specific, but now long rendered irrelevant, compromise.

No doubt, there were many dysfunctionalities in the RT-based constitutional system, and various 'checks and balances' represented incoherencies in the system rather than deliberate restrictions on powers. For instance, there were cases where the Sejm would *refuse* to dismiss a minister whose dismissal was demanded by the prime minister and occasionally even by the minister concerned.[7] In fact, as some scholars observed, the constitutional system brought about by the RT did not implement any coherent pattern of separation of powers.[8] But some of the most anachronistic provisions of the old Constitution (including the official name of the state) had been removed through the amendment of 29 December 1989, and its most important provision, modelled partly on the *Rechtsstaat* clause of the German Basic Law, was incorporated: 'The Republic of Poland is a democratic state, ruled by law and implementing principles of social justice'. Hence, the constitutional grounds for democratic transition had been firmly laid down.

The basis for transition immediately materialized in the first elections held on 4 and 19 June 1989. Solidarność, re-institutionalized for the purposes of the elections as citizens' committees, ran an extraordinarily well-designed and managed campaign, with Wałęsa as a powerful unifying symbol, re-energized by his success in the RT. By contrast, the communists, who were clearly uncomfortable with the very idea of 'competitive elections', ran a near-suicidal campaign—disjointed and lethargic. Solidarność won all seats reserved for it in the Sejm (35 per cent) and all but one seat in the Senate. This decisive victory thoroughly demoralized the communists (General Jaruzelski is said to have admitted to his top aides, '[o]ur defeat is total'),[9] and compelled the anti-communist opposition to reshape their ideas as to the lessons drawn from the RT, and to move quickly towards refashioning the compromise with their communist counterparts—a compromise which now seemed much too timid and deferential. In this way, the elections thoroughly changed the political landscape, including the original context for the RT compromise, which now seemed to belong to pre-history. As Andrzej Rapaczynski put it a few years later:

> [b]oth sides believed that the compromise [at the RT] guaranteed the communists effective control over the political system, but also gave the opposition a possible veto over communist initiatives. No one had imagined that the election, held on June 4, 1989, would bring such a crushing defeat to the communists that its aftermath would transform the whole Round Table agreement beyond recognition.[10]

Based on a slogan by Adam Michnik propounded in the newly established, independent, daily *Gazeta Wyborcza,* 'Your President, our Prime Minister', the first non-communist government on this side of the Iron Curtain was formed, under the leadership of Tadeusz Mazowiecki, a Christian-democratic politician and thinker, formerly one of the top advisers of the Solidarity movement

The 'Small Constitution'

The aspiration of quickly adopting a brand new, comprehensive constitution was clearly present from the beginning of the transition, and the opposition's overwhelming victory in the first elections of June 1989 was the source of much enthusiasm. In December 1989 a Constitutional Committee of the Sejm was established, followed by its counterpart in the Senate. From the start, however, there was a clear rivalry and certainly a lack of collaboration between the two committees, both of which ended up presenting their own, mutually incompatible constitutional proposals.[11] The Senate's vision focused on fundamentally classical liberal rights and a presidential model of government, while the Sejm's proposal offered a more generous catalogue of social rights and endorsed a parliamentary model. After the presidential elections of 25 November and 9 December 1990 (conducted as direct popular elections thanks to a constitutional amendment of that year) which elevated Lech Wałęsa to the top position, and the fully free parliamentary elections of October 1991, a single, bicameral constitutional committee was established, composed of fifty-six Sejm members and ten Senators. The Constitutional Act of 23 April 1992 stipulated that the new constitution would be adopted after three readings and a national referendum.

The window of constitutional opportunity finally seemed wide open, with the charismatic revolutionary hero endowed with popular legitimacy as president, and the freely elected parliament fairly representing all of the main political forces of the nation (including the new-look post-communists, trying to find their place in a new political landscape after the relatively painless dissolution of the PZPR in 1990). But it soon became clear that the prospects for a quick adoption of a comprehensive constitution were dim, largely due to the growing divisions and subdivisions in what was earlier the Solidarność camp, and so '[t]he need for reform combined with political divisiveness within parliament led to a strategy of gradual or "step-by-step" constitution-making'.[12] Two documents were to be adopted prior to a comprehensive constitution: a bill of rights and a constitutional act on the relationship between the legislature and the executive. The former did not see the light of day due to the unpopularity of President Wałęsa's draft Charter of Rights and Freedoms, a thoroughly liberal document, clearly distinguishing between fully justiciable liberal rights, on the one hand, and provisions on the socio-economic duties of the state, on the other. In an economically backward Poland, additionally traumatized by the shock therapy of the economic reforms designed by energetic Deputy Prime Minister Leszek Balcerowicz, a bill of rights strong on individual liberties but weak on socio-economic rights may have had intellectual integrity, but it was of no use to social movements propounding egalitarian or populist messages. By contrast, the latter document was adopted on 17 October 1992 as a so-called Small Constitution (this informal name referred to the previous 'small', or interim, constitutional texts adopted in Poland in times of political transition: in 1919, after regaining independence after the First World War, and in 1947, in the process of establishing a communist regime after the Second World War). From that time, three constitutional acts were in force until 1997: the Small Constitution, the old Constitution of 1952, and the Constitutional

Act of April 1992 on the procedure for adopting a new constitution; one old and two new constitutional statutes.

The Small Constitution was a self-consciously transitional document; indeed, its Preamble stated that it was to be in force only 'pending the passage of a new Constitution'. Its scope was limited to the regulation of relations between the legislative and executive branches, and, more marginally, the local government and the judiciary. It kept in force many of the provisions of the 1952 Constitution as later amended (including, importantly, procedures for the amendment of the Constitution, as well as on the CT, Tribunal of State, National Council of Broadcasting and TV, etc.). Symbolically, it was important that the Small Constitution enshrined the principle of separation and balance of powers between the three branches of government right in its first Article, thus formally abandoning the infamous doctrine of 'the unity of power'. The government was given a role in drawing up legislation through a right to issue regulations that had the force of law, without requiring approval by the parliament, but certain spheres were excluded from control by such regulations (such as the electoral law or the rights and freedoms of citizens). When it came to the legislative process, the Small Constitution reduced the Senate's power of oversight by eliminating its power of veto over the Sejm's laws, and allowing the Sejm to overrule the Senate's objections by an absolute majority.

Directly elected for a five-year term (with the possibility of one re-election), the president had his powers somewhat extended: he received a limited legislative role with the right to issue official acts (requiring, however, the countersignature of the prime minister or a relevant minister; presidential actions not requiring the consent by the government were exhaustively enumerated). Further, the president was given a larger role in appointing and dismissing the government; the Constitution stipulated that ministers of foreign affairs, internal affairs, and national defence could only be appointed with the president's consent, thus paving the way to the controversial concept of 'presidential portfolios'. The president also obtained more extensive powers regarding the right to dissolve parliament if the National Assembly failed to appoint a government or adopt a budget within a given time frame. A complex mechanism for appointing the government, requiring a degree of cooperation between the president and the parliament, was set up, giving the president the power to initiate the whole sequence by nominating the prime minister, who would then present a list of candidates for ministerial positions for approval by the president, followed by a presentation of the programme and the cabinet to the Sejm; an absolute majority was required for a vote of confidence. An intricate procedure was also designed for cases where there was a failure to win such an absolute majority; fortunately, in practice, it has never had to be applied. Similarly, the requirement of an absolute majority was also established for a vote of no confidence in the government as a measure to secure government stability.

As Professor Wyrzykowski characterized it, the Small Constitution 'installed a "rationalized parliamentary system" including unusual procedures such as the multi-stage cabinet formation as well as a distribution of powers typical of parliamentary-cabinet and semi-presidential systems'.[13] Another scholar called it 'a hybrid case with elements of both parliamentary and presidential systems interchangeable'.[14] Whatever the characterization, the mixed system of government historically embedded in the contingencies of the RT was now constitutionally confirmed and reinforced. With rather minor changes and fine-tuning brought about by a more permanent constitution, the system would survive until 2015. Whether that is proof that it served Poland well during the crucial post-transition quarter of a century, or that it carried the seeds of its own self-destruction, is a matter of individual opinion. It is probable that both interpretations are equally plausible, and complement each other.

Constitutional Tribunal pre-1997

One bizarre thing about Polish constitutionalism was that the Polish CT, a body that would become a robust defender of rights and liberties, was established by a constitutional amendment on 26 March 1982, i.e. at the height of repressive martial law. (The actual setting up of the tribunal on the basis of the statute on the CT had to wait until April 1985, and the tribunal began actual work from 1 January 1986.) The establishment of the court could be seen more as part of a disingenuous 'charm offensive' by General Jaruzelski and his team than a genuine wish to bring in democratic changes. The tribunal was no threat to the government because, with a strictly limited range of actors who could initiate review (and, of course, no availability of constitutional complaint at the time), there was no risk that the state's officials would dare to challenge any important law in the constitutional court. So before 1989 the role of the tribunal was basically limited to ascertaining the relationship between statutes and sub-statutory legal acts, and also restricting legislative production by the executive—not an insignificant task, but far from anything resembling vigorous constitutional scrutiny. By focusing on the compliance of sub-statutory laws with parliamentary acts, in accordance with the intention of its founders, the CT could be seen more as an aid to, rather than a controller of, parliament.

Soon after 1989 the CT acquired a role not necessarily anticipated for it by its designers and, in the absence of a comprehensive and coherent constitution, became an active partner and controller of the legislature and executive through its filling in the blanks in the constitutional text. Despite its major structural limitation— the fact that its judgments could be overridden by a qualified two-thirds majority of the Sejm—which it inherited from a pre-1989 era, the tribunal became a valuable, often enthusiastic constitutional actor, especially after the Small Constitution of 1992 was adopted. But even prior to that, a constitutional amendment of

December 1989 gave the tribunal a significant textual basis for many of its judgments in the form of the clause that declared Poland 'a state ruled by law', or the Polish equivalent of the German *Rechtsstaat*. Perhaps one of the most significant early judgments in this period was handed down on 22 August 1990 in which the CT derived, from the rule of law clause of the amended Constitution, the principle of non-retroactivity, protection of vested rights and what it called 'the principle of citizens' confidence in the state'.[15]

The tribunal was actively supplied with work by Ewa Łętowska, the outstanding first Ombudsman, who occupied the post from 1989, and who was involved in initiating many of the most important challenges. In a timely coincidence, six judges out of twelve completed their terms at the end of 1989, which opened up vacancies for reform-oriented judges, including the charismatic Janina Zakrzewska, a long-term legal dissident. Some of the CT's judgments soon after the transition concerned questions of the separation of powers, basic democratic rules of the game, and legislative procedures. The reinvigorated tribunal, inter alia, established rules about party parliamentary caucuses (explaining the basis for establishing a minimum number of MPs necessary to establish a caucus);[16] fine-tuned the role of the Senate in the legislative process (strictly confining its role to a secondary legislative function vis-à-vis that of the Sejm);[17] and defined the competences of the president concerning the dismissal of the president of the National Broadcasting Council, saying that the extinguishment of the latter's constitutional term of office was only allowed in exceptional circumstances, i.e. in the case of a gross violation of law (judicially confirmed).[18] Importantly, in the latter decision, the tribunal rejected the concept of 'implied' presidential competences, allegedly based on some other, expressly conferred powers, and argued that the powers of the top executive (or of any other constitutional official for that matter) cannot be enlarged in this way. Other judgments of the early period of the CT concerned constitutional rights, and were related to matters such as abortion, lustration, religion in public schools, and the status of electronic media. Former CT judge Leszek Garlicki is adamant that '[w]ithout any doubt, in that period the position of the [CT] as an important participant in the process of governing was stabilised'.[19]

The Constitution of 1997: The Process

The story of the Polish Constitution of 1997 confirms an old truth that the *process* of constitution-making may be as important as the outcome. The process, while it may be seen (and *was* seen) to have been unwieldy, messy, and unnecessarily drawn out, ex post appears to be almost a model of wise compromise-seeking.

After the unexpected fall of the government and dissolution of the parliament, the parliamentary elections of September 1993 marked a fresh start: any constitutional work undertaken so far had been extinguished by the premature ending of the parliamentary term. The new Constitutional Committee was dominated by the left and centre-left, reflecting the new composition of the parliament. The act of April 1994 amending the procedure for constitution-drafting opened up the possibility of presenting constitutional drafts to extra-parliamentary forces, including parties not represented in the parliament and the Solidarność trade union. As a result, seven proposals were presented to parliament, and, after the first reading, the Constitutional Committee (now chaired by the energetic Democratic Left Alliance (*Sojusz Lewicy Demokratycznej* (SLD)) leader, Aleksander Kwaśniewski) was expected to draw up a single draft.

The final draft resulted from a lengthy process in which the seven initial drafts were considered by both the subcommittees and plenary meetings of the Constitutional Committee, and was a compromise document based on the SLD and Solidarność drafts, with strong input from the Polish Peasants' Party (*Polskie Stronnictwo Ludowe* (PSL)) and the Freedom Union (formerly, the Democratic Union), a predecessor of the Civic Platform (*Platforma Obywatelska* (PO)). Seeking compromise was not only seen as a matter of principle, but also a practical requirement: while the governing SLD-PSL coalition had the required constitutional majority of two-thirds in the National Assembly, it fell short of the two-thirds majority in the Constitutional Committee required for the adoption of a project of the Constitution (due to vagaries of the election of members of the committee). In the end, right-wing parliamentary parties connected to Solidarność refused to take part in the constitutional coalition, which had eventually reached a compromise in the committee and undertook a public campaign in favour of the draft. By a partisan political logic, right-wing parties refused to support the draft constitution and led a vigorous public campaign against it, with the active support of the Catholic Church, showing that there were, after all, limits to the scope and depth of the compromise.

It was in these circumstances that the final draft was passed in the third reading in the Sejm on 2 April 1997, and by the National Assembly with 461 votes in favour, 31 against and 5 abstentions. The political campaign leading up to the referendum had become particularly nasty, with Solidarność leading the 'No' campaign and accusing the authors of the draft constitution of treason, intention to install tyranny, and anti-religious sentiments. Their demand to have their own draft (dubbed the 'citizens' draft', with an impressive 900,000 signatures) presented to the referendum alongside the parliamentary draft failed, as it had no foundations in the constitutional law governing constitution-making, or in general international practice. The norm is to submit a single text rather than a choice between two texts to a referendum. In the end, the referendum of 25 May 1997 accepted the parliamentary proposal. While the majority of 53 (versus 43) per cent was reasonably strong if not resounding, the low turnout of 47.86 per cent meant that in fact only 22.6 per cent of eligible voters turned up at the ballot box for the new Constitution—fortunately for its supporters, the constitutional law provided no minimum threshold for the validity of the referendum. Notwithstanding this fact, some persons contested the outcome of the referendum (there were over 400 protests lodged to the Supreme Court) claiming that the turnout of one-half of eligible voters is an implied prerequisite[20]—but the Supreme Court rejected those claims, and confirmed the validity of the referendum. According to some scholars, it was a regrettable decision. Bruce Ackerman believes that a requirement of a 50 per cent turnout at the referendum would have forced the constitutional drafters to make more concessions to Solidarność and to the church in order to gain broader support in a referendum, thus enhancing the Constitution's legitimacy.[21] But this is, of course, mere speculation, and it may well be that such further concessions would have rendered the Constitution altogether incoherent, or that a 50 per cent rule would have resulted in the failure of the draft at the referendum anyway. Eventually, the Constitution was signed by President Kwaśniewski on 16 July 1997 and entered into force on 17 October of that year.

In the opinion of Mirosław Wyrzykowski, 'the process of constitution drafting was quite open and inclusive, reflecting the various interests of a diverse society'.[22] This is a compelling assessment. The Constitutional Commission, in its latest iteration, worked for a year and a half on the final, multi-variant draft, based on separate initial drafts. Both parliamentary and extra-parliamentary parties and groups had their drafts considered by the committee. A detailed, book-length account of these works[23] presents a picture of quite in-depth deliberation, article by article, of the Constitution. This is not to say that the procedure was ideal. The authors of the detailed account just mentioned indicate certain defects of the procedure: occasionally there was a low turnout by members of the committee at its meetings, and its methodology of eliminating proposals that received the least support in the committee was questionable.[24] Another scholar who participated as an expert in the Constitutional Committee reported that opening up the range of constitutional drafts to extra-parliamentary parties 'resulted in at least some of the constitutional drafts becoming rallying points for political camps who were unwilling to make compromises'.[25] Yet another expert expressed concern that the crucial subcommittee on institutions was dominated by persons connected with the old regime, 'partly because most Polish experts in the area came from the once-tightly controlled university law faculties'.[26] But these defects do not undermine the high deliberative quality of the procedure leading up to the adoption of the Constitution. In a non-ideal world, the 1997 Polish Constitution was born of a process that ticked many of the boxes of the deliberative democratic ideal.

The Constitution of 1997: The Substance

As already mentioned, much of what (rightly) came to be seen as a principled, even if imperfect, constitutional compromise of 1997 was in fact prefigured by the purely pragmatic, contingent, and context-sensitive political compromise of 1989. For instance, the Senate, presented grandiosely in 1997 as a 'body of reflection' designed to mitigate the possible excesses of the Sejm, in fact had its roots in the 1989 split between a semi-democratic parliamentary lower chamber (with only 35 per cent of seats up for grabs) and a fully and freely elected higher chamber. The Senate had been deliberately established to test the real electoral support for the non-communists and to satisfy the then democratic opposition by giving it a weak veto over the communist-dominated 'Round Table Sejm'. According to some scholars, in these new circumstances, not resembling those of 1989, the Senate was a redundant and unnecessary body, in search of proper tasks and structure.[27] Similarly, the model of semi-presidentialism adopted in 1997 as a wise combination of a directly elected presidency appreciated by Poles and a strong parliament reflecting democratic pluralism in fact goes back to 1989. This was when the pragmatic compromise occurred between the guarantee for overall oversight by communists encapsulated in the presidency tailored for Jaruzelski and a genuine political role for democratic opposition— a compromise subsequently modified by adding a directly elected presidency when Jaruzelski's time was coming to an end in late 1990 (not as a matter of institutional design but of political contingencies), and when Wałęsa's elevation to office was clearly on the cards.

This is not to debunk the value of the 1997 compromise—it was a real achievement, despite its limitations. It is important, however, to keep in mind that the Constitution of 1997 was marked by path dependence and was embedded in the context of 1989 transition to a much higher degree than some commentators are willing to admit. But some dimensions of the compromise were of a more recent pedigree. In particular they concerned the relationship between the state and the Catholic Church, which was pressing for constitutional recognition of its special role, trying to entrench itself in the face of what was seen to be the inevitable secularization accompanying the democratization of Poland. The most famous—and widely applauded as inclusive and noble[28]—compromise has its symbolic articulation in the Preamble; the church insisted on the *Invocatio Dei* while the left preferred the absence of any reference to God and religion. The ingenious compromise solution, authored by Tadeusz Mazowiecki and a group of Christian liberal intellectuals around him, was to refer in the Preamble to citizens 'who believe in God as the source of truth, justice, goodness and beauty, as well as those not sharing such faith but respecting those universal values as they arise from other sources'— arguably one of the most important contributions of Poland to world constitutionalism. As the saying goes, one candle to God and another to the Devil. This is not the only religious reference in the Preamble: there is also a reference to 'Christian heritage of the Nation' (though supplemented by 'universal human values') and to the constitution-makers' 'responsibility before God' (though with an alternative of responsibility 'before one's conscience').

Still on the issue of the church–state relationship, a reference to the state's 'neutrality' on religious matters turned out to be another stumbling block: the church saw this formula as a Trojan horse bringing into the constitutional language the dreaded conception of a French-style *laïcité*. In the end, the concept of 'impartiality' was adopted (Art. 25 (2)), because it was allegedly friendlier to the church (and acceptable *by* the church) than that of 'neutrality'. This was, in addition, accompanied by a special reference to the Catholic Church which affirms that the relationship between the state and *this* church is regulated both by an international treaty with the Holy See (i.e. a concordat) and a statute (Art. 25(4)), while the relationship between the state and *other* churches is only regulated by statutes, enacted on the basis of agreements between the government and representatives of these churches (Art. 25(5)). In fact, a reference to a concordat (*sans le nom*) was merely recognition of reality: a concordat between Poland and the Vatican had been signed and ratified back in 1993.

Generally speaking, the Constitution incorporated many of the church's demands but certainly stopped short of turning Poland into a denominational state. Rather, in describing the relationship between the state and churches as based on the 'autonomy and independence of each', and urging the 'cooperation for the good of humankind and for the common good' (Art. 25 (3)) between the state and all denominations, the Constitution established a framework for a friendly church—state separation—though, significantly, the word 'separation' is never mentioned. This was also one of the concessions made towards the church. In addition, the committee gave in to pressure from the church by including a definition of marriage as 'a union of a woman and a man' (Art. 18), and by dropping sexual orientation from the list of expressly prohibited grounds of discrimination, instead opting for a general prohibition against discrimination 'for any reason' (in Art. 32).

A mixed system or semi-presidentialism combined the not insignificant powers of the president with a strong role for the cabinet generated by the parliamentary majority. The president has the power of suspensive legislative veto that may be overridden by a three-fifths majority in Sejm, thus marginally strengthening the position of the Sejm vis-à-vis the president compared to what it was in the Small Constitution, which required a two-thirds majority to overrule. Further, he (insofar as it has always been 'he') enjoys special supervision over the armed forces, a right to initiate ex-ante control of laws and international agreements by the CT, and to call early elections in certain circumstances. While the government and its prime minister are appointed by the president, they must enjoy the confidence of the parliamentary majority. In practice, this means that the winning political parties and their coalitions form governments. If a vote of no confidence is passed regarding the entire government, it is effective only if the Sejm elects a new prime minister (the so-called constructive vote of no confidence), which along with other measures (such as the electoral threshold of 5 per cent for parties and 8 per cent for coalitions) helps to maintain government stability. It is fair, however, to say that notwithstanding the strong legitimacy derived from direct elections and a relatively long five-year term (with the possibility of one re-election), the role of the president is rather limited and can be described as being basically 'an independent monitor of other state actors' and 'a check on the rest of the state'.[29] This is reflected, inter alia, in the requirement that the president must obtain the prime minister's countersignature for all official acts, except those specifically described by the Constitution as presidential 'prerogatives' (Art. 144 (3)). That is why some constitutional scholars have argued for reducing the discrepancy between legitimacy and competences by introducing the election of the president by a national assembly.[30]

The model of a charter of rights was also very much a compromise between a liberal system of justiciable personal rights and a relatively generous list of socio-economic rights, most of which are nevertheless subject to the 'by law' proviso. The fact that, in addition to all standard 'liberal' rights, the Constitution also contains a broad list of socio-economic rights, can be partly explained by the drawn-out and compromise-oriented drafting process: compromises between parties involved in the drafting usually consisted of accepting *additional* rights demanded by one party as a trade for that party accepting the other parties' constitutional ideas. This type of horse-trading in reality meant expanding the scope of constitutional 'benefits' popular in the electorates of various parties.[31] This also explains why socio-economic rights are included in the chapter on rights (Chapter 2 of the Constitution) rather than being articulated as directives or guidelines for state policies. So, the Constitution also contains:

- core socio-economic rights to social security, health care, and education (Art. 67, 68, 70)
- the rights to a choice of employment, minimum remuneration, and a state duty to pursue full employment (Art. 65)
- the rights of people with disabilities to special aid (Art. 69)
- the state's duty of pursuing 'ecological safety' and the right of citizens to be provided with full information about protection of the environment (Art. 74)
- consumer rights (Art. 76)
- a state duty to pursue housing policies in order to combat homelessness (Art. 75).

All of these rights and state duties are indiscriminately listed in a separate subsection in Chapter 2 of the Constitution ('Economic, Social, and Cultural Freedoms and Rights') but some of these (e.g. minimum remuneration) are specifically singled out as being subject to 'limitations specified by law' (Art. 81) and, in a rather messy case of legal drafting, some additional rights—even when not singled out in a provision of Art. 81—carry with them a 'by law' clause (e.g. Art. 70.4, regarding the rights of students for financial aid). As a consequence, it was left to the CT to more clearly determine the legal status and conditions for the justiciability of socio-economic rights.[32]

In its articulation of certain rights, the compromise acquired the form of 'deciding not to decide'.[33] One of the most symptomatic examples of this approach is Article 38 of the Constitution, which declares the legal protection of life, with the related controversial question of the regulation of abortion being left open. The proposals submitted in this regard to the Constitutional Commission were quite divergent in details: the majority of drafts adopted a general formula according to which everybody has an absolute and inviolable right to life (projects of the president, of the Freedom Union, of the PSL and Labour Union (*Unia Pracy* (UP)) coalition (PSL-UP), of the SLD, of Solidarność and of the Confederation of Independent Poland (*Konfederacja Polski Niepodległej* (KPN)). In its current shape, Article 38 contains a general framing of the right with an imprecise wording of the rule and an implicit delegation (and, hence, postponement) of the precise delimitation of the right to a separate statute. Article 38 merely announces that '[t]he Republic of Poland shall ensure the legal protection of the life of every human being'. As has been observed:

> The deliberately vague wording in Article 38 reflects a compromise, with the result that the responsibility for the regulation of abortion is passed effectively to the Sejm. As written, the provision would arguably seem to permit a restrictive law on abortion as well as a liberal law. In this regard, it should be noted that proposals to protect human life explicitly from the moment of conception were not accepted.[34]

This way of resolving the axiological conflict around the right to life has led, however, to a long-lasting and intense controversy, which continues to this day. The problem in question also became one of the components in the process of renegotiating the constitutional compromise after 2005 (and, in particular, in the ongoing constitutional crisis from 2015) in spite of a landmark judgment of the CT, which had not satisfied either side of the dispute.[35]

The most important constitutional change regarding the CT was the removal of the possibility of legislative override, as introduced by the Small Constitution. The discontinuation of that possibility (which had only been successfully used by Parliament on eleven occasions)[36] was applauded as a success for the constitutional judges, who had been pressing for such change. Parliamentary override in Poland by a qualified, two-thirds majority, likened by an observer to a constitutional amendment,[37] had never been popular among legal scholars, not to mention CT judges, and its withdrawal has not attracted much attention in debates around the new Constitution. Constitutional scholar and former prime minister, Hanna Suchocka, when applauding the change brought about by the new Constitution, even asserted that the previous system of parliamentary override 'was clearly a relic of the concept of unity of power and the dominant position of Parliament', and as such was 'in conflict with the principle of separation of powers'.[38] (It may be added that the only other post-communist state with the institution of parliamentary override, Romania, abolished it in 2003.) Further, and significantly for the future, the Constitution maintained the system of election of CT judges by a simple majority in the Sejm for a non-renewable term of nine years.

Finally, the Constitution provides for a limited number of instruments of direct democracy, of which two are truly important: a referendum for the approval of constitutional changes (Art. 235 (6)), and a national referendum on 'issues of special importance for the state' (Art. 125). A constitutional referendum *may* be called on the demand of the president, the Senate, and a group of members of the Sejm, to approve constitutional acts changing some specified parts of the Constitution (on the general foundations of the Republic, Chapter 1; on rights and freedoms, Chapter 2; and on constitutional amendments, Chapter 12). In turn, a referendum on issues of special importance may be called by the Sejm or by the president with the consent of the Senate. What may appear curious are the differences between the turnout and majority requirements for the two types of referenda. For the latter, the result is binding if at least 50 per cent of those eligible turned out, which, as many observers noted, is much too high, especially now that several million Polish citizens have since emigrated to other EU countries and yet still count as eligible voters.[39] The constitutional referendum, in contrast, is binding if at least one half of those voting approve the constitutional change—but there is no minimum turnout requirement. This may sound ironic: surely, the constitutional referendum should be seen as the most important of all. Nevertheless, the laxity in defining its conditions can be well explained by the drafters' scepticism in 1997,, especially in view of a huge propaganda campaign against the project, about the turnout. And they were prescient in this regard.

The Challenge of 2005–7

Despite its less-than-remarkable pedigree—the main aspect of which was a disappointingly low turnout in the referendum—the Constitution proved to be quite robust, if measured by the acceptance of its legitimacy by all the main political forces, including those that had argued against its adoption in 1997.

Perhaps the most difficult period of challenge was in 2005–7 when the Law and Justice (*Prawo i Sprawiedliwość* (PiS)) party first came to power. The electoral results of 2005 marked an important reconfiguration of political forces in Poland: the Freedom Union (*Unia Wolności* (UW)) did not win any seats in Parliament at all, and the SLD (post-communist left) was substantially weakened. Hence, the two main pillars of the 1997 constitutional compromise, encapsulating the worldview of the liberal-minded intelligentsia and middle class, were largely shattered. More generally, public preferences moved significantly to the right, which challenged the constitutional compromise. PiS leaders symbolically emphasized their distance from the Constitution by, for instance, referring to the state as the 'Fourth Republic', knowing full well that the Constitution describes it (in the Preamble) as the 'Third Republic'. In the 2005 electoral campaign they openly argued for constitutional change, even putting forward their own constitutional draft, envisaging much stronger presidential powers, reducing the rights of religious freedom, and radically limiting the powers of the Ombudsman. When elected, however, and knowing that they had failed to gain a constitutional majority and that its coalition partners (Samoobrona and the League of Polish Families) also had produced their own constitutional drafts during their campaigns, which were inconsistent with the PiS proposal, PiS never seriously returned to the idea of a comprehensive change to the Constitution. Instead it only dealt with two amendment proposals: one successful (amending the constitutional provision for the non-extradition of a Polish citizen, to accommodate the rules regarding the European Arrest Warrant)[40]; and one unsuccessful: PiS chose to reject a constitutional amendment proposed by its coalition partner, the League of Polish Families, which wanted to establish the constitutional protection of human life 'from the moment of conception'.

Several times during its short rule, PiS adopted laws that breached the Constitution of 1997, with the CT usually repairing the damage. For example, PiS attempted to empower the Broadcasting Council to establish journalistic ethics rules on the restriction of speech.[41] It adopted a law on lustration that would affect several hundred thousand persons by restricting their rights to privacy, non-discrimination, and the presumption of innocence.[42] It adopted a law punishing the attribution to the Polish Nation of co-responsibility for Nazi or communist crimes[43] (thus prefiguring the equivalent law of 2018). The statute on crisis management introduced the possibility for the government to suspend individual rights in vaguely defined 'crisis situations' beyond constitutionally defined emergencies. Several times the state breached the constitutional precepts of impartiality of the state on religious matters, for instance, by providing a large subsidy in the budget of 2006 and 2007 for construction of the Church of Divine Providence in Warsaw (totalling some sixty million PLN, or fourteen million euros) as well as financing or co-financing several religious schools and universities.

Right at the outset of its parliamentary term, the PiS government and President Lech Kaczyński breached the Constitution by improperly electing the president of the Broadcasting Council, based on a hastily adopted statute of 29 December 2005, which had terminated the term of office of the current members of the council and increased the number of its members, as well as giving the president an exclusive right to appoint and dismiss the president of the council. The CT later found the statute unconstitutional in all such respects, but abstained from demanding the dismissal of the improperly appointed president and members of the council.[44] Minister of Justice Zbigniew Ziobro breached, with impunity, the rule of presumption of innocence by publicly declaring in June 2007 the criminal guilt of a medical doctor accused (and then declared innocent by a court) of the manslaughter of his patient.[45] There were many openly homophobic, hateful public statements by high government officials.[46] President Lech Kaczyński, his twin brother and leader of PiS, Jarosław Kaczyński, the government, and the PiS leadership often expressed their open hostility towards the CT. President Kaczyński never challenged a single statute in an ex-ante procedure to the CT, thus showing his discomfort with the institution as a whole, and Jarosław Kaczyński frequently made insulting and offensive statements about the CT, for instance, implying that the CT should not consider the lustration law because 'each of its judges may be under suspicion', and that it puts its own 'corporate interests' above the interests of society.[47] Overall, however, and thanks to the active and vigilant role played by the CT, the harm caused by PiS's cavalier attitude to the Constitution was not that considerable, and was reversible after the 2007 elections, which brought the PO-PSL coalition to power.

The Constitution in Action

Overall, the damage done by the rule of PiS in 2005–7 to the 1997 Constitution was limited. Even though PiS later came up with its own draft of a new constitution in 2010, it remained a virtually unknown document, and was never seriously debated, either within PiS or in a broader political forum. It remained a text known only to constitutional experts, and after some time was even removed from the official PiS website, to be largely forgotten. The result was that all of the main political forces in Poland accepted—some more grudgingly than others—the legitimacy of the 1997 Constitution, and shaped its political actions and strategies by reference to it, clearly assuming its durability. With the exception of two minor amendments, which were pushed through remarkably smoothly (one amendment, of September 2006, regarding an extradition, already mentioned, and another, of March 2009, denying those sentenced to imprisonment for an intentional indictable offence eligibility to stand in parliamentary elections), no one seriously questioned the Constitution—until 2015. It turned out to be a document equally useful to the successors of its drafters as to the successors of its original opponents.

The only important political initiative for substantial constitutional amendment came from President Bronisław Komorowski soon after taking office. In November 2010 he proposed to add a European chapter, called 'Membership of the Republic of Poland in the European Union' which would declare the general rules regarding Polish membership, and more particularly, create conditions for the adoption of euro. The proposed chapter would also establish procedures for a decision on exiting the EU (the decision by the government, confirmed either by the Sejm with a two-thirds majority and the Senate with an absolute majority, or by a national referendum). The special parliamentary commission concluded its report in July 2011 but the prospect of general election (which were held in October 2011) put an end to the project.

Among constitutional scholars, a near-consensus has emerged—that the Constitution is quite adequate, and there is no need for any major amendments, much less a brand new Constitution. Even when constitutional scholars made proposals for constitutional amendments, these concerned rather marginal issues and were not accompanied by any suggestions for a major constitutional overhaul. In 2010 a leading Polish constitutional scholar, Professor Piotr Winczorek, offered the following suggestions for desired constitutional amendments: (1) abolition of the Tribunal of State as a body that 'turned out to be a dead institution';[48] (2) a reduction of the number of members of the Sejm and Senate; (3) the transformation of the Senate into a chamber representing various professional and territorial self-governmental entities; (4) changes to the law-making process, such as introducing decrees by the president and Council of Ministers, under the supervision of Parliament and with a limited scope of subject-matter; (5) corrections to the constitutional regulation of referenda, in a way as to make valid results binding upon Parliament; (6) further opening up access to constitutional complaints; (7) removing some so-called socio-economic rights, which are in fact directives for state policy, to a separate chapter in the Constitution, 'devoted to the main directions of the state policy'.[49] While the list is quite long, none of these suggestions was made by Professor Winczorek as a matter of urgency or with any great degree of confidence, but rather as questions worth considering in future. One immediately realizes that none of the suggestions is really central to the operation of a constitutional system of governance. Indeed, these proposals were preceded by a statement that the Constitution 'is not in itself the cause of political difficulties and [of] the not very efficient operation of the state institutions and mechanisms'.[50]

Much the same has been the *communis opinio* of constitutional scholars since the time when Winczorek sketched his evaluation, namely at the height of the post-2015 constitutional crisis. It is interesting to report the results of a constitutional survey conducted among constitutional scholars in 2017.[51] It may well be that the views of the scholars surveyed are largely coloured by their observations about the PiS assault on the Constitution.[52] On the other hand, it may be that their responses are also tainted with dismay that the Constitution has not created stronger self-protections, which is an important finding in itself. The overall result of the survey—which is reasonably representative of constitutional scholarship in Poland[53]—is positive about the Constitution. Only 4 per cent believe that a brand new Constitution is needed, while 72 per cent are in favour of the view that only partial amendments are needed; and 6 per cent believe that no change is needed at all.[54] To the question as to whether 'there is currently a constitutional moment in Poland', 84 per cent answered negatively.[55] At the top of the list of matters pinpointed as requiring change are rules regarding the liability of public officials for breaches of the Constitution; a hefty 82 per cent believed that these rules are currently inappropriate.[56] Only 16 per cent believed that the human rights provisions should be changed.[57] It is interesting to note some of the anonymous views expressed in the 'open' part of the survey:

> Respondents emphasized … that 'the constitutional crisis is not … an effect of imperfections of the Constitution' and that 'the Constitution of 1997 is not a source of the so-called constitutional crisis around the CT and courts'. The source of the crisis is in 'the breaches of the Constitution by the parliamentary majority, the government and the resident of the Republic'.[58]

The views by constitutional scholars are, by and large, echoed by general public opinion. A highly reputable polling organization recently conducted a survey to portray social comprehension and assessment of the Constitution twenty years after it was adopted.[59] The majority of the respondents (68 per cent) recognized the Constitution as one of the key elements of public order, having a significant impact on the life of individual citizens, while only 22 per cent have the opposite view of its role.[60] Furthermore, only 30 per cent of respondents support the claim that the Constitution should be changed, with 49 per cent of respondents opposing this possibility. The overall proportion of 'reformers' and 'conservers' in society has evolved in the last two decades in favour of the latter group: in 2004 and 2008 45 per cent were in support and 37 per cent were against altering the Constitution.[61] What is more, a significant majority of respondents (65 per cent) claim that the Constitution should prevail in the case of every political or regulatory dilemma—even if following its provisions would result in leaving a particular social problem unresolved. It all warrants a proposition that the Constitution's role has become largely consolidated in public consciousness, and that breaches of the Constitution are not with societal tolerance.

Lastly, a relatively large fraction of respondents (60 per cent) claim that its provisions are not complied with (while only 28 per cent express the opposite view).[62] Equally interesting is where the respondents locate these infringements: only infrequently do they complain of breaches of personal freedom. They mainly find constitutional violations in political regime-related matters, such as the principle of the division and balance of power, and the (mal-)functioning of the CT.[63]

But note the year when this survey was conducted: 2017.

Notes

1. Historian Jerzy Eisler, having recently studied the archives, established that Stalin made some fifty corrections to the draft Constitution of Poland, see Jerzy Eisler, *Czterdzieści pięć lat, które wstrząsnęły Polską* (Czerwone i Czarne 2018) 148.

2. Cited in Mark Brzezinski and Leszek Garlicki, 'Polish Constitutional Law' in Stanislaw Frankowski and Paul B. Stephan III (eds), *Legal Reform in Post-Communist Europe* (Martinus Nijhoff 1995) 21, 24.

3. A vague and ritualistic reference to the 'leading role' of the party was introduced in an amendment of 1976.

4. Adam Przeworski, 'Ruling Against Rules' in Tom Ginsburg and Alberto Simpser (eds), *Constitutions in Authoritarian Regimes* (CUP 2014) 21, 34.

5. See Bruce Ackerman, *The Future of Liberal Revolution* (Yale University Press 1992).

6. Bruce Ackerman, *Revolutionary Constitutions: Charismatic Leadership and the Rule of Law* (Harvard University Press forthcoming 2019) ch. 9.

7. Ryszard Chruściak and Wiktor Osiatyński, *Tworzenie konstytucji w Polsce w latach 1989–1997* (Instytut Spraw Publicznych 2001) 126.

8. Brzezinski and Garlicki (n. 2) 30–1.

9. Quoted by Rett R. Ludwikowski, *Constitution-Making in the Region of Former Soviet Dominance* (Duke University Press 1996) 151.

10. Andrzej Rapaczyński, 'Constitutional Politics in Poland: A Report on the Constitutional Committee of the Polish Parliament' (1991) 58 *University of Chicago Law Review* 595, 600.

11. See Mirosław Wyrzykowski, 'Legitimacy: The Price of a Delayed Constitution in Poland' in Jan Zielonka (ed.), *Democratic Consolidation in Europe*, vol. 1 (OUP 2001) 431, 437–8.

12. Ibid. 439.

13. Ibid. 445.

14. Ludwikowski (n. 9) 207.

15. Judgment K 7/90 of 22 August 1990.

16. Judgment U 10/92 of 26 January 1993.

17. Judgment K 5/93 of 23 November 1993.

18. Resolution W 7/94 of 10 May 1994.

19. Leszek Lech Garlicki, 'The Experience of the Polish Constitutional Court' in Wojciech Sadurski (ed.), *Constitutional Justice, East and West* (Kluwer Law International 2002) 265, 267.

20. See Chruściak and Osiatyński (n. 7) 308.

21. Ackerman *Revolutionary Constitutions* (n. 6) ch. 10.

22. Wyrzykowski (n. 11) 454.

23. Chruściak and Osiatyński (n. 7).

24. Ibid. 284.

25. Piotr Winczorek, 'The Political Circumstances of the Drafting of the Republic of Poland's Constitution of 2 April 1997' in Mirosław Wyrzykowski (ed.), *Constitutional Essays* (Institute of Public Affairs 1999) 15, 21.

26. Rapaczyński (n. 10) 603.

27. Andrzej Bałaban, 'Odpowiedź na ankietę konstytucyjną' in Bogusław Banaszak and Jarosław Zbieranek (eds), *Ankieta konstytucyjna* (Instytut Spraw Publicznych 2011) 13, 19.

28. See e.g. Joseph Weiler 'Invocatio Dei and the European Constitution' (*Project Syndicate*, 8 December 2003) <https://www.project-syndicate.org/commentary/invocatio-dei-and-the-european-constitution> (accessed 21 August 2018).

29. Susan Rose-Ackerman, *From Elections to Democracy* (CUP 2005) 62.
30. Marek Chmaj, 'Odpowiedź na ankietę konstytucyjną' in Bogusław Banaszak and Jarosław Zbieranek (eds), *Ankieta konstytucyjna* (Instytut Spraw Publicznych 2011) 41, 46.
31. For this observation, see Winczorek (n. 25) 28.
32. For discussion of CT case law on this matter, see Wojciech Sadurski, *Rights Before Courts*, 2nd edn (Springer 2014) 269–71.
33. On the strategy of postponing decisions on controversial issues during constitution drafting, see Rosalind Dixon and Tom Ginsburg, 'Deciding Not to Decide: Deferral in Constitutional Design' (2011) *International Journal of Constitutional Law* 636.
34. Ryszard Cholewinski, 'The Protection of Human Rights in the New Polish Constitution' (1998) 22 *Fordham International Law Journal* 236, 261–2.
35. Judgment K 26/96 of 28 May 1997. Note that the judgment, which still defines the current legal status quo in Poland regarding abortion, was based on the old Constitution because the 1997 version had not entered into force by the time the judgment was handed down. Based on the judgment, only pregnancies caused by a crime, or that are threatening to the life or health of the mother, or with a seriously defective foetus, may be lawfully terminated.
36. See Sadurski (n. 32) 110.
37. Herman Schwartz, 'The New East European Constitutional Courts' in A.E. Dick Howard (ed.), *Constitution Making in Eastern Europe* (Woodrow Wilson Center 1993) 208.
38. Hanna Suchocka, 'Checks and Balances under the New Constitution of Poland' in Mirosław Wyrzykowski (ed.), *Constitutional Essays* (Institute of Public Affairs 1999) 131, 143.
39. See e.g. Marek Chmaj, 'Odpowiedź na ankietę konstytucyjną' in Bogusław Banaszak and Jarosław Zbieranek (eds), *Ankieta konstytucyjna* (Instytut Spraw Publicznych 2011) 41, 45.
40. Constitutional amendment of Art. 55(1) of September 2006, in implementation of the CT judgment P 1/05 of 27 April 2005.
41. The law of 29 December 2005, Art. 6(1)(a), invalidated by the CT, judgment K 4/06 of 23 March 2006.
42. The law of 18 October 2006, amended 14 February 2007, invalidated in part by the CT, judgment K 2/07 of 11 May 2007.
43. Article 132 (a) of Penal Code, introduced on 18 October 2006, invalidated by CT, judgment K 5/07 of 19 September 2008.
44. Judgment K 4/06 of 23 March 2006.
45. See Wojciech Sadurski, 'Porządek konstytucyjny' in Lena Kolarska-Bobińska, Jacek Kucharczyk, and Jarosław Zbieranek (eds), *Demokracja w Polsce 2005–2007* (Instytut Spraw Publicznych 2007) 13, 42.
46. Ibid. 45–8.
47. Ibid. 57.
48. Piotr Winczorek, 'The Polish Constitutional System and the Law Making Process' in Jacek Kucharczyk and Jarosław Zbieranek (eds), *Democracy in Poland 1989–2009: Challenges for the Future* (Institute of Public Affairs 2010) 13, 27.
49. Ibid. 29.
50. Ibid. 27.

51. See Monika Florczak-Wątor, Piotr Radziewicz, and Marcin W. Wiszowaty, 'Ankieta o Konstytucji Rzeczypospolitej Polskiej. Wyniki badań przeprowadzonych wśród przedstawicieli nauki prawa konstytucyjnego w 2017 r.' (2018, 6) 73 *Państwo i Prawo* 3.

52. Ibid. 25.

53. Invitations to take part in the survey were addressed to all professors and doctors of legal science employed in the universities and research institutions dealing with constitutional law, as well as members of the Polish Association of Constitutional Law, altogether 186 scholars, of whom 72 responded (i.e. over 39 per cent of those invited), see ibid. 6. Among the respondents, younger scholars (with the title of Dr iuris) constitute 51 per cent while the medium-level scholars (with the title Dr hab) constitute 34 per cent of respondents and professors only 14 per cent, ibid. 6.

54. Ibid. 14.

55. Ibid. 16.

56. Ibid. 10.

57. Ibid. 15.

58. Ibid. 25.

59. *Dwudziesta rocznica uchwalenia Konstytucji RP. Komunikat z badań nr 37/2017* (CBOS, 2017) [PDF] <https://www.cbos.pl/SPISKOM.POL/2017/K_037_17.PDF> (accessed 12 August 2018).

60. Ibid. 3.

61. Ibid. 6–7.

62. Ibid. 8–9.

63. Ibid. 14.

3

Dismantling Checks and Balances (I): The Remaking of the Constitutional Tribunal

As argued in Chapter 1, populist backsliding in Poland should be seen as a comprehensive system in which particular aspects are mutually interconnected and reinforce each other. When a problematic change is introduced in a broadly liberal democratic structure, the larger constitutional environment cushions its potentially anti-liberal effects, and the system produces protections for individual liberties and checks and balances. In Poland, however, it is the opposite: a broad assault upon liberal democratic constitutionalism produces a cumulative effect, and the whole is greater than the sum of its parts. For example, the disempowering of the Constitutional Tribunal (CT), to be discussed in this chapter, should not be seen as a phenomenon in itself, lamentable but confined in its negative effects, but rather as having importantly disabled the constitutional review of liberal rights such as freedom of assembly.

Jarosław Kaczyński, leader of the Law and Justice (*Prawo i Sprawiedliwość* (PiS)) party, candidly admitted that the so-called reforms of the CT were needed in order to ensure there were no legal blocks on government policies. At the height of the struggle by PiS to capture the CT in December 2016, Kaczyński said—using a par excellence populist argument—that 'the reforms of the constitutional court' were needed 'to ensure there are no legal blocks on government policies aimed at creating a fairer economy'.[1] As Polish constitutional scholar Tomasz Tadeusz Koncewicz correctly noted: 'The Constitutional Court was targeted first because that would ensure that next phases would sail through without any scrutiny from its side. Who cares that the new legislation flies in the face of the constitution since there is no procedural and institutional avenue to enforce constitutional rules?'[2] This explains why PiS's most immediate and spectacular anti-constitutional action was addressed against the CT.

Constitutional Tribunal Before 2015

Prior to 2015 the CT had established itself as a strong protector of democratic processes and of limits upon legislative and executive powers—as presented in Chapter 2 with regard to the pre-1997 period. This is not to say that its entire case

Poland's Constitutional Breakdown. © Wojciech Sadurski 2019. Published 2019 by Oxford University Press.

law is unimpeachable from the point of view of a strong liberty-protective ideal. Many of its judgments were controversial and lacked the necessary vigour, as many observers have pointed out. For instance, the CT was almost always feeble when it came to insisting on the constitutionally entrenched separation of church and state and the principle of the secularity of the republic: it was all too willing to give in to various church demands for its active and ideologically slanted interference in the shape of law, whether it be in relation to the place of religion in public schools, the presence of religious symbols in the public sphere, or general conceptions about the privileged role of religious freedom vis-à-vis other individual liberties.[3] The CT was not sufficiently protective of media freedom and freedom of speech when a statute, for instance, declared that it was the duty of broadcasters to respect Christian values, or introduced a restrictive statutory regime of defamation law.[4] It was insufficiently protective of linguistic minorities when it endorsed the law on the official language that was majoritarian in spirit.[5] Perhaps most appallingly, the CT invalidated a reasonably liberal law on abortion and brought in a very restrictive policy on the matter, thus heralding subsequent oppressive legislation on abortion.[6] In all of these and many other instances, the CT either sought to find (often misguidedly) a compromise between competing values, or to track the dominant attitudes in society, or to give expression to the sincerely held conservative views of the majority of judges. But this is only natural, and there is no court in the world—no matter how independent and robust—in which its case law attracts unanimous support.

What matters is that, on balance, the CT had established itself as a constructive and valuable actor defending human rights, monitoring the alignment of Polish law with European Union (EU) standards, and explaining the rules of democratic governance. Here are some examples of the contribution of the CT in these three areas. *First*, when it came to human rights, the CT, for instance, found the partial unconstitutionality of the Penal Code provision that had extended criminal liability for producing, recording or importing, purchasing, storing, possessing, presenting, transporting or sending—for the purpose of dissemination—printed materials, recordings or other objects being carriers of fascist, communist or other totalitarian symbols.[7] It pronounced on the unconstitutionality of a provision of an Aviation Law that gave the authorities the right to permit shooting down a passenger aircraft in the event of special risk to national security.[8] It established the strongly libertarian constitutional status of spontaneous[9] and other assemblies, finding unconstitutionality in a provision of the Road Traffic Act that required permission for a public road assembly. It also took the opportunity to pronounce several general propositions about the freedom of assembly, the most important of which being that the lawmakers and administrative authorities may not sit in judgment on which substantive messages pronounced by the participants of assemblies are contrary to 'public morality'.[10] It strengthened the rights of criminal defendants, pronouncing, for instance, on the unconstitutionality of a provision of the Code of Civil Procedure that excluded legally incapacitated persons from the class of subjects entitled to put forward a motion to revoke the declaration, or change the scope, of legal incapacitation.[11] *Second*, the CT helped align the Polish legal system with EU laws and standards, for instance, by finding unconstitutionality in Poland's ratification of the Accession Treaty[12] and Treaty of Lisbon,[13] and in recommending a constitutional amendment allowing Poland to join the system of the European Arrest Warrant.[14] *Third*, the CT made important and positive contributions to democratic governance. For instance, it:

- clarified the relationship between the legislative and executive branches, elucidating the notion of the autonomy of parliament, and the controlling functions of the parliament[15]
- limited the role of the Prime Minister in determining the composition of the Council of the Civil Service, against a general discussion of the principle of separation of powers[16]
- determined, in some detail, the circumstances in which courts may refuse to register a political party[17]
- identified the limits of the right to set up associations[18]
- determined details of the process of legislative initiative[19]
- determined details of the duty of social consultation in the lawmaking process[20]
- clarified the scope of amendments that the Senate could introduce to a statute already adopted by the lower chamber of Parliament (Sejm)[21]
- established that the president has no prerogative to appoint or revoke the president of the National Broadcasting Board[22] etc.

Even this highly selective selection of judgments and doctrines by the CT demonstrates how active and positive an actor it had become in Polish constitutional politics.

Moreover, PiS had several of its legislative initiatives blocked by the CT in its first period of rule, between 2005 and 2007, as discussed in Chapter 2. Most importantly perhaps, the CT invalidated key aspects of its signature piece of legislation of that time, the so-called lustration law, which it found unconstitutional in 2007.[23] But there were also many other judgments of the CT in that period that put the CT on a collision course with the president, Lech Kaczyński, and the parliamentary majority, and which PiS at the time found annoying, though it failed (or was not capable) to take radical steps to curb the CT's powers. For instance, the CT invalidated the amendment of a law on the Broadcasting Council, which enabled the new government to appoint its own protégé as chairperson of the council;[24] it invalidated the provision of the law on public assembly according to which local authorities (including Lech Kaczyński, when he was still president of Warsaw) could refuse permission for gay pride parades to take place;[25] and it struck down a pet project of the new minister of justice concerning the reduction of the Bar Association's control over access to the legal profession.[26]

All in all, PiS had good reasons (from *its* point of view) to dislike the CT as it had frustrated some of PiS's legislative proposals. The memory of these collisions between the PiS government and the CT in 2005–7 certainly coloured PiS's attitude to constitutional review when it returned to power in 2015. But its antipathy was more generalized, not limited to specific judgments. The very existence of a body that may invalidate laws adopted by the majority seemed anathema to the institutional design in which the 'sovereign' embodied in the parliamentary majority could implement all its political wishes. The element of contingency, instability and revocability of 'reforms' inherent in any robust system of judicial review, uncontrollable by the executive and/or parliamentary majority, is something that an illiberal authority cannot tolerate. The example of Poland provides strong confirmation of this general proposition.

The capture of the CT by the ruling party after 2015 took place in two main stages. The first stage was paralysis, and took the form of several actions aimed at rendering the CT powerless to curb arbitrary power. Once this aim was achieved at the end of 2016, the second stage began: that of the actual proactive use of the CT against the opposition and in support of the ruling party. In contrast to the traditionally anti-majoritarian mission of constitutional courts, the CT became an active assistant of the parliamentary majority. While the first stage gave some reason to believe that the very existence of the CT was at stake, and that all PiS wanted was purely a façade rather than a fully functioning institution, the second iteration of the tribunal—as an active collaborator in anti-constitutional assault by PiS—showed that, perhaps contrary to initial attempts at destroying the CT as such, the rulers had identified a function for the CT in their design for democratic backsliding. The fact that PiS does not really consider realistic the prospect of alternating parties in power, and hopes to govern for an indefinite period, helps to explain why it is not interested in having an independent CT. Under Tom Ginsburg's 'insurance theory' of judicial review, parties that are uncertain about their future rule may seek insurance against future electoral losses by empowering a constitutional court.[27] But PiS apparently does not consider this a serious possibility, so at least *this* argument for judicial review would not apply to their calculus of costs and benefits.

The two stages of the emasculation and transformation of the CT will be considered in turn.

Stage One: Paralysing the Tribunal by Court-packing

Immediately after coming to power, PiS engaged in energetic court-packing, which after one year resulted in gaining a majority over the tribunal. The PiS-appointed judges and quasi-judges effectively paralysed the CT, rendering it unable to subject new laws to effective constitutional scrutiny.

The most important step by the new ruling majority was to fail to recognize three properly appointed judges, elected to their positions at the end of the previous term of the Parliament, and to elect into those seats three new quasi-judges, who were fully loyal to PiS. The story of this development is quite complex, and will be described here in some detail. The account may sound laborious and pedantic, but it is necessary to explain the details in order to understand the way in which PiS combined outright breaches of the Constitution with statutory constitutional 'amendments', using existing law for purposes opposite to this law's rationale.

Shortly before the 2015 parliamentary elections, on 8 October 2015 (i.e. close to the end of its seventh term, by which time expectations that PiS would win the elections were quite widespread; remember, this followed the the PiS candidate's victory in the presidential elections), the Parliament elected *five* new judges, based on a recently amended statute on the CT, which had entered into force on 30 August 2015. It was a dishonest move on the part of the then ruling coalition, PO-PSL, formed by the Civic Platform (*Platforma Obywatelska* (PO)) and Polish Peasants' Party (*Polskie Stronnictwo Ludowe* (PSL)). As it turned out later, but could have been anticipated, it was also a constitutional breach, but only, so to speak, a two-fifths breach. Only three new judges should have been elected at the time because three positions were to become vacant while still under the seventh parliamentary term. Electing all five was a deliberate act to block the possibility of the new Parliament (in its eighth term) from electing two additional new judges to positions that would become vacant in December 2015, hence in the new parliamentary term. Electing those two extra judges (for simplicity: the 'December judges') by the 'old' Sejm (the lower chamber of Parliament) was clearly improper, as subsequently stated by the CT in its judgment of 3 December 2015 (see below, in the next paragraph). In contrast, the election of the *three* judges by the Sejm in the previous term (namely, Roman Hauser, Andrzej Jakubecki and Krzysztof Ślebzak, or the 'November judges') was correct because these three vacancies fell on 6 November, while the first day of the new term of the Sejm (which is the day of the first session) was 12 November.

President Andrzej Duda refused, however, to take oaths of office from all five. After the parliamentary elections the PiS-dominated new Parliament adopted an unusual and arguably unlawful resolution on 25 November 2015 that declared that the whole process for electing all *five* justices (including the three correctly elected) on 8 October was irregular, and so the elections of all five would be null and void. On that basis new Parliament later (on 2 December 2015) forced through the appointment of five new judges (rather than only two), loyal to the ruling party. The Constitution does not recognize the possibility of such a resolution annulling an earlier election of judges, a resolution that effectively adds a new, extra-constitutional method of extinguishing the judicial term of office.

In its judgment of 3 December 2015 (K 34/15), the CT established that the law on the CT of 25 June 2015 was constitutional as far as the election of the *three* November judges is concerned, but unconstitutional as far as it purported to elect the *two* December judges.[28] Both these parts of the verdict were based on the simple principle that the election of new judges should be conducted by a Sejm of the term during which the vacancies to their positions occurred. The tribunal itself also pointed out that the newly elected parliament had no power to invalidate the elections of previous Justices and was not authorized to elect new Justices for the already occupied seats.

Further, on 9 December, the CT found unconstitutionality in the provisions of the new law on the CT of 19 November 2015 on the basis of which three judges were elected by the Sejm to replace the judges whose term ended on 6 November 2015.[29] The joint implications of the two judgments of December 2015 were that only the two judges elected by PiS majority on 2 December (Julia Przyłębska and Piotr Pszczółkowski) were properly elected while the elections of three other judges on the same day were invalid because the seats had already been filled by the elections on 8 October 2015. Since CT judgments are immediately binding, the formal situation *up to now* is that the election of three out of the five judges of the CT 'elected' on 2 December 2015 was, in light of the Constitution and the CT case law, irregular because the seats had already been filled by the three correctly elected judges in October 2015.

Fast forward to 24 October 2017. Nearly two years after the momentous events of November–December 2015, the 'new' CT handed down a judgment in October 2017[30] in which it 'cleansed' the improperly elected judges by creatively reinterpreting the K 34/15 judgment. Formally speaking, the tribunal ruled on (and affirmed) the constitutionality of two of the three laws on the CT adopted at the end of 2016.[31] This re-interpretation was done in order to legitimize the three unconstitutionally elected judges on 2 December 2015. First, according to the CT, 'a judge of the Tribunal who has been elected by the Sejm and who has taken the oath of office before the President may perform judicial duties, which means that s/he may be assigned to cases for adjudication'.[32] Secondly, the Tribunal pointed out that the K 34/15 judgment did not refer to the position or status of current judges because the subject matter of that judgment only concerned a hierarchical inconsistency of norms, without any operative consequences (whatever that may mean). Third, the tribunal did not agree with the argument that the Sejm in its eighth term elected three persons to seats already filled by the Sejm of the seventh term because the election of the previous judges was invalidated by the Sejm of the eighth term. Moreover, according to that judgment and in contradiction with Article 194(1) of the Constitution[33] and its well-established interpretation (that had also been applied by the K 34/15 judgment), the most important and constitutive moment for a CT judge election is an oath before the president. Significantly, two of the three improperly elected judges were part of the panel that handed down this judgment, including one (Mariusz Muszyński) as the president of the panel, thus breaching the fundamental principle *nemo iudex in causa sua*.[34]

Going back to the end of 2015, the gambit of 'electing' three judges to the already filled seats, and of not recognizing the three judges properly elected before PiS gained a parliamentary majority, would not have succeeded except for the active collaboration of President Duda. The president swore in the five PiS-elected judges, including three quasi-judges[35] elected to the already-occupied judicial posts hours after the election, in the middle of the night of 2/3 December 2015, thus earning them the film-noir sounding name of 'midnight judges'.[36] The swearing-in took place hours before the CT determined that the grounds for the election of the three judges by the *former* term of Sejm were constitutional, which was equivalent to saying that the three October judges were 'proper' judges, while three persons elected in their place by the new Sejm were not elected correctly, despite the swearing-in ceremony in the president's office.[37] Incidentally, there had been a discussion among experts about whether a swearing-in by the president of the Republic is a constitutive act or merely a symbolic confirmation of the parliamentary election. The majority view endorses the latter position, inter alia on the basis that a swearing-in by the president is not even envisaged by the Constitution but established by a statute. The judgment of 3 December 2015 (K 34/15) also considers the status of the act of swearing-in, and announces that the relevant statutory provision about it is unconstitutional unless it is understood as 'providing for the obligation on the President of Republic to swear in immediately any judge of the Tribunal elected by the Sejm'.

The three quasi-judges sworn in by President Duda in the early hours of 3 December 2015 (namely, Henryk Cioch, Lech Morawski and Mariusz Muszyński) to the positions already filled by the three November judges, were assigned offices in the tribunal building and put on the payroll immediately after entering the building of the CT the following morning. (According to reliable sources trusted byme , the whole group of new judges and quasi-judges came accompanied by security officers, just in case.) They were not, however, included on judging panels throughout 2016 until the retirement of Andrzej Rzepliński as president of the CT on 19 December 2016. Almost immediately upon Julia Przyłębska taking office in December 2016 as 'acting president' (a position newly established by statute, not known to the Constitution and arguably contrary to it),[38] the three quasi-judges were included on panels and on the General Assembly of Judges of the CT which then elected her as president of the CT. The first 'judgment' by a panel which included quasi-judges was the decision of 8 February 2017,[39] and since then, many other such 'judgments' have been handed down, the fact which may, in the future, result in them being deemed invalid. It should be added that by refusing to swear in some of the elected judges, the president de facto changed the constitutional system of the appointment of CT judges: headded a new stage to the parliamentary procedure of election, namely a presidential veto to the election of judges. The pre-rogative of such veto is invisible to the Constitution.

In a book-length interview two years later, Andrzej Rzepliński revealed that, early in 2016, at the height of the crisis, he had proposed a compromise solution to Kaczyński's emissary, namely that the president would take the oath of office from the three properly elected judges—Hauser, Jakubecki, and Ślebzak, successively—only as the new vacancies appear (the first such vacancy would arise on 27 April 2016 with the stepping-down of Judge Mirosław Granat). In this way, as Rzepliński now explains, there would be an incremental 'return onto the constitutional ground'.[40] This proposal was never taken up by PiS, however, and any contact be-tween Chief Justice of the CT and PiS representatives was discontinued.

The election of Julia Przyłębska as the new president of the CT on 21 December 2016 was also tainted by irregularities, although her status as a *judge* of the CT is uncontroversial (she was one of the two new judges elected in December 2015 to positions which were genuinely vacant, alongside Pszczółkowski). To start with, the competence of Przyłębska to convene the General Assembly qua a so-called acting president is highly questionable because that position is arguably unconsti-tutional,[41] in view of the presence of a constitutionally recognized vice-president who was very much alive and well at the time. Further, Judge Przyłębska was nom-inated as a candidate by the General Assembly of CT Judges which included three irregularly elected quasi-judges (Messrs. Cioch, Morawski, and Muszyński), in the absence of one of the 'old' judges (Judge Rymar) who was not given sufficient time to return to Warsaw from a short leave, and so the meeting was not quorate be-cause eight judges (a majority of judges on the CT) refused to vote. All these cir-cumstances, combined, ensured a majority of votes for Przyłębska, and since the General Assembly gave the second candidate, a quasi-judge Muszyński, only one vote, the absence of even one judge could make all the difference, because the law provides that the president of the Republic chooses the president of the CT from a list of two candidates submitted by the General Assembly of Judges of the CT. Hypothetically speaking, Judge Rymar, if he were given an opportunity to vote, might have voted for a third person (neither Przyłębska nor Muszyński), which would have resulted in a tie between two candidates for a second position on the list, and in the need for a second vote, with unknown results. To make things worse, and contrary to Article 21 of the statute of 13 December 2016 on the CT—that is, the very law adopted by a PiS majority to produce a new CT—the thus constituted 'General Assembly' failed to even take a formal resolution about the candidates presented to the president: Judge Przyłębska simply sent a letter signed by her to President Duda specifying the outcome of the vote, but not certifying whether, after the vote, a resolution was passed (it was not). According to constitutional and statutory provisions, there had to be *two* votes and two resolutions of the General Assembly (first, concerning the election of the candidates and, second, submitting candidates to the president of the Republic by General Assembly).[42] According to the minutes of the meeting on 20 December 2016, however, Judge Przyłębska decided to take one vote and only signed one document, which cannot be recognized as a resolution of the General Assembly (referred to in Art. 194(2) of the Constitution). The second stage of proceedings was ignored by Judge Przyłębska, and it is unclear whether this failure was due to her incompetence, high emotions, or her intention to avoid the embarrassment of having to reveal a lack of quorum— probably all three. Despite all these irregularities, President Duda immediately (the following day) appointed Przyłębska as the new President of the CT.

The uncertainties surrounding the election of Przyłębska also had a short and inconclusive reflection in the 'regular' courts. In an act of courage and judicial integrity, the Court of Appeal in Warsaw in February 2017 addressed a 'legal question' to the Supreme Court (SC) asking for the resolution of a legal problem, in connection with verifying Przyłębska's credentials as the President of the CT in a civil law case before the court. As the Court argued, 'An act issued by the President may fail to constitute an act of appointing a person to that position if a judge of Constitutional Tribunal indicated in that act was not presented by the General Assembly of Judges of the Tribunal as a candidate for the position [of President of the Tribunal]'.[43] In its justification for the decision, the Court of Appeal listed a full litany of reasons for its question: there was no formal resolution by the General Assembly of the CT when voting for the candidates; persons deemed to be candidates did not gain the majority of votes of the General Assembly; not all judges of the tribunal took part in the assembly; some persons who did participate had been elected to the already filled seats on the CT; one of those persons was presented to the president of Republic as a second candidate for the presidency of the CT; the meeting of the General Assembly was not convened by the vice-president of the CT nor chaired by him, as should be the case when the position of President is vacant. The implication was clear: Przyłębska may have been 'presented' to the president in a procedure that did not amount to the requisite act by the General Assembly. Rather opportunistically and on problematic procedural grounds, however, the SC on 12 September 2017 avoided taking a stance on the issue, arguing that the Court of Appeal had not established 'a real legal question' but rather that it was a purely abstract issue, not ripe for legal determination by that court. (The legal question, in reality, was perfectly ripe: it was whether the official letters signed by Przyłębska in the trials before common courts may be recognized as the official letters of the president of the CT.)

Nevertheless, the SC abstained from saying whether, in *other* circumstances, common courts could scrutinize the legality of elections for president of the CT— something that the 'new' CT strenuously denied. It should be added that the administrative courts, including the Supreme Administrative Court, which according to some scholars[44] would have been the most obvious court to determine this matter, completely avoided dealing with this issue, even though they were invited to do so several times by parties to administrative litigations (e.g. in response to official letters by Przyłębska acting as president of the CT who addressed questions by non-governmental organizations (NGOs) regarding the functioning of the CT within the procedure of freedom of information). Whenever the administrative courts were seized to clarify the legal status of Przyłębska, they refused to agree that it was within their jurisdiction. This attracted the attention of a commentator who observed that 'the administrative courts bury their heads in the sand'.[45] This is all the more problematic since the administrative courts had never expressed any doubts in any other case regarding their standing to scrutinize the legality of representing a given institution by a particular person—except for the president of the CT. After all, it was the administrative court in Warsaw that had initiated (on 8 February 2017) a procedure before the SC of controlling the legitimacy of election of Przyłębska. But in March 2018, in a final and binding judgment, the Supreme Administrative Court declared that it would be ultra vires for any administrative court to pronounce on that matter.[46]

This is not the end of the story of court-packing. By a shrewd manoeuvre, namely collusion between the new president of the CT and the minister of justice (who is ex officio prosecutor general), three 'old' judges were removed from judging in a case that was actually of no great political importance, chiefly as a show of force by the minister of justice. In a formal motion of 11 January 2017, Minister Zbigniew Ziobro, a leading politician of the ruling coalition, questioned the regularity of the election of three 'old' judges: Stanislaw Rymar, Piotr Tuleja and Marek Zubik back in 2010, on the basis that they were allegedly elected *en bloc* rather than separately (an evidently false allegation considering that the parliamentary minutes of their elections identify three different numbers of votes obtained by each candidate). The mere fact of such a challenge was, however, used to support a subsequent motion to depose all three judges from a full court panel because, allegedly, they may be prejudiced against the prosecutor general as an ex officio party to proceedings before the CT, even if often his role is purely perfunctory when he is not the author of a constitutional challenge in a given case.[47] A panel of three 'new' (PiS-elected) judges endorsed this claim as an interim measure before the minister's motion was considered on merits (case U 1/17, currently pending) and how long it will be 'pending' is entirely at the discretion of the president of the CT who clearly does not see any urgency in considering the status of three judges of her court. In itself it is scandalous because the matter should be fast-tracked and considered as most urgent since it concerns the very composition of the CT. In an extraordinary argument, the prosecutor general said in his motion that since *he* 'questioned the legitimacy ... of the judges to adjudicate, this may raise doubts as to the objectivity of those judges in their assessment of opinions submitted by the prosecutor general in particular matters considered by the Tribunal'.[48]

How disingenuous this trick is may be demonstrated by a simple thought experiment: if you have a right to participate as party to CT proceedings (e.g. because you are the prosecutor general, who is, by the nature of its office's merger with that of the minister of justice, an active politician of a ruling party) you can de facto exclude *any* judge from the CT by claiming that s/he was elected improperly (the soundness of the claim is immaterial), and then, on the basis of this claim, argue that a judge may be prejudiced against you, as a party to CT proceedings, because you questioned his/her status, and so should be removed from judging. All it takes is an appropriately compliant president of the tribunal.

The last aspect of court-packing already orchestrated under the chairmanship of Julia Przyłębska was the de facto removal of Professor Stanisław Biernat, a prominent judge and vice-president of the CT, from the CT from 1 April 2017 until the end of his judicial term of office; that is, the end of June 2017 (a period of intense legislative production by PiS). Biernat, the most vocal defender of the traditional functions and independence of the tribunal after the stepping down of President Rzepliński, was told by the new president of the CT that he *must* use his holiday leave entitlement which, as it turned out at the time, amounted to several months. Biernat argued that the entitlement is precisely that, an entitlement, which a judge may but does not have to take. Nevertheless, Przyłębska presented her decision as based on the concern for the CT budget (untaken holiday leave would have to be paid back to the judge in cash at the time of his retirement) and decreed the compulsory holiday of Professor Biernat, thus removing a truly outstanding 'older' judge from the tribunal.[49]

While still on the issue of the composition of the CT, an extraordinary fact was that in its new internal rules, adopted by resolution on 27 July 2017, the CT (by the votes of a new majority) had adopted an unusual gag rule which prevents any dissenting judges from making any comments about an improperly constituted panel in their dissenting opinions. (This may be the side effect of the judgment on the National Council of the Judiciary ((*Krajowa Rada Sądownictwa* (KRS)) of March 2017 (see Chapter 4), when in their dissenting opinions, publicly broadcast on CT streaming video, three of four dissenting judges[50] voiced strongly worded criticisms of the improperly—as they believed—constituted panel in this judgment, because it contained some persons who were not judges, legally speaking, and failed to include some judges who were entitled to be on the panel.) The new rules, signed by Julia Przyłębska, provide that 'the dissenting opinion may concern only the outcome and the justification (reasons) of the judgment. A dissenting opinion cannot apply to the rubrum of the judgment'.[51] The 'rubrum' is a preliminary part of the judgment, which includes the name of the case and the names of the judges sitting on the panel. From now on, judges are formally prevented from saying that some of the 'judges' have been included improperly in the panel. The matter is perhaps marginal, but indicative of the new order in the CT.

So much for court-packing: as one can see, it was successful due to collusion between the parliamentary majority, the president, and the newly elected judges (including quasi-judges) supported by the PiS majority. And it achieved its purpose: all the new judges and quasi-judges elected by PiS parliamentary majority, with a single exception,[52] have so far behaved predictably and voted in lockstep for the government's positions in all cases considered by the tribunal. It was greatly assisted by the fact that Przyłębska thoroughly changed the composition of panels in pending cases, including the judges-rapporteurs, by removing 'older' judges from the responsibilities of being rapporteurs in many panels in which they had already been working on a draft judgment for some time. Since taking her office, Judge Przyłębska has taken ninety-eight decisions on the composition of panels in pending cases, fully disregarding the statutory requirement of respecting alphabetical order when designing the panels.[53] An analysis indicates that as a result of these changes: (1) quasi-judges have been included in numerous panels; (2) the panels are composed so as not to have them dominated by 'older' judges; and (3) many changes also relate to the identity of judges-rapporteurs. Perhaps one of the most striking cases involving the manipulation of the composition of panels was as regards one considering a politically sensitive case on the law on surveillance. An 'old judge', Sławomira Wronkowska-Jaśkiewicz, who had been a judge-rapporteur in the case from the beginning, was replaced at the last minute by a 'new' judge, Jarosław Wyrembak, with the consequence that the entire panel only consisted of new judges, elected by the PiS parliamentary majority.[54]

The following data is telling. In 2017, the first full year of Przyłębska's presidency of the court, there were six cases that may unquestionably be described as politically sensitive. In one of these cases (concerning the law on assembly, discussed in Chapter 6)[55] the tribunal sat in full court, but thanks to the exclusion of three 'old judges', as described, the new judges and quasi-judges had a clear majority.[56] In all other five 'political' cases the tribunal deliberated in five-judge panels, and in three of these cases, the panels consisted exclusively of new judges,[57] while in two others, the composition was made up of four new judges and one 'old judge'.[58] This shows how the manipulation of panels by Przyłębska ensured the 'political correctness' of the judgments. By contrast, the president of the CT generously assigned 'old judges', allowing them to constitute the majority of panels in cases such as those concerning local taxes and tax on real estate,[59] the powers of the Social Insurance Institution (*Zakład Ubezpieczeń Społecznych* (ZUS)) regarding the basis for calculating pensions,[60] the protection of tenants in the case of death of co-tenants,[61] and the principles of issuance of licence (certificate) of an engineer of renewable energy.[62] The bottom line is: in *all* politically sensitive issues, the panels have a majority of PiS-elected judges and/or 'quasi-judges'.

Quasi-judge Mariusz Muszyński, elected 'vice-president' of the CT, has played a particularly prominent role in assuring the politically correct line of CT case law and is widely considered to be the real *éminence grise* of the tribunal, de facto in charge of its functioning. Muszyński has sat on a disproportionately high number of panels (seventy-one, from late 2016 until 10 June 2018), and was judge-rapporteur in twenty-seven cases. More importantly, Muszyński was judge-rapporteur in the most politically sensitive cases, which were all initiated by PiS politicians (either by the prosecutor general or by MPs belonging to the parliamentary majority), such as those regarding the right to assembly,[63] the election of members of the KRS,[64] and regarding the election of the chief justice of the SC.[65] All these judgments were fast-tracked, with the time between lodging a challenge and final judgment taking between two and three months. All ended in judgments favourable to the parliamentary majority, either to validate the laws enacted by PiS majority (as in the case of right to assembly), or to invalidate pre-PiS laws, which were seen as an obstacle to unconstitutional actions by the ruling elite (as in the cases regarding the KRS or chief justice). The true significance of Muszyński's role becomes more apparent if one knows that the media have reported that he had been an active agent in the Polish intelligence services, and was even expelled from his office in the Polish Embassy in Berlin by German authorities for illegal actions as diplomat in that country. Moreover, at the time Muszyński was stationed in the Polish Embassy in Berlin as a 'diplomat', Julia Przyłębska was also working there.

The relentless manipulation of the composition of panels by Judge Przyłębska led to an unprecedented protest on 28 June 2018 by the remaining 'old judges' (and one new judge, Piotr Pszczółkowski) who wrote a joint letter (leaked to the press shortly after) to Przyłębska urging her to explain why she constructs panels in a way inconsistent with the CT rules.[66] The letter, signed by seven judges was highly emotional ('We can no longer stay silent … '), and charged the president of the CT with the following objectionable practices: (1) using unclear criteria for appointing judges-rapporteurs and chairpersons of panels; (2) frequently changing the composition of already appointed panels (including the elimination of judges-rapporteurs at a time by which they would have already prepared their drafts); (3) not providing any rationale for changes to the panels; (4) almost completely omitting to appoint certain judges to panels. This is the only case known to me in which nearly half of the constitutional court contested fundamental decisions made by the head of the court. To this, Przyłębska simply responded that the charges are 'groundless', and that whenever there were changes in the composition of panels, they were dictated by 'operational requirements'.[67]

Stage One, Continued: Legislative Bombardment 2015–16

Court-packing was not the only process employed by PiS to prevent the CT from scrutinizing PiS legislation. Throughout 2016 (or to be exact, between November 2015 and December 2016), the Parliament adopted no fewer than six statutes regarding the CT, some of which abrogated parts of the older laws, and replaced them with new provisions. Bombarded by these new laws, the CT was compelled to deal mainly with laws about itself rather than substantive laws adopted at the same time.

The saga of the subsequent new laws on the CT in fact began as early as 2015, with the law of 19 November 2015 amending the statute regarding the CT, which referred mainly to the terms of office of the president and vice-president of the CT, and to the commencement of terms of office of judges of the CT. The main point of the statute was to remove the president and vice-president of the CT from their of-fices within three months, as well as give the president of the Republic more leeway in deciding when to take oath of office from newly appointed judges (he would be given one month for this action).[68] As may have been expected, the CT reacted im-mediately. On 9 December, in judgment K 35/15, the CT struck down a number of provisions of the amending statute, regarding the possibility of the re-election of the president of the CT (on the basis that it would give the executive scope for un-lawful interference with the actions of the CT), the provision that a person elected to the position of a judge of the CT is to take the oath before the president of Poland within thirty days of the election (on the basis that it would postpone a newly elected judge taking office), and the provision that would extinguish the terms of office of the current president and vice-president of the CT three months after the statute's entry into force (on the basis that it constitutes interference by the legisla-ture with judicial functions, and also with the powers of the president of Poland to appoint president and vice-president of the CT).

The next was the statute of 22 December 2015, which contained many of the restrictive provisions that would be repeated in the statutes in 2016,[69] and which will be discussed below. In judgment K 47/15 on 9 March 2016, the CT ruled on the unconstitutionality of the entire statute on the CT, a rare occurrence in thirty years of CT case law.

The highlights of legislative production of that year began with a statute of 22 July 2016 that implemented legal rules very similar to the provisions that had been assessed as unconstitutional in earlier CT case law.[70] As a result, in judgment K 39/16 on 11 August 2016, the CT found the statute partly unconstitutional (nine out of ten challenged provisions were struck down) precisely on that basis, and reiterated that the government had no authority to decide which CT judgments it would publish and which it would not. Due to violations of the principle of separation of powers, the constitutional requirement of cooperation between constitu-tional state authorities, the constitutional guarantee of the independence of courts and tribunals, as well as all the norms and principles that underlie the constitu-tional order of the state, the CT ruled unconstitutional the provisions that:

a) enacted the requirement that a full bench of the Tribunal should adjudicate in situations where three judges of the Tribunal will file a relevant motion in this re-spect within 14 days from the date of receiving the certified copies of constitu-tional complaints, applications, or questions of law;[71]
b) made consideration of a case contingent upon the attendance of the Prosecutor-General;[72]

c) regulated the terms on which judges of the Tribunal may raise an objection to a proposed determination with regard to a case considered by a full bench of the Tribunal;[73]

d) imposed the obligation that the Tribunal must consider all cases commenced by constitutional complaint or question of law within one year from the date of entry into force of the 2016 Act.[74]

This statute was followed by a trio of statutes in November and December of that year: two statutes of 30 November 2016 (on the Organisation of the Constitutional Tribunal and the Mode of Proceedings Before the Constitutional Tribunal, and on the Status of the Judges of the Tribunal), and one of 13 December 2016 (the Introductory Provisions to the Act on the Organisation of the Constitutional Tribunal and the Mode of Proceedings Before the Constitutional Tribunal, and to the Act on the Status of the Judges of the Tribunal). By that time, the composition of the CT changed fundamentally, and PiS had obtained a majority of judges (and quasi-judges), so the last three statutes have been partly recognized as constitutional by the new CT.[75]

The relentless production of new laws on the CT compelled the tribunal to deal almost exclusively with the laws concerning itself. If we add the interventions by the Venice Commission[76] (VC) and the European Commission,[77] and subsequent governmental responses to the Opinions of the VC,[78] the various drafts and laws that have produced a mosaic of interlocking provisions (some of which were invalidated by the CT, but with some of these invalidating judgments remaining unpublished), we end up with a picture totally obscured and incomprehensible to the general public, which was probably the precise purpose of the whole exercise.

Looking at the totality of the provisions contained in the laws of late 2015 and 2016, one can divide them into three categories (with a caveat that there is clearly an overlap between categories (1) and (2)): (1) provisions exempting recent PiS legislation from constitutional scrutiny, (2) provisions paralysing decision-making by the CT, and (3) provisions enhancing powers of the executive and legislature towards the CT. These are now described in turn.

(1) Provisions exempting recent PiS legislation from constitutional scrutiny. Perhaps the main rule belonging to this category was the requirement to strictly respect the sequence of judgments according to the time the motion reached the CT.[79] With an already existing backlog of over a hundred cases, this rule would effectively postpone consideration of the new laws enacted by PiS by many months, probably years. The VC lucidly recognized the true reason for the sequence rule: 'constitutional courts have to be able to quickly decide urgent matters also in cases concerning the functioning of constitutional bodies, for instance when there is a danger of a blockage of the political system, as is the case now in Poland'.[80] Another provision in this category was the requirement to consider a motion no *earlier* than three months (and in the cases decided by full bench, six months) after

notifying the participants of the proceedings of the relevant date.[81] The VC saw right through it: 'Mandating such long time lapses for hearings could deprive the Tribunal's measures of much of their effect, and in many cases even make them meaningless'.[82] Another device, invented in a law passed in mid-2016, was the requirement of the compulsory passage of time between the adoption of a statute and its constitutional review (thirty days), but four judges (hence, the number that PiS already safely controlled in the court at the time) may demand postponement of the deliberation by three months if they disapprove of the main lines of the proposed judgment, and they may make such a demand twice, which extends the passage of time to six months.[83] The same statute required the postponement of proceedings if the prosecutor general does not attend,[84] combined with a list of cases in which the presence of the prosecutor general is compulsory (including in all cases before a full bench) even if he were properly notified, thus giving the minister of justice/prosecutor general (hence, an active politician of the governing party) the power to prevent consideration of a case by simply staying away. These provisions should be viewed in combination with PiS's practice of adopting new laws without any *vacatio legis*, hence effectively immunising them from review. Perhaps the most shocking case of such failure to admit a *vacatio legis* was when the amendments of 22 December 2015 to the law on the CT provided for its immediate entry into force: it contained a required quorum of thirteen judges for valid decisions; but since the tribunal at the time had only twelve sitting judges, it would not have been able to consider a case if it were to apply the amendment in reviewing the amendment itself.

(2) *Provisions paralysing decision-making by the CT.* Here, one of the key provisions was the requirement of a difficult-to-achieve qualified majority of two-thirds for the General Assembly for judgments of the CT.[85] Note that the Constitution provides that the CT takes its decisions 'by a majority of votes',[86] which was always understood to mean a simple majority, because whenever a special majority for votes by any institution is required, the Constitution (and not a statute) says so explicitly. In the same act in which such a stringent majority was introduced, the provisions were accompanied by a heightening of the minimum number of judges required for judgments initiated by abstract review from nine to thirteen out of fifteen.[87] A combination of these two voting rules virtually ensured that a new judicial team on the CT could veto any decision invalidating a new statute. The law of December 2015 also introduced a requirement to set newly composed panels for cases already under consideration, which effectively applied to all cases from the beginning of the process.[88] An additional device for paralysing the CT was a requirement to judge in the full panel of fifteen judges if at least three judges demand it,[89] or if the president of the tribunal deems a matter 'particularly complex'.[90]

(3) *Provisions enhancing the powers of the executive and legislature towards the CT.* The president and minister of justice obtained the right to move a motion for disciplinary process against a judge of the CT;[91] and the Sejm could decide on a

disciplinary removal of a judge.[92] In addition, the same statute established that the president must agree to the extinguishment of a judge's term of office on disciplinary grounds, even if the CT-based disciplinary panel has made that decision. As a leading think tank properly observed:

> A requirement to obtain a consent of the President [of Poland] may in a particular case mean that the executive will compel the CT to admit to adjudicating panels a judge who was deemed by the General Assembly of the CT not deserving to fulfil that function. In this way, the President of the Republic would become a super-umpire and an appellate body positioned above the top court in our country.[93]

The role of the president of the Republic in appointing the president of the CT was also to be strengthened by increasing, from two to three, the number of presidential candidates to be presented by the CT to the president of Poland.[94] In combination with the method of voting in the General Assembly of Judges of the CT (each judge having a single vote), this amendment meant that even a judge with very low support—possibly even his/her own only—could make it to the list, thus allowing him/her to become the president of the CT. Another means of enhancing the powers of the executive branch vis-à-vis the CT was a provision that CT judgments shall be published in the official gazette (Journal of Laws) upon 'an application' by the president of the CT to the prime minister,[95] seemingly giving the prime minister a potential basis for denying publication.[96]

Most of these provisions were eventually found unconstitutional by the CT,[97] but in the process, the CT became effectively paralysed by having to mainly consider laws on itself ('existential jurisprudence').[98] The government tried to disable the tribunal from invalidating these provisions by claiming that the procedure for scrutinizing them must be based *on the very laws under scrutiny* (this, on the basis of the doctrine of the presumption of the constitutionality of statutes and the principle that a law is immediately binding unless it contains a *vacatio legis* provision, which these laws, as a rule, did not). This created a catch 22 situation for the CT: in assessing constitutionality of a statute, it had to use the rules provided by that very statute. As Professor Stanisław Biernat, vice-president of the CT at the time, observed in his oral reasons for one of the judgments (of 9 March 2016), one and the same law cannot be the *basis* and the *subject matter* of scrutiny at the same time. The tribunal refused to fall into this trap and found that it could not, in its judgments, use the very provisions that it scrutinizes for unconstitutionality, and that the only proper approach is to apply the Constitution directly.

There is, incidentally, a clear constitutional textual basis for the direct application of the Constitution in general (Art. 8(2)): 'The provisions of the Constitution shall apply directly, unless the Constitution provides otherwise'; and by the CT in particular: Article 195(1) of the Constitution provides that judges of the CT are subject only to the Constitution, significantly omitting their subjection to statutes, in contrast to an equivalent provision regarding all other judges who are, according to Article 178(1), subject to the Constitution *and* statutes. As Mirosław Wyrzykowski, a renowned constitutional law scholar and an ex-judge of the CT later opined:

> The construction of the direct application of the Constitution was used [by the CT when considering these laws] in urgent circumstances, i.e. in an attempt to save the constitutional order ... As the supreme norm, the Constitution cannot be helpless when its most fundamental principles are violated.[99]

And the VC made very much the same point: 'A simple legislative act, which threatens to disable constitutional control, must itself be evaluated for constitutionality before it can be applied by the court'.[100]

These legislative assaults on the tribunal only continued up to the moment when PiS acquired a majority on the CT (eight out of fifteen judges). Half a year after the election of Julia Przyłębska as the president of the CT, the process of creating a PiS majority on the tribunal was completed as a result of 'old judges' stepping down at the end of their terms. The governing party had elected nine judges by that time. Four of them were properly elected to vacant seats (Judges Zbigniew Jędrzejewski, Michał Warciński, Grzegorz Jędrejek, and Andrzej Zielonacki). They replaced judges whose terms of office drew to a close in the end of 2016 and in the first part of 2017. The other two judges were elected by parliament back in December 2015, also to vacant seats (Judges Julia Przyłębska and Piotr Pszczółkowski). Three other persons were illegally elected by the Sejm of the eighth term to already-filled seats (Mariusz Muszyński, Lech Morawski, Henryk Cioch; the latter two deceased, and replaced by new 'quasi judges' Justyn Piskorski and Jarosław Wyrembak). In this way PiS achieved the fundamental aim of court-packing to control the majority on the court. At that time, all of the legislative innovations discussed here were dropped and forgotten because they had become unnecessary. In fact, they would have constituted a hindrance to the tribunal in playing its new role, that is, that of the government's enabler.

The current law on the CT, based on two statutes of 30 November 2016[101] and one of 13 December 2016,[102] is in many respects a restoration of the *status quo ante* and does not contain any of the inventions that PiS was trying hard to introduce throughout 2015 and 2016. The earlier rules that seemed so defective to PiS when it did not have a majority on the CT turned out to be perfectly satisfactory once it had captured the majority.

Stage One, Continued: Refusal to Publish Judgments

In addition to court-packing and paralysing the CT by subsequent new bills on the tribunal, the government illegally refused to publish the CT judgments that it deemed improperly handed down. According to the government, they were taken irregularly because they contradicted laws on the CT under scrutiny in these judgments, as those laws allegedly enjoyed the 'presumption of constitutionality' during the process of review. Still under the presidency of Andrzej Rzepliński, and until the takeover of the CT by PiS-appointed majority, the government simply refused to publish judgments in the official gazette.

After the K 47/15 judgment of 9 March 2016 invalidated the statute on the CT of 22 December 2015, the government argued that all CT judgments were delivered in violation of that statute and could not be published in the Journal of Laws. The grotesque character of the situation should not be missed: *the government refused to publish the judgments handed down allegedly in violation of a statute, which was itself invalidated in the very judgment which the government refused to publish.* In that period the Tribunal reviewed the constitutionality of statutory provisions on: (1) electoral districts and decisions of the National Electoral Commission;[103] (2) customs officers returning to service;[104] (3) VAT refunds;[105] (4) the scope of parliamentary immunity;[106] (5) decisions on refundable treatment and rehabilitation;[107] (6) reimbursement for costs of court proceedings;[108] (7) limited access to public information;[109] (8) limitation of the right to a fair trial under a bankruptcy law;[110] (9) material obstacles for persons with disabilities during a driving license exam;[111] (10) disciplinary dismissal of a police officer;[112] (11) administrative enforcement costs;[113] (12) rights of fully incapacitated persons and standards for social care homes;[114] (13) appealing under the law on juvenile justice;[115] (14) the return of a rehabilitation allowance;[116] (15) the scope of the right to sickness benefit;[117] and (16) the rights of detainees in prisons and persons held in detention centres.[118]

All of these judgments, *except for the critically important judgment K 47/15,* were eventually published after the statute of 22 July 2016 entered into force. But there was a controversial side to the statute: it divided the CT's judgments into those that were to be published in the Official Journal (Journal of Laws) and those that did not deserve such attention; the statute included a stigmatizing statement about the tribunal's rulings 'issued in breach of the provisions of the Constitutional Tribunal Act of 25 June 2015'.[119] Soon after, on 11 August 2016, the tribunal issued ruling K 39/16 in which it said, in relation to the statute: 'Not only did the legislature exceed the scope of its systemic competence by making such a statement, it also failed to provide any factual or substantive grounds in support thereof. Such interference of the legislature with the realm of the judiciary ... is inconsistent with the standards of a state ruled by law'.[120] As could be expected, the judgment of the CT did not impress the government, which kept maintaining its position and decided to delay the publication of five more judgments.[121] Judgment K 47/15 of 9 March 2016 that invalidated the law on CT of December 2015,[122] K 39/16 of 11 August 2016 that invalidated the statute on CT of 22 July 2016,[123] and K 44/16 of 7 November 2016 that invalidated the rules regarding the election of the president and vice-president of the CT contained in the statute of 22 July 2016[124] *were not published until 5 June 2018.* As journalists established much later, the prohibition against publishing these three judgments was personally issued by Prime Minister Beata Szydło herself.[125] In addition, they were removed from the tribunal's official journal, and, in an Orwellian gesture of erasing any information about the very fact that these judgments were ever handed down, they were removed from CT websites and the judgments database as soon as Julia Przyłębska became president of the CT. It was perhaps the first time in the practice of any constitutional court, worldwide, that all traces of the fact that certain judgments had been issued in the past were carefully removed, as if they never existed. The tribunal's office refused to answer the question, addressed to it through a Freedom of Information request, as to *who* actually made the decision to remove these judgments from the official database—perhaps because, in Poland, the removal of an official document by a person who has no competence to do so is a criminal offence, an abuse of office penalized by Article 231 of the Criminal Code.

The refusal to publish (incidentally, not even communicated by way of explanation to the CT, which instead was informed about it by the media) violated a clear and imperative constitutional requirement that demands that the government publishes judgments 'immediately', and does not give the government any power to control the judgments submitted to it by the CT for publication.[126] It is an absolute and unconditional obligation of the government. The government here plays the role of a printing press, nothing more. Usurpation of the authority to refuse to publish a verdict clearly put the government on a collision course with the CT, and with the Constitution for that matter. It was the first time in the history of the CT that another body (here, the executive) usurped the power to decide which judgments of the CT had been properly taken and which merely constituted non-binding opinions. Much later, the prosecutor's office refused to undertake an investigation regarding the government's dereliction of duty, arguing that the government's failure to publish into official circulation the judgments was dictated by its unwillingness to include the judgments that are contrary to legal order. As Professor Wyrzykowski aptly observes, under the institutional system since enactment of the new law on the prosecutor general's office of 6 March 2016 (see Chapter 4 of this book), the complaint was addressed to a person who reports to the official who is the target of the complaint: the Prosecutor General, merged with the Minister of Justice, is subordinate to Prime Minister.[127] As the ex-president of the CT, and current Polish judge at the Court of Justice of the EU, Professor Marek Safjan declared that this was the point at which the rule of law in Poland definitely ended.[128]

The continued non-publication of some of the judgments, with the passage of time, was defended by the government on the basis that these judgments referred to statutes that were no longer in force, and hence publication would be redundant. But this is wrong, both legally and politically. Legally, a judgment referring to a statute that is no longer valid still maintains its legal effect in that it is the basis for invalidating individual decisions issued on the basis of that old statute (as provided by the Constitution, Art. 190(4)). Politically speaking, the publication of judgments on abrogated statutes is important because it indicates the ways in which the CT was paralysed in fulfilling its constitutional functions.

The issue of the (non-)publication of CT judgments had a minor but significant postscript in 2018. After the formation of the new government of Mateusz Morawiecki—presented by governmental propaganda as a pragmatist and moderate, somewhat distancing himself from the harsh and dogmatic image of his predecessor Beata Szydło—there was some hope within the opposition that one of the conciliatory moves of the new government would be to publish immediately three judgments, that of 9 March 2016 (K 47/15), of 11 August 2016 (K 39/16), and of 7 November 2016 (K 44/16). The symbolism of that act would have had a real importance because at issue was a fundamental matter of principle: can the government effectively arrogated to itself the power to assess which CT judgments measure up to the criteria of properly issued judgments? Hopes, however, were crushed. In December 2017, Artur Dunin, a Civic Platform (the main opposition party) member of Parliament, raised a formal parliamentary interpellation to the prime minister, inquiring whether and when the government would publish the judgments. The response—not provided by the prime minister himself but, with his authorization, by Tomasz Dobrowolski, a low-level governmental official—basically repeated previous justifications for non-publication, stating that the 'competence of the Prime Minister to publish the Journal of Laws' is 'an independent competence which compels the Prime Minister to establish whether an act supplied for publication is a document issued by a proper or properly composed institution'.[129] Significantly, however, an additional argument was provided in the response to the MP in a parliamentary question time: it pointed out that the judgments were absent from an online collection of judgments administered by the CT. In this way, Przyłębska's rewriting of history by erasing the past judgments of the CT that were embarrassing to her and to the ruling elite became an additional reason for the government not to publish them.

In the end, however, and clearly as a result of pressure by the European Commission, the Morawiecki government decided to publish the three remaining judgments in the official gazette (Journal of Laws) on 5 June 2018, but, rather oddly, with an annotation: 'The ruling issued in violation of the statute of 25 June 2015 about the Constitutional Tribunal ... which concerned a normative act which is no longer valid'. So there were at least three provisos attached, showing the distance of the government towards the judgments: 1) they were not described as judgments but as a ruling (in Polish: *rozstrzygnięcie*)—a concept not visible in the Polish statute about the CT or in the Constitution; (2) the judgments were alleged to have been issued improperly; and (3) the judgments were described as concerning laws no longer in force. So, over two years after the judgments were issued, the government was compelled to perform its basic obligation—but did so, characteristically, in a disingenuous and dishonest way.

Stage Two: Turning the CT into the Government's Enabler

The paralysis and disempowerment of the CT achieved by the ruling elite in Poland after 2015 via the means just described brought about a fundamental effect: the extinguishment of effective constitutional scrutiny of its laws. Once the combination of court-packing through the inclusion in the tribunal of three improperly elected judges and through natural attrition due to the terms of office ending for the 'old judges' (including President of the Court Andrzej Rzepliński and Vice-President Stanisław Biernat) produced a PiS majority on the CT, the measures for paralysing the tribunal turned out to be no longer necessary. And rather than existing as a body incapable of taking any decisions at all, the tribunal has been transformed into a positive, active aide of the government and the parliamentary majority. The government has found the CT to be a useful means for legitimizing its power, and at the same time has legitimated the CT by activating it with its own motions. As Martin Krygier put it well, 'The government sends petitions to the Tribunal so that it can lend legal legitimacy to purely political inroads on the system of justice and the Constitution.'[130] Moreover, the judgments of the CT, on their merits, have produced very convenient legal circumstances, which serve to aid the legislative and political agenda of PiS. Four examples will illustrate this new, 'positive' role of the CT as the government's enabler.

The first is a judgment of 20 June 2017[131] on the KRS. In this judgment, the new CT found the existing statute on KRS—dating back to 2001 and not raising any doubts so far—unconstitutional because, as the CT alleged, it discriminated against judges of the lower courts by improperly differentiating the procedures for appointing the judges-members of the KRS by the level of courts they represent. The problem with this argument was that the Constitution does not mandate any particular method of selection by the judges of their representatives on the KRS. The specific design of elections by the judiciary was clearly within legislative discretion. The argument of the tribunal was therefore a post-factum rationalization, without any rational basis. The CT also found the system of 'individual' terms of office for particular judges-members of the KRS unconstitutional, claiming that the Constitution requires a 'joint/collective' term of office. The Constitution implies no such thing. Moreover, nothing in the existing statute rendered judicial terms individual rather than collective.

These constitutional objections were clearly pretextual, designed to pave the way for a new statute on the KRS, which was to become one of the cornerstones of the broad design of subordinating courts to the politicians (see Chapter 4). The usefulness of this judgment to the ruling party became apparent when the parliamentary majority, and then the president (having vetoed the initial PiS bill), eventually brought their bills on the KRS: the argument by the proponents was that since the CT invalidated the old law, a new statute must be enacted. These new measures included extinguishing the constitutionally guaranteed terms for the judicial members of the KRS and changing the overall mode of recruiting judicial members away from election by judges towards parliamentary election, giving majority politicians a decisive say in the composition of the KRS. In defending the discontinuation of the KRS members' terms of office halfway through the term, notwithstanding the constitutional guarantee of a four-year term, parliamentary majority spokespersons and the president repeatedly pointed at the CT judgment of 20 June 2017 that deemed unconstitutional the statute under which those judicial members were elected.[132] The fact that there was no relationship between the alleged constitutional defects of the old statute (alleged discrimination against some categories of judges due to differentiation between the election of KRS members by different levels of the judiciary; the allegedly 'individual' terms of office) and the proposed changes to the manner in which judicial members of the KRS were elected (after all, the response to alleged discrimination in election modes by the judiciary cannot consist of removing the power of electing judicial members of the KRS altogether) did not seem to bother the authors of the new bills on the KRS. In their view, the judgment of the CT gave them *carte blanche* to fundamentally alter the relationship between the KRS and Parliament. (There is more about the 'reforms' of the KRS in Chapter 4.)

The second example is a pending case before the CT regarding the president's prerogative to grant pardons.[133] The background was that soon after coming to office, President Duda conferred the benefit of pardon upon the former head of secret services, Mariusz Kamiński, who was sentenced in a *non-final* judgment (prior to the conclusion of appellate proceedings which were underway at the time) for criminal abuse of office. (The same applies to Kamiński's deputy, Maciej Wąsik). If the judgment had stood, this would have made it impossible for Kamiński, one of Jarosław Kaczyński's closest collaborators, to serve on the new government (in the same position, more or less, as the one the execution of which earned him a criminal punishment). The SC, in considering the appeal of one of the parties to the same proceedings (an alleged victim of Kamiński's conduct), had to decide whether the presidential act of pardon regarding a non-final and therefore non-binding judgment was legally effective; it determined that it was not. PiS reacted with anger, and the speaker of the Sejm lodged a motion to the CT on the basis of a so-called contest of competencies (*spór kompetencyjny*) between the CT and the president, which is one of the constitutionally defined powers of the CT.[134] This motion was supported by a group of PiS MPs along with the minister of justice/prosecutor general. According to the submission, the SC had no power to pronounce on the circumstances and limits of the constitutional prerogative of president. However, a startling aspect of this motion was that it was *not* a controversy regarding competencies at all: the SC did not claim any presidential competencies. The SC only provided a legal characterization of the constitutional right of mercy in response to a legal question addressed to it by a lower panel because it was essential for judicial proceedings pending before the SC. Whatever the judgment turns out to be (the case is pending at the time of writing), the case confirms a pattern of conduct of PiS vis-à-vis the CT in which the ruling party uses it as a vehicle for its own political plans, and in particular as an ally in confrontation with other bodies, such as the SC.

The third example is provided by the CT judgment of 24 October 2017[135] on the statute on the SC and the resolution of the General Assembly of Judges of the SC of 14 April 2003 (note the year!) on the regulations regarding the selection of candidates for the position of chief justice of the SC. The true target of the motion was the outspoken Chief Justice of the SC, Professor Małgorzata Gersdorf. Again, a group of PiS MPs (supported by the minister of justice/prosecutor general and the speaker of the Sejm) claimed that the statutory provisions regarding the election of candidates for the position of chief justice (the candidates to be presented to the president of the Republic for his choice in nomination) were unconstitutional because they improperly delegated some details of the election to an internal act of the SC, namely to an ordinance that is a sub-statutory act and as such should not affect any actions concerning external bodies (here, the president). The motion concerning a law that was in operation and left unchallenged for fifteen years, and under which the two predecessors of Chief Justice Małgorzata Gersdorf were elected, was absurd because all the important matters regarding the elections were actually determined by the *statute* (such as the number of candidates to be presented to the president, the required quorum and majority of votes, as well as a requirement of a secret ballot), while the SC internal regulations merely further concretized them with regard to minor, technical details, such as the design of the ballot paper etc. But the CT gladly accepted the arguments of unconstitutionality, and only refrained from concluding that the election of Gersdorf CJ was ineffective on the basis that as she was the president's choice (it was President Bronisław Komorowski at the time), this presidential choice somehow superseded the unconstitutionality of the first stage of the nomination/election process.

The best explanation for this puzzling decision (how a presidential decision following an allegedly unconstitutional procedure can bring about a constitutionally proper outcome) is that, by the time the judgment was handed down, it was already known that Gersdorf CJ would be a victim of the new compulsory retirement age of 65, contemplated in negotiations between Duda and the PiS regarding the law on SC at the time (see Chapter 4), so there was no point in implicating the CT in such a shocking act as the removal of the chief justice of the SC. Nevertheless, by pronouncing on the unconstitutionality of an important element of her election (namely, the nomination by her peers on the SC), the CT significantly weakened her legitimacy in the eyes of her opponents. In delivering the oral argument for the judgment, Vice-President of the CT Mariusz Muszyński (an improperly elected 'quasi-judge'), ominously alluded to the possibility of bringing the past president of the Republic, Bronisław Komorowski, before the Tribunal of State (a body charged with dispensing constitutional liability for violations of law by top officials), thus casting a shadow of doubt upon the legacy of a vocal opponent of the PiS rule.

The fourth example is the CT judgment affirming a newly adopted statute on assemblies[136] (discussed in Chapter 6). What is important to note at this point is that, in its judgment, the CT has fully endorsed a law on peaceful assemblies that adopts a hierarchy, giving special priority to 'cyclical' assemblies, and protecting them against counter-assemblies. While, as summarized in this way, the law may sound neutral, in fact it is not: the purposes of the legally prioritized cyclical assemblies are defined in such a way as to give preference to pro-government or religious assemblies over those that express anti-PiS sentiments. In particular, the law, validated by the new CT, was directly triggered by Kaczyński's irritation with the counter-assemblies during the monthly rallies to commemorate his twin brother and other victims of the plane crash near Smolensk on 10 April 2010.

So far, I have only been discussing the *judgments* of the CT. It should be added, however, that the new leadership of the CT also actively supports the government in their extra-curial pronouncements. This applies in particular to the president of the CT. Julia Przyłębska has been an active supporter of governmental legal drafts, regardless of the possible conflict of interest she may encounter if those laws eventually come before the tribunal. For instance, in the middle of July 2017, when public controversy was at its apex regarding the judiciary bills, and on the eve of President Duda's decision concerning the veto, Przyłębska pronounced confidently on governmental television that the bills 'do not threaten the separation of powers' and that they 'meet the expectations of the entire society'.[137] In the same interview, she criticized the opposition for allegedly provoking 'unwarranted' views by foreign observers that the rule of law in Poland is endangered.[138] Later, in January 2018, when the government proposed and quickly enacted its controversial legislation on defending the good name of the Polish nation (see Chapter 6), Julia Przyłębska again publicly defended the law, notwithstanding that it was probable that it would come before the CT for consideration, as it eventually did. (The abrogation of the key provisions by the government, under foreign pressure, rendered consideration by the CT moot.)

An unusual action was taken by one of the quasi-judges, Mariusz Muszyński, who as 'vice-president' of the CT is largely viewed as the key actor in the tribunal. In March 2018 the Ombudsman, Adam Bodnar, decided to withdraw one of his earlier challenges to the law on surveillance by police (discussed in Chapter 6), namely the challenge of 18 February 2016, on the basis that the composition of the panel had, in the meantime, been unlawfully modified by Przyłębska, and also on the basis of inclusion in the panel of persons elected irregularly to the CT—of course, Bodnar had in mind the 'quasi-judges'. (This, incidentally, was not the only withdrawal of his earlier challenge by Dr Bodnar.) The CT had no choice but to discontinue its proceedings: when an applicant withdraws his/her challenge, the CT cannot proceed.[139] Muszyński chose, however, to attach a "separate opinion" to the ruling, strongly attacking Dr Bodnar for his withdrawal and even suggesting that this may be a proper basis for removing Dr Bodnar from office.

The separate opinion was unusual for at least two reasons. First, it was irregular from a formal point of view. The law on the proceedings before the CT permits judges to lodge separate opinions solely when they disagree with the merits of the ruling or with the reasoning of the tribunal. No such disagreement was raised by Muszyński: in no way did he disagree with the discontinuation or the reasoning, the latter being purely formal and confined to mentioning the statute on CT, which obliges the tribunal to discontinue its proceedings in such circumstances.[140] So it was really not a 'separate opinion' in the terms recognized by the statute. Second, Muszyński used this platform as a vehicle by which to strongly attack Dr Bodnar, accusing him of dereliction of duty by failure to respect the protection of human rights. In a nutshell, Muszyński's argument was that if Bodnar was concerned with the statute's effect on citizens' rights, as implied by his original challenge, then the withdrawal of the challenge was symptomatic of his disregard for human rights. This led Muszyński to the conclusion that Bodnar breached the terms of his oath, and this breach 'constitutes a premise of removing him from his function.'[141]

The true meaning and function of this curious document becomes clear once we realise that Dr Bodnar has been a real *bête noir* of the PiS after the party came to power: having been elected to his position by the Sejm under the Civic Platform (*Platforma Obywatelska* (PO)) government, Bodnar maintained his independence, courage, and critical attitude to the PiS government. There was speculation in the media that the PiS establishment was considering the possibility of impeaching Bodnar, though Jarosław Kaczyński has never explicitly made such a statement. Muszyński's 'separate opinion' could be used as a legal argument for the impeachment of an adversary generally hated by the PiS should a 'political decision' be made (i.e. a decision by Kaczyński) to remove Bodnar from public life. It could always be activated—and the leading member of the new team installed in the CT may be a helpful enabler of such a decision, even though the form of Bodnar's 'impeachment' would require a qualified majority that the PiS does not have. (There is another side to this coin, though. As some commentators have observed, the PiS now has an easy way of protecting its laws against challenges by Bodnar: assign some quasi-judges to the case, thus compelling Bodnar to withdraw his challenge.[142] That such a scenario is plausible is a measure of the crisis of constitutional justice in Poland.)

The decline and transformation of the CT has again raised the prospect of the direct application of the Constitution by regular courts, and the transplant of a 'diffuse' (or 'decentralized') model of constitutional review into Poland. In fact, some motions for constitutional scrutiny have been withdrawn from the tribunal (with the effect that the Tribunal is unable to consider them) precisely in order to enable regular courts to apply the Constitution directly, as it would be difficult (or even impossible) for them to do so after an affirmative judgment by the CT. This is precisely what happened with the Ombudsman's motion to the CT for scrutiny of the 'surveillance act' (discussed in Chapter 6). Several months after lodging a motion against the statute adopted in 2016, Dr Bodnar decided in March 2018 to withdraw it, having realized that the composition of the panel set up to consider it included two quasi-judges. But the main rationale for the withdrawal was that if the CT were to uphold the constitutionality of the statute, it would render it much more difficult for regular courts to apply the Constitution directly in cases involving the improper surveillance of citizens. In this way, the transformation of the CT by the regime, ironically, may have contributed to the more direct engagement of regular judges with the Constitution. By sidestepping the CT, the Ombudsman encouraged the courts to conduct such scrutiny that would have certainly been almost impossible if the CT was given an opportunity to consider the law, and upheld it.

Conclusion: The Uses of the Incapacitated Tribunal

After the electoral victories of 2015, the PiS transformed the CT from an effective, counter-majoritarian device to scrutinize laws for their unconstitutionality, into a powerless institution paralysed by consecutive bills rendering it unable to review new PiS laws, and then into a positive supporter of enhanced majoritarian powers. In a fundamental reversal of the traditional role of a constitutional court, it is now being used to protect the government from laws enacted long before PiS rule. Whatever else constitutional courts around the world are expected to do, there is no doubt that their first and primary function is 'to ensure adherence to a ... constitution and its protection against legislative majorities'.[143] In Poland, the CT became a defender and protector of the legislative majority. This changed role, combined with a general distrust of the CT and concerns about the legitimacy of its judgments, explains the extraordinary drop in the number of its judgments.[144] For all practical purposes, the CT as a mechanism of constitutional review has ceased to exist: a reliable aide of the government and parliamentary majority has been born.

The difference between the Polish and Hungarian cases of dealing with the constitutional court may be instructive. In Hungary, the change penetrated more deeply: in addition to court-packing, the constitution-making majority introduced important restrictions to the sphere of competences and the modes of decision-making by the constitutional court. Most importantly, the powers of the court were restricted on fiscal matters, the *actio popularis* has been abolished, the scrutiny of constitutional amendments was only allowed for procedural defects, and the Court was prevented from referring to any of its precedents based on the pre-Fidesz constitution. No such changes were introduced in Poland; although, knowing the modus operandi of PiS in the parliament, they could have easily introduced any such, or similar, restrictions in a statutory mode. They just did not consider them useful. Having captured the majority on the CT, they were confident that it would be an obedient servant of the executive branch, and would not dare decide contrary to political expectations. Restricting its powers could have even been seen as counterproductive (though this is only speculation as no statements to that effect are known to me) because it may have impeded the new role the CT is performing, namely that of legitimating the new statutes and delegitimizing the old ones.

But this is not to say that the disarmament, capture, and transformation of the CT into the government's ally is an unqualified benefit to authoritarian rule. Quite apart from all other political costs, domestic and international, a fully dependent court is of no use for the government in a blame game—a function that constitutional courts may otherwise perform, to the benefit of the executive or the party controlling the parliamentary majority. Governments may often find it useful to dump certain decisions on courts: when a decision by the government is costly in one way or another, the constitutional court may perform the decision-making role while absorbing the political costs. This function is occasionally played by constitutional courts, both in democratic and authoritarian systems. But in the latter, the plausibility of that effect is contingent upon the general belief that a court is at least relatively independent of the government; if it is not, the blame game does not work because everyone knows that whatever the court decides is a reflection of political decisions by the rulers. As Tamir Moustafa and Tom Ginsburg put it, using somewhat different vocabulary, and considering a scenario whereby an authoritarian government wishes to abandon some of its policies that are popular but considered too costly, 'The strategy of "delegation by authoritarian institutions" will not divert blame for the abrogation of populist policies unless the courts striking down populist legislation are seen to be independent from the regime'.[145]

This is the case of the CT in PiS's Poland. As an example, having enacted a speech-restrictive Holocaust law in haste in March 2018 (discussed in Chapter 6), the government realized after the fact how costly this law was internationally for the regime. At the same time, not wanting to alienate its hard-line electorate, it chose a strategy of engaging the CT. (Under pressure from abroad, the government eventually changed its strategy and removed the most problematic aspects of the law, rendering the CT challenge moot.) But whatever the CT may have decided, no one in Poland or abroad would have blamed *the tribunal* for the outcome because the full dependence of the majority judges on the ruling party rendered a 'blame game' ineffective: it is general knowledge that actual decisions are being taken elsewhere, and that the CT is just a spokesperson for the ruling elite. An inability to benefit from shifting even part of the blame on the tribunal, if it is so dependent on the regime, is at a real cost to the regime—but a cost that the PiS has consciously accepted to pay.

There is another consequence of the disarming of the CT, this time at an international level, and more specifically to the relations between Polish subjects and the European Court of Human Rights (ECtHR). Normally, the use of constitutional complaint is considered by the ECtHR as one of the domestic remedies that must be exhausted before an aggrieved party can turn to the ECtHR for protection. But this presupposes the existence of an independent constitutional court. As Adam Bodnar observes, 'if the Constitutional Court is not any longer an "independent court", then applicants may not be obliged to use this remedy before turning to the ECtHR'.[146] In such a case, a (perhaps) ironic consequence for Poland will be that some legislative acts now can be 'subject to a more stringent verification by the ECtHR than previously'.[147] Whether the Strasbourg Court will indeed strengthen its scrutiny, and release Polish parties from the need to show that they had tried to use a 'constitutional complaint' as a domestic remedy, remains to be seen. (More about the ECtHR role vis-à-vis the Polish constitutional crisis in Chapter 8.)

A more general reflection may be in order. The constitutional designers of the '3rd Republic' (a term designating post-communist Poland) saw the CT as the centrepiece for the protection of the rule of law, and constitutional checks upon majoritarian politics. That was when the tribunal was largely peopled by civil-libertarian lawyers of the highest standards. Their judgments eventually created a canon of liberal constitutionalism in Poland. In contrast, constitutional designers in Poland disliked the 'dispersed' model of constitutional review because 'ordinary' judges (many tainted by their service in the previous regime) were not to be trusted with the protection of new values. Or such was the near-consensus among liberal constitutionalists.[148] But if one places all one's trust in a small, fifteen-person body to carry the enormous burden of the constitutional control of politics, one makes it easy for populists to quickly dismantle the system by hitting at its centrepiece. Slovenian constitutional scholar Bojan Bugarič writes correctly about 'the institutional fragility of constitutional courts when they are targeted by illiberal forces'.[149]

This is exactly what happened in Poland. The incapacitation of the CT was one of the earliest and most spectacular actions by the PiS. With hindsight, it would have been much more difficult for them to succeed had a legal culture been generated under which all judges, low and high, could refuse to apply a statute they deemed unconstitutional. There is a textual basis for the 'dispersed' control of the constitutionality of statutes: Article 8 of the Constitution proclaims its 'direct applicability', but there were no habits, culture or skills among the judges to act accordingly. The years of hubris by the CT and its acolytes (granted, often for the best of reasons) made the 'regular judiciary' less constitutionally empowered.

Would a different design of CT render it less vulnerable to the capture by the ruling party? It is of course a counter-factual, which is very difficult to demonstrate, but one may consider a line of reasoning such as that offered not a long time ago (on the eve of Polish transformation) by Stephen Gardbaum. He suggests that the adoption of 'weak judicial review', that is, a review stopping short of categorically invalidating a law by a constitutional court, is a better design for new, non-consolidated democracies because it minimizes these courts' clashes with political branches and thus reduces the likelihood of effective assaults upon judicial independence. The independence of judges is the paramount value, Gardbaum asserts, and it is more immune to being undermined when courts exercise only weak review, that is for instance overridable by the legislature (as in Canada, or Poland pre-1997) or limited to findings of incompatibility (as in the UK). As Gardbaum claims, 'as far as courts are concerned, the most important, basic, and essential goal for new democracies in their transition to becoming stable ones is *not* establishing the power of one or more courts to invalidate legislation, but establishing and maintaining the overall independence of the judiciary'.[150]

It is difficult to speculate whether such a design would have prevented the undoing of the Polish CT. Perhaps when considering Gardbaum's conception, one point to begin with is by contesting his confident view that judicial independence is a paramount value while robust judicial review is merely a contingent measure which may or may not be needed. In my opinion, judicial independence is more of an instrumental measure than a valuable tool in itself: judicial independence combined with (for the sake of argument) judicial impotence, is of no great benefit to society.[151] A totally independent judge whose judgments are not complied with makes no contribution to the rule of law. In this sense, Gardbaum may be guilty of what is sometimes called 'goal displacement', which occurs when means are substituted for ends. So if one presupposes, as Gardbaum does, that judicial independence is indeed a paramount and inherent value, the recommendation of the adoption of weak review may be logical. But the presupposition is questionable. To understand why, consider a scenario raised by Martin Krygier: 'One difficulty [with judicial independence as a key to the rule of law] is that measures designed to enhance institutional autonomy [of courts and judge], or at least justified in those terms, might well shield incompetence, political affiliations, and corruption'.[152]

It is, after all, not a coincidence that new, transitional democracies usually opt for a robust constitutional court, with a power of binding and non-overridable review, while *all* the examples of weak review (the Commonwealth model, famously described and analysed by Gardbaum)[153] are of consolidated strong democracies. The empirical data therefore seems to contradict Gardbaum's recommendation. But putting this observation to one side, one may suggest that weak review qua a method of avoiding head-on clashes between constitutional judiciary and political branches, and thus treated as a judicial independence protection device, may apply to situations in which the tension between the court and the executive (and/or the legislative) is set at a relatively low level of intensity. When political branches are *moderately* hostile to constitutional review and insist on having the last word on constitutional disputes, conferral upon courts of weak competencies, for instance of making merely non-binding findings of the incompatibility of the law with the

Constitution, may make good sense. In such circumstances, the scenario envisaged by Gardbaum may indeed be realistic:

> it may be better that the political institutions have a lawful outlet for their disagreements with specific judicial decisions on (some or all) constitutional issues rather than leaving them with only the blunter instruments of general tampering with judicial powers, jurisdictional grounds, composition, or routine constitutional amendment.[154]

When the conflict is intense, however, like when the executive is determined to disregard constitutional restraints on its powers, and the government is strongly committed to dismantling all checks and balances including, but not limited to, constitutional courts, no amount of 'weakness' of constitutional review will save the court. This is the case of Poland. Even if the judgments were overridable by a stronger parliamentary majority, the ruling party would fight the court if it did not control the requisite qualified majority of votes in the parliament, or would happily override any judgments if it did. Judicial independence, so lauded by Gardbaum, would perhaps be intact, but at the cost of rendering the court totally irrelevant as a device for policing constitutional constraints on the government. But even the hypothesis with regard to rescuing judicial independence is unrealistic: as the empirical evidence shows, newly formed courts (such as constitutional courts in transitional systems) are viewed by anti-democratic forces as a fundamental challenge to their rule, and are unlikely to persist as independent and robust institutions.[155]

Notes

1. Pawel Sobczak and Justyna Pawlak, 'Poland's Kaczynski Calls EU Democracy Inquiry an "absolute comedy"' *Reuters Online* (New York, 23 December 2016), <http://www.reuters.com/article/us-poland-politics-kaczynski-democracy/polands-kaczynski-calls-eu-democracy-inquiry-an-absolute-comedy-idUSKBN14B1U5?utm_campaign=trueAnthem:+Trending+Content&utm_content=585c5c2204d30126992cd8d9&utm_medium=trueAnthem&utm_source=twitter> (accessed 7 November 2017).
2. Tomasz Tadeusz Koncewicz, 'Farewell to the Separation of Powers – On the Judicial Purge and the Capture in the Heart of Europe' (*VerfBlog*, 19 July 2017) <http://verfassungsblog.de/farewell-to-the-separation-of-powers-on-the-judicial-purge-and-the-capture-in-the-heart-of-europe> (accessed 2 January 2018).
3. See Wojciech Sadurski, *Rights before Courts: A Study of Constitutional Courts in Postcommunist States of Central and Eastern Europe*, 2nd edn (Springer 2014) 188–93; Aleksandra Gliszczyńska-Grabias and Wojciech Sadurski, 'Freedom of Religion versus Humane Treatment of Animals: Polish Constitutional Tribunal's Judgment on Permissibility of Religious Slaughter' (2015) 11 *European Constitutional Law Review* 596.
4. See Sadurski, *Rights before Courts* (n. 3) 239–40 and 243–4.

5. See ibid. 318–20.
6. See ibid. 178–9.
7. Constitutional Tribunal judgment K 11/10 of 19 July 2011.
8. Judgment K 44/07 of 30 September 2008.
9. Judgment P 15/08 of 15 July 2008.
10. Judgment K 21/05 of 18 January 2006.
11. Judgment K 28/05 of 7 March 2007.
12. Judgment K 18/04 of 18 May 2005.
13. Judgment K 32/09 of 24 November 2010.
14. Judgment P 1/05 of 27 April 2005.
15. Judgment K 8/99 of 14 April 1999.
16. Judgment K 3/99 of 28 April 1999.
17. Judgment W 14/95 of 24 April 1996.
18. Judgment K 12/95 of 21 November 1995.
19. Judgment K 37/03 of 24 March 2003.
20. Judgment K 3/98 of 24 June 1998.
21. Judgment K 5/93 of 23 November 1993 and K 11/02 of 12 June 2002.
22. Judgment K 4/06 of 23 March 2006.
23. Judgment K 2/07 of 11 May 2007.
24. Judgment K 4/06 of 23 March 2006.
25. Judgment K 21/05 of 18 January 2006.
26. Judgment K 6/06 of 19 April 2006.
27. See Tom Ginsburg, *Judicial Review in New Democracies* (CUP 2003) 22–33.
28. Judgment K 34/15. In the same judgment, the CT also held that the President of Poland was under the obligation to accept their oath.
29. Judgment K 35/15.
30. Judgment K 1/17 of 24 October 2017.
31. The Introductory Provisions to the Act on the Organisation of the Constitutional Tribunal and the Mode of Proceedings Before the Constitutional Tribunal, and the Act on the Status of the Judges of the Tribunal.
32. Judgment K 1/17 of 24 October 2017, Part III.4.6.
33. 'The Constitutional Tribunal shall be composed of 15 judges chosen individually by the Sejm for a term of office of 9 years from amongst persons distinguished by their knowledge of the law. No person may be chosen for more than one term of office'. Note that the Constitution does not say anything about the oath before the president; it was a statutory addition.
34. The tribunal refused the Ombudsman's request to exclude Henryk Cioch and Mariusz Muszyński (two quasi-judges) from the Tribunal's consideration of the case.
35. A term used in Polish journalistic language (by those who believe that the election of the three 'judges' to the already-filled places was improper) is '*dubler*' (which corresponds, roughly, to a 'double', as in 'body double' in a film, or to an understudy in a theatre production). I will be using here the word 'quasi-judges' as a rough, but in my view most adequate, translation of the Polish word '*dubler*'.
36. See Anna Śledzińska-Simon, 'Midnight Judges: Poland's Constitutional Tribunal Caught between Political Fronts' (*VerfBlog*, 23 November 2015)

<http://verfassungsblog.de/midnight-judges-polands-constitutional-tribunal-caught-between-political-fronts> (accessed 9 January 2018).

37. Judgment K 34/15.

38. This is the view of the group of legal experts of the Batory Foundation, see 'Stanowisko Zespołu Ekspertów Prawnych przy Fundacji Batorego w sprawie ostatnich zmian prawnych i faktycznych dotyczących Trybunału Konstytucyjnego', Warszawa 26 January 2017 (unpublished document, on file with the author) 1–2. Unconstitutionality is seen in the fact that the statutory 'acting president' sidesteps the constitutional position of vice-president.

39. Judgment P 44/15.

40. Andrzej Rzepliński, *Sędzia gorszego sortu* (Prószyński 2018) 29.

41. See, similarly, ibid. 210.

42. On the two-stage proceeding in accordance with the Art. 194(2) of the Constitution, see judgment K 44/16 of 7 November 2016. It had been originally published in the Constitutional Tribunal's official journal, but after Julia Przyłębska's election, the K 44/16 judgment was removed from the journal as well as official CT databases. The main thrust of the K 44/16 judgment was about the General Assembly's obligation to take two votes and two resolutions in order to submit candidates for the president of the Tribunal position.

43. Ruling of Court of Appeal in Warsaw of 8 February 2017, I ACz 52/17.

44. Dr Ryszard Balicki, quoted in Małgorzata Kryszkiewicz, 'NSA ostatecznie kapituluje w sprawie prezesa TK', *Dziennik Gazeta Prawna* (Warsaw, 9 April 2018) 8.

45. See Małgorzata Kryszkiewicz, 'Administracyjne sądy chowają głowę w piasek', *Dziennik Gazeta Prawna* (Warsaw, 1 February 2018) 5.

46. Judgment I OSK 657/16, discussed in Małgorzata Kryszkiewicz, 'NSA ostatecznie kapituluje w sprawie prezesa TK', *Dziennik Gazeta Prawna* (Warsaw, 9 April 2018) 8.

47. Judgment Kp 4/15 of 5 October 2017.

48. Wniosek Prokuratora Generalnego z 7 marca 2017 o wyłączenie ze składu orzekającego w sprawie Kp 1/17 (A motion by Prosecutor General for exclusion of judges from the panel in case Kp 1/17, 7 March 2017).

49. See Marek Domagalski and Tomasz Pietryga, 'Interview with Julia Przyłębska', *Rzeczpospolita* (Warsaw, 14 January 2017) <http://www.rp.pl/Sedziowie-i-sady/301149987-Prezes-TK-Julia-Przylebska-o-Trybunale-Konstytucyjnym.html> (accessed 9 January 2018); the vice-president of the Constitutional Tribunal Stanisław Biernat's statement of 14 March 2017 < https://www.tvn24.pl/wiadomosci-z-kraju,3/oswiadczenie-stanislawa-biernata-do-prezes-julii-przylebskiej,726397.html> (accessed 10 January 2018).

50. Judges Kieres, Pyziak-Szafnicka, and Wronkowska-Jaśkiewicz.

51. Para. 54 of the Constitutional Tribunal Internal Rules, Annex to the Resolution of the General Assembly of Judges of the Constitutional Tribunal of 27 July 2017 (Official Gazette of the Republic of Poland 2017, item 767; available in Polish at <http://trybunal.gov.pl/fileadmin/content/dokumenty/Akty_normatywne/Regulamin_TK.pdf> (accessed 8 January 2018). It is not clear how particular judges voted in respect of the Internal Rules as the only person who signed the act is Julia Przyłębska. See also Łukasz Woźnicki, 'Sędziowie Trybunału Konstytucyjnego ocenzurowani', *Gazeta Wyborcza* (Warsaw, 10 August 2017) 4.

52. Judge Pszczółkowski. The reasons for his 'defection' are unclear, and a hypothesis of personal integrity cannot be rejected outright. As Andrzej Rzepliński later reminisced, Pszczółkowski kept himself apart from the rest of the PiS judges from the very beginning, and did not socialize with them, see Rzepliński (n. 40) 212.

53. The law of 30 November 2016 on the proceedings before the CT, Art. 38 (1).

54. Małgorzata Kryszkiewicz, 'Tylko nowi sędziowie TK skontrolują władze', *Dziennik Gazeta Prawna* (Warsaw, 19 February 2018) 1.

55. Judgment Kp 1/17 of 16 March 2017.

56. The exclusion of three 'old judges' (decided by a panel composed of three new judges) in addition to the compulsory leave taken by Vice-President Stanisław Biernat, resulted in a full panel of eight new judges and six 'old judges'. Therefore, it was only thanks to the exclusion of three 'old judges' that the judgment on the constitutionality of the law on assemblies was assured.

57. Judgments K 5/17 of 20 June 2017 (on the statute on KRS), K 10/17 of 11 September 2017 (on the election of president of CT), U 3/17 (on creation of communes and its borders).

58. K 1/17 (on the statute on CT); K 3/17 (on the statute on SC, regarding the election of chief justice of SC). In both these cases there was the same 'old judge', Leon Kieres, who was generally considered to be the most acceptable to the new majority on the Tribunal, as he issued very mild dissenting opinions.

59. SK 48/15 (three old judges).

60. P 9/15 (three old judges).

61. P 13/16 (five old judges).

62. K 16/15 (four old judges).

63. Judgment Kp 1/17 of 16 March 2017.

64. Judgment K 5/17 of 20 June 2017.

65. Judgment K 3/17 of 24 October 2017.

66. See Anna Wójcik, ' "Nie możemy dłużej milczeć". Siedmiu sędziów TK żąda wyjaśnień od Julii Przyłębskiej' (*Archiwum Osiatyńskiego*, 6 July 2018) <https://archiwumosiatynskiego. pl/wpis-w-debacie/nie-mozemy-dluzej-milczec-siedmiu-sedziow-tk-zada-wyjasnien-od-julii-przylebskiej/?preview=true> (accessed 9 July 2018). The article contains a facsimile of the letter signed by seven CT judges: Judges Kieres, Pszczółkowski, Pyziak-Szafnicka, Rymar, Tuleja, Wronkowska-Jaśkiewicz, and Zubik.

67. Agata Łukaszewicz, 'Sędziowie nie chcą już milczeć i żądają wyjaśnień', *Rzeczpospolita* (Warsaw, 6 July 2018) 15.

68. Invalidated partly by the CT on 9 December 2015, judgment K 35/15.

69. Invalidated by the CT on 9 March 2016, judgment K 47/15.

70. In the cases K 34/15, K 35/15, and K 47/15.

71. Judgment K 39/16 of 11 August 2016, Part III.6.2.

72. Ibid. Part III.6.5.

73. Ibid. Part III.6.6.

74. Ibid. Part III.8.3.

75. Judgment K 1/17 of 24 October 2017. Note that the 'judgment' was delivered with the participation of quasi-judges in the panel.

76. Opinion on Amendments to the Act of 25 June 2015 on the Constitutional Tribunal of Poland, adopted by the Venice Commission at its 106th Plenary Session (Venice, 11-12

March 2016), Opinion no 833/2015, CDL-AD(2016)001; Opinion on the Act on the Constitutional Tribunal, adopted by the Venice Commission at its 108th Plenary Session (Venice, 14–15 October 2016), Opinion no. 860/2016, CDL-AD(2016)026.

77. The European Commission Opinion Concerning the Rule of Law in Poland (Brussels, 1 June 2016); The European Commission Rule of Law Recommendation on the situation in Poland (Brussels, 27 July 2016).

78. See the expert report on issues regarding the CT, commissioned by the speaker of the Sejm, Marek Kuchciński, presented on July 2017 (English text: <http://www.marekkuchcinski.pl/wp-content/uploads/2016/09/EN-Raport-Zespo%C5%82u-Ekspert%C3%B3w-do-spraw-problematyki-Trybuna%C5%82u-Konstytucyjnego-wersja-angielska-1.pdf>, accessed 10 January 2018).

79. Article 1(10) of the statute of 22 December 2015; Art. 38(3–6) of the statute on the CT of 22 July 2016.

80. Opinion on Amendments to the Act of 25 June 2015 on the Constitutional Tribunal of Poland, adopted by the Venice Commission at its 106th Plenary Session (Venice, 11–12 March 2016), Opinion no. 833/2015, CDL-AD(2016)001 para. 63.

81. Article 1(12)(A) of the statute of 22 December 2015.

82. Opinion of the Venice Commission Opinion of 11–12 March 2016 (n. 80) para 87.

83. Article 68 (5–7) of the statute on the CT of 22 July 2016.

84. Article 66(6) of the statute on the CT of 22 July 2016.

85. Article 1(3) of the statute of 22 December 2015.

86. Article 190(5).

87. Article 1(9) of the statute of 22 December 2015.

88. Article 2 of the statute of 22 December 2015.

89. Article 26(1)(g) of the statute on the CT of 22 July 2016.

90. Article 1(9) of the statute of 22 December 2015.

91. Article 1(5) of the statute of 22 December 2015.

92. Article 31(3) of the statute of 22 December 2015.

93. 'Stanowisko Zespołu Ekspertów przy Fundacji im. Stefana Batorego w sprawie projektu ustawy o Trybunale Konstytucyjnym', 5 July 2016 (unpublished manuscript on file with the author) 1.

94. Article 16 of the statute of 22 July 2016.

95. Article 80 of the statute of 22 July 2016.

96. See Opinion of the Venice Commission of 14–15 October 2016, Opinion no 860/2016, CDL-AD(2016)026 para 75.

97. In particular by the judgments of 9 December 2015 (K 35/15), 9 March 2016 (K 47/15), and of 11 August 2016 (K 39/16).

98. For this term, see Tomasz Tadeusz Koncewicz, 'The Court is Dead, Long Live the Courts? On Judicial Review in Poland 2017 and "Judicial Space" beyond' (*VerfBlog*, 8 March 2018) <https://verfassungsblog.de/the-court-is-dead-long-live-the-courts-on-judicial-review-in-poland-in-2017-and-judicial-space-beyond/> (accessed 9 July 2018).

99. Mirosław Wyrzykowski, 'Antigone in Warsaw' in Marek Zubik (ed.), *Human Rights in Contemporary World: Essays in Honour of Professor Leszek Garlicki* (Wydawnictwo Sejmowe 2017) 370, 381.

100. Opinion of the Venice Commission of 11–12 March 2016 (n. 80) para. 41.
101. The statute on the organization of and proceedings before the CT, and the statute on the status of judges of the CT.
102. This is an essentially transitional statute; its name is 'The provisions introducing the statute on the organisation of and proceedings before the CT and the statute on the status of judges of the CT'.
103. Judgment P 5/14 of 6 April 2016, unpublished for four months (see Journal of Laws 2016, item 1232).
104. Judgment P 2/14 of 6 April 2016, unpublished for rour months (see Journal of Laws 2016, item 1233).
105. Judgment SK 67/13 of 6 April 2016, unpublished for four months (see Journal of Laws 2016, item 1234).
106. Judgment K 2/14 of 21 April 2016, unpublished for four months (see Journal of Laws 2016, item 1235).
107. Judgment U 1/15 of 26 April 2016, unpublished for four months (see Journal of Laws 2016, item 1236).
108. Judgment SK 37/14 of 17 May 2016, unpublished for three months (see Journal of Laws 2016, item 1238).
109. Judgment K 8/15 of 7 June 2016, unpublished for two months (see Journal of Laws 2016, item 1239).
110. Judgment P 62/14 of 8 June 2016, unpublished for two months (see Journal of Laws 2016, item 1240).
111. Judgment K 37/13 of 8 June 2016, unpublished for two months (see Journal of Laws 2016, item 1241).
112. Judgment SK 18/14 of 14 June 2016, unpublished for two months (see Journal of Laws 2016, item 1242).
113. Judgment SK 31/14 of 28 June 2016, unpublished for one month (see Journal of Laws 2016, item 1244).
114. Judgment K 31/15 of 28 June 2016, unpublished for one month (see Journal of Laws 2016, item 1245).
115. Judgment SK 24/15 of 29 June 2016, unpublished for one month (see Journal of Laws 2016, item 1246).
116. Judgment P 131/15 of 5 July 2016, unpublished for one month (see Journal of Laws 2016, item 1247).
117. Judgment SK 40/14 of 12 July 2016, unpublished for one month (see Journal of Laws 2016, item 1248).
118. Judgment K 28/15 of 12 July 2016, unpublished for one month (see Journal of Laws 2016, item 1249).
119. Article 89 of the statute on the CT of 22 July 2016.
120. Judgment K 39/16 of 11 August 2016.
121. See judgments SK 11/14 of 27 September 2016; K 24/15 of 11 October 2016; P 123/15 of 18 October 2016; SK 71/13 of 25 October 2016; SK 28/15 of 11 October 2016.
122. Published on an 'alternative' website in English <http://citizensobservatory.pl/wp-content/uploads/2016/03/TK_wyrok_09032016_ang.pdf> (accessed 26 October 2018).

123. Published on an alternative website in English <http://niezniknelo.pl/trybunal/en/news/press-releases/after-the-hearing/art/9311-ustawa-o-trybunale-konstytucyjnym/index.html> (accessed 10 January 2018).

124. Published on an alternative website in English <http://niezniknelo.pl/trybunal/en/news/press-releases/after-the-hearing/art/9433-zasady-powolania-prezesa-i-wiceprezesa-trybunalu-konstytucyjnego/index.html> (accessed 10 January 2018).

125. Ewa Ivanova, 'Premier Szydło: Nie publikować wyroku Trybunału!', Gazeta Wyborcza (Warsaw, 30 November 2017).

126. Article 190(2) of the Constitution.

127. Wyrzykowski (n. 99) 385.

128. See Gazeta Wyborcza (Warsaw, 22 February 2017) online edition.

129. Gazeta Wyborcza (Warsaw, 20 January 2018) online edition.

130. Martin Krygier, 'Institutionalisation and Its Discontents: Constitutionalism versus (Anti-) Constitutional Populism in East Central Europe', Democratic Politics in Global Crisis? Challenges, Approaches, Resistances, lecture delivered to Transnational Legal Institute, King's College London, Signature Lecture Series, 17 November 2017; manuscript on file with the author, 5.

131. K 5/17.

132. Remarks by President Andrzej Duda in a TV interview (TVN24, 26 November 2017).

133. Case file no. Kpt 1/17.

134. Article 189 of the Constitution.

135. K 3/17.

136. Judgment KP 1/17 of 16 March 2017.

137. 'Julia Przyłębska: ustawy o sądach wychodzą w kierunku o którym mówi całe społeczeństwo', Rzeczpospolita (Warsaw, 17 July 2017) <http://www.rp.pl/Sadownictwo/170729671-Julia-Przylebska-Ustawy-o-sadach-wychodza-w-kierunku-o-ktorym-mowi-cale-spoleczenstwo.html> (accessed 7 January 2017).

138. Ibid.

139. Ruling of CT K 9/16 of 22 March 2018.

140. Article 59(1)(1) of the statute of 30 November 2016 about organization of and procedure before the CT.

141. Separate opinion by Mariusz Muszyński to the Ruling of CT K 9/16 of 22 March 2018, para. 4.

142. Małgorzata Kryszkiewicz, 'Sędziowie dublerzy użyteczni dla władzy', Dziennik Gazeta Prawna (Warsaw, 29 May 2018) 7.

143. Andrew Harding, Peter Leyland, and Tania Groppi, 'Constitutional Courts: Forms, Functions and Practice in Comparative Perspective' (2008) 3/2 Journal of Comparative Law 1, 4.

144. In 2017, 284 motions (including constitutional complaints, concrete review initiated by courts, and abstract review) were lodged in the CT, while in 2014, 2015, and 2016, the annual numbers were, respectively, 530, 623, and 360. In 2017, the CT handed down 36 judgments while in 2014, 2015, and 2016, 71, 63, and 39, respectively. See Dominika Wielowieyska, 'Układ Julii Przyłębskiej', Gazeta Wyborcza (Warsaw, 14 February 2018) 12. In other words, in 2016, the first full year of the process of capturing the Tribunal, the Tribunal received 42 per cent fewer motions than in the previous year

(2015), while in 2017, 22 per cent fewer than in 2016, which already had noted a record decline. In comparison with 2015, the number of motions in 2017 fell by 55 per cent.

145. Tamir Moustafa and Tom Ginsburg, 'Introduction: The Functions of Courts in Authoritarian Politics' in Tom Ginsburg and Tamir Moustafa (eds), *Rule By Law: The Politics of Courts in Authoritarian Regimes* (CUP 2008) 1, 13.

146. Adam Bodnar, 'Protection of Human Rights after the Constitutional Crisis in Poland' 66 (2018) *Jahrbuch des öffentlichen Rechts der Gegenwart* 639, 644, footnote omitted.

147. Ibid. 644.

148. For an account and critique, see Sadurski, *Rights Before Courts* (n. 3) 40–3.

149. Bojan Bugaric, 'Populists at the Gates: Constitutional Democracy Under Siege?' (*ResearchGate*, 21 September 2017) <https://www.researchgate.net/publication/319955332_The_Populists_at_the_Gates_Constitutional_Democracy_Under_Siege> (accessed 1 January 2018) 17.

150. Stephen Gardbaum, 'Are Strong Constitutional Courts Always a Good Thing for New Democracies?' (2015) 53 *Columbia Journal of Transnational Law* 285, 303, emphasis in original.

151. See, similarly, Martin Krygier, 'The Rule of Law: An Abuser's Guide' in Andras Sajó (ed.), *Abuse: The Dark Side of Fundamental Rights* (Eleven 2006) 129, 144–5.

152. Ibid. 144.

153. Stephen Gardbaum, *The New Commonwealth Model of Constitutionalism* (CUP 2013).

154. Gardbaum, 'Strong Constitutional Courts' (n. 150) 312.

155. For this proposition, and the evidence to support it, see Douglas M. Gibler and Kirk A. Randazzo, 'Testing the Effects of Independent Judiciaries on the Likelihood of Democratic Backsliding' (2011) 55 *American Journal of Political Science* 696.

4

Dismantling Checks and Balances (II): Judges and Prosecutors

In a lecture delivered in Karlsruhe, on 21 July 2018, by the invitation of her German counterpart, Chief Justice of the Polish Supreme Court Małgorzata Gerdorf gave the best summary of what has happened to the Polish system of justice since the Law and Justice (*Prawo i Sprawiedliwość* (PiS)) party came to power. The central and most dramatic passage is worth citing at length:

> Damage is regrettably extensive and there seems to be no hope for remedy in the near future. The independence of the Polish constitutional court has been destroyed, its judiciary panels manipulated in response to expectations of the governing party. The Minister of Justice is also Prosecutor General. He now holds all instruments allowing real impact on all judicial proceedings, under criminal law in particular. Court presidents report to him; to add insult to injury, he has staffed over one-half of the National Council of the Judiciary with people without constitutional mandates, who now owe him everything. The party machine can crown or destroy anyone and everyone at the whim and will of those in rule. The Supreme Court has undergone a cleansing masked by a retrospect change to the retirement age. The content of vital judiciary-related legislation changes incessantly, within a few days as of the motion date, with no consultations or opinion seeking exercise.[1]

This chapter offers a detailed account of the developments which have been described in a nutshell in this passage from Gersdorf's lecture.

The 'Regular' Judiciary Under Assault

After the Constitutional Tribunal (CT), the second main target of the populist assault has been the 'regular' judiciary. While it was relatively easy to handle a fifteen-person body like the CT, there are some ten thousand judges in Poland. And while it was generally accepted under the 'old' CT that the CT had a near-monopoly on constitutional adjudication,[2] the elimination of the CT as a device of constitutional review triggered a debate about dispersed, or decentralized, constitutional review

Poland's Constitutional Breakdown. © Wojciech Sadurski 2019. Published 2019 by Oxford University Press.

performed by all courts, US-style. This debate was prefigured by some jurispruden-
tial discussions in Poland after the fall of communism, but conventional wisdom
prevailed, under which the conditions of transition necessitated a centralized
system of abstract review performed by a robust and activist constitutional court.
When the latter has, however, been dismantled and turned into an aide of the government, judges and scholars have returned to the idea of a decentralized and concrete review.

There *are* some constitutional grounds for such a practice. For one thing, the
Constitution proclaims the direct application of the Constitution (Art. 8)—which
means that if, in the view of a judge, a sub-constitutional provision clashes with
the Constitution, the former should be disregarded and the latter applied directly. For another thing, the Constitution states that judges are 'subordinate to the
Constitution and statutes' (Art. 178(1)), which clearly refutes the anachronistic
view that only statutes are directly binding upon the judiciary. Further, the established and popular practice of 'concrete' review by the CT—conducted at the initiative of a judge who has doubts as to the constitutionality of a statute and stays
the proceedings until the CT provides an authoritative response to the question—
means that judges are acquainted with the idea that responsibility for applying
only those statutory provisions that are consistent with the Constitution rests
with them. In recent years there have been some examples of a judicial set-aside
of statutory rules on the basis of constitutional provisions and values. On the basis
of the principle of the direct application of the Constitution, the Court of Appeal
in Wroclaw determined that the use of the 'fruits of a poisonous tree', as permitted
by the code of criminal procedure, is unconstitutional because it violates the constitutional principles of dignity and privacy. According to the Court, the statutory
regulation on 'poisoned tree' evidence was not binding in this particular case, and
so defendants might be finally acquitted.[3] More ominously for the PiS elite, more
and more scholars and judges expressed their admiration for the idea of decentralized review, as it is compatible with the Constitution and necessitated by the disempowerment of the CT. The spectre of regular judges conducting a review of PiS
laws in the process of concrete adjudication provided a special incentive for PiS to
fundamentally transform the common courts, including the Supreme Court (SC);
however, this was not the only reason.

Regular courts were recalcitrant and not amenable to handing down 'correct'
judgments in politically sensitive matters, such as the sentencing of the already-
mentioned Mariusz Kamiński for abuse of duties as minister in charge of special
services, or a court ordering the prosecutor to reopen a case involving the alleged
violation of rules of parliamentary procedure by the PIS majority during the lower
chamber of Parliament (Sejm) vote on the annual budget Act in 2016.[4] In addition,
the SC and many lower courts openly sided with the 'old' CT during the crisis of
2016. For instance, on 27 April 2016 the General Assembly of the SC adopted a
resolution stating that the judgments of the CT are binding even if they are not

published. (Taking its cue from the SC's view, several local self-government entities also declared that they would apply the unpublished judgments of the tribunal.) All in all, the PiS ruling elite concluded that the courts may become—or already have become—a countervailing power, which may check and control the legislation and politics of the hegemon. Hence, PiS proposed a comprehensive package of judicial 'reforms'.

In a sequence of events characteristic of other 'reforms', PiS's legislative proposals were preceded by a well-orchestrated propaganda campaign against judges. All of a sudden, pro-PiS media and in particular public TV channels began publicizing particular cases of alleged corruption or petty offences committed by judges. In one infamous instance, a judge was shown to have stolen a sausage from a grocery store: subsequently it turned out that the judge in question had long been removed from the profession and that she suffered a nervous disability at the time of committing the theft. This was followed by a government-funded smear campaign against judges (big billboards in public spaces), accompanied by top politicians attacking the judiciary. Prime Minister Beata Szydło referred to the judiciary as a 'judicial guild' (or 'caste') and said that 'everyone knows someone who was hurt by the judiciary system'.[5] The minister of justice (MJ) said that the case law of the SC is directly linked to the communist times.[6] This was the prelude to a legislative package.

As will become apparent from a survey of the package in this chapter, none of the 'reforms' was addressed against the judicial system's main failure depicted by PiS propaganda as the principal reason for reforms: that is, excessive delays in the proceedings, often raising a sense of unfairness. This is a universal problem for courts around the world. Interestingly, none of the devices proposed by PiS was related to the promptness of the judicial process, and, on the contrary, some of them will definitely lengthen proceedings and inflict possibly hundreds of thousands of new cases upon the courts (this is the case, for instance, for the so-called extraordinary complaint – see 'The Law on the National Council of the Judiciary (KRS)' of this chapter). All these 'reforms' have a simple common denominator: they have been designed to change the *cadres* of the judicial system, and establish stronger control by the political branches, mainly the ministry of justice, president, and both PiS-dominated chambers of parliament over the judicial system personnel. In other words, the 'reforms' mean massive purges. This is consistent with Jarosław Kaczyński's dominant idea that all the wrongness of the old system related to the people who served in it: replace the people with better ones and you will change the system. And 'better' means more controllable by the dominant party, more loyal, more in tune with the programme of PiS.

This logic led to three statutes that together make up a comprehensive legislative package on the judiciary. One of these laws was enacted immediately (the statute on common courts of 27 July 2017), while the other two (on the National Council of the Judiciary (*Krajowa Rada Sądownictwa* (KRS)), of 8 December 2017 and on the SC, also of 8 December 2017), were only enacted after President Duda vetoed initial bills on 31 July 2017 and collaborated in the preparation of the final bills. It is no credit to the president that the vetoes were most probably influenced by mass protests against the new laws held in two hundred Polish cities: rather, the bills that he drafted himself were (as will be shown below) just as unconstitutional as the laws he vetoed. (According to Andrzej Rzepliński, the two vetoes were influenced by the persuasion of top church officials who wanted to avoid the escalation of mass protests.)[7] Rather than 'listening to the people', vetoes were just disingenuous measures to outmanoeuvre democratic activists and at the same time strengthen the position of the president in the electorate without relaxing the umbilical cord connecting him with PiS. They cannot therefore be seen as 'successes' of the opposition, as some observers would like to see them.[8] Rather, as one astute observer of the Polish political scene suggests, '[t]he vetoes marked not a change of heart, but a tactical retreat'.[9]

Notwithstanding a massive propaganda assault on the courts that preceded the legislative package, and in particular the dominant argument that the legitimacy of courts in society is very low, more detailed studies show that the social perceptions are more positive than the government paints it. For instance, a survey about courts conducted by pollster CBOS in 2017 shows that there is only a slight prevalence of negative views (50 per cent) over positive views (45 per cent) among individuals who have actually had personal experience with the court system—and importantly, less than one-fifth (18 per cent) of respondents based their judgment on their own personal experience, while hefty 54 per cent based theirs on media reports.[10] In the same poll, 24 per cent expressed a 'negative attitude to Polish judges', with a large plurality (45 per cent) declaring a 'neither positive nor negative' attitude to judges.[11] Surveys about corruption show the Polish judiciary in a relatively good position (an indicator of 0.86, with 1.00 being an ideal result), compared to the much worse position of the legislature (0.52).[12] In addition, 'hard' statistics, that is, those based not on perceptions but on actual data from court archives, show that the length of proceedings puts Poland in the middle of EU standards.[13] Hence, the evidence used in the propaganda assault upon judges to justify the 'reforms' was highly selective and inconclusive, and certainly not related to actual changes included in the legislative package (which, for instance, would do nothing to shorten court proceedings).

The Law on the National Council of the Judiciary (KRS)

The first of the three laws in the judiciary package concerned the KRS, a constitutionally designated body with a key role in judicial nominations. It has the power to nominate all candidates for judicial positions in the nation, and propose them to the president of the Republic (Art. 179 of the Constitution). It is a matter of controversy under constitutional law as to whether the president may reject the KRS nominations. Since the 1997 Constitution entered into force and until 2008, presidents invariably accepted KRS proposals under Article 179 of the Constitution and did not claim any competence to influence or reject KRS motions. 2008 brought about a new practice, when in a decision on 3 January 2008, President Lech Kaczyński for the first time rejected the KRS nominations without a legal basis and for political reasons. This case established a precedent and started a long judicial saga that, inter alia, involved the CT's and the Supreme Administrative Court's decisions on the lack of judicial competence to control the prerogatives of the president.[14]

The KRS also has some additional powers regarding the judiciary, namely to safeguard the independence of courts and judges;[15] apply to the CT regarding the constitutionality of normative acts on courts and judges;[16] adopt a code of ethics governing the judicial profession; express an opinion on drafts of normative acts concerning the judiciary; select a disciplinary prosecutor for judges; and express an opinion in the case of the dismissal of the president of a court.[17]

From the very beginning of its campaign against the judiciary, PiS considered the judicial component of the KRS to be the main obstacle to its reform. According to the Constitution, the KRS consists of fifteen judges. The remaining members are the chief justices of the SC and Supreme Administrative Court, the MJ, a representative of the president, four MPs 'elected by the Sejm', and two senators 'elected by the Senate'. The Constitution does not explicitly provide that the judges on the KRS are to be elected by the judiciary—it only says that fifteen members are 'chosen from amongst the judges' (Art. 187)—but so far it has always been understood that they are elected by the judiciary itself, and, accordingly, the statute on the KRS established a complex mode of elections for the different types and branches of the judiciary. Importantly, the 'new' CT judgment of 20 June 2017 that found the statute unconstitutional (and in which some quasi-judges participated) did not object to the very principle that the judges are elected by judges, but only objected to different methods of inter-judiciary elections at different levels of the courts (see Chapter 3).

As said, the principle that the judicial component of the KRS is a representative of the judiciary and must therefore be elected by judges has not been challenged until now. It is also considered to be a European norm. As the Consultative Council of European Judges (CCJE), a body affiliated with the Council of Europe, said in its recent report:

> [T]he Committee of Ministers of the Council of Europe took the position that not less than half the members of Councils for the Judiciary should be judges chosen by their peers from all levels of the judiciary and with respect for pluralism inside the judiciary.[18]

The same was emphasized by the Venice Commission (VC), which adopted the view that 'a substantial element or a majority of the members of the Judicial Council should be elected by the Judiciary itself'.[19] In addition to the principled argument for maintaining the constitutional custom of letting judges elect the judicial component of the KRS, there is also a textual argument from the Polish Constitution: with regard to MPs sitting on the KRS, the Constitution explicitly provides that they are 'elected by the Sejm' (and, similarly, with regard to the Senators, that they are 'elected by the Senate'), so if the Constitution-makers wanted to allow or mandate the election of judges-members of the KRS by the Sejm, they would have said so openly.

In addition, one may observe that the principle that the judges themselves elect the judicial component of the KRS *precedes* the current Constitution: it was first adopted in December 1989 by the first statute on the KRS in post-communist Poland establishing this institution. This model of the KRS, which goes back to the agreement of the Round Table in early 1989, was later embraced as self-evident by the Constitution of 1997.

This principle of judges electing judges was eventually rejected by PiS in its bill on the KRS, and also by President Duda in his own bill proposed after vetoing the original PiS bill. Both PiS and Duda wanted the fifteen judges on the KRS to be elected by the legislature rather than by the judges themselves, as was the case until 2018. The only disagreement was about the majority needed for their election: PiS proposed a simple majority while Duda proposed a three-fifths majority (i.e. more than PiS currently enjoys), on the basis that it would let the opposition have some influence upon the composition of the KRS. In the end, the law voted on by the Sejm on 8 December 2017 and the Senate on 15 December 2017, and signed by the president on 20 December 2017, envisaged that the fifteen judges in the KRS would be elected by the Sejm by a three-fifths majority, but that if this mode does not result in a full list of fifteen, the remaining members would be elected by a simple majority. This gives the ruling party a decisive say in the composition of the KRS, and indirectly, in the nominations of judges; in effect, it is a return to the proposals initially vetoed by the president. The candidates may be proposed by groups of citizens (minimum 2,000) or groups of twenty-five judges. Then on that basis, each of the parliamentary party caucuses can nominate up to nine candidates, after which a parliamentary committee selects fifteen candidates to be presented to the Sejm.

Taking into account the ex-officio members of the KRS as well as representatives of the president, Sejm, and Senate, this means that *politicians elect twenty-three out of twenty-five members* of the KRS. A remark by the VC, addressed to an earlier draft, applies well to the law eventually adopted: the mechanism of assuring compromise in the vote for members 'would not be effective if in the second round candidates supported only by the ruling party may be elected by a simple majority of votes'.[20] As the elections of members of a 'new' KRS in 2018 have shown, the parliamentary majority now enjoys full, unmediated, and unconstrained power of appointment to the institution that appoints all Polish judges, and the KRS has thus been turned into 'a subservient body to rubberstamp nominations by the Minister [of Justice]',[21] to use the words of Andrzej Rzepliński, ex-president of the CT.

The law also envisaged the pre-term removal of all judges sitting as members of the KRS at the time the law entered into force, despite their constitutionally guaranteed term of office (of four years). President Duda never questioned the unconstitutional termination of the constitutional term of office when he vetoed the initial bill, and this arrangement has been maintained in the statute. In the original PiS version—adopted by Parliament on 12 July 2017 but vetoed by the president on 31 July—the KRS was to be divided into two chambers: a 'judicial' and a 'political' one. There was a requirement of consensus by both chambers for any binding decision, which would give politicians an extra power of veto against KRS decisions on, for instance, judicial nominations. But even abandoning this idea, the ruling party's politicians and judges elected by PiS together obtained a comfortable majority on the KRS. The VC stated the obvious: the combination of a new parliamentary method of electing judges to the KRS with the termin-ation of the currently serving members' terms of office 'is going to weaken the independence of the Council with regard to the majority in Parliament'.[22] In fact, it is an understatement. In conjunction with the new Act on the SC and on the ordinary courts, it amounts to the full capture of the council of judiciary by the ruling party.

The law on the KRS caused a great deal of controversy within the judicial profes-sion, especially with regard to the judicial candidates for membership in the KRS, with ensuing polarization between the large majority of judges critical of the 're-forms' and a small minority loyal to the authorities. Professors Adam Strzembosz and Andrzej Zoll, two doyens of the Polish judiciary and legal scholarship, issued a statement in March 2018 in which they boldly affirmed that the new KRS is un-constitutional, and therefore that 'its decisions by their nature will be invalid'. As a result, the judicial appointments determined by the new KRS will need to be re-viewed in the future for their validity.[23] Later, in a press interview one of the signa-tories, Professor Zoll (an ex-president of the CT and an ex-Ombudsman) added that judges-members of the new KRS will one day have to face disciplinary pro-ceedings on the basis that 'they had agreed to be candidates in elections conducted by the Sejm even though it is not the legislature that should elect them to the [KRS]'; he also expressed a belief 'that such [disciplinary] proceedings will be held after the alternation in power'.[24] As the president of the association of judges (*Iustitia*) said, only about three to four per cent of all judges supported the legislative changes.[25] The dominant view was that the elections to KRS should be boycotted, and the *Iustitia* even adopted a resolution that any judge agreeing to be a candidate for the KRS would be excluded from the association. The *Iustitia* promptly acted upon this rule, for instance excluding Ms Dagmara Pawełczyk-Woicka, a newly appointed president of the regional court in Cracow and a KRS candidate (later to be elected a member of the KRS).

In the end, only eighteen judges agreed to be candidates, and the newspapers quickly discovered that a large majority of them were judges 'delegated' to the ministry (hence subordinate to the MJ) and also new presidents of courts, recently nominated by Minister Ziobro (hence, his beneficiaries). To make matters worse, contrary to the constitutional requirement of the KRS representing courts of all levels, there were no judges representing the SC or the Supreme Administrative Court and no judge from a court of appeal or a military court on the list of eighteen candidates. The whole process of generating candidates was shrouded in secrecy, and the names of supporters were never publicly announced, which confirms the degree of embarrassment and shame that the candidates (and their supporters) must have felt. In this way, one of the main official rationales for the changes, namely to make the appointment process more democratic, has been discarded. What is worse, by making the lists of those who supported and seconded the candidates secret, it is impossible to verify whether each of the candidates indeed had the required number of supporting judges. In particular, it is impossible to say whether the judges elected to the KRS enjoy the support of their peers because no judicial self-government has in any way had an impact upon recommendations for KRS candidates. And after having constituted the new KRS, the KRS itself opposed a motion to reveal the names of supporting judges (the parliamentary motion by the opposition), with some judges-members of the new KRS claiming that it would enable a 'witch hunt' in the courts.[26]

In the end, fifteen members of the KRS were elected on 7 March 2018, and echoing the list of candidates, a large majority of the judges elected were either direct beneficiaries or recent subordinates of Minister Ziobro, thus undermining the very rationale for having the KRS in the first place, which is to protect independence of the judiciary.[27] The composition is badly skewed toward lower ranks of the courts. In addition to PiS, only a de facto satellite party of PiS called Kukiz-15 decided to propose candidates (PiS proposed nine and Kukiz six, in an act of collusion aimed at avoiding any 'surprises' in the election) with all other opposition parties boycotting the election. Thanks to the boycott, no second round of elections was necessary, and all fifteen were elected with a super-majority.

Immediately after the election, the media featured profiles of the new members, highlighting their unimpressive qualifications and, at the same time, connections to the minister. By way of example: prior to his election to the KRS, Judge Paweł Styrna was appointed a deputy president of the district court (second instance) in Cracow, but had been unsuccessful five times in his applications for promotion, based on the large number of judgments delivered being quashed on appeal. Out of seventy judgments delivered in 2017 by another judge, Mr Marek Jaskulski, reasons for the judgment were produced after the statutory deadline in sixty-four cases, and nineteen of his judgments were quashed or changed on appeal.[28] These are judges who are supposed to evaluate the skills and character of candidates for judicial positions.

On the day of the election of the new KRS, the incumbent ex officio President of KRS, Chief Justice of the SC Małgorzata Gersdorf resigned from her function in the KRS. There had been some hope among PiS critics that Professor Gersdorf—an ex officio convenor of the inaugural meeting of the KRS—would refuse to convene it on the basis of the new law on the KRS's unconstitutionality, and because of uncertainties surrounding the names of the supporters of candidates. In the end, after some public agonizing, she decided to convene it, arguing (incorrectly, in my view) that not to do so would amount to an act of civil disobedience, an act that it is improper for a chief justice of the SC to perform. The first meeting took place on 27 April 2018, and it was opened by a short statement from Professor Gersdorf who declared that she had no doubts as to the *un*constitutionality of a premature shortening of the terms of previous KRS members and of the election of new members—after which she left the meeting. This gesture did not impress the KRS members who proceeded to select its board and chair, Judge Leszek Mazur. Journalists quickly found out that he is the brother of Judge Witold Mazur who was recently appointed by Minister Ziobro to the position of president of the Court of Appeal in Katowice.[29] Similarly, the new spokesperson of the KRS, Judge Maciej Mitera, is a recently appointed (since January 2018) president of the regional Court in Warsaw, having served before as a judge 'delegated' to the ministry.

The dilemma experienced by judges in the face of a 'new' KRS was not limited to deciding whether to nominate for membership of the KRS, but also whether to apply to the KRS for the office of a judge or for a promotion to a higher court—that is, activate the most essential task of the KRS. Significantly, soon after the constitution of the new KRS, quite a number of judges who had applied to the old KRS for promotions withdrew their applications, probably ('probably' because the withdrawals contained no reason for such action)[30] on the basis that they did not want to be evaluated by a body carrying the stigma of unconstitutionality. For instance, in one of the first meetings of the new KRS, on 13 June 2018, no fewer than twenty-one old applications were declared to have been withdrawn and the procedure for evaluating these applications extinguished. The dilemma was well captured by one of the judges:

> This is a devilish alternative. I can understand the judges who say: let us hold off on it, we shall not appear before this KRS, but on the other hand, many of these judges deserve a promotion. I do not know what they should do.[31]

One of the high-profile judges in Warsaw, Mr Wojciech Łączewski, said: 'In full knowledge that the statute on the KRS is unconstitutional but there is no possibility of challenging it because the CT is a fiction these days, I do not intend to apply for promotion.'[32] This approach has been supported by some legal scholars. Professor Marcin Matczak opined: 'The lack of application [for promotion] will be a clear sign that Polish judges do not accept the unconstitutionality [of the KRS].'[33]

The first months of the 'new' KRS have shown it to be a fully reliable assistant to the government. In its zeal, it even went beyond its sphere of competence, for instance by adopting a collective opinion about the draft law prepared by the opposition, which would legalize civil unions between same-sex partners. The ideological message was certainly consistent with the government's official position, but the strange thing was that the KRS has no general competence to provide opinions on legislative drafts in general, only those regarding the judiciary—this bill had nothing to do with judges. When it came to adopting official positions on laws regarding the judiciary, the KRS fully supported the government's law on the SC in its opinion of 13 July 2018.

In its core activity related to the appointment of judges, the KRS fully supported governmental actions aimed at quickly removing unwanted judges from the SC, including Gersdorf CJ (KRS unconditionally endorsed the government's line that Gersdorf's term of office expired in July 2016, despite clear constitutional provisions otherwise), and replacing them with the new ones, submissive to the government. The KRS agreed to fast-track the process of evaluating applications. Contrary to its early announcements that it would meet in September 2018 to consider its recommendations to the president, it unexpectedly decided to meet in late August, and run a parody of the procedure for interviewing candidates. Each candidate was given about ten to twenty minutes for the interview, and the final list of recommendations seemed to everyone to have been pre-approved. In August, the KRS recommended forty persons for appointment, mainly to the two new chambers. Many of the persons recommended are closely linked to the Minister of Justice/Prosecutor General Zbigniew Ziobro or to other PiS politicians, including Mr Kuchciński, the speaker of the Sejm. Waves of KRS recommendations continued in August and September, with the president appointing each subsequent batch of nominees.

In the process of nominations and appointment, an interesting legal matter occurred: the Supreme Administrative Court (SAC), until that time not known for its courage in slowing down the dismantling of the rule of law, suspended the implementation of six nominations by the KRS.[34] The suspensions were adopted in response to the motions by unsuccessful candidates who questioned the legality of the entire procedure, by (rightly) claiming that it violated their constitutional right to equal and fair access to public positions as well as their right to fair trial. The SAC ordered on interim measures, demanding suspension of all these nominations until the SAC judgment on merit. The obvious implication was that the president should abstain from appointing the recommended candidates to these positions, but he refused to do so, claiming that, not being a party to the administrative procedure, he is not bound by the judgment on interim measures. In this way he has shown his utter disregard for court decisions—including those by a court which had been so far extremely cautious and unwilling to enter into political controversies.

By way of conclusion to this part, it should be said that not only in its design, but also as evidenced by the first couple of months of activity, the KRS (suspended on 17 September 2018 from the European Network of Councils for the Judiciary, based on the assessment that it was no longer the guardian of independence of the judiciary),[35] has been transformed from an institution constraining the executive and the legislature in defence of judicial independence into a faithful, unwavering enabler of the government in its feud with recalcitrant judges. And this observation was not lost on judges: in a recent survey among common court judges, ninety-one per cent of judges said that the KRS is 'more dependent upon political pressure than under the former Minister of Justice'.[36]

The Law on the Supreme Court

The initial bill by PiS envisaged a scorched-earth tactic regarding the SC: extinguishment *ex lege* of the terms of office of all judges, with the MJ having the right but no duty to reappoint particular judges upon their request, and appointment of all remaining judges by a 'new' KRS. This seemingly outraged the president who vetoed the bill. Whether the outrage was a propaganda trick or a sincere expression of a sense of humiliation by the president, the Presidential bill transferred the power of consent to continue in a judicial position from the minister to the president himself. Further, only those who reached the newly lowered retirement age of sixty-five would have to step down unless their terms were extended with presidential approval. This solution was adopted in the law eventually enacted.

The new retirement age meant that 37 per cent of judges of the SC—and of course, this included the most experienced ones—found themselves in retirement zone, or were compelled to make a humiliating declaration to the president, who maintains discretionary power on the matter: he may refuse the request by a judge to continue beyond sixty-five years of age without giving any reasons. In itself, reducing the age of retirement and effectively shortening the term of office during the term itself may be considered unconstitutional, as has been found with regard to a similar situation in Hungary by the Hungarian Constitutional Court[37] and by the Court of Justice of the European Union (CJEU),[38] though in Poland effective constitutional challenge is no longer available.

Under pressure from the European Commission, the Sejm introduced cosmetic changes to the regime of retirement in May 2018: now when deciding whether to accede to an SC judge's request for extension, the president has to seek the opinion of the KRS. Considering that by this time the composition of the KRS had been totally subjected to political will of the majority party, the change does not make any difference and does not diminish the executive's control over the retirement situation of SC judges. In addition, the opinions by the KRS on that matter are not binding on the president.

Out of seventy-three judges of the SC, twenty-seven judges reached the age limit of sixty-five by the time the new law entered into force. Eleven of them retired willingly and sixteen judges expressed a will to continue in office, but there was a significant division within this group: only nine submitted declarations required by the new law, accompanied by medical certificates. Four within this group were subsequently negatively assessed by the KRS while five were accepted. The remaining seven adopted a different strategy: they merely made declarations that, in accordance with the Constitution, which guarantees judicial irrevocability (Art. 180 (1)), they intend to complete their service until the age of seventy. They did not present the declaration in the form of applications to the president (nor did they present the medical certificates required by the new statute) but as declarations lodged with the office of the chief justice of the SC. One of those judges, Stanisław Zabłocki (head of the Criminal Law Chamber), explained later that his declaration is not an application to the president or to the KRS, but merely articulates his 'readiness to perform the function of a judge of the SC in accordance with the principle of the irrevocability of judges'.[39] On 12 September 2018, the president 'informed' all of them about their retirement (just like the four who had made declarations in accordance with the new law, but were nevertheless negatively assessed). So the bottom line is that out of twenty-seven SC judges (including the chief justice) who reached the lowered retirement age of sixty-five, only five will continue in their office.

The chief justice is one of the twenty-seven SC judges who reached the age of sixty-five, but her case is special and requires a more detailed description. The extinguishment of the term of office subject to presidential permission upon request is said to also apply to Chief Justice Małgorzata Gersdorf (who turned sixty-five in 2018), notwithstanding the fact that her term of office as chief justice is constitutionally defined as six years (Art. 183(3)), and should therefore run until 30 April 2020. As President Duda explained in a TV interview, the retirement age (brought about by a statute) takes precedence over the constitutional term of office.[40] When asked by the journalist conducting the interview whether he himself should worry that, if the opposition party comes to power, they may want to use this precedent and shorten his own term of office, Duda responded that he has a long way to go before reaching the age of sixty-five, clearly failing to grasp the nature of the problem.

This is one of the most striking instances of changing the Constitution by statute. As one commentator noted:

If a parliamentary majority ... may, by enacting a statute, at any time 'recall' the Chief Justice of SC and in this way influence the functioning of the most important court in our judicial system, no other judge or court in Poland may feel 'safe'. It produces a serious risk of creating so-called chilling effect among judges ... which evidently threatens judicial independence ...[41]

The zeal with which PiS attacked Małgorzata Gersdorf, and seemed prepared to violate the express term of office of the chief justice can be explained not only by a personal animosity to herself—known as a strong critic of PiS—but must also have something to do with the fact that the chief justice is, ex officio, the president of the Tribunal of State,[42] a special body charged with dispensing constitutional liability for acts committed by top officials in connection with their official duties.

Before the cut-off date of 3 July 2018 (which, according to the MJ and the president, was the last day in office for those judges aged over sixty-five who had not requested an extension) she announced that she intended to complete her term, which ran until 2020, and that she was not going to request permission from the president because it is an unconstitutional condition, both as it creates a restriction on an explicit constitutional term of office of six years, and also subjects the fate of a judge to the discretionary will of the executive branch. The chief justice obtained massive support from her own colleagues: on 28 June 2018, almost at the eleventh hour before the statute-dictated purge, the General Assembly of Judges of the SC declared unanimously (with sixty-three judges participating in the meeting) that she must remain the chief justice until 30 April 2020. The resolution is just one-sentence long and is worth citing:

> We, the justices of the Supreme Court ... mindful of the oaths of office we made and allegiant to the Constitution of the Republic of Poland, which is the supreme law of the Republic of Poland, state that Justice of the Supreme Court, Professor Małgorzata Gersdorf ... shall remain – according to Article 183 section 3 of the Constitution ... directly applied under Article 8 section 2 of the Constitution ... – the First President of the Supreme Court, heading of [sic] the institution in which we perform our service to the public, by 30 April 2020.[43]

The second resolution adopted at that meeting states that the provisions of the new statute, which would remove

> a large number of judges from the SC ... constitutes an obvious violation by the legislature of one of the fundamental guarantees of the independence of the judiciary and will soon significantly disrupt the normal functioning of the Supreme Court. Justices who began their service on the Supreme Court before the Act of 8 December 2017 on the Supreme Court came into force, should continue such service until the age of 70 without any additional conditions.[44]

The crisis came to its climax, with a good deal of theatrics, on 3 July 2018, which according to the statute was the last day of service for all over sixty-five-year-old judges who failed to make their application to the president for prolongation. On that day, PiS and the president declared that they believed Professor Gersdorf to have completed her term of office, while Gersdorf herself, supported by her colleagues on the SC, maintained that she would continue to serve as chief justice. A rather puzzling thing happened on that day: both Professor Gersdorf and President Duda nominated (ostensibly, separately and independently of each other) Judge Józef Iwulski, the most senior judge on the SC (and the president of Labour Law Chamber) as a 'deputy, during periods of her absence' (in the language of Professor Gersdorf) or as an 'acting Chief Justice' (in the words of President Duda). The difference in nomenclature is significant: under Article 14(2)) of the existing law on the SC, in the part not abrogated by the new law, chief justice may appoint another judge to be her deputy at a time of her absence. In turn, President Duda *could have* cited the provision related to transitional arrangements under the new (PiS-enacted) law, which mandates the president to appoint an acting chief justice (Art. 111 (4) of the new statute on the SC) for a period before a permanent chief justice is nominated (i.e. before the SC has the requisite number of judges for such a vote). Clearly, however, he could not find any judge on the SC willing to undertake this task, so he simply referred to the same provision that Gersdorf did, but with a clear proviso that Gersdorf's mission is terminated, so Iwulski was not her deputy but rather an interim successor. Nonetheless the old statute under which Gersdorf nominated her deputy provides no role for the president at all; rather, it is a routine provision about an official (here, a chief justice) appointing a replacement for a limited period of illness or other absence from office. There were no legal grounds for Duda to jump on the bandwagon already set up by Gersdorf, and to say that Judge Iwulski enjoys full confidence of the president.

For President Duda, nominating Judge Iwulski was fraught with legal inconsistencies: Iwulski is older than Gersdorf (he was sixty-six years old on that day), hence he belongs to the group of judges in the retirement zone, and he did not make an application to the president in the procedure provided by the new law, but (as many other 'intransigent' judges did) made a declaration of his will to continue, with direct reference to the Constitution. In addition, Judge Iwulski was one of the signatories of two resolutions of the SC of 28 June 2018, already mentioned, including the one declaring full support for Gersdorf as the continuing chief justice. This means that President Duda accepted the continuation in office of a judge who, under Duda's own law, had his term of office terminated because he had reached retirement age and did not ask the president for the right to continue in office! By using Article 14 of the old law (on standing in for the current chief justice) rather than Art. 111(2) of the new law (on interim successor, i.e. acting chief justice), the president, perhaps unwillingly, accepted that Małgorzata Gersdorf was still chief justice. And to make matters even worse, Duda failed to hand Professor Gersdorf any written declaration regarding her stepping down, even though the law (Art. 39 of the statute on the SC) requires that such a declaration be issued by the president (with an implication that it needs to be countersigned by the prime minister because it does not belong to the constitutional list of the president's own prerogatives) regarding any SC judge stepping down from his/her active duty. It was speculated that this incoherent action by the president was made in order to stop the procedure of infringement against Poland in the CJEU; that is, if Professor Gersdorf was still a chief justice (though her functions are performed by her deputy), what is the point of an infringement action? But this argument is clearly inconsistent with the president's frequently repeated official conviction that Gersdorf terminated her mission on 3 July 2018.

The following day, 4 July 2018, Judge Gersdorf, surrounded by her colleagues and applauded by hundreds of demonstrators, returned to the SC building, thus symbolically showing her disregard for official statements about the expiry of her term of office. As of the writing of this book, the stand-off continues: Gersdorf claims (including in her conversation with the author of this book, on 26 September 2018 in Warsaw) that she considers herself to be chief justice, and intends to perform this function until 2020, while the government, the president, and the KRS declare that she is a retired judge and has no right to occupy the office of chief justice.

***

There is one other significant change in the new law on the SC compared to the status quo: under the new statute, the president of the Republic would choose the chief justice of the SC from five candidates (currently: only two) presented by the General Assembly of the SC. This obviously increases the control of the president over the SC, reduces the impact of the SC upon the election of its own chief justice, and opens up the possibility that a judge chosen by the president will only enjoy minimal support from the judges of the SC: if judges have to nominate three candidates, it is likely that candidate number three, considering the number of votes obtained, would have made it to the list with very meagre support.[45] The election of a new chief justice, according to the new statute, was initially tied to the condition of filling 110 judicial positions on the SC, which may have taken quite a lot of time, and it meant that the acting chief justice, directly appointed by the president, could have led the SC for as long as the president and PiS wanted because there were no deadlines for the appointment of all 110 judges. What seemed like a clever gambit from the point of view of PiS turned out to be counterproductive, because no one on the old SC would agree to perform the role of acting CJ, succeeding Professor Gersdorf whose term of office was unconstitutionally terminated according to the same SC. In itself, it is a tribute to the integrity of the 'old' judges, and their loyalty to the chief justice and to the institution. When the rulers realized this, they rushed through a new amendment to the 'new' statute in July 2018 (by which time this was the fifth amendment to the statute), and radically lowered the bar for the number of judges of the SC required to propose candidates to the president. It was decided that two-thirds of the composition of the SC (i.e. eighty judges) may, in a general assembly, adopt a list of five candidates to be presented to the president. It means that they went from one extreme to another in order to tailor the law to suit their political needs. PiS politicians made it clear that they made this change in order to prevent the judiciary from blocking the procedure by sending a large number of applications to the KRS, and thus overwhelming it with paperwork.[46]

At the same time, the July 2018 amendments relaxed the criteria of eligibility to the judgeship of the SC, and also neutralized the effects of an appeal from a negative decision by the KRS regarding an appointment to the SC: from now on, such an appeal to the Supreme Administrative Court will not block the appointment of another candidate to a given seat on the SC, which effectively renders the appeal meaningless.[47] In a Kafkaesque arrangement, if the KRS chooses to deem an application inadmissible on 'formal grounds', no appeal from such a determination is possible at all, including challenging the KRS's characterization of inadmissibility as based on formal grounds. Such an administrative decision is then final with no avenue for judicial review of the decision. These hastily adopted changes make it much simpler for PiS to quickly appoint new judges to the SC; all the more so since the criteria of eligibility have been greatly expanded, making it possible for public prosecutors, advocates, and notaries public to apply for seats on the SC, if they are over forty years old and have at least ten years' professional experience.

In addition, the law envisaged a huge increase in the number of judges on the SC (from 93 to at least 120). Combined with the forced stepping-down of a large number of judges over sixty-five, according to conservative assessments, this created vacancies of *about 60 per cent* of all judgeships on the SC, to be appointed by the president on the recommendations of the 'new' KRS. In this ingenious way, the law produced a brand new composition in the top court, peopled largely by judges selected by the parliamentary majority, with PiS handing itself a decisive control over the SC.

In June 2018, after subsequent amendments to the law on the SC, President Duda formally advertised an initial forty-four positions on the SC, predominantly to new chambers, staffed entirely by new judges. Over two hundred lawyers initially applied but some withdrew their applications, largely under pressure from their professional associations, so in the end 182 candidates applied, of which there were 70 judges of lower courts, 31 barristers/advocates, 38 commercial lawyers, 22 legal academics and 12 public prosecutors. There was a consensus in the legal profession that candidates generally were of a very low quality, often unknown in their professional settings. This was made possible by the lowering of formal qualifications of eligibility, but also by the composition of the KRS (see the section of this chapter, 'The Law on the National Council of Judiciary (KRS)'), the non-transparent and perfunctory character of 'interviews' (lasting about fifteen minutes per candidate), and the general perception that the outcome had been predecided by PiS politicians (it was general knowledge that some candidates were 'blacklisted' by PiS, and that one PiS MP—a member of the KRS—circulated a list of 'incorrect' candidates).[48] The list of candidates positively recommended by the KRS contained a number of persons very closely linked to Minister Ziobro, and included some persons who had disciplinary proceedings against them. Asked by the media for the reasons why such judges were recommended, the Vice-President of the KRS Wiesław Johann admitted that 'errors may be committed' when one acts in haste, but defended the list of recommendations as mostly good, and hoped that President Duda would sift out inadequate candidates.

The action by the KRS was accompanied by an accelerated purge managed by the president. At the time of the writing, President Duda has issued only five positive responses regarding permission to continue in office and nine negative ones, following the KRS recommendations. To give an example of a judge purged by the KRS and Duda, one may look at the figure of Wojciech Katner. Judge of the Civil Law Chamber of the SC since 2009, Katner is a senior professor at the University of Łódź, author of nine monographs, two textbooks, and some one hundred and twenty articles in academic journals. On 12 July 2018 the KRS submitted a negative recommendation to the president regarding whether Katner should judge beyond the age of sixty-five on the basis that (quoting from the justification provided) 'agreeing to continuation of his position is contrary to the interest of the system of justice, to important public interest, and in particular with rational use of human resources of the Supreme Court and the needs arising out of the caseload in the Civil Law Chamber of the Supreme Court'.[49] This rationale simply cites, verbatim, the provision of the law on the SC describing the grounds on which the recommendation by the KRS and the decisions by the president should be made, regarding permission to continue in office.[50] The disingenuousness of the rationale provided is manifested by the fact that (quite apart from professional skills and experience of Judge Katner), as the media reported around that time, in the Civil Law Chamber there are actually twenty active judges (and thirty-five judicial positions), and that the backlog has increased as a result of understaffing. As president of that Chamber, Judge Dariusz Zawistowski said, the number of cases of cassation awaiting judicial resolution has risen from about thirty to over a hundred.[51]

So much for the cadres of the SC. Structurally, the new law brings about some important developments, in particular the creation of two new chambers, peopled by new judges (hence, appointed fully through the newly politicized procedure), including a twenty-judge chamber on 'extraordinary review and public affairs' tasked with, *inter alia*, determining the legality of election results (note the connection between the ruling party having the dominant say in the composition of this chamber, via a 'new' KRS, and its interest in adjudicating electoral disputes). As the Venice Commission observes, the result of this design will be that 'judges appointed by a [KRS] dominated by the current political majority would decide on issues of particular importance, including the regularity of elections, which is to be decided by the Extraordinary Chamber'.[52] The second new chamber, dealing with disciplinary proceedings against judges (and other legal professions), is a device to focus public opinion on judicial accountability. It has been widely publicized that the budget of the SC envisages a 40 per cent bonus for judges serving on that chamber, but no rationale for such an immense privilege has been ever produced, and the only reason one may think of is creating incentives for candidates to apply to a body viewed with disgust by a large number of lawyers. The chamber has a separate budget, and all budgetary changes made by the president of the SC will require consent from the president of this new chamber. What is more, the budget is huge: roughly one half of the entire SC budget, even though it will only have sixteen judges out of the projected 120 in the entire SC.[53] The president of the chamber, in addition to its enormous budgetary powers, will also possess the powers of the chief justice of the SC vis-à-vis his/her judges: they will be subordinate only to him/her, rather than to the chief justice. It all shows that the new disciplinary chamber will constitute, for all practical purposes, a separate court within a court.

Associations of judges—such as *Iustitia* and *Themis*—appealed to judges to boycott the call for nominations to the new chamber (just as they had earlier appealed to boycott the new KRS), but PiS had anticipated this problem and had included a provision that public prosecutors with at least ten years' experience of office are eligible to become judges of the SC in the new law on the SC. Thanks to this new rule, PiS may recruit new SC judges (in particular, to the disciplinary chamber) among prosecutors subordinate to the MJ. As prominent legal commentator Ewa Siedlecka notes:

> The proposal [to become a judge of SC] is very tempting [for prosecutors]: much less work than they have now, and a salary which is 40 percent higher than that of the other judges of the SC ... In this manner, prosecutors who are habituated to hierarchical subordination and compliance with their superiors' commands will become disciplinary judges [of the SC].[54]

In addition, both new chambers will have panels including lay judges, elected by the Senate (a panel will consist of two professionals and one lay judge). The only eligibility criterion is a high school certificate, age between forty and sixty, and non-employment in a state institution as well as non-membership in a political party. This mode of recruiting lay judges assures, again, the dominant influence of PiS, which has a comfortable majority in the Senate. There is no other explanation for including lay judges in the SC, for the first time in its history, which is inconsistent with the role of the SC as a court 'of law' and not 'of facts', dealing normally with extremely complex legal issues. The procedure of recruiting lay judges has so far been a big fiasco: by the final application deadline of 24 May 2018, only nineteen candidates had applied for thirty-six seats. After initial hearings in the Senate (boycotted by the opposition), only thirteen have been vetted as meeting the formal criteria.

In his new version of the law on the SC, President Duda granted himself considerable powers of control over the SC, including 1) the right to appoint the chief justice (the prerogative already held by the president, but now extended because he will be able to choose from five rather than two candidates presented to him by the assembly of judges of the SC), 2) the discretion to reappoint a chief justice for a second term, 3) conferral of the internal rules of functioning upon the SC, and 4), as already mentioned, the power to grant an extension of the term of office to judges who have reached the age of sixty-five. The vetoes and the resultant presidential amendments to the law were therefore entirely self-serving and concerned reallocation of executive powers of control over the SC from the MJ to the president.

A clearly populist innovation, proposed by the president and incorporated into statute, is the new appellate instrument—the 'extraordinary complaint'—in addition to the three stages of appellate measures already existing in Polish law. This type of appeal may be lodged against every final judgment over the last twenty years (with very few exceptions, such as judgments concerning divorce) during the transitional period of three years, and over the previous five years after the transitional period. A minor change to the regime on extraordinary complaint was introduced in May 2018, in the hope that it will placate the European Commission: the list of officials entitled to initiate the procedure has been narrowed from eight to two, namely the prosecutor general (PG) and the Ombudsman. But this only applies to judgments handed down before the law's entry into force; as far as future judgments are concerned, the list of authorized initiators is much longer.[55] In effect, it means that almost any legally binding judgment dating back to the time of the introduction of the new Constitution of 1997 can be reopened, and will be considered again by judges of the SC appointed by the ruling party (via its control over the KRS), with participation of lay judges appointed by the Senate with the votes of the majority party. Critics note that, in addition to being redundant (there are already some instruments of special appeal in Polish law, such as cassation), the new procedure will possibly flood courts with hundreds of thousands of cases, resulting in delays in judicial proceedings much worse than the current ones, which figure in governmental propaganda as the main rationale for the 'reforms'. The new instrument was presented by the president as meeting justice in the popular sense, but in reality it will greatly undermine the sense of judicial stability, *res judicata*, and in consequence, the rule of law.

The new law on the SC created severe moral dilemmas for the older judges who faced a choice: either make a request to the president for an 'extension' beyond a newly lowered retirement age or accept the inevitable and step down. As with so many times in Polish history, arguments of high principle were mixed with pragmatic considerations, with no self-evidently good choices. On the one hand, it was argued that the duty of a judge is towards the citizens, and that judges placed in the highest court should continue to perform their role as long as the circumstances allow. A 'boycott', some argued, would be immoral and would be tantamount to surrendering professional duty in exchange for a high pension while not having high stress connected with performing judicial duties. If the president refuses an extension, so be it, and let him carry the odium of the decision, the argument went.[56] On the other side of the argument, it was maintained that judges should not humiliate themselves and subject themselves to the president's will, while knowing full well that the president's prerogative had been established in a statute that is unconstitutional.[57] As a judge of a district court puts it, empathizing with his colleagues in the top court, 'The matter is not all that simple because one has to choose between a more honourable solution, which is to retire, and a more pragmatic one, which is to remain in active service. The latter solution would be chosen not for one's own benefit but in order to save the current acquis of the Supreme Court'.[58] Discontent among judges reached such a level of intensity that the SC itself, in an unusual resolution of its General Assembly, found it necessary to declare (on 16 January 2018) that any decision of a judge regarding retirement or application to the president for a right to continue in office should be 'respected'.[59] In the same resolution, the SC stated, however, that the statutes on the SC and on the KRS, adopted by the parliament and signed by the president, are 'in many respects contrary to the binding norms of the Constitution of the Republic of Poland and violate the principles of tripartite division of powers, independence of courts, judicial independence and irrevocability of judges'.[60]

The law on the KRS and that on the SC have to be considered jointly: their cumulative effect is that the judges elected by judges-members of the KRS, who are in turn elected by the politicians, will occupy a large number of seats on the SC (perhaps around 60 per cent), including all seats on the new special super chambers of the SC. This gives the parliamentary majority and the president (who obtains large discretionary powers over the composition of the SC, enhanced power over the selection of the chief justice, and the power to adopt the rules of procedure of the SC) great new controls over the apex court of the Polish judicial system.

The Law on the Organization of Common Courts

The statute of 27 July 2017, the only one in the package that was signed by the president without vetoing it first, gave the MJ/ PG additional great powers in respect of the national judicial system, in addition to the already expansive powers that the minister enjoyed. Before the new law entered into force, the minister had the power to assign new judges to individual courts; establish divisions of courts; establish or abolish courts; determine territorial jurisdiction areas; authorize transfers of judges to other courts or secondments to other state institutions; request disciplinary proceedings against a judge, as well as lodge an appeal against the decisions of a disciplinary court, etc. The new law put the court system under the effective control of the MJ to an even higher degree, in particular by giving the MJ/ PG the power to appoint and dismiss the presidents of all courts within six months of the law's passage. The MJ could exercise this power to extinguish their previously set terms, without the need to give any reasons and without having to take into account the opinion of the general assembly of judges of the affected court. Under the earlier law, the MJ had to obtain the approval of the general assembly of judges of the relevant court, or in a case when such approval was denied, of the KRS; if the latter also refused a candidate, the minister had no authority to appoint him/her. In practice, it meant that presidents of courts were appointed upon the recommendation of judges themselves.

The new law ended this judicial control over presidents of courts, and the Minister of Justice Mr Zbigniew Ziobro has enthusiastically made use of this new opportunity, replacing some one-fifth of all the senior management of all courts (158 out of 730 court presidents and vice-presidents).[61] The bare statistics do not reflect the depth of the changes, which is better revealed by their structure: presidents in ten out of eleven appellate courts were replaced, and one should bear in mind that the appellate courts exercise administrative control over district courts. Even the form of discharge was undignified: the decisions were very often sent to courts by fax or delivered by couriers, and the process lasted until the final hours of 12 February 2018, which marked the end of the transitional period.

According to some commentators, due to the depth of the purges this law turned out to be the most important of the three reforms, even if it attracted the least attention.[62] The breadth of purges took many judges by surprise. After the period of discharges without grounds by the minister ended, *Iustitia*, the association of judges, declared: 'We express our thanks to all [court] presidents who were discharged, and we remind all new court presidents that their promotion is based on provisions which are contrary to the Constitution.'[63]

After a transitional period of six months, the MJ has maintained the power to dismiss court presidents under vague standards of 'serious or persistent failure to comply with the official duties' or 'other reasons which render remaining in office incompatible with the sound dispensation of justice', that is, on easily manipulable grounds to suit the minister's wishes. Under a cosmetic amendment brought about in April 2018, however, the MJ can only do so with the approval of the court's college (*kolegium*) and of the KRS. The change is generally positive, but considering the composition of the 'new' KRS, is not much of a change in reality, given that it comes after a massive purge in top court positions, unconstrained by any requirement to consult with the KRS. In addition, court 'colleges' have been redesigned to enhance the role of the MJ: so far they have consisted only of judges elected by their colleagues, but now they include judges appointed by the MJ to the position of president and the most senior vice-presidents of the courts, hence judges dependent on the MJ.[64] In addition, by July 2018, amendments to the law on common courts greatly reduced the competences of the colleges. For instance, the power they had so far to consider complaints by judges regarding the court president's decisions concerning allocation of tasks have been transferred to the newly politicized KRS. In addition, the quorum requirement for college decisions was abandoned so that from now on, a college consisting of the president and vice-president of a court can take a valid decision. Overall, the changes in the top positions of the courts were badly received by judges: in a recent survey only 12 per cent of judges said that they have a higher confidence in their new court presidents, while 45 per cent trusted the old presidents more.[65] New court presidents have therefore been perceived as meeting the minister's, rather than their colleagues', preferences.

Control over the appointment of court presidents is a very important power if one realizes that, in Poland, court presidents have tight control over judges in their courts and play an important role in the case-management process. In particular, they assign judges to divisions and set out their duties, which gives them the power to ensure that 'unreliable' judges will not deal with politically sensitive issues, such as in criminal law. They also assign and replace judges hearing a case, and may alter the composition of a judging panel. How this change operates in practice, was revealed immediately after the new statutory regulation entered into force. Judge Waldemar Żurek, generally considered to be one of judges most hated by PiS (and a former spokesperson for the old KRS), has had his responsibilities in the Cracow District Court radically modified against his wishes by a new court president, Ms Dagmara Pawełczyk-Woicka, recently appointed by Minister Ziobro. He was transferred from an appellate chamber of the court to a first-instance chamber, which is a de facto demotion for a judge. As one legal commentator observed, this is just a symptom of a more general trend: regular judges will have to appeal to a 'body they do not trust' (the new KRS) against these types of decisions by their superiors: 'What will they do if it turns out that the sole purpose of a transfer of a judge to a different court department is to remove them from a case which, for some reason, politicians consider important?'[66]

Żurek's case is not the only one to show that the minister-appointed presidents of courts have understood the political tasks expected of them very well, and that they have complied with the minister's wishes. As an example, one particular case is meaningful: a judge of a district court in the north-eastern town of Suwałki was subjected to judicial disciplinary proceedings by a newly appointed president of his court in a politically sensitive matter. The case concerned a peaceful demonstration by members of the Committee of Defense of Democracy (*Komitet Obrony Demokracji* (KOD)) during an event that formed part of a supplementary election campaign in March 2016 for Ms Anna Maria Anders, a PiS senatorial candidate (eventually, successfully elected to the Senate from the Suwałki district). One of the protesters was charged with an alleged physical assault against a minor during a skirmish, and Judge Dominik Czeszkiewicz was in charge of the court proceedings, which began on January 2018. The PiS put the pressure on for a speedy and exemplary punishment, and the prosecutors were unhappy about an alleged delay in setting the date for a trial by the judge (to be exact, eight days later than the prosecutors demanded). Eventually Judge Czeszkiewicz acquitted the defendant for lack of evidence, but the decision was quashed by the court of second instance, and remanded for reconsideration by the district court. (In the end, on 23 May 2018, the court punished the defendants but abstained from execution of punishment—an arguably bizarre judgment.) The newly appointed (by Minister Ziobro, under the new statute) court president Jacek Sowul (incidentally, the same judge who had quashed the first instance sentence) initiated a disciplinary case against Judge Czeszkiewicz, for an alleged procedural error in setting the trial date with undue delay. The matter became a *cause célèbre* in Poland, and showed clearly that the new presidents of courts are willing to comply with the minister's political expectations.

There were other cases of that type.[67] Retired judge Małgorzata Kluziak, who agreed to act as counsel for Czeszkiewicz in the disciplinary trial against him, said: 'There have not been situations so far whereby the minister has influence on the appointment of the presidents [of courts], who then can decide whether to lodge disciplinary actions in proceedings against judges'. She added, addressing a journalist: 'You should realize that in this disciplinary proceeding the prosecutor is a disciplinary plenipotent elected by judges, but at every stage of disciplinary proceedings the spokesperson can be replaced by the Minister of Justice if he considers that the general direction of proceedings clash with his own expectations'.[68] In the end a disciplinary judge discontinued the disciplinary procedure at the end of May 2018.[69]

The new law introduced a new disciplinary hierarchy among court presidents, with the MJ on top. Each higher court's president may issue a critical notice about the president of a court lower in rank in his/her area, with the minister having the power to uphold or dismiss such a 'notice'. Furthermore, the MJ himself can issue such critical remarks. In both cases, the MJ has the power to reduce the allowance linked to the post of president. Furthermore, all presidents of courts of appeal must submit to the MJ annual reports, with the minister entrusted with 'grading' the reports, and depending on the grade, the minister may reduce or increase the court president's allowance. As the VC observed, as a result, 'all court presidents become a part of a pyramid, with the [MJ] on top. The Minister performs the function of the highest disciplinary authority in the "chain of command" composed of court presidents'.[70] The minister's power to interfere with court presidents' salaries based on his evaluation of their work, without the participation of the judiciary in the process, is a blatant interference with judicial independence.

There have also been acts of harassment and persecution carried out by the executive and the prosecutor's office, which have specifically targeted the most outspoken judges protesting against the reforms. A true *bête noire* of the minister and his entourage turned out to be the already mentioned Judge Waldemar Żurek, of Cracow, who was also a spokesperson of the KRS (in its previous iteration) and the spokesperson of the Cracow Regional Court. The newly appointed president of the latter court immediately dismissed Żurek from his function as a spokesman, but the assembly of representatives of judges of that court undertook a robust defence of their dismissed colleague. In a strongly worded resolution, they listed a number of intimidating actions undertaken by the prosecutor's office and by the Central

Anti-corruption Bureau (*Centralne Biuro Antykorupcyjne* (CBA)) against the out-spoken judge: these actions included the CBA questioning of Żurek's neighbours and his tax adviser, the interrogation of the judge's elderly parents and his wife, and the reopening of an old and long-closed case against Żurek concerning his fi-nancial disclosure declarations, etc.[71] Clearly, the aim was to produce evidence to discredit the judge.

The same resolution by Cracow judges provides a rare insight into a number of actions carried out by the PG against recalcitrant judges, and these actions go beyond the *ad personam* attacks on Judge Żurek. As the judges declare, several of their colleagues both in Cracow and elsewhere in Poland have seen criminal or disciplinary proceedings launched against them by the prosecutor's office on the basis of the *substance of their judgments*. For instance, two judges of the court in Szczecin (Judges Agnieszka Poświata and Małgorzata Czerwińska) had a criminal case brought against them by the prosecutor's office because they had denied the prosecutor's motion for the provisional arrest of former members of the board of a chemical plant. Another case cited in the resolution is a *criminal* case pending against a Cracow judge, Agnieszka Pilarczyk, in connection with her conduct as a judge in a case of an alleged medical error concerning the late father of Minister of Justice Ziobro. Similarly, in September 2016, Deputy Minister of Justice Patryk Jaki initiated a disciplinary procedure against Judge Alicja Fronczyk of the Warsaw Regional Court, in connection with her conduct in a civil case against himself.[72] This is worth highlighting: rather than restricting themselves to normal appellate procedures, prosecutors and members of the executive branch now resort to dis-ciplinary or even criminal actions against judges who hand down judgments dis-liked by the MJ/PG.

The use of formal disciplinary proceedings against judges as a reprisal for ju-dicial decisions has accelerated over time, creating a strong chilling effect upon judicial functions, and de facto establishing the political control of judges. For in-stance, on 20 September 2018, the deputy disciplinary prosecutor questioned Ewa Maciejewska, a judge of the Regional Court in Łódź, for over two hours after Judge Maciejewska decided to refer a question to the CJEU as to whether the new discip-linary proceedings were compatible with EU law.[73] After the questioning, Judge Maciejewska said that it 'verged on the breach of a judge's professional privilege', and that 'the way it was carried out confirmed her concerns over the political pres-sure on judges'.[74] In a similar action on 14 August 2018, the deputy disciplinary prosecutor summoned Judge Igor Tuleya of the Regional Court in Warsaw in rela-tion to his judgment in a case involving opposition MPs who had filed a complaint about their exclusion from a parliamentary session in December 2017.[75] Judge Tuleya is among the judges most hated by the executive: he is a vocal critic of the reforms, and just like Judge Maciejewska, he had also submitted a request for a pre-liminary ruling from the CJEU, asking whether the legislation removing guaran-tees of impartiality in disciplinary proceedings against judges is consistent with EU law, and in particular with Article 19 of the Treaty on European Union, regarding the member states' obligation to ensure remedies sufficient to ensure effective legal protection. (For more on preliminary questions to CJEU from Polish judges, see Chapter 8.)

These actions were partly made possible by the radical changes to disciplinary proceedings against judges. The changes enabled the minister to affect such procedures and thus influence the judges' conduct. Before the change, only a judge could be a disciplinary plenipotent (*rzecznik dyscyplinarny*, i.e. an equivalent of a prosecutor in disciplinary proceedings) in disciplinary cases against other judges, and the minister was only competent to make non-binding recommendations as to the need to initiate such a procedure in a given case. The new law[76] made it possible for public prosecutors—that is, officials directly subordinate to the MJ/PG—to perform that role. They will now be formally obliged to initiate a case whenever the minister demands it, even if the case was initially discontinued. The minister now has the power to appoint a 'disciplinary plenipotent' and his/her deputies; he needs to ask the KRS for advice but the advice is non-binding, and in any event, the KRS is now fully compliant with the will of PiS. This, in addition to the fact that the minister has acquired the power to nominate *judges* to disciplinary courts means that the minister 'appoints the person who presents the accusation in disciplinary cases, and also judges who decide such cases'.[77] The appointment of several judges by the MJ to the position of 'disciplinary judge' without their knowledge and consent[78] quickly resulted in numerous protests by the judges concerned, who only found out about their appointment *ex post facto*, and who also found out, to their bewilderment, that the new law does not provide for any right of appeal against such an unwanted appointment.

There are many other disturbing aspects of the newly revised procedure for disciplinary proceedings against judges, including a provision that will make it possible to carry out a disciplinary case even in the justified absence of the judge concerned and his/her counsel,[79] which is a blatant violation of the right to defence. Equally inconsistent with the right to defence is a provision that a request by a judge to have a legal representative appointed by a disciplinary panel due to the defendant's illness does not stay proceedings, which in practice means that the procedure may be concluded before the legal representative takes up his/her functions.[80] There is also the possibility of using evidence obtained without judicial control and even in violation of the law, including evidence obtained as a result of operational control of telephone conversations.[81] All in all, the executive branch has obtained huge powers to indict judges in disciplinary proceedings. As one prominent Polish judge said: 'All disciplinary proceedings [against judges] will be de facto managed by one person, i.e. the Minister of Justice ... With the provisions constructed in this way, it is clear that when political will is present, a judge can be indicted instantly, and removed from office.'[82] Finally, disciplinary appeals are to be considered by a new chamber of the SC which, as already explained, has been entirely composed of new judges elected by the 'new' KRS, the majority of whom are persons close to the MJ. The president of the new chamber will be appointed by the president of the Republic. Appeals will be considered by judges accompanied by lay judges, elected by the Senate, dominated by PiS.

The new law also lowers the retirement age for judges from seventy to sixty-five, but the MJ has acquired the power to extend the term of office beyond retirement age, with the law not specifying the length of time for which such an extension may be granted, thus allowing for a discretionary power to refuse an extension or to only grant a short-term extension, making the judge vulnerable to pressure.[83] As one can see, this is a mirror image of the president's prerogative vis-à-vis SC judges. After the new law entered into force, several known cases have arisen where the MJ has refused judges' applications for renewal beyond the new retirement age, without giving any reasons.[84] The subtitle of a newspaper article, 'Judges at the mercy of the Minister of Justice', summarizes the state of affairs in the 'transitional' period.[85] By 20 December 2017, only two months after the new law entered into force, twenty-nine judges received a negative response to their request to continue at work, with no reasons provided. According to Deputy Minister for Justice Łukasz Piebiak, with responsibility for judiciary issues in his portfolio, about a third of all judges requesting an extension are likely to receive a negative decision from the minister.[86] In April 2018, however, under pressure from the EU Commission, a change was introduced: the new retirement age became uniform for men and women at the age of sixty-five (initially, it was sixty for women). Each judge approaching that age may make a declaration of their intention to continue in the job, and these declarations will be considered by the KRS, which has obtained the power of making final and binding decisions on the matter.

The lowered retirement age created a high number of judicial vacancies to be filled by the newly politicized KRS. Over the two years directly preceding the new law, the MJ deliberately failed to propose new judges in proceedings before the KRS under its previous institutional design, the result of which was that some six hundred to seven hundred judicial positions were kept vacant. When added to the several hundred judges currently working in the ministry of justice (as 'delegated judges'), this amounts to about one thousand judicial positions (10 per cent of all judges) waiting to be appointed now that the executive has obtained effective control over the KRS. The vacancies were advertised, wholesale, after the new law's entry into force. To begin with, in January 2018 the minister advertised over four hundred positions to be filled according to the new rules by a 'new' KRS.[87] In the meantime, however, an absurd situation arose: while the officially avowed reason for judicial reforms was to increase the effectiveness and efficiency of judicial proceedings, the effect of transferring a large number of judges to the newly established conditions of retirement and refusing their requests to continue, hugely exacerbated the shortage of judges.

This brings us to the issue of the executive branch's control over judges at the commencement of their careers. The dominant profile of new judges (in addition to the barristers and law professors who are also eligible) is that they are alumnae of the National School of the Judiciary and Public Prosecution in Krakow. Set up in 2009, the school is under the full control of the MJ who appoints its director and the board of supervisors, and can veto the appointment of any lecturer. Appointed by Minister Ziobro in 2016, the current director is his former deputy minister. The MJ appoints graduates to the position of junior judge and, after a few years in that position, they may apply to become full judges. The MJ at this point has a power of veto, and if he does not exercise it, the application is subject to recommendation by the KRS before it goes to the president of Poland for a final decision. Two authors who recently discussed the path of a judicial career in Poland summarize it in this way: '[T]he minister of justice has power over his education, over his appointment as a junior judge, over his court presidents who manage his work; the minister can punish him and has a lot of influence in disciplinary cases. The Minister is a member of the [KRS] and a parliamentarian of the governing majority, which chooses the majority of the [KRS]'.[88]

Despite the avowed rationale for the 'reform' of courts, none of the changes translates into visible improvement in the effectiveness of the courts, especially as far as the length of proceedings is concerned. The only evident outcome is the 'revolution in cadres' and the further subordination of judges to the MJ. The alleged revolution in assigning judges to particular cases, which is supposed to be managed by random allocation, is a big unknown because the algorithm that controls the assignment has never been revealed, and many judges express scepticism as to whether it indeed prevents individual control by presidents of the courts.[89] One thing that *is* known is that the algorithm also has some other basic defects—for instance, it does not distinguish between complex, time-consuming, and easy cases.[90] In any event, the idea of random allocation has been largely undermined by an amendment of July 2018 that provides for the right of a court president (practically speaking, the minister's confidant) to change the composition of a panel determined by random allocation, at any moment up to the first session of a trial. So court presidents, not a lottery, have the final say on the composition of panels to decide each specific case.

The only thing that is clear and certain is that, from now on, both admission to the judiciary and progress of judicial careers depends on politicians. The consequences for judicial impartiality and independence are already visible. One significant example is a case concerning a traffic accident. On 10 February 2017 the armoured car carrying Prime Minister Beata Szydło collided with a small passenger car. The event immediately hit the headlines, largely due to awkward propaganda attempts by the government aimed at blaming the driver of the other car, probably on the basis of a theory that, if the prime minister's driver was at fault, it would somehow badly affect her reputation. Normally, this kind of case would be a routine, minor issue to be decided by the lowest court. It turned out, however, that a judge of the local court in Oświęcim (where the accident happened) asked to have the case transferred to a higher court, based on the case's alleged legal complexity. This rationale was clearly disingenuous and the only explanation for the bizarre decision was that the local judge was simply worried about his judicial career prospects if he handed down a judgment contrary to the government's expectations.

Perhaps this kind of judicial opportunism may happen everywhere. What mattered here, however, was that the local judge's concerns were perfectly justified, considering the politicization of decisions about the status of judges in Poland. As an experienced judge from the Regional Court in Łódź observed: 'So far, judges could have been concerned about criminals, media pressure, and their colleagues' opinions. Now they are concerned about what politicians will think of them. This is the price of making the judiciary dependent upon the legislative and executive branches.'[91]

In summary, as a result of legislative changes, politicians of the ruling party have acquired immense control over the judiciary. Politicians make decisions on 1) the composition of the KRS, and hence indirectly about who may be appointed to a judgeship (this is determined by a parliamentary majority); 2) the appointment and discharge of presidents and vice-presidents of all courts (MJ); 3) which judge is 'delegated' to the ministry of justice (MJ); 4) which judge is delegated to particular courts (MJ); 5) who may continue as judge after reaching the retirement age (president or MJ); 6) which courts may be established or extinguished (MJ); 7) who may be elected as lay judges in the SC (this is decided by the Senate); 8) what the budget is of any particular court (MJ); 9) who sits on the panels for disciplinary suits against judges (MJ); and 10) how many judges there should be on the SC, the division of the number of judgeships between its particular chambers, and the internal organization of the SC (president). These are considerable powers, decisively upsetting the idea of the separation of powers and mutual checks and balances. It also renders absurd talk about strengthening judicial independence. And, despite the avowed rationale for the changes, namely (in addition to its effectiveness) to improve public respect for the judiciary, the effect has been the complete opposite: surveys show that the ratio of those who do not believe that the courts are fully independent has grown, from 2017 to 2018 (that is, in the period of reforms) by a huge 9 per cent, from 38 to 45 per cent of respondents.[92] This perception is certainly shared, even more consensually, by the judges themselves. According to a recent survey, some 90 per cent of judges believe that after the reforms of 2016–18, Polish courts are 'more politicized' than before; about 30 per cent of judges have heard about specific instances of political pressure upon judges, while 15 per cent have experienced such a pressure themselves.[93]

The three judiciary-related statutes enacted by the PiS majority contain many very questionable features, as listed, but their truly nefarious effect is produced by accumulation. The new laws create a system in which the threat to the independence of the judiciary in one provision in one statute is amplified by another provision of the same or another statute. For instance: the lowering of the age of retirement in the statute on the SC combined with the new composition of the KRS allows for a large influx of politically dependent and vulnerable judges to the SC; the creation of two new chambers of the SC entrusted with politically sensitive matters (including election results) is compounded by the participation of lay judges in those cases, elected by a simple majority of the Senate. A possible measure for controlling the executive in one act is disarmed by a measure in another act; for instance, the power of the KRS to control the ministerial dismissal of a court's president is weakened by the political composition of the KRS and the requirement of two-thirds majority of votes for such a decision, which is highly unlikely to be obtained.

A cumulative effect also arises from the interaction of the judicial package with other statutes, including the new law on the public prosecutor's office. This act will now be discussed.

The Law on the Public Prosecutor's Office (*prokuratura*)

The major function of the new law on the *prokuratura* of 28 January 2016[94] was to merge the hitherto separate positions of the MJ and PG, and to endow the newly merged position with enhanced, substantial prerogatives. The 2016 law put an end to the principle of the independence of public prosecutors, which was the declared aim of the earlier law of 2009.[95] In contrast, the new law, tailored specifically to the ambitions of Minister of Justice Zbigniew Ziobro, was defended on the basis of the need for effective management and centralized subordination within the overall system of public prosecution. The system of the public prosecutor's office was incorporated into the executive branch and explicitly politicized, with its head being a member of the government.

The new competences of the PG/MJ mean that he can now intervene in prosecutorial investigations at any stage, and *give orders regarding specific cases*. He can transfer cases from one prosecutor to another, change and annul a decision of any subordinate public prosecutor, inspect documents collected during the course of any preparatory proceedings, reveal details of non-final investigations to public authorities and to 'other persons' (including media), etc. As a journalist summarizes:

> Zbigniew Ziobro has prepared a law which allows him to do anything which might have been illegal or legally doubtful under the previous PiS rule [in 2005–7]. He may show the files to whomever he wants. He may publicly reveal selected pieces of the files. He may control every prosecution and is immune to charges of influencing and affecting the independence of prosecutors…. As prosecutor general, he may change every decision of every prosecutor. He also has informal

means of pressure by which he may compel any prosecutor to do whatever the PG wants him or her to do.[96]

As an example of such informal pressure, there is the new, legal possibility of delegating any prosecutor to another office, at a lower hierarchical level and far from the prosecutor's place of residence for up to *twelve* months of the year (which means, de facto, permanently). Several prosecutors (no fewer than 200, according to *Lex Supra Omnia*, the association of prosecutors) who appear to be unwilling to sheepishly follow any requirement issued by the PG have been subject to such involuntary transfers.[97]

This is a degree of interference by the MJ unknown to any other European system. As the VC observes, 'Even if there are a few systems [in Europe] where the Minister of Justice can give instructions, the Polish system stands out because of the competence of the Public Prosecutor General to act personally in each individual case of prosecution ... '.[98] In connection with the law on common courts, already discussed, and in particular in light of the MJ's increased powers over court presidents (who have a strong influence on the composition of panels in their courts), the merging of offices means that a party to the proceedings (*qua* a public prosecutor subordinated to the PG) will at the same time have huge control over judges (*qua* the minister). Further, having obtained, in the new law on the SC, a right to initiate a procedure of 'extraordinary review' (*qua* the PG), the same person will have a strong say over who sits in the new, super chamber of the SC that will consider these complaints (*qua* the minister, a member of the ruling coalition with a decisive say on the composition of the new SC chamber, and also an ex officio member of the KRS). In sum, the PG, who is an active politician as a result of the merger with the office of minister, has total authority regarding the prosecutorial system. Arguably, this is a power unparalleled in public prosecutorial institutions in democratic states elsewhere.

Incidentally, to an outside observer, a clause allowing the PG to reveal operational information to public authorities *and other persons* may sound puzzling—who are 'the other persons' whom the PG may wish to inform on cases processed by public prosecutors? The puzzle disappears if one notes that Zbigniew Ziobro, who was also MJ under the first PiS government in 2005–7, allegedly discussed specific, politically sensitive cases with the leader of PiS, Jarosław Kaczyński, who had no legal right at the time to be informed about ongoing investigations. Now this right has been acknowledged in the statute, private discussions between the PG and his political superior will no longer carry the stigma of illegality.

The merger of the offices of PG and MJ is also in direct contravention of the Constitution, which forbids public prosecutors (inter alia) from also being MPs, in order to attempt to prevent the overt politicization of the office. But the PG, *qua* MJ, *is* a political official and an MP. Defenders of the new law claim that PG is not a prosecutor within the meaning of Art. 103(2) of the Constitution,[99] but this is a disingenuous defence. For one thing, the new law occasionally refers to the PG as a public prosecutor (e.g. in Art. 1(1)); for another, the whole point of the merger was to improve the efficiency of the prosecutor's office by including it in the executive branch. If the PG is not a prosecutor, the rationale for the merger largely collapses.

In the two years since the law's entry into force, changes within the prosecutor's offices have been comprehensive and deep. The structure has been turned into a military-like system, with submissive prosecutors promoted to higher offices (without any competitive process and in a purely discretionary way, contrary to the practice before 2016) and rewarded with huge financial gains, while recalcitrant ones are punished with demotion (in the official language, 'delegation') to lower positions and often to offices far away from their place of residence.[100] In order to facilitate these changes, the names of particular levels of the prosecutorial institutions have been changed (e.g. the central level *Prokuratura Generalna* has been replaced by *Prokuratura Krajowa*) even if the structure remains the same. This has allowed Zbigniew Ziobro to appoint, reappoint or dismiss whomever he likes in the entire system. The structural change was in many cases fictional, for the real purpose was the 'verification' of cadres, that is, purges. For instance, twenty-two persons from the top office (*Prokuratura Generalna*, renamed *Krajowa*) were demoted to a lower position, and ninety-one others from 'appellate public prosecutors offices' (*prokuratura apelacyjna*, renamed *regionalna*) met the same fate. One-third of all prosecutors in these offices have been subject to fictional 'liquidation'.[101] Normally, demoting a prosecutor to a lower position is a disciplinary penalty requiring a special procedure, but a simple trick with reorganization allowed Ziobro to punish some prosecutors and reward others, depending on who is obedient enough, without any procedural constraints. Prosecutors who were willing to open investigations on matters inconvenient to the government—for instance, regarding the non-publication of CT judgments—saw those cases removed from them and reassigned to other prosecutors, who were willing to follow the party line.[102] As a result, the media occasionally reported bizarre decisions. A prosecutor who decided to discontinue an investigation into violence against a group of women who protested against a nationalistic march that took place on 11 November 2017, affirmed that the purpose of the violent men was not to cause harm to the protesting women but merely to 'demonstrate displeasure' about their messages.[103] The prosecutor, Magdalena Kołodziej, was promoted to a higher rank.

At the same time, the post-reform period has clearly shown that the changes have been counterproductive from the point of view of the avowed purpose of the changes: to improve the efficiency of law and order institutions. The length of time spent on prosecutorial pre-trial investigations conducted by prosecutors has, on the whole, increased rather than shortened:[104] the system has become much more centralized and politically malleable, but is less efficient in its core functions. This, in fact, is the story of both the *prokuratura* and the court system: reforms have meant purges, and little else.

Notes

1. Lecture by Małgorzata Gersdorf, 'Speech to Mark the Occasion of the Conference Organised by the Federal Court of Germany (*Bundesgerichtshof*): Polish Rule of Law: Missed Opportunities? (Sąd Najwyższy, 20 July 2018) [PDF] <http://www.sn.pl/aktualnosci/SiteAssets/Lists/Wydarzenia/NewForm/Wyst%C4%85pienie%20 PPSN%20w%20Karlsruhe%20-%20wersja%20ang.pdf> (accessed 22 July 2018), 4.

2. See Wojciech Sadurski, *Rights before Courts: A Study of Constitutional Courts in Postcommunist States of Central and Eastern Europe,* 2nd edn (Springer 2014) 40–3.

3. The Court of Appeal in the Wrocław judgement of 25 April 2017, case no. II AKa 213/17.

4. District Court in the Warsaw decision of 18 December 2017, VIII Kp 1335/17.

5. See CCJE Prov5, 'Report on Judicial Independence and Impartiality in the Council of Europe Member States in 2017' (Strasbourg, 3 November 2017), para. 324.

6. Ibid. para. 326.

7. Andrzej Rzepliński, *Sędzia gorszego sortu* (Prószyński 2018) 107.

8. See e.g. Yascha Mounk, *The People vs. Democracy* (Harvard University Press 2018) 187.

9. Christian Davies, 'Hostile Takeover: How Law and Justice Captured Poland's Courts' (Freedom House, Nations in Transit Brief, May 2018), 5.

10. Komunikat z badań, 'Społeczne oceny wymiaru sprawiedliwości' (Centrum Badania Opinii Publicznej, March 2017) [PDF] <https://www.cbos.pl/SPISKOM.POL/2017/K_031_17.PDF> (accessed 11 July 2018), 4–5.

11. Ibid. 11.

12. World Justice Project, 'Rule of Law Index 2017–2018' <http://data.worldjusticeproject.org/#/groups/POL> (accessed 11 July 2018).

13. European Commission, The 2017 EU Justice Scoreboard, COM(2017) 167 final, 7–8.

14. See the Constitutional Tribunal judgment SK 37/08 of 19 June 2012; the National Administrative Court judgment I OSK 1891/12 of 9 October 2012; for discussion see Michał Ziółkowski, 'Prerogatywa Prezydenta RP do powoływania sędziów (uwagi o art. 144 ust. 3 pkt 17 i art. 179 Konstytucji)' (2013/1) *Przegląd Sejmowy* 59, 66–76.

15. Article 186(1) of the Constitution.

16. Article 186(2) of the Constitution.

17. Article 3 of the statute of 12 May 2011 on the National Council of the Judiciary.

18. The Opinion of the CCJE Bureau of 12 October 2017 on the draft legislation on the Polish National Council of the Judiciary presented by the president of Poland (CCJE-BU(2017)9Rev) para. 14.

19. Report of the Judicial Appointments and the Report on the Independence of the Judicial System, quoted in the opinion on the draft act amending the act on the National Council of Judiciary, on the draft act amending the act on the Supreme Court, proposed by the president of Poland, and on the act on the organization of ordinary courts No. 904/2017, adopted by the Venice Commission at its 113th Plenary Session (8–9 December 2017) para. 17.

20. Ibid. para. 22.

21. Rzepliński (n. 7) 10.

22. Opinion of the Venice Commission (n. 19) (904/2017) para. 31.

23. 'Oświadczenie prof. Strzembosza i prof. Zolla ws. nowego składu KRS', *Onet.pl* (Warsaw, 8 March 2018) <https://wiadomosci.onet.pl/kraj/oswiadczenie-prof-strzembosza-i-prof-zolla-ws-nowego-skladu-krs/t22wjb4> (accessed 22 July 2018).

24. Wojciech Tumidalski, 'Zniszczone trudno naprawić', *Rzeczpospolita* (Warsaw, 13 March 2018) 1 (interview with Andrzej Zoll).

25. Małgorzata Kryszkiewicz, 'Mentalność służebną mieli sędziowie w czasach PRL', *Dziennik Gazeta Prawna* (Warsaw, 8 February 2018) 6.

26. Agata Łukaszewicz, 'KRS przeciw polowaniu na czarownice', *Rzeczpospolita* (Warsaw, 11 May 2018) 15.

27. This point was forcefully raised by a judge of the regional court in Łódź, Tomasz Krawczyk. See Tomasz Krawczyk, 'Co zapowiadają złe początki Rady', *Rzeczpospolita* (Warsaw, 13 March 2018) 2.

28. JSZ, 'Protegowani Ziobry i nieudacznicy. I oni mają pilnować sędziów?', *Fakt*, on-line edition (Warsaw, 7 March 2018) https://www.fakt.pl/wydarzenia/polityka/sejm-wybral-w-glosowaniu-15-sedziow-krs/2q2z8fw (accessed 1 February 2019).

29. Łukasz Woźnicki, 'KRS wybrana przez PiS już działa', *Gazeta Wyborcza* (Warsaw, 28 April 2018) 5.

30. Agata Łukaszewicz, 'Kandydaci wycofują się z konkursów na sędziów', *Rzeczpospolita* (Warsaw, 14 June 2018) 12.

31. Łukasz Woźnicki, 'KRS ma problem', *Gazeta Wyborcza* (Warsaw, 14 June 2018) 6, quoting Judge Jarosław Gwizdak of the Regional Court in Katowice Zachód.

32. Ibid., quoting Judge Wojciech Łączewski of the Regional Court Warszawa-Śródmieście.

33. Ibid.

34. The SAC decisions of 25 September 2018, case no. II GW 21/18, no. II GW 24/18, and of 27 September 2018, case no. II GW 26/18.

35. See <https://www.encj.eu/node/495> (accessed 17 October 2018).

36. 'Stan niezależnego sądownictwa w Polsce: Raport z badań i analiz', *Stowarzyszenie Sędziów Polskich Iustitia* (Warsaw, October 2018).

37. Decision 33/2012 (VII. 17) of 16 July 2012.

38. Case C-286/12, European Commission v. Hungary.

39. Cited in Łukasz Woźnicki, 'Wyrok na sędziów odroczony', *Gazeta Wyborcza* (Warsaw, 26 June 2018) 5.

40. Remarks by President Andrzej Duda in a TV interview (26 November 2017, on TVN24).

41. Mateusz Leźnicki, 'Konstytucja czy karykatura?', *Rzeczpospolita* (Warsaw, 8 February 2018) 20.

42. Article 199(2) of the Constitution.

43. Resolution of the General Assembly of the Justice of the Supreme Court of Poland on the term of the First President of the Supreme Court, 28 June 2018, on file with the author.

44. Resolution of the General Assembly of the Justice of the Supreme Court of Poland on the removal of Supreme Court Justices, 28 June 2018, on file with the author.

45. See, similarly Venice Commission Opinion 904/2017 (n. 19) paras 73–7.

46. See interview with a PiS MP Mr Stanisław Piotrowicz, 'Prawo uprzedzi obstrukcję', *Nasz Dziennik* (Warsaw, 20 July 2018) 2.

47. See Paweł Wroński, 'PiS przegłosował ustawy sądowe w Sejmie otoczonym jak twierdzą', *Gazeta Wyborcza* (Warsaw, 20 July 2018) online edition.

48. For such an opinion, see e.g. Tomasz Krawczyk, 'Z tej mąki będzie zakalec', *Rzeczpospolita* (Warsaw, 23 August 2018) 17. (The author is a judge in Łódź.)

49. 'Wiesław Johann wyrzuca Wojciecha Katnera z SN z ważnego interesu społecznego', *Monitor Konstytucyjny* 18 July 2018, http://monitorkonstytucyjny.eu/archiwa/4989 (accessed 1 February 2019).

50. Article 2 (2) (b) of the statute of 10 May 2018.

51. 'Duda blokuje nominacje', *Gazeta Wyborcza* (Warsaw, 6 September 2018) 5.

52. Venice Commission Opinion (n. 19) (904/2017) para. 43, footnote omitted.

53. Małgorzata Kryszkiewicz, 'Izba dyscyplinarna rośnie w siłę', *Dziennik Gazeta Prawna* (Warsaw, 5 April 2018) 6.

54. Ewa Siedlecka, 'Grillowanie sędziów', *Polityka* (Warsaw, 16 May 2018) 20.

55. See (unsigned article) 'Skarga nadzwyczajna zawężona', *Rzeczpospolita* (Warsaw, 11 May 2018) 14.

56. This was a view expressed by an ex-member of the KRS and a chairman of the NGO INPRIS (*Instytut Prawa i Społeczeństwa*), Mr Łukasz Bojarski, in Łukasz Bojarski, 'Sędziowie, liczymy na Was', *Dziennik Gazeta Prawna* (Warsaw, 23 January 2018) 2.

57. For an account of this attitude, see e.g. Wojciech Tumidalski, 'Kiedy zejść ze sceny', *Rzeczpospolita* (Warsaw, 9 January 2018) 2.

58. Mariusz Królikowski, 'Być albo nie być, czyli trudne wybory sędziów', *Rzeczpospolita* (Warsaw, 9 January 2018) 3. The author is a judge in the District Court in Płock, and chair of the Płock branch of the Association of Polish Judges *Iustitia*.

59. Resolution of the General Assembly of Judges of the Supreme Court, 16 January 2018, para. 6.

60. Ibid. para. 1.

61. More specifically, seventy-five presidents and seventy-three vice-presidents of common courts, two presidents and eight vice-presidents of military courts.

62. Tomasz Pietryga, 'Czystki bez precedensu', *Rzeczpospolita* (Warsaw, 8 February 2018) 2.

63. Łukasz Woźnicki, '"Dożynki" w sądach. Ostatnią dymisję przyniósł goniec', *Gazeta Wyborcza* (Warsaw, 14 February 2018) 3.

64. Małgorzata Kryszkiewicz, 'Kolegia sądów do wygaszenia – tak uznało prezydium KRS', *Dziennik Gazeta Prawna* (Warsaw, 14 June 2018) 6.

65. See 'Stan niezależnego sądownictwa w Polsce: Raport z badań i analiz' (n. 36) 5.

66. Małgorzata Kryszkiewicz, 'Gra toczy się o niezawisłość', *Dziennik Gazeta Prawna* (Warsaw, 2 August 2018) 6.

67. For a description of this and another, similar case, see Ewa Ivanova, 'Grillowanie sędziów', *Gazeta Wyborcza* (Warsaw, 31 January 2018) 1. See also 'Stan niezależnego sądownictwa w Polsce: Raport z badań i analiz', *Stowarzyszenie Sędziów Polskich Iustitia* (Warsaw, October 2018), for a number of other instances of disciplinary actions (or threats of such actions) against judges, usually by Minister Ziobro.

68. TV interview with Judge Kluziak, 'Nie spotkałam się z tak dyskusyjnymi zarzutami dyscyplinarnymi', <https://www.tvn24.pl/wiadomosci-z-kraju%2C3/sedzia-kluziak-nie-spotkalam-sie-z-tak-dyskusyjnymi-zarzutami-dyscyplinarnymi%2C837702.html> (accessed 17 May 2018).

69. 'Sędzia Czeszkiewicz nie zawinił. Winni są prokurator i przewodniczący wydziału' (*Gazeta Prawna Online*, 29 May 2018) <http://prawo.gazetaprawna.pl/artykuly/1126921%2Csprawa-sedziego-czeszkiewicza-winny-prokurator> (accessed 15 June 2018).

70. Venice Commission Opinion (n. 19) (904/2017) para. 114.

71. Resolution of the Assembly of Representatives of Judges of the regional Court in Cracow of 26 February 2018, unpublished document on file with the author.

72. See 'Stan niezależnego sądownictwa w Polsce: Raport z badań i analiz' (n. 36) 15.

73. Amnesty International, 'Update: "Reform" of the judiciary in Poland', 9 October 2018 1 (on file with the author).

74. Ibid. 1.

75. Ibid. at 1–2.

76. The amendment of 8 December 2017 to the statute on common courts; the amendment entered into force at the beginning of April 2018.

77. See interview with Judge of the SC and former Chairman of KRS Dariusz Zawistowski, in Tomasz Kwaśniewski, 'Sędziowie się ważą', *Gazeta Wyborcza*, section Duży Format (Warsaw, 12 February 2018) 14, 16.

78. See Małgorzata Kryszkiewicz, 'Sędziowie nie chcą sądzić kolegów', *Dziennik Gazeta Prawna* (Warsaw, 12 June 2018) 7.

79. Article 115, a, para. 3, of the new statute on common courts.

80. For a critique of a new disciplinary procedure along these lines, see interview with Chief Justice of the SC Małgorzata Gersdorf, 'Pędzimy ku przepaści', *Gazeta Wyborcza*, section *Duży Format* (Warsaw, 2 July 2018) 8.

81. Article 115(c) of the new statute on common courts.

82. The quoted opinion is by Mr Krystian Markiewicz, President of the Association of Judges (*Iustitia*), see Małgorzata Kryszkiewicz, 'Postępowania dyscyplinarne sędziów w rękach polityków', *Dziennik Gazeta Prawna* (Warsaw, 20 March 2018) 7.

83. See similarly Venice Commission Opinion (n. 19) (904/2017), para. 109.

84. See Agata Łukaszewicz, 'Minister często mówi sędziom „nie"', *Rzeczpospolita* (Warsaw, 10 January 2018) 15.

85. Małgorzata Kryszkiewicz, 'To nie jest kraj dla starszych sędziów: Sędziowie na łasce ministra sprawiedliwości' *Dziennik Gazeta Prawna* (Warsaw, 17 January 2018) 5.

86. Ibid.

87. Małgorzata Kryszkiewicz, 'Konkursy odblokowane', *Dziennik Gazeta Prawna* (Warsaw, 22 February 2018) 5.

88. Piotr Buras and Gerald Knaus, 'Where the Law Ends: The Collapse of the Rule of Law in Poland – and What to do', *Report by Stefan Batory Foundation and European Stability Initiative* (Berlin-Warsaw, 28 May 2018) 14.

89. Piotr Mgłosiek, 'Sąd Najwyższy, ale jaki?', *Dziennik Gazeta Prawna* (Warsaw, 30 March 2018) 5. The author is a judge of the Regional Court in Wrocław.

90. Ewa Ivanova, 'Sądolotek Ziobry do poprawki', *Gazeta Wyborcza* (Warsaw, 24 May 2018) 3.

91. Tomasz Krawczyk, 'Wokanda: uniki ze strachu przed władzą', *Rzeczpospolita* (Warsaw, 25 May 2018) at 20. Mr Krawczyk is a judge of the District Court in Łódź.

92. Małgorzata Kryszkiewicz, 'Pogłębia się kryzys w postrzeganiu sędziowskiej niezawisłości', *Dziennik Gazeta Prawna* (Warsaw, 30 May 2018) at 6.

93. See 'Stan niezależnego sądownictwa w Polsce: Raport z badań i analiz' (n. 36) 5–6.

94. Adopted by the Sejm on 28 January 2016, by the Senate on 30 January 2016, signed by the president 12 February 2016, and entered into force on 4 March 2016.

95. It is true that prior to 2009, and based on the previous law on the public prosecutor's office of 1985, both offices were merged and, in that sense, the period of 2009–16 of institutional separation can be seen as a non-typical episode. It would be ironic, however, for a strongly anti-communist leadership to refer to the law originating under communism as a model. Further, the earlier merger was at a time when the PG's competences were much narrower than under the law of 2016, for instance, regarding the instructions that the PG can issue to every prosecutor on any particular case.

96. Przemysław Pokrycki, 'Prokuratura umiera w ciszy', *Polityka*, online edition (Warsaw, 25 May 2018).

97. See ibid.

98. Opinion on the act on the public prosecutor's office as amended adopted by the Venice Commission at its 113th plenary session (Venice, 8–9 December 2017), Strasbourg, 11 December 2017, opinion 892/2017 para. 42, footnote omitted.

99. Ibid. para. 31.

100. See the report by the Lex Super Omnia association of prosecutors published 7 June 2018 (in Polish), '"Dobra zmiana" w prokuraturze', <lexso.or.pl> (accessed 17 June 2018). All information in this paragraph is based on this report; the facts have never been denied or challenged by the authorities.

101. Ibid. 22.

102. Eva Ivanova, 'Prokuratura pod butem', *Czarna Księga, Gazeta Wyborcza* (Warsaw, 17 October 2018) 12, 13.

103. Ibid.

104. As evidenced by the number of 'protracted investigations' (defined as investigations the length of which is over six months and under one year): in 2015, there were 6,351 such cases; in 2016, 7,419; and in 2017, 9,073. For cases in which investigations have lasted over five years, the respective numbers were 106, 173, and 209; see report of *Lex Super Omnia* (n. 100) 10.

5

Undoing the Institutions of
the Democratic State

The Constitutional Tribunal (CT), courts, and other institutions of the system of justice have been the main target of the Law and Justice (*Prawo i Sprawiedliwość* (PiS)) party's assault on the liberal democratic state—but are, by far, not the only targets. In its revolutionary zeal, PiS chose to undermine many other elements of the state apparatus and civil society. Five democratic institutions were targeted from the very beginning: the parliament with its principles for the recognition of the role of the opposition; the professional and neutral civil service; the free media; the electoral institutions; and the institutions of civil society. All these institutions provide a buffer for the population from the arbitrary will of politicians, and that is why PiS could not tolerate them. All five assaults will be discussed in this chapter. Another critically important aspect of the state is its electoral system, which is discussed in Chapter 6, being directly relevant to civil rights to vote.

Parliament: Silencing and Delegitimation
of the Opposition

Parliamentary and extra-parliamentary opposition is an important element of checks and balances in any democracy, and the treatment of the opposition by the ruling parties is a test of how seriously they take the idea that alternation in power is a crucial criterion of democratic governance. In Poland under PiS, the opposition parties—with the exception of some 'friendly' opposition in the form of a populist-nationalist party 'Kukiz-15'—have been treated as an alien body in politics, and in particular in Parliament, where they have been systematically marginalized and intimidated. In addition to the large number of slurs and insults that have been inflicted on the three main parliamentary opposition parties—Civic Platform (*Platforma Obywatelska* (PO)), 'Nowoczesna', and the Polish Peasants' Party (*Polskie Stronnictwo Ludowe* (PSL))—the primary way in which the opposition have been denied a meaningful political role is through the legislative process, which PiS have turned into a voting machine. The opposition parties have been reduced to a marginal role, as irritants treated with open hostility rather than vehicles of possibly helpful amendments to legislative drafts.

Poland's Constitutional Breakdown. © Wojciech Sadurski 2019. Published 2019 by Oxford University Press.

This has mainly been achieved by a favourite device of PiS, namely that of legislative fast-tracking, as well as proposing some of the most significant items of legislative changes as private members' bills rather than governmental initiatives, even
if de facto they were very much elaborated and put forward by the government.
(Indeed, a similar trick is often used in Hungary, PiS's role model in so many ways,
where after highly secretive drafting, the new constitution of 2011 was proposed to
Parliament as a public member's bill, thus eliminating consultation rounds and allowing for extreme fast-tracking.) The expedited procedure was never defended as
being warranted by the urgency of the subject matter: indeed, no such excuse was
even thought necessary. In 2016, the first full year of rule by PiS, over 40 per cent
(76 out of 181) of PiS legislative proposals were submitted as private members' bills
(in the two previous parliamentary terms, the percentages were respectively 15 and
13 per cent).

Mere statistics do not fully reflect the size of this change: this method was
adopted to push through some of the most important pieces of legislation,
including laws concerning the common courts (which, as we have seen, conferred
huge new powers upon the minister of justice) and the Supreme Court (SC). In
addition, with regard to the bills that did go through the process of consultation,
expert opinion, and impact statements, the requirement of publishing all opinions
on the parliamentary website was dropped, which meant that the general public
had no way of knowing whether any negative opinions were supplied.[1] As an example of legislative fast-tracking, consider the law on the public prosecutor's office, discussed in Chapter 4. Even though the Ministry of Justice de facto prepared
the law, it was formally presented as a private members' bill. Notwithstanding that
a number of entities produced opinions about the bill, including the SC and the
National Council of the Judiciary (*Krajowa Rada Sądownictwa* (KRS)), they were
disregarded during the legislative process.[2]

The frantic pace with which some of the most important legislative acts were
forced through parliamentary commissions and in the plenary debates of the Sejm
and Senate silenced the opposition through the use of devices such as gag rules
during 'deliberations', placing new items on the agenda without any notice, and
speeding up the deliberation, often late into the night or early morning, ignoring
critical expert opinions, etc., with this speed not being justified by any substantive
urgency to the proposals. Occasionally, the chairman of the parliamentary commission, which considered the draft laws on the KRS and the SC, when subjecting
the opposition's proposed amendments to vote, would not allow the opposition
MPs to explain what the amendments were about—hence the members of the
commission were unaware of what they were voting on. The silencing was literal: it
was achieved by the simple method of turning the microphone off.[3]

In the hurried pace of pushing through some of the most momentous changes,
such as the law on the SC, even the MPs representing the ruling party limited
themselves to the most perfunctory statements, knowing full well that whatever

they said ultimately did not matter because it would be followed by a vote based on party lines. In one of the most important legal changes (to the law on the SC), the 'speech' by a representative of the PiS proponents of the bill in the Sejm plenary session on 20 July 2018 lasted *seven* seconds.[4] Requests by opposition members for intervals in the committee meetings in order to have time to get acquainted with the newly submitted drafts were summarily refused. Under the new parliamentary rules, the Sejm Presidium (dominated by PiS) may set a limit on the number of questions raised by members in the discussion of a bill—the number is a function of the size of a parliamentary party caucus, which obviously disadvantages opposition parties. The new rules also exclude any plenary Sejm discussion on amendments proposed by the Senate to a new bill. The silencing of the opposition and of experts also took place in the Senate, despite its avowed role as a 'chamber of reflection'. For instance, during Senate debates concerning the laws on the courts, some senators wanted to continue after an interval as planned, by questioning experts and listening to invited guests such as the Ombudsman, but the speaker unexpectedly interrupted debate and carried out a motion to immediately proceed to a vote on the laws, thus putting an end to the debate.[5]

A non-governmental organization (NGO) called Civic Legislative Forum[6] lists the following examples where the voice of the opposition in the Sejm was reduced: the limiting of speeches to one minute (but one should add that occasionally, the speakers were given a limit of thirty seconds for their 'speeches');[7] the method of voting *en bloc* on amendments where all of the amendments were bundled together, not on the basis of their subject matter, but on the basis of which party proposed them (in order to make it easier for the MPs of the ruling party to know which amendments to reject); failure to provide enough time to read some proposed amendments; working late into the night; failure to respond to observations of legislative mistakes in the bills, etc.[8] In addition, opposition MPs have occasionally been excluded from the parliamentary floor on disciplinary grounds. Various other procedural tricks have been used to sidestep the opposition. For instance, the 2017 budget was not adopted in the Sejm assembly hall but transferred on 16 December 2016 to a smaller room where the so-called parliamentary session was immediately held as a follow-up to the PiS parliamentary caucus meeting, where no reliable counting of votes was possible, and with many credible allegations that opposition MPs were not allowed in. Another trick used in parliamentary commissions was to repeat the vote ('reassumption') when the outcome of the original vote was not favourable to PiS.

Yet another device used to silence the opposition was to prevent it from asking ministers questions during parliamentary question time. For instance, on 12 June 2018 the main opposition party, the PO, was denied the right to ask Prime Minister Mateusz Morawiecki a question regarding the prospects of the European Union's (EU's) use of the Article 7 procedure and the risk of financial sanctions against

Poland. The PiS used a simple trick by announcing, at the last moment, that its member of Parliament had 'his own' question to the government (as it turned out, a friendly question regarding Poland's use of EU subsidies in health care). Although a custom had been established that all political parties had the right to ask a question on a rotating basis in subsequent sessions of Parliament, the Speaker Marek Kuchciński (PiS) departed from custom on this occasion. Although it was the PO's turn, under the pretext that more than one question were foreshadowed, but that there was only time for one question and governmental response, the speaker subjected the matter as a point of order to a vote on the floor of the Sejm. Of course, the Sejm voted to allow the PiS MP to speak, and deny the PO its voice. In this way, a constitutional custom was extinguished, and the opposition effectively gagged.

A symbolic instance of penalizing the opposition occurred at the beginning of June 2018 when one of the most outspoken opposition MPs, Mr Sławomir Nitras (PO), was denied the right to go to a pre-election mission in Turkey on behalf of the Parliamentary Assembly of the Organization for Security and Cooperation in Europe. The denial was issued by the deputy speaker of the Sejm, Mr Ryszard Terlecki (PiS). The decision was expressly based on Mr Nitras's conduct during a parliamentary debate on the vote of no-confidence in Deputy PM Beata Szydło, in which the Information Centre of the Sejm established laboriously that Mr Nitras interrupted PM Morawiecki's speech thirty-two times.[9] This type of sanction is unprecedented in the history of the Sejm. As of the writing of this book, eight MPs (including only one PiS MP) have been fined for their conduct during this parliamentary term (beginning 2015) (just to provide some perspective, in the entire previous parliamentary term, 2011–2015, such fines were imposed only twice).

The marginalization of the opposition has also been reflected in the governance of parliamentary work. Contrary to custom so far, one of the opposition parties (the PSL) was denied a seat on the Presidium of the Sejm—a body in charge of agenda-setting for plenary meetings, among other things. Equally contrary to established patterns, the principle of 'rotation' in chairing the highly sensitive parliamentary commission for secret services has been abandoned, and the chairmanship has been reserved exclusively for PiS MPs. The main advisory parliamentary institutions have also been captured by PiS: the Bureau for Parliamentary Analyses (an analytical body providing advice and information to MPs) and the parliamentary journal *Przegląd Sejmowy* (Parliamentary Review) have seen their leadership transferred to PiS party loyalists (respectively, to Professors Wojciech Arndt and Waldemar Paruch, both active PiS intellectuals). Finally, in a move reminiscent of Stalin's practices, where the entire central administration adjusted its office hours to suit Stalin's daily programme, the commencement of plenary meetings have been delayed from 9a.m. to 11a.m. (and closure respectively extended) because Jarosław Kaczyński gets up late and goes to sleep late at night.

Dismantling of a Neutral and Professional Civil Service

After the 1997 Constitution entered into force, a new civil service regulation, designed to guarantee the efficiency of state administration regardless of the political situation and changing governments (see Art. 153 of the Constitution), was introduced by the statute of 18 December 1998 on civil service. It had been amended several times until the Sejm adopted a new statute on 25 August 2006 after PiS's first electoral victory, in order to increase the political impact on the civil service. After a change of government, the just-mentioned PiS statute was replaced by a new statute of 21 November 2008 during the seventh term of the Sejm. It was generally approved by scholars and recognized as an important step on the road to building a professional and independent civil service.[10]

After PiS had won the 2015 election, however, the issue of the civil service quickly became part of the parliamentary agenda again. PiS members of Parliament submitted a draft of a new law during the first month of the Sejm's eighth term. As with so many other bills, all changes to the amendment proposed by the opposition parties during parliamentary proceedings were rejected, while all PiS-proposed changes were approved. Less than one month later (on 30 December 2015) substantial and complex changes in the statute on the civil service were introduced. The real aim of the amendments and justification for frenzied parliamentary works were rather honestly articulated during the public debate by the advocates of the new law. They argued that it was important to employ new civil servants in order to ensure support of the government from people who 'identify'[11] with its policy— that is, that they should be party loyalists.

The idea of the neutrality of public service and merit-based recruitment has been abandoned. The statute of 30 December 2015 removed the obligation to carry out tenders for high-level positions in the civil service. Employment is based now on political appointment only. For lower positions in the civil service, there are two other ways of being nominated (either taking state exams or graduating from the National School of Public Administration named after Lech Kaczyński). The requirements for candidates have been substantially changed in order to employ new people who are politically aligned with PiS even though they may lack the necessary experience. Candidates for high-level positions do not have to prove long-term service any more. They also may be members of political parties up to the moment before appointment. The previous civil service regulation required either six or three years' service experience for candidates (depending on the rank to which they are appointed), and excluded those who had been members of political parties in the five years prior to recruitment. Further, according to the statute of 30 December 2015, candidates for high-level positions in the civil service are not required to have a clean criminal record. They may be nominated after having been sentenced as long as the sentence is not final.

After the new statute entered into force, all employment relationships at higher levels of the civil service came *ex lege* to an end. New conditions of employment might have been offered to some but not all outgoing officials. Perhaps most emblematic was the change in the mode of appointing the head of the public service. Under the previous dispensation, he/she must have had at least five years' experience in a senior management post, five-years non-membership to a party, and a positive recommendation by the Council of Public Service. All these requirements were abolished (and the council extinguished), with the appointment made dependent exclusively on the will of prime minister.

The law of December 2015 was the epicentre, but not the only act, in a dense legal infrastructure that PiS brought about in order to institute a massive purge in public administration and state bureaucracy. There were a large number of so-called personnel statutes (*ustawy kadrowe*) the sole aim of which being to help replace the cadres in virtually every state institution. As of March 2018 some thirty-seven such 'personnel statutes' were enacted, sometimes in haste, and many of them (54 per cent, to be exact) proposed as private members' bills in order to avoid the need for public consultation and various expert opinions, impact assessments etc.[12] No public institution was spared. The purges concerned such majestic bodies as the Military Academy (*Akademia Sztuki Wojennej*) and the Institute of National Remembrance (*Instytut Pamięci Narodowej* (IPN)), as well as such minor bodies (with all due respect to film historians and horseracing fans) as the National Film Archives or Polish Council of Horseracing. No public or state-controlled institution was left untouched where nominees of the *ancien régime* could have been found and PiS loyalists placed.

Often, the new statutes (prefiguring what happened to the constitutional terms of KRS members or the chief justice of the SC) terminated the statutory terms of office guaranteed to the incumbents, thus speeding up the purge. This was the case, for instance, of the Institute of National Remembrance (IPN); its council members had six-year terms of office, which were extinguished by the statute of 29 April 2016. The council was replaced by a new body called the College (*Kolegium*), in which the members were elected by a simple majority (the result being that only the candidates nominated by PiS were elected), with a term of office of seven years. The College, among other things, appoints the head of the IPN. Members of the College (in contrast to the members of the previous council) do not need to have academic degrees—and indeed some do not. It was then no surprise to anyone that the College appointed Dr Jarosław Szarek, a zealously nationalistic history scholar (known mainly for his books for children on Polish history) as the head of the IPN tasked with running an ideological 'historical policy' promoted by PiS.

As a result of these thirty-seven statutes, over eleven thousand positions (including over six thousand senior management positions) were vacated and immediately refilled with PiS cadres. (This compares to two 'personnel statutes' adopted in the comparable period of the first half of the previous parliamentary term, resulting in the discharge of nineteen persons in the institutions subject to liquidation.) In some institutions, entire senior echelons were discharged (as in the Chambers of Fiscal Control, public media and customs offices) or demoted to lower ranks *ex lege* (as in the public prosecutor offices). Just as an example, as a result of the statute on broadcasting of December 2015 (adopted only two days after the bill was proposed to the Sejm), all 118 senior management positions in public radio and TV, both in the central and regional bureaus, changed hands. In a complex of institutions related to agriculture (including social security for farmers and the agency of agrarian real estate), 768 positions were released and then filled by new office-holders appointed without an open competition procedure. The same applied to health administration, education, tax and customs, etc.

This was perhaps the most thorough, and at the same time least publicly and internationally visible, aspect of the state capture by PiS: the policy of spoils and patronage that far exceeded any of the clientelistic practices of the sixteen former governments in post-communist Poland. The only analogy that comes to mind is that of an occupied country, in which all the positions paid from the public purse go to the colonizers. As Professor Leszek Balcerowicz said, 'In no democracy known to me have there been such massive top-down changes [in public administration] as they occur in Poland now.'[13] And statistics provided above do not accurately show the scale of clientelism under PiS because they do not focus on the top (and the best paid) public positions, that is, those in state-controlled companies (companies of State Treasury). If one considers the thirty-two largest of such companies, in the first five months of its post-2015 rule, PiS replaced all but one of the CEOs of these companies with its own protégés.[14] In addition, a practice emerged of multiple and frequent changes to the top executives of the largest state companies, obviously not based on considerations of merit (the appointments were purely political and without any open competition) but to maximize the number of persons benefiting from enormous financial privileges connected with occupying (even for a very short time) such positions.[15] Many of them had no relevant professional background and no experience in corporate governance, capital markets, or anything else even vaguely related to their prominent new positions.[16]

Media: National, Not Public

Almost overnight, the public media was transformed into a governmental propaganda machine, with no attempt to pretend that opposition views would be presented objectively and neutrally. Immediately after PiS came to power, some two hundred journalists were purged from public TV and radio, and replaced mainly with journalists coming from fringe right-wing media, belonging, in the most part, to the 'media empire' of Fr. Tadeusz Rydzyk, the founder of the fundamentalist Catholic Radio Maryja and TV Trwam.

The regulatory and supervisory system was changed by statute even though the Constitution provides for a National Council of Radio and TV Broadcasting (*Krajowa Rada Radiofonii i Telewizji* (KRRiTV)) tasked with oversight of all TV and radio, both public and private. The new, five-member Council of National Media (*Rada Mediów Narodowych*) elected by the president, has three representatives from PiS and, as was demonstrated at least once, takes instructions directly from Jarosław Kaczyński.[17] In addition, the KRRiTV is now staffed exclusively by members supported by PiS, in contrast to a custom practised up to 2015 that the opposition also elects its members, though in minority. The KRRiTV has made it known that it will treat private media severely, and one example of this was the hefty financial penalty (PLN 1.5 million or EUR 350,000) imposed upon a major news and current affairs private TV channel, TVN24, for reporting the demonstrations around Parliament in December 2016. The official justification for the fine was that the broadcaster allegedly 'promoted illegal activities' and 'encouraged conduct that threatened security'. While the penalty was eventually withdrawn after TVN24 announced that it would go to court over the regulator's action, the very fact that it was imposed sent a strong signal to reporters and journalists that merely reporting expressions of anti-government views could be penalized. Significantly, the original penalty was imposed on the basis of an 'expert opinion' solicited by the KRRiTV from Ms Hanna Karp, an employee and collaborator with the Catholic media empire run by Fr Tadeusz Rydzyk. As a commentator for the moderately conservative newspaper *Rzeczpospolita* observed in this context: 'After having appropriated the public media, the ruling party is now reaching for the private ones, in an attempt to enjoy a monopoly [over the media].' And having added that the cassation appeals from the KRRiTV's judgments would be considered by a newly established Chamber of the Extraordinary Control and Public Affairs of the Supreme Court, fully appointed by the parliamentary majority, the commentator adds: 'It looks as if PiS has designed an extremely effective machine for restricting freedom of speech and media pluralism.'[18]

Even more ominously, the government announced that it would propose legislation aimed to 'repolonize' and 'deconcentrate' private media. What this may mean specifically is at present anyone's guess, but no doubt PiS will attempt to find ways of reducing the influence of the very vibrant private media, both electronic and press, in Poland. The Polish media structure makes it relatively easy to 'deconcentrate' them and, in the process, transfer ownership to those who would be friendly to, or dependent on, the PiS government. Currently, the printed press and major Internet portals are to a large degree in German and Swiss ownership (Bauer, Ringier Axel Springer, and Passauer Neue Presse) while control an important segment of the TV market is in American hands (the Discovery Channel owns a large part of the TVN group, including TVN24); in turn, the French control a large share of the radio market. This makes it easy for PiS to depict and criticize foreign control over the media.

In speaking about the need to 'deconcentrate' media, PiS talks of the need for a greater media pluralism, but without mentioning that anti-monopolistic provisions are already enforced in Poland, which block anything above a 40 per cent market share—PiS is allegedly thinking of lowering the threshold to 20 or 25 per cent. The critics fear that '[i]nstead of deconcentration, there will be media concentration in the hands of PiS'.[19] One expert believes that there is a plan for the consolidation of twenty vibrant regional newspapers published in the largest Polish cities by the Polska Press group belonging to Passauer Neue Presse. One scenario apparently envisaged is to create rich investment vehicles based on state-owned companies, which would then offer foreign publishers and broadcasters 'proposals they cannot refuse'.[20]

It should be added, however, that around mid-2017 official work on the 'deconcentration' or 'repolonization' of the media, carried out under the auspices of the Minister of Culture, slowed down on the basis that there had been no 'political decision' (i.e., decision by Jarosław Kaczyński) as to whether such a law would be adopted in the current parliamentary term. This is one of very few instances in which Kaczyński has decided to limit the number of fronts in PiS's battle for the monopolization of control over all independent centres of societal power. Private media in Poland, vibrant and independent, has yet to be colonized by PiS.

The Electoral System

It is well known that the manipulation of the electoral competition mechanism, aimed at entrenching the hegemony of the ruling party and denying fair chances to the opposition, may prevent the alternation in power which is the main definitional criterion of democracy: as many theorists of democracy like to say, the true test for democracy is not the first but the second election.[21] In the elections of 2015, the disproportion between the number of raw votes obtained by PiS (37.6 per cent, with an electoral turnout just under 51 per cent) and the number of parliamentary seats won (235 out of 460, or 51 per cent) suggested to many observers that PiS would attempt to further consolidate its control over the electoral process to its own advantage. Following in the footsteps of its role-model, Orbàn's Hungary,[22] PiS proposed massive changes to the electoral law at the end of 2017, introducing enhanced control by the parliamentary majority and executive over the mechanisms for conducting elections, the 'de-judicialization' of the electoral institutions, as well as entrusting new-style 'commissioners', who are no longer judges, with full authority (albeit as from elections after the next) to redraw electoral boundaries.

What was suspicious was the frenzy accompanying the enactment of the new law; in fact, PiS has never produced any serious explanation as to the need to change the electoral law in the first place. Despite hard-line PiS propaganda claiming that in various previous elections, which PiS kept losing, some allegedly monstrous irregularities had been committed, nothing of the sort has ever been demonstrated. Indeed, the only (and rather marginal) incident happened back in 2005 in which the SC found the elections to the Senate in one district invalid.[23] Apart from that, the courts have not found any of the electoral protests to be of such a nature that would impact the electoral process.

As with everything that PiS has addressed in its 'reforms', the main focus of the changes in the electoral law are the cadres: reforms equal purge. Under the new law, adopted by the Sejm on 11 January 2018,[24] the main body in charge of elections, the National Electoral Commission (*Pańtwowa Komisja Wyborcza* (PKW)) is to be completely restructured as of the beginning of the next parliamentary term. (It should be added that the importance of the PKW goes well beyond the election itself, as it deals with the allocation of funds to political parties—a huge source of income for those parties that make it to Parliament.) Rather than, as was the case so far, being composed of nine judges appointed in equal numbers by three presidents of the top courts: the CT, the SC, and the Supreme Administrative Court (SAC) (from among the judges of those courts), the new PKW is to be composed of just two judges of the CT and SAC, accompanied by seven members *appointed by the Sejm*. Under the new law, the head of the National Electoral *Bureau* (not to be confused with the commission), which is an executive arm of the PKW, is appointed by the new PKW from among three candidates *submitted by the minister of interior*; he/she is capable of being dismissed by the PKW *with consent of the minister of the mnterior*. Until now, the main official responsible for the actual nuts and bolts of the elections was appointed by the PKW, at the motion of the chairperson of the PKW. It had its logic: the head of the bureau was responsible to the PKW which, itself, has no resources, bureaucracy, budget or capacities to actually run the elections (all this is done by the bureau). Now, losing the power of full control over the appointment of the head of the bureau, the PKW's supervisory role is illusory, and the head of the bureau owes his/her appointment directly to the minister. On 21 February 2018, the election of this official confirmed fears that the office would be politicized: the PKW elected one of the three candidates the minister of interior presented to it. Prior to her appointment, the new Head of the Bureau, Magdalena Pietrzak, worked in a high administrative office reporting to the prime minister as deputy director of the department of parliamentary affairs of the office of prime minister—a certainly well-placed person in the governmental bureaucracy under PiS. But the other two candidates were even closer to PiS party politics, so the PKW (still, in its judicial version) was faced with a choice among three politically positioned candidates, all very close to (and dependent upon) top PiS politicians.

The responsibility for local electoral districts falls upon 100 'commissioners' appointed by PKW, but again, from among the candidates proposed by the minister of interior (with the additional proviso that if the PKW fails to appoint them within 100 days after the the law enters into force, they are to be appointed directly by the minister). By their pedigree, those commissioners are therefore representatives of the minister rather than of PKW in their districts. Most importantly, these commissioners, as well as chairpersons of the electoral commissions at the district level, do not need to be judges (as they currently have to be). Hence, the judicial penetration of the electoral administration—starting at the top with the PKW, and all the way down—which has been a strong fixture and achievement of the Polish electoral system since 1991, has now been terminated.

An additional power conferred upon public administration is the competence to redraw the boundaries of electoral districts. According to the new law, local self-governments (communes) are obligated to redraw the boundaries within sixty days of its entry into force. If they do not do so, the commissioners will perform this task (i.e. officials appointed from the lists supplied by the minister). If they do redraw the boundaries, the head of state administration at the level of *voivodship* (a large region) has the right to change these boundaries. Either way, government officials will make the final decision about electoral boundaries— which, of course, raises the real spectre of gerrymandering. Further, after the next round of elections, the commissioners will maintain a right to change the boundaries. At the same time, it needs to be recalled that electoral disputes will be heard by a new chamber of the SC, composed exclusively of judges appointed by a 'new' KRS, with the majority of members (twenty-three out of twenty-five) elected by the parliamentary majority. All this shows that the electoral process will be thoroughly controlled by the ruling party, either by the parliamentary majority or by the minister of interior who is a member of a narrow party leadership (at the time of the writing, it is Mr Joachim Brudziński, who is considered to be Jarosław Kaczyński's number one adviser, and is tipped by some to become his successor).

In addition, there is a new, rather ominous, change regarding the technicalities of ballots which, according to some critics, is a cause for concern.[25] Up to now, a ballot card is valid only if there is an 'x' placed next to the name of a candidate chosen by the voter, and any other signs, characters, symbols, additional notes etc. render the ballot card invalid. It was a guarantee against a third person placing a sign next to another name and erasing or changing the original 'x'. Under the new law of December 2017, this guarantee is gone, and a ballot with one sign crossed out and another added may still be considered valid, with the local electoral commission having the discretion when evaluating such ballots, thus opening up a space for arbitrariness and even electoral fraud.

Most importantly, however, the de facto subordination of the electoral personnel to the politicians of the ruling party (via the minister for interior) combined with the elimination of judges both in the PKW and as commissioners in the electoral districts, completely erodes the process of its integrity. In addition, taking into account some of the PKW's politically sensitive functions outside the elections themselves, namely the supervision of the spending of state subsidies by parliamentary parties (with sanctions in the form of refusing public funds to parties where financial irregularities have been found; in the extreme, the PKW can initiate the procedure for banning a party), entrusting these functions to representatives of politicians may be catastrophic for the freedom of political parties and for the democratic process generally. As the (old) KRS stated in its opinion on the draft electoral law, 'With the new composition of the National Electoral Commission, large parliamentary parties will be able to hinder the day-to-day functioning of their political opponents, which constitutes a real threat to the functioning of the democratic system in Poland.'[26]

The best characterization of the changes in this system was offered by the Chairman of the PKW, Mr Wojciech Hermeliński (earlier, a conservative politician and a judge of the CT):

> This is a departure from a judiciary-based system which guaranteed the transparency and impartiality of the elections, and a move in the direction of commissioners who may be close collaborators of political parties. ... The changes in the electoral [law] are dangerous for the impartiality of electoral process ... Up to now the rulers have not explained why they have opted for the party-governmental system.[27]

And they have not explained this choice since, after Hermeliński made this point, and before completing this book. We do not know yet whether the next national elections will be free and fair, but what we know for sure is that the mechanism is rigged against the opposition, and may easily be used against the opposition's chances of prevailing in the future.

Finally, it is interesting to note that, as already mentioned, by amending the electoral law to its advantage, the PiS regime followed in the footsteps of Orban's Hungary, which had thoroughly changed its electoral law in December 2013, a few months prior to the 2014 parliamentary elections. But there is a difference: while the main thrust of Polish changes was on the cadres and the electoral machine, the Hungarian changes were focused on the substance of the electoral process. By a combined mix of a reduction in the number of parliamentary seats (from 389 to 199), an increase to the threshold for entering the parliament (10 per cent for a party and 15 per cent for a coalition), and a massive redrawing of electoral districts having all the traits of shrewd gerrymandering, Orban attained a situation under which 45 per cent of raw votes for Fidesz translated into 66 per cent of seats, while the Socialist Party's 25 per cent of votes translated into 19 per cent of seats. But, in Poland, the huge powers of redrawing the districts conferred upon the 'commissioners' who owe their positions to the government, directly or indirectly, suggests that we should 'watch this space', and that PiS is preparing further steps to adjust the electoral process to suit its political needs.

Civil Society

The last aspect of checks and balances not directly controlled by PiS is a richly tex-tured civil society in Poland: a large network of NGOs, think tanks, social organ-izations ranging from foreign policy to free soups for the homeless, from rights of refugees to protection of historical cemeteries. And, as Jan-Werner Müller ob-served, the existence of an independent civil society raises a special challenge to populists in power, 'for the opposition from within civil society creates a particular moral and symbolic problem: it potentially undermines their right to exclusive moral representation.'[28] It took PiS two years to come up with legislation that helps subordinate civil society to the political hegemon. Negative assessments of the new bill made, inter alia, by NGOs[29] and the Ombudsman Office,[30] did not stop the governmental majority. Moreover, all motions and proposals that members of the opposition or NGOs' representatives had submitted as part of the legislative pro-cess were rejected by PiS.

The reform was based on two acts: the amendment of the statute of 24 April 2003 'on activities for the public good and voluntary service', and the introduction of the statute of 15 September 2017 on the National Institute of Freedom. Two new institutions were created: the Committee for Public Benefit (the Committee), and an institution with an Orwellian title—The National Institute of Freedom – Centre for the Development of Civil Society—in order to centralize state control over gov-ernment funds for NGOs.[31]

The former institution is composed mostly of members of the government (the president of the Committee (who is also a member of the Council of Ministers)[32] secretary of state in the Chancellery of the Prime Minister, ministers, and director of the National Institute of Freedom).[33] As one of the governmental administra-tive bodies, the Committee is responsible for 'coordination of cooperation between NGOs and public administration'.[34] Statutory competences and membership render the Committee (on which no NGOs representatives sit) the highest polit-ical body on all matters concerning the financing and control of civil society by the government. The leading role is centralized in the office of the president of the PKW, who has financial and management oversight of the Fund for Supporting the Development of Civil Society, exercises statutory supervision over public benefit organizations, has a right to appoint and dismiss the director as well as deputy dir-ector of the National Institute of Freedom, conducts supervision of the Institute, and has a right to appoint and dismiss members of the Public Benefit Council (comprising local government and NGO representatives with a consultative in-volvement in the Committee's activity).

The general objective of one of these institutions (the National Institute of Freedom) is to support the financing and development of civil society in accord-ance with governmental guidelines.[35] Within a long list of the institute's statutory tasks, it is important to note a normative preference for supporting or financing projects concerning the Christian heritage of national and local tradition.[36] The statute unfortunately does not guarantee a sufficient level of pluralism, legal certainty or lack of arbitrariness. First, the institute is charged with the implementation of tasks defined on a case-by-case basis by the president of the Committee —giving this person (a member of the government) and the prime minister (to whom s/he reports) enormous power over dispensing grants to NGOs. Second, the governance model of the institute is fully subordinate to the government: the majority of members of the institute's council are appointed by the governmental Committee for Public Benefit, and so indirectly by the prime minister. Although there are to be some NGO representatives on the council, they are in a minority (five out of eleven), and in any event the council has only an advisory role.[37] To make matters worse, the 'NGO representatives' are appointed by the president of the Committee (let us recall, a member of the government) who has full discretion over whom to appoint from among candidates proposed by NGOs. Considering the great pluralism within Polish civil society, there is no obstacle towards appointing only or mainly representatives of right-wing or Christian organizations. Third, there is no statutory obligation for the institute always to call for applications concerning programmes of civil society. It is a choice for the institute whether to perform statutory tasks by itself or to organize an open competition.[38] The statutory criteria for bidding for grants in a competition are very vague, and do not provide an anti-discrimination clause or any other guarantees for equal access by different subjects of civil society to public finances.[39]

Importantly, a preamble to the new law mentions 'Christian values', which may indicate a built-in bias in the system towards faith-based NGOs. But even before the new law entered into force, there was a clear shift in priorities: those with a Christian, conservative agenda have been privileged in reallocation of funds after PiS came to power while those with more 'liberal' or 'left' agendas have been disfavoured. For instance, various women's rights organizations, such as the Women's Rights Centre concerned with domestic violence, have been denied funds, on the basis that their programmes discriminate against male victims of domestic violence. Similarly, NGOs concerned with asylum seekers and refugees have been denied funds. The centralization of all state grants for NGOs by the setting-up of the Committee and the institute, structured in such a way as to make them fully subordinate to the prime minister, will make it possible to consolidate the trend of favouring the 'correct' NGOs and starving 'incorrect' NGOs of funds.

This was not the only way in which the PiS government attempted to undermine the independence and resources of NGOs critical of its policies. In a separate bill of February 2018, it put forward a new regulation regarding the public collection of money that is a large source of many NGOs' funding.[40] The law would give the minister of interior the power to refuse or block the carrying-out of public collection on the basis of the vague criteria of 'breach of principles of social coexistence or an important public interest'. The law would also give the administration the power to decide, in an arbitrary and discretionary way, what can and what cannot be funded by public generosity as expressed by a donation to street collections. In case some moneys had already been collected in an action subjected to this sort of administrative interference, the minister would have the right to devote the money collected to a 'social goal' of his/her choice; in other words, the money may be diverted to another charitable purpose than the one known to the donors. It should be added that this bill proposed to add a new, politically motivated criterion to the permissibility of collections 'because, under the already existing law, the administration has sufficient power to scrutinize the *legality* of collections and, in particular, whether the collection is consistent with the declared aims of a given NGO. Such a law, therefore, not only would starve certain NGOs of their funds, but also violate the freedom of choice of donors. In the end, in March 2018, the Ministry of Interior withdrew the bill under pressure from NGOs and the Ombudsman, but the very fact that it had been proposed gives a good insight into the thinking of PiS politicians about how to best control NGOs.

***

As this chapter has shown, PiS has not confined itself to an assault on the courts, including the CT, the SC, regular courts and the strategically critical institutions of law enforcement, as described in Chapters 3 and 4. The neutering of the judicial system was accompanied by a thorough hollowing-out of the structures and institutions of Poland's democratic state, which are intended to ensure that when a party wins domination over the parliament, the winner does not take all. PiS views such cushioning-off of the institutional constraints upon partisanship as an irritant, and something to be dispensed with, hence prompting a broad assault upon institutions that are meant to be resilient and beyond the reach of the winning party: parliamentary opposition, a neutral and professional public service, an independent public media, impartial electoral institutions, and a civil society supported by a democratic state. Each of these institutions has been colonized by the PiS state. In addition, it has centralized the governance of the state by reducing the powers of local self-government. For instance, the competences of local entities regarding agriculture, the environment, as well as minor but often sensitive matters like naming the streets, have been removed. Sources of revenue for local self-government have also been reduced.[41] Against this background, PiS could take on some of the rights of citizens identified by it as a challenge to its rule—to be discussed next.

Notes

1. See Piotr Szymaniak, 'Coraz gorsze standardy tworzenia prawa', *Dziennik Gazeta Prawna* (Warsaw, 16 November 2017) 6.

2. See Opinion on the act on the public prosecutor's office as amended adopted by the Venice Commission at its 113th plenary session (Venice, 8–9 December 2017), Strasbourg, 11 December 2017, opinion 892/2017 para. 24.

3. See Dominika Wielowieyska, 'Piotrowicz wziął opozycję za twarz', *Gazeta Wyborcza* (Warsaw, 29 November 2017) 2.

4. Paweł Wroński, 'PiS przegłosował ustawy sądowe w Sejmie otoczonym jak twierdza', *Gazeta Wyborcza* online edition (Warsaw, 20 July 2018).

5. See Łukasz Woźnicki, 'Senator PiS: Ustawa o SN łamie konstytucję', *Gazeta Wyborcza* (Warsaw, 15 December 2017) 7.

6. See Stefan Batory Foundation, Civic Legislative Forum, <http://www.batory.org.pl/en/operational_programs/anti_corruption/civic_legislative_forum> (accessed 2 October 2018).

7. This was the case in a parliamentary committee meeting debating the draft amendments to the law on the Supreme Court and regular courts on the night of 19/20 July 2018, see Paweł Wroński, 'PiS przegłosował ustawy sądowe w Sejmie otoczonym jak twierdza', *Gazeta Wyborcza* online edition (Warsaw, 20 July 2018).

8. Obywatelskie Forum Legislacji—Fundacja im. Stefana Batorego, 'Jakość stanowienia prawa w drugim roku rządów Prawa i Sprawiedliwości: X Komunikat Obywatelskiego Forum Legislacji o jakości procesu legislacyjnego na podstawie obserwacji w okresie of 16 listopada 2016 do 15 listopada 2017 roku' (2017) 2 and 11.

9. 'Poseł Sławomir Nitras ukarany obcięciem pensji i zakazem wyjazdu' (*Wprost online*, 7 June 2018), <https://www.wprost.pl/kraj/10130566/posel-slawomir-nitras-ukarany-obcieciem-pensji-i-zakazem-wyjazdu.html> (accessed 17 June 2018).

10. See Agnieszka Łukaszczuk, *Kształtowanie się modelu ustrojowego służby cywilnej w Polsce* (Wydawnictwo Sejmowe 2014) 320.

11. Report from the 5th plenary session of the Sejm of the 8th term on 17 December 2015, p. 223.

12. All data in this and the next paragraph are from Janusz Paczocha, 'Raport: Partia w państwie: Bezprecedensowa wymiana kadr w administracji rządowej', *Forum Obywatelskiego Rozwoju* (Warszawa, February 2018).

13. See 'Kadrowa miotła PiS. W administracji zwolniono w sumie 11 tys. osób' (*Business Insider Polska*, 28 February 2018) <https://businessinsider.com.pl/finanse/zmiana-kadrowa-pis-raport-for/n571tk1> (accessed 4 March 2018).

14. See Grażyna Kopińska, 'Stanowiska publiczne jako łup polityczny. Polityka personalna w okresie od 16 listopada 2015 do 31 października 2017 roku', *Fundacja im. Stefana Batorego* (Warsaw 2018) 8. To compare this with similar practices of former governments, the biggest changes were made by the SLD government in 2002–5 (55 per cent of CEOs) and the first PO-PSL government of 2007–11 (56 per cent). The second PO-PSL government of 2011–15, the directly preceding government before PiS victory in 2015, replaced 20 per cent of CEOs, see ibid. at 8.

15. Grażyna Kopińska provides some examples of such frequent changes: for instance the CEO of the Bank Ochrony Środowiska changed five times between December 2015 and July 2017; gigantic state-owned companies KGHM, Lotos, Jastrzębska Spółka Węglowa, and Enei saw their CEOs replaced twice in that period, ibid. 15–16.

16. See ibid. 17.

17. See Chapter 1 for an account of Kaczyński prevailing over members of the council to un-dismiss the chairman of TVP (public TV).

18. Zuzanna Dąbrowska, 'Wolność mediów? Wolne żarty', *Rzeczpospolita* (Warsaw, 13 December 2017) 2.

19. Michał Kobosko, 'The Shadow over Media' (*Visegrad Insight*, 1 December 2017) <http://visegradinsight.eu/the-shadow-over-media/> (accessed 20 May 2018).

20. Ibid.

21. See Samuel Issacharoff, *Fragile Democracies* (CUP 2015) 129.

22. In Hungary between 2010 and 2014, the boundaries of electoral districts were changed in a shameless gerrymandering exercise, and a number of other changes favourable to Fidesz were introduced. For example, a ban on paid campaign advertisements in the private media concentrated campaigns in the public media, strongly controlled by the government. In both 2010 and 2014 elections, Fidesz benefited from a discrepancy between the number of raw votes and the proportion of seats won: in 2010, a 53 per cent majority of voters translated into 68 per cent of seats for the coalition Fidesz/KDNP; in 2014, 45 per cent of voters helped achieve only 1 per cent fewer seats.

23. See the resolution of the Chamber of Labour, Social Security and Public Matters of the Supreme Court (Poland) of 15 December 2005, III SW 199-200/05.

24. Note an Orwellian title of the law: 'The statute on improvement of citizens' participation in the election and control of public bodies'.

25. See Wojciech Hermeliński, 'Sędziom przy wyborach już dziękujemy', *Rzeczpospolita* (Warsaw, 9 January 2018). It should be added that the author has been the chairman of the National Election Committee; formerly a judge of the CT.

26. 'Opinia Krajowej Rady Sądownictwa z dnia 7 grudnia 2017 w przedmiocie poselskiego projektu ustawy o zmianie niektórych ustaw w celu zwiększenia udziału obywateli w procesie wybierania, funkcjonowania i kontrolowania niektórych organów publicznych', unpublished document, 7 December 2017, on file with the author.

27. Jacek Nizinkiewicz, 'Wojciech Hermeliński: Nie trzeba psuć procesu wyborczego', *Rzeczpospolita online* 31 January 2018, https://www.rp.pl/Rzecz-o-polityce/301319994-Wojciech-Hermelinski-Nie-trzeba-psuc-procesu-wyborczego.html accessed 20 April 2018.

28. Jan-Werner Müller, 'Populism and Constitutionalism' in Cristóbal Rovira Kaltwasser, Paul Taggart, Paulina Ochoa-Espejo, and Pierre Ostiguy (eds), *The Oxford Handbook of Populism* (OUP 2017) 590, 597.

29. See, inter alia, the Organization for Security and Cooperation in Europe Office for Democratic Institutions and Human Rights, opinion of 22 August 2017, <file:///C:/Users/Micha%C5%82/Downloads/303_NGO_POL_22Aug2017_pl.pdf> (accessed 16 January 2016).

30. See Polish Ombudsman's Opinion of 13 of July 2017 <https://www.rpo.gov.pl/sites/default/files/Do%20Marsza%C5%82ka%20Sejmu%20w%20sprawie%20projektu%20o%20Narodowym%20Instytucie%20Centrum%20Rozwoju%20Spo%C5%82ecze%C5%84stwa%20Obywatelskiego%2013.07.2017.pdf> (accessed 16 January 2016).

31. Previously, decision-making on allocation of funds was shared between different ministries, and this facilitated distribution to multiple beneficiaries.

32. On 11 December 2017 Minister of Culture Piotr Gliński was appointed Chairman of the Committee for Public Benefit by President Duda. Minister Gliński, who is also deputy prime minister, is known for his numerous restrictive actions against (what he sees as) left-liberal and non-patriotic trends in theatre, cinema, and museums.

33. Article 34a of the statute of 24 April 2003 as amended.

34. Articles 1a and 34a of the statute of 24 April 2003 as amended.

35. Article 1(2) of the statute of 15 September 2017.

36. Article 24(3) subpar 4 and the Preamble of the statute of 15 September 2017.

37. For a criticism of this regulation, see Helsinki Foundation of Human Rights, 'HFHR Opinion on National Freedom Institute Bill', 18 August 2017, <http://www.hfhr.pl/en/hfhr-opinion-on-national-freedom-institute-bill/> (accessed 10 January 2018).

38. Article 24(5) of the statute of 13 October 2017.

39. Article 30 of the statute of 13 October 2017.

40. A draft law by the minister of interior and administration of 26 February 2018, available at <http://legislacja.rcl.gov.pl/projekt/12308652> (accessed 8 March 2018).

41. See Witold Gadomski, 'Recentralizacja', *Czarna Księga, Gazeta Wyborcza* (Warsaw, 17 October 2018) 46.

6

An Assault on Individual Rights

Illiberal populism is impatient with human rights. This is probably best seen when populists express their hostility towards the rights of defendants in the criminal process, claiming that these rights constitute a charter for criminals and are insensitive to the claims of the victims. Expressions of rage against human rights are also well reflected in populists' use of measures against terrorism. Populists in power deeply dislike non-governmental organizations (NGOs), in particular those dealing with human rights regarding women, domestic violence, the rights of children, of refugees, of ethnic minorities, etc. As noted in Chapter 5, the Law and Justice (*Prawo i Sprawiedliwość* (PiS)) government has radically reduced financial support for such NGOs, often to zero. This is in line with its overall worldview, which is basically nationalistic, xenophobic, misogynistic, and hostile towards much of the human rights agenda.[1] Another reflection of populist hostility towards human rights is visible in populist reactions against international or regional human-rights instruments and tribunals. In Europe, the European Court of Human Rights (ECtHR) has long been a target of populist dislike, to put it mildly. This dislike resonates with xenophobia and slogans against 'foreign interference'. The combined rhetoric against human rights and against international intervention produces a strong populist narrative of nationalism and of collective security allegedly threatened by the rule of cosmopolitan liberal elites who are said to be insensitive to the real concerns of the people.

No wonder that Dr Adam Bodnar, Poland's Ombudsman, noted recently that 'the legal environment [in Poland] is becoming more and more difficult to exercise political rights'.[2] So far, statutory changes regarding protection of constitutional rights have not been huge. However, the institutional infrastructure for protecting and enforcing those rights has been thoroughly dismantled, with the legislature (in fact, the extra-constitutional power concentrated in the hands of PiS leadership) having the final say on the rights of citizens. Henceforth, the interpretation of the legitimacy of statutory restrictions on constitutional rights will be the prerogative of the political leadership. In particular, for all practical purposes, the removal of the Constitutional Tribunal (CT) as the supreme body protecting rights against legislative and executive infractions means that the maintenance of rights is now a matter of the goodwill of ruling politicians.

When populists come to power, they characteristically attempt to tilt the political playing field in their own favour, and to disadvantage the opposition

Poland's Constitutional Breakdown. © Wojciech Sadurski 2019. Published 2019 by Oxford University Press.

in future elections, thus perpetuating their position as rulers of the country. They do so in various ways: by social policies, by propaganda, and as discussed at length in this book, by disabling institutional checks on their power. They also use legislation regarding civil rights to this effect, and the two most fundamental rights which they redesign and recalibrate for that purpose are those related to the political democratic process, namely the rights of assembly and of political speech. PiS has undermined and redesigned these rights for its party political purposes, and its actions in these dimensions are discussed in this chapter. In addition, PiS has endowed the police and secret services with a range of competences that are incompatible with the protection of the privacy of individuals in a liberal democratic state. This troubling phenomenon will also be described here.

Right of Freedom of Assembly

The new statute of 13 December 2016 (amending the Peaceful Assembly Statute of 24 July 2015) established priority for so-called cyclical manifestations and demonstrations. An assembly is recognized as cyclical when (1) it has the same organizer, and occurs at least four times a year, or once a year if it falls on an important national day; (2) it has its own history (i.e. it has taken place for at least three years); and (3) it is aimed at celebrating events of a high importance in Polish history. In this way, the law created a hierarchy of peaceful assemblies, establishing a priority for preferred ones. It is now legally impossible to organize a demonstration in the same location where a recognized 'cyclical assembly' organized by public authorities or churches is to take place. To be absolutely clear, the amendment expressly prohibits counter-demonstrations against periodic assemblies (counter-demonstrators must be distanced from the principal assembly by at least 100 metres). The purpose of the law was clear from the beginning: it was to prevent anti-government activists from registering their assemblies prior to PiS-sponsored assemblies (in particular, the monthly 'Smoleńsk marches'), thus reserving for themselves the space and time for assembly.

The effect of this new regulation is to ensure a privileged position for assemblies devoted to patriotic, religious, and historic events, which in Poland singles out governmental or government-supported assemblies in particular, such as the monthly events held up until 10 April 2018 to commemorate the Smoleńsk aircraft crash of 10 April 2010. These monthly manifestations, held in the centre of Warsaw and always culminating with a speech by Jarosław Kaczyński in front of the Presidential Palace, became hate rallies against the opposition and, understandably enough, provoked peaceful counter-assemblies. The effect of the new law made it illegal for counter-assemblies to take place within the immediate vicinity of the PiS regular assemblies. Similarly, though of lesser importance, is the priority given to the annual Independence Marches on 11 November (Polish Independence Day), which have been de facto appropriated by radical, extreme right-wing movements.

The hierarchy of assemblies formally endorsed by the new law is in direct conflict with the established, strongly libertarian regime of the law of assembly in Poland, based mainly on the CT judgment of 18 January 2006[3] (on the unconstitutionality of a provision of the Road Traffic Act that required permission for a public road assembly) and the judgment of 10 July 2008[4] (on the constitutional status of spontaneous assemblies). The former judgment was of especially great significance. The challenge by the Ombudsman was submitted at a time when local authorities had, on a few occasions, refused to grant permission for the holding of assemblies due to failure to fulfil the requirements indicated in the traffic law (this, for example, was the case of the 'Equality Parade' in Warsaw). In its judgment, the 'old' CT had relied on three main premises: first, a right to counter-demonstration cannot go so far as to undermine the citizens' rights to peaceful assembly; second, public authorities are obliged to ensure the protection of peaceful assemblies, regardless of the substance of the messages of these assemblies (as long as they are not illegal); third, 'public morality' as a constitutional basis for restricting a right to assembly must not be equated with the moral beliefs of public officials.[5] As a result, provisions of the Road Traffic Act 1997, insofar as they restricted those assemblies that could create hindrances or affect road traffic, were struck down. The judgment aligned fully with the guidelines established by the Organization for Security and Co-operation in Europe (OSCE), which stated that counter-demonstrations

> are a particular form of simultaneous assembly in which the participants wish to express their disagreement with the views expressed at another assembly. In such situations, the unity of time and place of two assemblies is an important element of the message that is to be delivered during both demonstrations.[6]

In March 2017 the new law on 'cyclical assemblies' found its way to the 'new' CT.[7] The applicant (who was, rather surprisingly, President Duda) argued that there had been a violation of freedom of assembly because of the statutory preference for the new type of public assemblies. The motion argued—correctly, in light of established case law in Poland[8] and in the ECtHR[9]—that the degree of constitutional protection of assemblies could not be made contingent upon the substantive purposes and messages conveyed. The new regulation also excluded a constitutional right of appeal against the decisions of public authorities regarding prohibition of public assembly. The CT (in a panel which consisted, inter alia, of quasi-judges, and with a quasi-judge Mariusz Muszyński as rapporteur) affirmed the constitutionality of the new statutory provisions. According to the judgment, assemblies of a cyclical nature have a constitutionally legitimate aim connected with the protection of national values proclaimed in the Preamble of the Constitution. The CT stressed that, due to 'the connection with the Nation's values and history', precedence over other assemblies should be guaranteed for this new type of assembly. The judgment's justification also confirmed the broad discretion of parliament in the field of freedom of assembly. In reasons provided orally by Mr Muszyński, it was claimed that the priority status of cyclical assemblies is properly 'counter-balanced' by the more stringent conditions required of the organizers when applying for such a status.

The judgment has been strongly criticized in dissents by 'old' judges,[10] and even by one of the judges elected in December 2015.[11] The dissenting opinions emphasized the unconstitutional composition of the CT: three legally elected judges were not allowed to adjudicate; the judgment was delivered by a panel in which three persons were not legally elected judges. Substantively, the dissenting opinions pointed out that the differentiation of the status of assemblies had a discriminatory effect; that the law wrongly entrusts administrative authorities with deciding which assemblies 'deserve' a higher status; that the law had improperly retrospective effects (because it made recognition of an assembly as cyclical dependent upon past events), and as such, it violated the principle of public trust in law.[12] The statute, fundamentally departing from the main canons of freedom of assembly established in Polish constitutionalism so far (such as non-discrimination because of content and viewpoint), had a clearly partisan purpose—and the CT's affirmation of this statute was just one more example of its enthusiastic collaboration with the ruling elite.

After the new law's entry into force, it became settled practice for local authorities to routinely ban 'counter-manifestations', usually at the last moment or even at the beginning of such demonstrations, making it impossible for the activists to challenge the bans in courts. Participants of counter-manifestations (relegated by the new law to the status of inferior assemblies) became subject to increasingly harsh persecutions and intimidation, with hundreds of people interrogated by police, and often treated brutally by the police and volunteer security teams of the PiS-sponsored assemblies. So it is not only the content of the law but also its actual *enforcement* that breaches the right of assembly. As Ombudsman Dr Bodnar has recognized in his recent reports, during the last few years 'all over Poland during the preparation and running of … assemblies, there have been many violations of the constitutional freedom of assembly by public institutions'.[13] For instance, in the so-called Independence March of 11 November 2017, police protected the organizers and activists of the principal march (even though several participants carried banners with clearly racist and neo-fascist slogans, which are banned under Polish law) while persecuting counter-manifestations, and also turning a blind eye to aggressive actions of marchers towards passive, peaceful protesters.[14] Implementing the aim of the law on 'cyclical assemblies', in particular the monthly commemorations of 10 April 2010, permits for counter-manifestations were routinely refused, and people assembling to protest against those 'privileged' manifestations were forcibly removed by police well before the time of the assembly.[15]

Many of the participants in anti-government rallies have been formally in-dicted: at the time of the writing, some one hundred and eighty such cases are pending. But the number of persons harassed and persecuted in various other ways is much higher: the NGO Obywatele RP (Citizens of the Republic of Poland) has over five hundred and sixty cases documented in which participants in various manifestations and marches have been fined for taking part in anti-government or anti-fascist assemblies, usually on the basis of an offence against public order.[16] Many were fined for damage to public property, for instance for slogans sprayed on pavements. Some were fined even for acting as an advocate for assisting those summonsed to the prosecutor's office for hearing.[17] Perhaps the most improbable was the indictment of a person who, as member of a counter-assembly during a Smolensk 'monthly assembly' held on 10 July 2017, had shouted the words 'Lech Wałęsa!'[18]

Freedom of Speech

As described in Chapter 5 of this book, the state has fully captured the public media, transforming it into a vehicle of primitive propaganda. In addition, there have also been attempts at silencing independent journalists and writers, and to produce a chilling effect by threatening them with legal action, often disproportionate to the alleged 'offences'. Perhaps the best-known attempt was the case of investigative journalist and writer Tomasz Piątek, who published a book[19] that was the product of his investigation into the allegedly suspicious contacts and professional relation-ships of the minister of defence Antoni Macierewicz[20]—(a vice-president of PiS, generally considered to be the leader of its hard-line faction). In response to the book, Mr Macierewicz instructed the military prosecution office (reporting dir-ectly to him) to launch an investigation under the Penal Code for the alleged of-fence of the 'use of violence or unlawful threat against a public official in order to take up or give up official duties' and 'insulting a public official'. After Macierewicz ceased to be minister at the beginning of 2018, the investigation was probably discontinued—there have been no official announcements about its progress—but the very threat surely had, or at least could have had, a strong chilling effect.

In a separate development, at the end of January 2018 parliament enacted a law amending the statute on the Institute of National Remembrance (*Instytut Pamięci Narodowej* (IPN)). The new law established an offence of publicly and falsely attrib-uting responsibility or co-responsibility to the Polish nation or the state for crimes against humanity committed by the Nazis during the Second World War, punish-able by up to three years in jail. The same law also provides civil sanctions for state-ments violating the reputation of Poland or the Polish nation. According to the law, the Institute of National Remembrance as well as NGOs shall be empowered to bring civil law actions in order to protect the good name of the Republic of Poland or the Polish nation. In the case of a judgment finding that there had been a viola-tion, the State Treasury shall be entitled to compensation.

The chilling effect of such penal and civil sanctions upon scholarly or journal-istic debates regarding the darker sides of Polish history is obvious, and the law clearly resonates with a nationalistic governmental rhetoric, under which Polish history is comprised exclusively of heroic acts and undeserved victimhood, and never of criminal deeds. The proposed law is sometimes referred to as 'lex Gross', referring to Professor Jan T. Gross of Princeton, whose books and articles depicting Polish crimes against Jews on German-occupied territories during the Second World War have provoked heated public debates in Poland over recent decades.

The government's publicly avowed motive for proposing this law was to coun-teract the admittedly unfortunate use of the concept of Polish concentration (or death) camps. This rationale, however, is manifestly insufficient to carry the burden of defending the law: while no one ever uses these words in Poland, the law would be utterly toothless with regard to foreigners committing this 'crime' in non-Polish media. In fact, both the further justification and plain meaning of the text of the law suggest that its intended reach was much broader: it covered statements other than 'Polish concentration camps', but also those which can be seen as 'attributing responsibility or co-responsibility' to the Polish nation for, inter alia, the crimes of Holocaust. But at which point does a statement about a large number of Polish criminals during the Second World War (including the so-called *shmaltzovniks*, i.e. those who brought certain death upon Jews by denouncing them to Germans) become an 'attribution' of co-responsibility to a nation as a whole? No one ever says that a particular action was committed by 'the nation'. These crimes were com-mitted by individuals. So how many individuals does it take to personify a nation as a whole? Will one be excused before the law if one makes a proviso that those individuals were a minority? The very fact of such questions arising immedi-ately suggests how vague and imprecise this provision is. In fact, it concerns not so much statements of fact, but rather an opinion: an opinion about (the alleged) responsibility of, say, passive onlookers. To punish for an opinion is an anathema to any system of freedom of expression—and this is precisely what the law would have done.

The defenders of the law pointed at two types of exceptions that were allegedly speech-protective. First, the punishment would be meted out only for the state-ments 'contrary to facts'. But the 'facts' are often disputed—including regarding the pogrom and massacre in Jedwabne in Eastern Poland on 10 July 1941, when over 300 (perhaps many more) Jews were burned alive by their Polish neighbours. While a group of 'old' IPN experts pointed at the active agency of Polish neighbours in murdering the Jedwabne Jews, the new chairman of the Institute, Dr Jarosław Szarek (appointed by PiS majority in the parliament), claims that Poles acted under coercion by Germans. This has never been demonstrated, but is an article of faith for the Polish nationalist right. The practical outcome is that prosecutors and judges will have to determine historical facts about which there is an ongoing dispute among historians. Second, 'scholarly and artistic' works will be exempt from liability. But this does not include journalism and the popularization of scholarship. Will a historian appearing in the media attract criminal responsibility, while lecturing in a classroom be exempt? All this shows how dangerous and malleable the new law was. In addition, rather than protecting the pride and 'good name' of Poland, the fact of enacting criminal sanctions for making 'improper' statements about Poland's past suggested to many that there must be some ulterior reasons— a sense of guilt?—for such an unusual, restrictive response to certain statements made in the course of public debate. As Tomasz Koncewicz observed, the law 'is the most recent proof that in Poland the past continues to be seen as a collection of indisputable truths, not open to divergent interpretations and historical debate'.[21]

The law quickly became a cause of major international embarrassment for the government, with both the US and Israeli governments reacting angrily. The former protested on the basis of the general violation of freedom of speech and academic inquiry. The latter objected that the law might silence the testimonies of many Holocaust survivors who remember the inhospitable (to say the least) attitude of their Polish neighbours during the German occupation. Oddly enough, President Duda both signed the law *and* sent it to the CT for a post-factum scrutiny: an arguably internally contradictory action. If the president has doubts about the constitutionality of the law, the constitutional convention requires him to send the law to the CT for an ex ante review; if the president signs the law, this signifies a lack of constitutional doubts on his part. The president, being formally a 'guardian of the constitution', must not promulgate a law that is putatively unconstitutional. The real reason for this incoherent action was an attempt to reconcile an appeal to nationalistic pressures within Poland with an attempt to placate observers abroad. Political opportunism once again resulted in a constitutionally scandalous action.

In the end, the CT did not get an opportunity to pronounce on the law because the government neutered the statute, on 27 June 2018. The most controversial provisions, namely the criminal punishment for an act described in the statute, and also a proviso that it applied also to acts committed abroad, were withdrawn. Incidentally, it shows that even PiS holds the CT in such disregard that, when political opportunism requires, they will conveniently ignore the fact that a matter is pending before the CT. In any event, major damage to the image of Poland was done, even though the government tried to present the short-lived law as its great success. Incidentally, the statute's neutering provided another example of extreme fast-tracking of legal change, without any real possibility for the opposition to discuss it. The amendment was introduced at the last minute in a parliamentary session with, officially, a completely different item on the agenda. The three required readings in the Sejm were held consecutively in a matter of a few hours, the discussion in the Sejm was purely perfunctory, with the opposition denied a right to a voice, all amendments proposed by the opposition were summarily rejected without discussion, the freshly adopted statute was immediately confirmed by the Senate, and signed by President Duda who happened to be on a state visit in Latvia on that day—the whole process took less than half a day.

One ironic and unintended consequence of the law, ostensibly aimed at protecting 'the good name' of Poland, was to draw the attention of domestic and international public opinion to those who really do damage Poland's reputation—namely the racists, neo-Nazis, and anti-Semites in Poland. Since Poland found it necessary to punish accusations against Poland for being, inter alia, anti-Semitic, there must be a reason for it, the argument went, and the reason must have had something to do with embarrassing aspects of the Polish past and present. Countries that have 'nothing to hide' have no need of criminal punishment to protect their reputation. This train of thought led to an enquiry into persistent extremist strains in Polish life—which were, alas, not too difficult to find. A serious recent study has shown that one of the by-products of the statute on responsibility for the Holocaust was that it triggered a huge increase of violently anti-Semitic themes in public discourse (as an example, one of the leading MPs of a parliamentary party Kukiz-15 said that 'Israel wants to appropriate to itself all the suffering which occurred during the Second World War'),[22] and especially on social media. The report, having studied the frequency of certain derogatory anti-Semitic descriptions and words, concluded: 'While before the debate about the law on IPN Internet conversations about "Jews" and "Israel" not necessarily had anti-Semitic character, after the commencement of the debate about the new law in posts about Jews and their state used [predominantly] anti-Semitic phrases and hashtags.'[23]

Privacy Rights vs Counter-Terrorism Measures and Police Act

Two laws adopted in 2016 greatly increased the discretionary powers of the special services and police: the statute of 10 June 2016 on counter-terrorist activities, and the statute of 15 January 2016 on the police.

The statute of 10 June 2016 established a vast but vaguely defined scope of powers for the Internal Security Agency (*Agencja Bezpieczeństwa Wewnętrznego* (ABW)) in order to protect the state against terrorism, as well as to control citizens and collect personal data without following normal statutory procedures. The Ombudsman questioned the constitutionality of a significant part of the statute before the CT just after the statute entered into force,[24] and before Julia Przyłębska assumed her function as president of the CT.[25] The motion of unconstitutionality was supported by the following arguments. First, there is no clear definition of the term 'terrorist act', even though the new law uses it as one of the most important statutory criteria for intervention by the anti-terrorist services. This term is also a part of another crucial statutory definition: 'anti-terrorist activities'.[26] A new database is to be created by the ABW in order to control persons associated with terrorist acts. There are, however, no clear statutory purpose, principles, or limits for such a database. The provisions do not guarantee efficient judicial control over it, nor do they allow any interested party to demand, correct, and delete false or incomplete data. The ABW may demand and shall have open (and in fact unlimited) access to data and information collected by all public agencies or bodies at the central as well as local level.[27] Mere risk of, or an attempt to commit a terrorist act shall be a sufficient justification to apply for pre-trial detention.[28] Moreover, under the new statutory provisions, the ABW may make orders to block internet services in order to prevent (undefined) terrorist acts.[29] The court's jurisdiction over ABW acts is strictly limited.

The second of the two laws (amending the Police Act) gives the police and its agencies access to internet data, including the content of communications, under court orders (for up to three months, but without a requirement of necessity or proportionality),[30] or to metadata without the need for court orders.[31] The latter provision especially is a cause for serious concern: metadata may be obtained without the prior consent of a court, and the only requirement is for an ex-post court review of a *generalized* (i.e. basically limited to statistics) report by the police on metadata collection. While metadata is theoretically not content-related, a combined analysis of various types of metadata (something which is not excluded by the law), collected secretly by law enforcement agencies, and which may be used against a person unaware of the fact of collection of those data, may significantly intrude into a person's privacy, and give insight into intimate aspects of a person's private life. As the Venice Commission noted, the law regarding collection of this information has no 'probability test' (no need for the police to have a specific reason to believe that a criminal activity is going on or being prepared), and no 'subsidiarity test' (a requirement that metadata collection be a subsidiary means of obtaining information).[32] In combination with no effective oversight of such activities, the law allows for very deep intrusion into a person's private life, without him or her even being aware of such surveillance.

Eventually, the Ombudsman withdrew his constitutional challenge, on the basis that the new president, Ms Przyłębska, had unlawfully tampered with the composition of the panels after she took over leadership of the CT, and also on the basis of the inclusion of quasi-judges in the panels. This compelled the CT to discontinue the case.

The final legal innovation worth mentioning in this context, though strictly speaking, made as an amendment to the Code of Criminal Proceedings, concerned the doctrine of the 'fruits of the poisonous tree'. On 11 March 2016, an amendment to the code was enacted making such evidence admissible in criminal trials even if it was collected illegally—for example, as a result of an illegal search or seizure, or illegal surveillance.[33] This reversed a major achievement of Polish criminal procedure, and brought back incentives for police and prosecutors to take shortcuts with the law of criminal evidence.

***

As this chapter has shown, there have been some very troubling developments in Poland in the field of human rights, especially those with direct implications for the political process, such as freedom of assembly. Political rights have been adversely affected by many statutory and political developments discussed in the previous chapter: for instance, voting rights—the most critical political right of all—have been drastically diminished by institutional changes which pack electoral system institutions with ruling party nominees, and which diminish standards of impartiality of electoral officials.

And it should be emphasized that the catalogue of human rights considered in this chapter is far from exhaustive. For instance, over the past few years especially, Poland has systematically violated the rights of asylum-seekers, particularly from Chechnya, Armenia, and Tajikistan, who—in violation of international law and also the Polish Constitution itself (Art. 56(2))—have been denied the right to enter upon Polish territory to seek asylum, or once they have, in most cases have been deported in an inhumane manner, without the right to judicial review of the deportation, and to places where their lives and security are endangered.[34] Speaking of deportation, Poland has also violated the rights of non-EU nationals against deportation, as was evidenced in the case of Lyudmyla Kozlovska, a Ukrainian national and wife of a Polish citizen, engaged in activities of Polish NGO 'Open Dialogue Foundation'. Long hated by the government because of her publicly stated anti-PiS views, she was given a Polish entry ban which was reported in the Schengen Information System, making her an 'inadmissible alien' within the entire Schengen area. Her expulsion, for reasons treated by Polish security services as classified, breached her rights to residence as family member of an EU citizen, of freedom of expression, family life, and effective judicial protection all in one go.[35]

Without denying the seriousness of the developments discussed in this and in previous chapters, in terms of infractions of fundamental rights, it would be fair to say that Poland's constitutional breakdown evidenced in this book, to use Dimitry Kochenov's words (not in the context of discussing Poland), proceeds via 'a well-executed dismantlement of the Rule of Law and the constitutional checks and balances ... [and] without bald violations of human rights'.[36] This combination is not something to be applauded. By dismantling the institutional protections of individual rights and liberties, the ruling party has paved the way for future assaults on rights—and if these happen, the institutions that would normally be expected to prevent this state of affairs from occurring will not be there.

Notes

1. For a characterization of the contemporary populist agenda as 'often avowedly nationalistic, xenophobic, misogynistic, and explicitly antagonistic to all or much of the human rights agenda', see Philip Alston, 'The Populist Challenge to Human Rights' (2017) 9 *Journal of Human Rights Practice* 1, 1–2, footnote omitted.
2. Adam Bodnar, 'Protection of Human Rights after the Constitutional Crisis in Poland' (2018) 66 *Jahrbuch des öffentlichen Rechts der Gegenwart* 639, 657.
3. K 21/05.
4. P 15/08.
5. The Constitutional Tribunal ruled on the unconstitutionality of such regulations. For a discussion see Wojciech Sadurski, *Rights before Courts: A Study of Constitutional Courts in Postcommunist States of Central and Eastern Europe*, 2nd edn (Springer 2014) 220–1.
6. See OSCE Office for Democratic Institutions and Human Rights, Guidelines on Freedom of Peaceful Assembly, 2nd edn, 17.
7. Judgment KP 1/17 of 16 March 2017.
8. Judgment of the Constitutional Tribunal K 21/05 of 18 January 2006.
9. See e.g. *Bączkowski and Others v. Poland*, App. no. 1543/06 (ECtHR, 3 May 2007).
10. Judgment KP 1/17 of 16 March 2017; see the dissenting opinions of Judges Leon Kieres, Małgorzata Pyziak-Szafnicka, and Sławomira Wronkowska-Jaśkiewicz.
11. See the dissenting opinion of Judge Piotr Pszczółkowski. His dissent was based, however, on the narrowest ground, namely on the absence of a means of reviewing an administrative decision concerning the prohibition of an assembly.
12. Dissenting opinions of Judges Małgorzata Pyziak-Szafnicka and Sławomira Wronkowska-Jaśkiewicz.
13. 'Wolność zgromadzeń w Polsce w latach 2016–2018', *Raport Rzecznika Praw Obywatelskich* (Warsaw, September 2018), 8.
14. For example, a group of twelve women sitting by the roadside with a 'Stop Fascism!' banner were beaten and spat upon by some marchers—to no reaction from the police.
15. Raport Rzecznika Praw Obywatelskich (n. 13) 10.
16. Magdalena Kursa, 'Obywatele ścigani za protesty', *Czarna Księga, Gazeta Wyborcza* (Warsaw, 17 October 2018) 14.
17. Ibid.
18. Ibid.
19. Tomasz Piątek, *Macierewicz i jego tajemnice* (Arbitror 2017).
20. Macierewicz ceased to be minister as a result of a governmental reshuffle on 8 January 2018, but maintained his position as vice-president of PiS.
21. Tomasz Tadeusz Koncewicz, 'On the Politics of Resentment, Mis-memory, and Constitutional Fidelity: The Demise of the Polish Overlapping Consensus?' in Uladzislau Belavusau and Aleksandra Gliszczyńska-Grabias (eds), *Law and Memory: Towards Legal Governance of History* (CUP 2017) 263, 271. Please note that the observations by Professor Koncewicz refer to an earlier iteration of the same law. However, the differences between the two versions of the law are insignificant.

22. Maria Babińska, Michał Bilewicz, Dominika Bulska, Agnieszka Haska, and Mikołaj Winiewski, 'Stosunek do Żydów i ich historii po wprowadzeniu ustawy o IPN', *Centrum Badań nad Uprzedzeniami* (Warsaw 2018), 8; the words are by Mr Marek Jakubiak. The report was commissioned by the Ombudsman.

23. Ibid. 20.

24. See 'Wniosek Rzecznika Praw Obywatelskich' (Warsaw June 2016), <https://www.rpo.gov.pl/sites/default/files/Wniosek%20do%20TK%20w%20sprawie%20ustawy%20antyterrorystycznej%2011%20lipca%202016.pdf> accessed 20 October 2018.

25. See case no. K 35/16, now discontinued.

26. Article 2(1) of the statute of 10 June 2016.

27. Article 11 of the statute of 10 June 2016.

28. Article 26(2) of the statute of 10 June 2016.

29. Article 38 subpara. 6 of the statute of 10 June 2016.

30. Article 19 of the statute of 6 April 1990 on the police, as amended.

31. Article 20c of the statute of 6 April 1990 on the police, as amended.

32. Venice Commission, Opinion on the Act of 15 January 2016 amending the Police Act and Certain Other Acts, adopted by the Venice Commission at its 10th Plenary Session, Venice 10–11 June 2016, Opinion No. 839/2016, paras 55–9.

33. Act of 11 March 2016 on amending the Code of Criminal Proceedings and Selected Other Acts.

34. See Chapter 8.

35. See Evelien Brouwer, 'Schengen Entry Bans for Political Reasons? The Case of Lyudmyla Kozlovska' (*Verfblog*, 30 August 2018), <https://verfassungsblog.de/schengen-entry-bans-for-political-reasons-the-case-of-lyudmyla-kozlovska/> (accessed 19 September 2018).

36. Dimitry Kochenov, 'The Acquis and Its Principles: The Enforcement of the "Law" versus the Enforcement of "Values" in the EU' in András Jakab and Dimitry Kochenov (eds), *The Enforcement of EU Law and Values Ensuring Member States' Compliance* (OUP 2017) 9, 22.

7

Why Did It Happen?

The Polish case (and the Hungarian case, for that matter) presents a puzzle regarding conventional wisdom on the sources of anti-constitutional populist backlash. There is a large body of literature in political science offering various explanations about what renders democratization *unlikely* and, once it happens, non-resilient. The best short summary of the scholarly *communis opinio* was well articulated in this passage by Steven Levitsky and Lucan Way, written on the eve of Polish antidemocratic transformation:

> According to a substantial body of research, stable democratization is unlikely in very poor countries with weak states (e.g., much of sub-Saharan Africa), dynastic monarchies with oil and Western support (e.g., the Persian Gulf states), and single-party regimes with strong states and high growth rates (China, Vietnam, Malaysia, Singapore). Our own research suggests that democratization is less likely in countries with very low linkage to the West (e.g., Central Asia, much of Africa) and in regimes born of violent revolutions (China, Ethiopia, Eritrea, Vietnam, Cuba, Iran, Laos, North Korea) ... While the recent stagnation on the overall number of democracies in the world may be normatively displeasing, it is entirely consistent with existing theory.[1]

As one can see, Poland does not fit any of these syndromes: it is not a very poor country with a weak state, not a single-party regime with impressive growth rate, it has high linkages to the West, it is not a regime born out of a violent revolution, it is not a dynastic monarchy, and it has, alas, no oil. These 'structuralist' explanations do not apply to the Polish case. So how to explain its unconstitutional populist backsliding?

The Paranoid Style in Polish Politics, Post-Smolensk[2]

In July 2017, soon after the government submitted to Parliament a legislative package aimed at full political control over the judiciary, Rafał Matyja, a conservative political scientist and public intellectual known for his independence of judgment, observed:

Poland's Constitutional Breakdown. © Wojciech Sadurski 2019. Published 2019 by Oxford University Press.

The changes which are being introduced in the judiciary are part of a ... logic which constitutes a serious danger for the state: a logic of total distrust towards institutional rules and willingness to replace them by mechanisms based on personal trust. At first sight, such logic may seem innocuous but in practice it means the creation of a model in which all important functions are filled by persons obedient to the will of the Chairman or at least those who are incapable of resisting him.[3]

Matyja's observations can be extended to all legal and state-related matters, not just those related to the political control over the judiciary. Poland offers a strong vindication of the explanatory power of the 'agentic' theories that emphasize the significance of the 'human factor' as a source of illiberal transformations. Quite apart from deeper societal sources (which I discuss in section 'Sources of the Emergence of Effective Populism'), much of the animus driving the erosion of liberal-constitutional checks on arbitrary power can be explained by the relentless will and obsession of one person, the leader of the Law and Justice (*Prawo i Sprawiedliwość* (PiS)) party Jarosław Kaczyński and his closest allies, who are deeply distrustful of any independent social powers, be they the judiciary, media, local self-government, non-governmental organizations (NGOs), non-partisan military, or a neutral civil service (but not yet the clergy, though that time may come), and who present the democratic mandate given to their party through the electoral choice of 2015 as a basis for extending personal control over all social powers.

In his article Matyja went on to draw an analogy between this ambition of Jarosław Kaczyński and the Polish People's Republic (*Polska Rzeczpospolita Ludowa* (PRL)) system, and continued: 'The evil of the PRL did not consist only in the fact that communists ruled. Much more important was the fact that they ruled within a system infused with paranoia.'[4] The mention of 'paranoia' evokes an important trope assisting in the analysis of Kaczyński's understanding of politics, and much of Richard Hofstadter's famous 1964 essay[5] (though not mentioned by Matyja) applies presciently to Poland 2017. Kaczyński indeed perceives the world as composed of largely hostile forces, plotting against the forces of the good, the latter personified in the leader who knows that any compromises with the enemy are a sign of weakness (or worse, of betrayal) which must lead to catastrophe. Polish politics and Polish state-controlled propaganda are based on the Manichean antinomy of good and evil, and a conviction that the good will not triumph if the forces of evil are allowed to maintain their strongholds in the judiciary, media, or NGOs. The opponents are simultaneously pathetically weak (because they are not in tune with the real society) and distressingly powerful (which justifies constant mobilization against them); the evil they represent is apocalyptic yet capable of being prevented; hence the need for continuous vigilance and struggle. Grotesque exaggerations, deep suspicion, and absurd conspiracy theories[6]—all aspects Hofstadter had detected in the paranoid political style—are abundantly present in Poland today. This recent characterization of PiS's opponents by Jarosław Kaczyński is typical: 'Our adversaries, our enemies, will not rest. They want to destroy our life, to bring about a deep crisis in our country.'[7]

As should be clear, I am not attributing to Kaczyński 'paranoia' in a clinical sense of the word but am borrowing it, just like Hofstadter did, for a political analysis. And I may repeat after Hofstadter, 'I have neither the competence nor the desire to classify any figures of the past or present as certifiable lunatics.'[8] But the dismantlement of constitutional checks and balances is a consequence of the paranoid style in Polish politics, and of the perception (so reminiscent of Stalin's late paranoia) that the more crushed the enemy is (and crushed he *is*—otherwise the struggle launched by the leader would turn out to be tragically misplaced, which is unthinkable), the more vicious and desperate, hence dangerous, he becomes. As Jarosław Kaczyński recently diagnosed: 'in our [social] life a lot of evil has appeared, evil which is more and more insolent, more and more aggressive, and enjoying more and more impunity.'[9] And if the enemy *is* dangerous, constitutional checks and balances render the struggle against him ineffective. All these obsessions, fears, and concerns by Kaczyński himself resonate with an important segment of the Polish electorate.

A special place in this paranoiac style of politics in Poland has been played by the horrendous air crash of an aircraft carrying ninety-six leading Polish politicians, military commanders, and religious and civic leaders, including then President Lech Kaczyński and his wife, on 10 April 2010 on its descent towards the airport in Smolensk, Russia. The visit was fraught with deep symbolism: it was meant to commemorate the memory of over twenty-one thousand Polish officers and soldiers murdered at Stalin's orders by the KGB in the five killing fields—one of them the forest of Katyń, not far from Smolensk, in April 1940. It was generally understood that Lech Kaczyński intended this visit to be the inauguration of his presidential election campaign, less than three months before the election, and at a time when his ratings were at an all-time low. For this reason, his visit was separated from Prime Minister Donald Tusk's visit to Katyń, who came with the official governmental delegation three days earlier and who was joined by then Prime Minister Putin: it seems that neither Tusk nor Kaczyński fancied a joint visit at a time when the *cohabitation* was particularly sour.

The causes of the crash were later well described by the state commission chaired by Minister for the Interior Jerzy Miller: it was caused by a combination of extremely bad weather (heavy fog, getting worse by the minute), human error on the part of the Polish pilots (uncertainty as to the real altitude of the plane, wrongful efforts to attempt to land despite having no visual contact with the airstrip etc.) and Russian airport personnel (lack of issuing a firm prohibition on landing), bad training and organization in the military air-force unit responsible for the flights of VIPs, interference in the cockpit by third persons who distracted and distressed the pilots, insufficient advance planning of the visit, and the appalling condition of the airport itself etc. There have been a great number of very serious findings by the committee but the bottom line was: the plane should have never taken off knowing the weather situation on arrival; once it had taken off, it should have been redirected to an alternative airport; once it had approached Smolensk, it should have abandoned any attempt to land. Just before the crash, it flew too fast, too low, and with no required minima of horizontal and vertical visibility.[10]

As one would expect, the disaster caused an outburst of emotion—anger, mourning, and distress—in Polish society. What is more relevant, however, is that PiS quickly decided to play the 'Smolensk card' in politics, by formally and with increasing strength rejecting the explanation of the causes of disaster by the Miller commission, and transforming a tragic but avoidable aircraft crash into a political mass murder. Jarosław Kaczyński, seized by a personal trauma and additionally irritated by his defeat in the presidential elections, which took place on 20 June and 4 July 2010, established the Smolensk disaster as the main platform to attack the Civic Platform (*Platforma Obywatelska* (PO)) government and the new president, Bronisław Komorowski. He shamelessly propounded conspiracy theories, which—in their strong version—blamed the Tusk government for complicity with the Russians in masterminding the crash, and—in their weak version—blamed the government for its alleged unwillingness to properly investigate the crash. One of the most (in)famous speeches by Kaczyński on the topic referred to his late brother and his co-passengers as having been 'betrayed at dawn', thus referring to a moving poem by the great Polish poet, Zbigniew Herbert.[11]

He found an enthusiastic executioner of this line of attack on the PO government in Antoni Macierewicz, an ex-head of military counterintelligence (in 2006–7). Macierewicz quickly set up an alternative commission for investigating the crash, which regularly kept coming up with new revelations, all of which suggested somebody's criminal intent and action, but none of which had even minimal plausibility. (Occasionally, even the absence of any available evidence was treated as evidence of how shrewd the wrongdoers were.) The workings of this commission, in conjunction with the monthly rallies in the centre of Warsaw on the 10th of each month, invariably culminating in front of the Presidential Palace with an angry speech by Kaczyński, formed the core of the 'Smolensk ritual', which infused Polish public life with a particularly toxic kind of paranoia and was an effective instrument for mobilizing the hard core of PiS supporters. In fact, the ritual did not end with the PiS victory in 2015. To the contrary, with Macierewicz becoming the minister of defence, and with his commission upgraded in status to an official governmental body, the 'Smolensk conspiracy' became part of the officialdom of Poland post-2015, with Macierewicz requiring the names of Smolensk victims be read at all important public events with military participation, urging North Atlantic Treaty Organization (NATO) involvement in a new investigation, and even proclaiming that the 'Smolensk assault' was the first act in a war waged by Russia against Poland. As Timothy Snyder describes with only a little exaggeration: 'After 2015, Smolensk became more important than the Katyn massacre that Polish leaders had wished to commemorate, more important than the Second World War, more important than the twentieth century.'[12]

This all began to wane by the end of 2017 and the beginning of 2018, when Macierewicz lost his governmental position (but not the chairmanship of the Smolensk committee, positioned within the Ministry of Defence), and rhetoric on the conspiracy was gradually extinguished. Kaczyński's speech on 10 April 2018 marked an end to the official monthly rallies, with his statement that the 'actual truth' about the accident may be impossible to discern in the near future, if ever, bringing closure to the ritual (even though Macierewicz and the hardcore pro-PiS media still regularly return to the matter, with nearly the same enthusiasm as before). The impact of the 'Smolensk religion' (as some critics came to call the conspiracy theory and practice around the matter) cannot be over-estimated, and notwithstanding Kaczyński's change of rhetoric in 2018, it still infuses Polish public discourse with hatred, suspicion, and paranoia. It has probably been the most polarizing issue in the deep ideological divisions of Polish society in and after 2010.

The paranoia-oriented interpretation of the causes for PiS victory in 2015 places a high explanatory burden on human agency: on the will and behaviour of political leadership, which is relatively contingent and relatively unconstrained by systemic factors. Political scientists Ellen Lust and David Waldner discuss and assess a hypothesis, attributed to Scott Mainwaring and Annibal Pérez-Liñán (generated by a statistical analysis of Latin American democracies) that democracy survives when political leaders seek moderate policies and have a normative preference for democracy.[13] Lust and Waldner observe, however, that this hypothesis does not 'account for the sources of elite preference'.[14] This, in my view, does not detract from the attractiveness of this theory, and does not undermine its negative implication: that democracy falls when a strong and dynamic leadership supplies a radical vision, and has no or low commitment to democratic principles. This is not to say that one should endorse excessive voluntarism and deny any role to structural determinants,[15] but rather that these structural factors often under-determine political phenomena, and the scope left by this under-determination is filled by the active role of political leaders and their enthusiastic followers.

This explanation belongs to what some political scientists call 'agentic theory' (defined in contrast to structural theories):

> In these theories, we lift the structural constraint so that political actors have a high degree of freedom of choice. We explain the outcome by reference to this relatively unconstrained choice or action; by calling an action or choice contingent, we assume that it could feasibly have been otherwise, given the sum total of external conditions.[16]

As Lust and Waldner further explain, agentic theories focusing on the role of political leadership 'imply causal interventions that are short term, directed at the supply side, and institutional', that is, where (1) changes occur almost immediately rather than in the long term, (2) causes are connected with the leadership 'supplying' political reforms (rather than to citizens demanding reforms), and (3) interventions directly shape political institutions (rather than operating via background factors, such as the economy or the cultural system).[17] With the proviso that all three distinctions allow judgments of degree rather than either/or alternatives, this 'supply-side' account befits the political leadership of Jarosław Kaczyński as an explanatory factor for anti-constitutional populist backsliding in Poland. The combination of a radical normative vision with a low commitment to constitutional democracy produces leadership that initiates and then perpetuates anti-constitutional backsliding.

But surely, to secure popular support for his paranoid politics, Kaczyński must have identified some real societal anxieties and concerns? In any comprehensive account, there is room for supply-side and demand-side analyses. Even if a leader skilfully supplies certain ideas, s/he will not be effective without strong predispositions on the part of the audience to accept them. Bart Bonikowski describes this source of populist success as 'resonance—that is, congruence between the content of the message and the predispositions of the audience' explaining 'a social movement's ability to mobilize supporters around the movement's core message'.[18] On the demand side, there is a process of crystallizing various concerns and fears around the slogans and ideas provided by a populist leader. This description by Bonikowski is worth citing in full as it describes the demand-side process of the populist phenomenon well:

> [It is] a process whereby populist, ethno-nationalist and authoritarian discourse leads those in the target public to connect their experiences (e.g., fears associated with social, cultural, and economic changes) with their pre-existing beliefs (e.g., ethno-nationalism, distrust of elites, scepticism toward democratic institutions), and to support candidates that offer radical solutions to the resulting problems (i.e., minorities, immigrants and politicians being jointly responsible for undesirable social changes).[19]

Sources of the Emergence of Effective Populism

Effective populism—that is, populism that attains power, as in Poland and Hungary, rather than populism that strives for power, as is the case of Marine Le Pen in France or Geert Wilders in the Netherlands—owes its success to the fact that it has managed to combine at least two of the following items on the checklist of contemporary populism's sources of appeal, and managed to seduce a large number of people into believing that those beliefs and concerns cohere into a complete package, capable of being articulated in very simple, attractive catchphrases:

- the sense of economic insecurity with a resultant loss of social cohesion
- xenophobic attitudes towards 'others', in particular migrants and refugees
- resentment towards globalization, internationalism, and a renewed support of nationalism (economic and other)
- cultural and religious resentment, expressed in a distrust of 'political correctness' and multicultural tolerance
- disenchantment with the current political elite and with the 'establishment', combined with the perception that the establishment is arrogant, remote, and insensitive to the needs of 'real people'
- impatience with liberal constraints on government, with checks and balances viewed as an institutional obstacle to 'getting things done' and to the expression of the will of the people.

Varieties of contemporary populisms may be viewed as usually resulting from different combinations of two or more of those sources of populist resentment, and the specific repertoire is country-dependent. In Poland all six have been salient in public culture to a degree, but Kaczyński's success is due to an effective combination of (2), (5), and (6) in particular (as well as a significant presence of (4), but only residual amounts of (1) and (3)).

Let me begin with the two factors that, I claim, had only a minimal effect on the success of PiS in 2015. Regarding factor (1), that is, an increased sense of economic insecurity and resultant decline in social cohesion: prima facie, such a hypothesis would be vindicated by a correlation between support for PiS and the voter's place in lower economic positions, often having been threatened by further relative deprivation. Indeed, in the first decade of the twenty-first century, party divisions in Poland have become more and more correlated with class and strata divisions. This is clear in respect of educational status (an important class indicator in Poland): only 9 per cent of PO voters finished their schooling at elementary level with 38 per cent going on to higher (university) education, but in the case of PiS voters, 25 per cent of voters have only an elementary education and 20 per cent have a higher education. Another dividing factor is between urban and country residence: 35 per cent of the PO electorate live in large cities, while only 19 per cent of the PiS electorate are big-city dwellers. PiS has the largest percentage of low-income earners: 60 per cent of PiS voters earn the lowest income (1,000 PLN or EUR 240 per month, per capita). Some 60 per cent of entrepreneurs declare a fear/concern that PiS will continue in government, and not one of them declares any fear related to a hypothetical return to power of the PO. These divisions tend to increase so it is fair to say that the main party schisms in Poland now roughly overlap with class divisions.[20]

However, it does not follow from this data that the electoral victory of PiS was largely due to a sense of economic insecurity. For instance, a large number of PiS voters were peasants (which also correlates with the variables of non-city dwellers and a lower educational status, as mentioned), and yet this social group is not overall plagued by a sense of economic insecurity, partly thanks to European Union (EU) agricultural subsidies. More generally, the emergence of ruling populism in Poland did *not* come as a result of economic crisis, but rather *despite* continued economic prosperity, and in that sense Poland may be seen as a counter-example to the conventional wisdom that anti-democratic reversals tend to come in periods of economic recession, while a high level of economic development reduces the risk of authoritarian reversals.[21] (Note, however, that as a general rule a correlation between high economic performance and low likelihood of democratic reversals applies uncontroversially only to coups d'état, not to anti-democratic reversals caused by the democratically elected incumbents unconstitutionally broadening their powers.)[22] Over the decade preceding PiS coming to power, unemployment systematically declined (in 2007, 15.1 per cent while in 2015, 10.2 per cent), real wages grew (over the decade up to 2015 by a hefty 50 per cent), and economic inequality began to decline after reaching its peak in 2005 (in 2011, the Gini coefficient was 31.1, hence very close to the European median of 30.7). The differences in standards of living between Poland and Western Europe became smaller: in 2005 the purchasing power of median salary in Poland was 46 per cent of that in France and 50 per cent of that in Spain, while in 2015 it was respectively 64 and 77 per cent.[23]

So while aspirations grew faster than the economic capacity to satisfy them, as is usually the case, real material conditions were far from catastrophic. In this sense, Polish populism may only be a partial vindication for the sociological theory that views the universal growth of populism as based on status anxiety by those (usually white uneducated men) who see themselves as economically underprivileged and at the same time (and relatedly) feel culturally distant from the dominant groups in society, and disapprove of such causes as multiculturalism, feminism, or the green movement.[24] As Noam Gidron and Peter Hall claim, the relative decline in the subjective social status of a group whose economic situation has deteriorated the most generates concerns that lead them to support parties of the populist right and reject the traditional political establishment. In Poland, however, while the 'cultural' segment of this syndrome seems to apply to the PiS electorate, the socio-economic part of it is less obvious. PiS voters have a sense of distance from the cultural values of the liberal elite, and in particular they feel anxiety related to immigration and multiculturalism, and this sense is not clearly correlated with their relative socio-economic deprivation. The anxieties and concerns of PiS voters are generated largely by their concerns about 'others', but not because those people are likely to take their jobs and wealth, but rather because they may impart unwanted cultural meanings to Polish collective life.

Regarding the other factor in my catalogue of populism-inducing structural factors that I claim only played a minimal role in Poland, namely factor (3) (anti-globalism and growth of nationalism), Poland is consistently among the most EU-enthusiastic societies in the EU. Immediately after the Brexit referendum, some 77 per cent of Poles were in favour of continued membership while only 16 per cent were against,[25] although pollsters claim that this enthusiasm is quite shallow and superficial, and quickly recedes when the polled person is asked questions relating to refugees. Over a third of Poles believe that EU membership places excessive restrictions on the sovereignty and independence of their state, while over half of Poles are of the opposite opinion.[26] This certainly does not show that Polish society became 'Eurosceptic', but does at least show that there is significant division on the value of integration within the EU, as it is now constituted. A report published by a renowned think-tank in January 2017 noted that the social consensus regarding the EU has all but collapsed: while there is still a large consensus (of about 80 per cent) on membership alone, it is no longer significant in the light of 'profound divisions in Polish society concerning various questions connected to the EU'.[27] But while nationalism is without any doubt an important part of PiS philosophy, as evidenced, inter alia, by frequent references to national pride, the need to defend the good name of Poland and the use of nationalistic rituals and slogans, the anti-EU aspect of nationalistic feelings present in many European societies has a rather low salience in Poland. In addition, the version of anti-globalism, which elsewhere (especially, in the United States) is reflected in anger at 'exporting jobs' to low-wage countries, or at powers of transnational corporations, has hardly registered in Polish public life so far. Specifically, it has not been visible in the PiS electoral programme, and has not moved PiS supporters to consolidate around that party.

Anti-globalism has to be distinguished from xenophobic attitudes (factor (2)) which were skilfully stimulated by PiS in the wake of the refugee crisis in Europe: the influx of migrants and refugees from Africa and the Middle East in 2015 was a God-given gift for Kaczyński who could stir up anti-migrant (often racist) attitudes in an ethnically and religiously homogenous Poland.[28] In the most infamous, but not atypical, philippic against admitting refugees, Jarosław Kaczyński warned that they would bring in various 'parasites' to which 'these people' are immune, but which may be deadly to their Polish hosts.[29] Analogy between this rhetoric and the language of Nazi propaganda in occupied Poland (claiming the Jews were bearers of typhoid and lice) was not lost on Polish critics of PiS.[30] Anti-immigrant impulses were inextricably related to racially tinged and anti-Muslim concerns.[31] The sense of self-esteem and dignity became somewhat perversely founded on the sense of superiority to those over whom we can for once exercise power, even if only by saying 'no' to their desperate pleas for admission to a safe place. Drawing national, cultural, and religious boundaries between 'us' and 'them' helped to exploit the fear of otherness and sustain a sense of self-esteem.

This is not an unusual combination. As Noam Gidron and Peter Hall report, there is some evidence that, for instance, 'men in the French and American working classes sustain their sense of dignity or status, in part, by drawing sharp boundaries between themselves and North African migrants or African Americans'.[32] How the inhumane resistance to accepting even a limited number of children and women from war-stricken Syria could have, in Poland, been squared with Christian benevolence and love in a nation where over 90 per cent identify themselves as Christians is an intriguing question, which is outside the bounds of this chapter. But it worked, partly thanks to the connection successfully drawn by government propaganda between being Muslim and being a terrorist; opinion polls found that '[t]he overwhelming majority of Poles connect Muslims with terrorism'.[33] As sociologist Maciej Gdula, reporting on his interviews with PiS supporters said, 'When it applies to strangers, the impulses of empathy are suspended and the language used unpleasantly resembles a liberal laissez-faire philosophy'.[34] He further explains that one of Kaczyński's sources of success is that he gave many people of lower ranks a sense of importance based on their superiority and strength by comparison with vulnerable others, as well as a sense of community 'the members of which are equal in their distinction from elites and from strangers'.[35]

This is combined with a sense that one's group (and not only oneself individually) is threatened in its dignity and self-respect by allegedly excessive concern for traditionally despised groups or, what comes to the same in this constellation of concerns, immigrants. This attitude is well summarized (though not with respect to Poland) by Bonikowski:

> The combined effects of economic, cultural, and social changes are perceived as impinging on the life chances, dignity and moral commitments of in-group members, who perceive themselves as increasingly sidelined by elites and mainstream culture and who view members of other groups as having been granted unfair advantages in society, often by those same vilified elites.[36]

By opposing the concern for the others, PiS restores (though in a perverse way) a sense of dignity and self-respect to those of their supporters who may acquire a sense of power and superiority from saying 'no' to immigrants.

Anti-establishment sentiments (factor (5)) were facilitated by a certain fatigue displayed by the PO by the end of its second term; by some embarrassing though not too odious corruption or quasi-corruption scandals; by the PO's ecumenical approach to ideology (stretching from left liberalism to traditionalist conservatism), which was initially its strength, but eventually came to be seen (correctly) as unprincipled pragmatism; and by a particularly inept, lethargic, and arrogant electoral campaign by President Komorowski in 2015. Two Polish political scientists, otherwise critical of PiS, wrote about 'Komorowski's "emotional-intelligence gap" and indifference to voter sentiments'.[37] What's more, there is a clear, even if somewhat ironic (because the two target groups seem at the antipodes of social status) link between anti-elite and anti-immigrant passions. The incumbent elite are seen not only as arrogant and corrupt, but at the same time so cosmopolitan and anti-national that they are willing, for whatever reasons (to allay their own sense of guilt?) to let in masses of migrants and thus dilute the sense of nation-based unity and community. In the end, both groups are strangers to the common folk; they are 'them' rather than 'us'.

In Stephen Holmes's description of elections bringing (or consolidating) populists to power, '[p]opulist voters, feeling ignored and victimized go to the polls to avenge themselves symbolically against out-of-touch elite and under-the-radar immigrants. Collective solutions to shared problems are not on their agenda.'[38] And elsewhere in the same essay Holmes adds:

> By clamoring against inner enemies, … [populist leaders] can channel voters' frustration and resentment away from themselves and toward two eminently targetable social groups: those who endorse liberal-humanitarian values as a matter of principle and those who benefit personally and concretely from a liberal *Wilkommenskultur*.[39]

This is a mechanism that was shrewdly if cynically employed by Jarosław Kaczyński, both before and after the 2015 elections, with the consequence that, among other things, Polish streets became highly dangerous to persons with darker skin colour, and newspapers described elementary schools in which some children of migrants were bullied and scolded by their peers as 'terrorists'. Holmes's graphic footnote to the last-quoted sentence applied unfortunately to Poland as well: 'After the leader "names the inner enemy", his most zealous private followers can take matters into their own hands, sending death threats to outspoken critics and stabbing unloved minorities on the street.'[40] When the large photos of six PO Euro-MPs who voted in Brussels for activation of Article 7 against Poland were symbolically placed on the gallows by ultra-nationalists in Katowice in November 2017,[41] or when students from Middle East or India were beaten up by nationalist gangs,[42] Holmes's prediction was vindicated.

Illiberal impatience (factor (6)) was best reflected in the notion of legal or constitutional 'impossibilism', a term coined by PiS leaders (mainly Jarosław Kaczyński) and meant to signify the obstacles and barriers that law erects, disingenuously, in order to render it impossible to carry out necessary and desirable reforms. Professor Jerzy Zajadło, a leading Polish liberal constitutional scholar and legal philosopher, notes an anachronistic character to the concept because it is an 'attempt … to undermine a progressive process of challenging the idea of legislative omnipotence'.[43] Paul Blokker describes this trait of populism as 'legal skepticism' which means that 'populists are wary of the institutions of and limits of liberal constitutionalism'.[44] But note that not all contemporary movements described as 'populist' necessarily espouse that form of legal scepticism; for instance, the pro-Brexit movement in the UK was not, by and large, critical of constitutional checks and balances.[45] In Poland, however, this factor played an important role in PiS rhetoric before and after the 2015 elections, and in particular was reflected in frequent references to the 'sovereign's will', which was meant to underlie an unrestrained majoritarianism.

Explaining how xenophobia, anti-establishmentarism, and illiberalism could have come together in a single package (for they do not necessarily imply one another) is key to a compelling story about the sources of Kaczyński's seduction of a significant segment of the Polish electorate. Internal coherence is not necessarily a virtue for which populists are known. Consider this account by a US journalist of the sources of Trump's success:

> Donald Trump's campaign was massively fuelled by racism and xenophobia. But racism and hatred and fear of foreigners were not irreconcilable with hatred of the arrogant establishment that controlled major-party politics. Many voters out there hated both, and some hated those latter folks with the heat of a thousand suns.[46]

Substitute in this passage Donald Trump for Jarosław Kaczyński, remove 'major party politics' with 'ruling coalition parties', and concretize 'racism' as 'anti-Islamism'—and you get a good account of PiS's social sources of victory. Internal coherence and credibility are not self-evident: after all, it may seem difficult to raise the spectre of Islam when there are no Muslims, to attack the establishment if you have been part of it for the entire history of democratic Poland, and to assault the very constitution that brought you to power. And yet PiS's appeal to so many voters hinged upon successfully (in the eyes of many voters, though not necessarily under some ideal standards of coherence) combining the three into a single story, which could identify the sources of legitimate anxiety as well as the ways out.

The next point about the sources of PiS's electoral success is the simplest: it has to do with the distorting effect of the Polish electoral system. Kaczyński's party won an absolute parliamentary majority allowing it to independently form government, with only 38 per cent of those voting—this is a substantial plurality but not a majority of voters. Whatever alternatives there are, and each has its defects, this fact speaks to the imperfections of the parliamentary/party/electoral system. Due to the inability of smaller parties (mainly on the left) to come to terms with the need to form effective and persuasive coalitions or party mergers, some 15 per cent of all voters saw their votes 'wasted'—their preferred parties did not make it to Parliament. This 15 per cent segment of 'wasted votes' (including the 11 per cent received by left-wing parties[47]) was decisive for Kaczyński's success, as he benefited greatly from the absence of the left in Parliament. If even a fraction of the 15 per cent of votes had translated into parliamentary parties (and with a 5 per cent threshold for a party, there is no reason why they could not), these parties would be natural coalition partners for the PO and other non-PiS parties (Nowoczesna, the Polish Peasants' Party (*Polskie Stronnictwo Ludowe* (PSL)), etc.). It is of course wrong to say that the electoral system had been designed in such a way as to specifically favour PiS, but one has to be aware that because of the Polish combination of PR and majoritarian system of vote-counting in the Sejm, and majoritarianism with single seat districts in the Senate, large parties enjoy a disproportionate 'bonus', both in terms of seats in Parliament and in terms of very high subsidies from the budget.

In addition, it has to be said that PiS had not revealed all its plans (if there *were* such plans) during the election campaign: there was never any blueprint about the Constitutional Tribunal (CT), regular courts, prosecutor's office etc. disclosed, beyond very vague statements about the need for a 'good change'. (In this, it may be added, it followed in the footsteps of its role model, Hungarian Fidesz, where the campaign in the momentous election of 2010 was run as a 'normal election', with no pledges of fundamental constitutional changes, which actually followed soon after Orbán's victory.)[48] Furthermore, in the last months of the campaign the 'hawks' in the PiS establishment, such as Antoni Macierewicz, were almost hidden from public view, and even Kaczyński made himself rather scarce, especially as he was not running for any of the highest official positions, while apparent moderates played a key role in the campaign. In this way, PiS represented itself as a 'normal' party, acting within the generally accepted democratic rules of the game, nicely distinguishable from the corruption-ridden (as the PiS propaganda maintained) PO and its allies. This trick with putting on a moderate and reasonable face was often accompanied by plain lies; in the eleventh hour of the campaign Beata Szydło (who ran as a candidate for the prime minister's position) declared, when pressed by a journalist, that the apparently moderate intellectual, Jarosław Gowin, would be her minister for defence. This was in response to a press speculation that Antoni Macierewicz (a generally disliked, radical politician, whose extreme views scared many PiS supporters except for the most radical ones) would be her minister of defence. Szydło's was an outright lie: Gowin had never been groomed by PiS for that position and, immediately after the electoral victory, he became minister for higher education, while Macierewicz became minister of defence. The speculations proved correct, but they were inconvenient to PiS during the campaign. This shows that the voters did not exactly get what they voted for in 2015.

The last factor that needs to be mentioned is that the incumbents ran a pathetically bad electoral campaign in 2015, both in the parliamentary and especially the presidential elections. The PO has shown signs of exhaustion after two terms in office, especially when its successful and politically shrewd leader (and founder) Donald Tusk left Poland in August 2014 to take up a top EU job (as president of the European Council). This was preceded by leaks of illegal recordings of private conversations between top officials, which exposed them as using vulgarities and contemplating questionable deals—not a scandal of major proportions, but low-level corruption, very skilfully exploited by PiS opposition and pro-PiS media (as Timothy Snyder notes correctly in the context of the Polish tape scandal of 2014, '[i]t is a rare politician who can survive his constituents knowing how he orders food or tells jokes'[49]—and PO politicians taped in a Warsaw restaurant were no exception). In making themselves so vulnerable to secret recording, the PO leaders' lamentable judgment and sense of arrogance was revealed, inexcusable for a democratic politician who should know better and be aware of the tabloids' thirst for such leaks.[50]

In the presidential office, Bronisław Komorowski assumed arrogantly that he needed no electoral campaign because his achievements would speak for themselves. In contrast to the buoyant, energetic, and power-hungry Andrzej Duda, Komorowski and the PO looked like they were surrendering any serious claim to re-election. Suddenly, in the eyes of many voters, traditional cultural roles were reversed: a liberal-cosmopolitan PO seemed to run out of steam while the conservative and lower-to-medium class PiS came to be seen as a carrier of dynamism and change. But of course in populism, this is the normal course of events.

Sources of Populism's Persistence

The sources of populist *victory* in Poland have to be distinguished from the sources of PiS's *continuing popularity* among the electorate. After all, the anti-establishmentarian, anti-elitist engine can last only so long; populists in power themselves become part of the 'establishment' and the 'elite', and an over-use of the anti-elitist tool may turn out to be counterproductive to them. Also, other negative motives—xenophobia and distrust towards liberal checks and balances—have limited benefits for the populist ruling party. Xenophobia's appeal is reduced by the fact that the government, true to its promises, resists admitting even a token number of refugees, so they stop figuring high in the public imagination; liberal checks and balances are no longer seen as an obstacle to effective governance as they become progressively dismantled or used by the ruling party by way of staffing institutions with its own cadres. This is not to say that these factors do not play any role—they do, and they have been skilfully upheld by governmental propaganda. But their usefulness is limited, and they have to be replaced or accompanied by other sources of appeal for the maintenance of public support for populists in power.

The main sources of persistent support (which after the elections and up to the time of completing this book, in late 2018, has vacillated around 35–44 per cent) are as follows.

First, the delivery of new welfare benefits. The programme known as '500+' (providing each family a monthly stipend of PLN 500, or EUR 120, per month for each child after the firstborn), with 2 million families as its beneficiaries, was ingenious in its simplicity. This is a typical instance of pork-barrel politics, employed with great shrewdness by PiS. While various benefits 'in kind' may be much more economically rational (free preschool facilities, improvement of public schools, public transport and infrastructure aimed at disadvantaged regions and groups, and in particular improvement in health services), their effects are delayed in time and are less tangible. In contrast, giving cash to every family with more than one child, no conditions attached, is instantly attractive; for instance, in a low-income family of three children or more, it may translate into a doubling of the family income. For many poorer families, it is a very significant injection of cash, and the prospect that PiS's electoral defeat may mean the end to this influx of money gives PiS a huge edge over the opposition (especially since the PO's promises to maintain and even increase the programme after its future victory do not sound credible).

These big social transfers are presented by PiS, and seen by its supporters, as a huge act of social justice and as recognition of the legitimate claims of people who felt harmed and humiliated by the post-1989 transformation—either in reality, or as an effect of skilful PiS anti-elite propaganda. Early criticism of the programme by the opposition and the liberal media who represented it as a massive bribe only helped to strengthen the perception that it is only PiS that understands, empathizes with, and helps ordinary people. The carefully cultivated image of PiS as a 'socially sensitive' party was partly shattered in April/May 2018 when the party demonstrated a cruel insensitivity to a strike, held on the premises of the Sejm, by carers of persons with disabilities: the government steadfastly refused to give in to most of their demands, and some officials even used offensive language to describe the protesters. The contrast between the manifest 'generosity' of child subsidies and insensitivity towards persons with disabilities may have been due to the fact that the latter—and their carers—offered a negligible dividend in terms of votes.

Second, PiS is viewed, partly correctly, as a party that fulfils its promises, and in the social sphere it indeed does: the '500+' handout; the lowering of the retirement age (thus undoing a major, politically costly though economically justified PO reform, and thereby winning a sizeable group of pre-retirement age voters); energetic and spectacular actions to protect tenants in recently 'reprivatized' buildings; legislative action aimed at a ban on Sunday trading presented by governmental propaganda less as religiously driven and more as a protection for underpaid personnel in the commerce industry. These and similar actions show the electorate that PiS is on the side of 'ordinary people'. Even if some reforms are clearly misplaced and hugely controversial (secondary education reform or health service changes), they all tend to support PiS's image as a 'can do' party, the perception of which is facilitated by a general economic boom, which has been largely externally driven. Much of the malaise in society under the former ruling elite was not about the *democratic* qualities of the state (which largely matched the European standards) but rather about its relative inefficiency in delivering important public goods, such as affordable housing, public health, labour rights (a notorious privileging of short-term contracts virtually with no guarantees for the employees), quality public schools, and quality media. As a result of Tusk's antipathy to a tax aimed at supporting public media, the main source of financing came from advertising, which led to competition with commercial media in pursuit of ratings, and the drastic lowering of standards.

That is why PiS's positioning to address these problems, even if wasteful and economically irrational in the long term, positively contrasts with the record of the PO in these fields in the short term,[51] all the more so since it is being rationalized by the government and its supporters in 'dignitarian' terms. Many non-ideological supporters of the PO became disgruntled by the end of its second term in office, and had good reasons to turn away from the party, which promised modernity but failed to deliver quality public goods such as just listed. The accompanying assault on institutional checks and balances, and in particular on the CT and the judiciary, is seen as an abstract issue, one that does not affect individuals directly, especially if the ostensible targets of the assaults are often viewed with scepticism and distrust; the institutions of democracy seem remote and aimed at the benefit of the ruling elite. Propaganda depicts anti-PiS protesters as beneficiaries of the former ruling system, frustrated by the loss of undeserved advantages. As Jarosław Kaczyński said, signalling this line of argument: 'In short, we are seeing a revolt against the fact that we are simply taking away the money that the elites had looted and divided up somehow.'[52]

The third factor is the effectiveness of relentless propaganda, especially on public TV which in some areas of Poland has no competition due to its superior territorial coverage. Propaganda, of course, further alienates opponents of PiS but that does not matter: its function is to consolidate its supporters, and to enhance their hatred towards PiS opponents. As long as that hatred is stronger and more widespread than the dislike of PiS by its opponents, propaganda performs its function. The PiS faithful cling to Kaczyński because they are confident that his critics are much worse. And it is not mere hatred but also fear: the propaganda machine presents the opposition as not only evil but also as extremely dangerous (claiming that they would bring millions of Islamists into Poland; they are capable of masterminding an airplane clash; they conspire with Poland's enemies in order to keep it subordinate and impoverished, etc.). There have not been, to my knowledge, any credible sociological studies of the actual effectiveness of governmental propaganda in Poland, but anecdotal evidence suggests that it has some effect, especially in consolidating the support for PiS among those undecided or only weakly predisposed to support PiS.

Fourth, and connected to the previous point, PiS unscrupulously appeals to negative emotions in the collective social psyche: fear (of 'others'), envy (of the 'elite'), resentment (based on a sense, quite justifiably, that democratic and market transformation resulted in disregard for the net losers, i.e. the relatively deprived groups), and anger (PiS's political rivals are treacherous, anti-Polish, non-patriotic, and even murderous).[53] These emotions are usually much stronger than positive emotions, and this particularly applies to anxiety, fear, anger, and hatred, because, in contrast to positive emotions (such as solidarity or empathy) they seem to raise quite basic existential concerns. All four were skilfully exploited by PiS not only to foment support for itself, but mainly to spread dislike of the opposition and disgust towards out-groups, such as prospective immigrants. That is why the opposition also feels compelled to appeal to negative emotions (being 'anti-PiS' as the only unifying ideology of the opposition) and in effect a downward spiral ensues in the political culture of public debate. But in this race to the bottom, PiS wins hands down: liberals and the left in Poland are much less effective at using negative emotions than the right-wing populists are. At the same time, PiS's arguments, addressed to 'ordinary Poles', tired of cosmopolitan liberal elite, have a certain appeal based on flattery: there is nothing wrong (they are being told) with being anti-refugee or anti-Islamic. In fact, these attitudes may be a basis for pride because they reflect a sense of identity and commitment to one's nation.

This connects with the fifth factor: an unprecedented level of political polarization in Poland. This polarization is to a large degree generated by the two previous factors: relentless propaganda and manipulation of social fears and hatreds. But of course Poland was already highly polarized when PiS came to power, and PiS further aggravated divisions in Polish society. It is a plausible theory in political science that the higher the degree of polarization, the higher the support for incumbents bent on undemocratic transformation, even by those voters who are initially committed to the general principle of democracy. In addressing the question of why voters who routinely profess pro-democratic values simultaneously support incumbents intent on subverting democracy, Milan Svolik, a political scientist at Yale University, answers that when voters are highly partisan in their policy preferences, they are more willing to accept non-democratic practices and reforms by incumbents as long as they expect their partisan interests to thereby be furthered.[54] This is the case even where those voters express a strong preference for democratic government or democratic norms. By contrast, an electorate with a high percentage of centrists is more likely to react negatively to incumbents who introduce non-democratic reforms, and to vote them out of office, because their attachment to particular policies or interests is weaker than their commitment to democratic norms.

While Svolik provides support for his thesis mainly from Venezuela at the peak of Chavez's rule, a high tolerance for 'the gradual subversion of democracy by an initially democratically elected incumbent'[55] is an attitude characteristic of many PiS supporters, who are prepared to look the other way, or downplay assaults on checks and balances, considering it the necessary and proper price to pay for blocking the return of the despised PO to power. The Faustian choice between PiS, democratically objectionable but appealing by virtue of its policies, and the PO, politically disliked though enjoying strong democratic credentials, in a situation of high polarization is for many PiS supporters a no-brainer. This is especially since the act of withdrawal of loyalty to a party for which a person only a few years ago voted is an act that often comes with a moral and psychological cost to the voter. People sometimes tend to stick to the political preferences expressed in their recent votes because they do not like to admit to themselves that they were wrong or, worse, they were duped.

The sixth factor is the weakness and precariousness of institutions, and unreliability of 'veto points' such as bicameralism, semi-presidentialism, judicial review, and decentralization. None of the four potential veto points just listed turned out to be effective in Poland. The Senate, as a 'chamber of reflection' was meant to put a brake on the laws produced by the lower chamber, but when dominated by the same party as the Sejm, became a rubber stamp. Semi-presidentialism contributed very few meaningful vetoes to the legislative production. Judicial review was easily dismantled, as evidenced earlier in this book (Chapter 3). Decentralization, lacking strong constitutional entrenchment, and a political will to support local authorities, fell victim to centralization tendencies, mainly in the fiscal field. Part of the weakness was the mere newness of democratic institutions: 'political scientists have found that the sheer amount of time that a democracy has existed is positively related to its chances for survival'.[56] The younger a democratic system is, the more likely it is to collapse or backslide.

That durability is a good predictor of resistance to non-democratic change is natural. Institutions, whether parliaments, constitutional courts, electoral commissions, central banks or political parties, take time to shape their roles and responsibilities, to develop habits and conventions, to win societal support and legitimacy for itself, to establish 'institutional memories', to overcome volatility by showing positive trends in a *longue durée*, in a word—to consolidate.[57] 'Durable, independent, and confident state institutions are more likely to be able to withstand and resist capture than newer, dependent, and insecure institutions'[58]—these words by Noah Feldman ring true, and additionally, they (correctly) imply that the factor of longevity of institutions may be primary, in that it supports and enhances their independence and sense of confidence. The process of acculturation to legal and cultural norms that underlie those institutions may take time, and these norms are not only about specific institutional tasks, but also about second-order values such as regularity, independence, and transparency. Here, the human factor turns out to be crucial: when there are not enough people sufficiently committed to defending and respecting institutions, no institutional design is immune to attack, however pluralistic and equipped with veto points and defences.

Institutional Design and the 'Human Factor': General Observations Occasioned by the Case of Poland

No institution is *absolutely* resilient. As Aziz Huq and Tom Ginsburg say in relation to the United States:

> The decisions of party leaders and activists on both sides to prioritize the continuance of democracy as an ongoing concern, and their willingness to allow transient policy triumphs to offset concerns about antidemocratic behavior, will be of dispositive importance ... Constitutions are, after all, just pieces of paper that take their force from the intersubjective understandings of elites and citizens. It is this quality that leads us to suggest that the current moment may be a dangerous one, and to identify public support for the norms and conventions pf democratic politics as the critical factor.[59]

But the human factor is all the more significant in new, transitional democracies, where there was simply a shorter time in which people had the opportunity to become convinced about the advantages of democracy; democracy is stable when its citizens believe that it is 'the only game in town' and that non-democratic alternatives are illegitimate.[60]

This is not to suggest that the shape and design of institutions do not matter: there are ways of prompting, and ways of minimizing the need for, inter-party dialogue and compromise through institutional design. As Jeremy Waldron notes, with regard to the United States: 'The constitutional structure—bicameralism, the president's veto, advice-and-consent, and perhaps also judicial review—means that any party "in power" has to coordinate and usually compromise with leaders of other persuasions.'[61] These and other factors of institutional design (notably, federalism) constitute jointly what Samuel Issacharoff calls 'the structural dimensions of democratic stability,'[62] such as districted elections and presidential rather than parliamentary governance.[63] Admittedly, most of the elements of election-related design and presidentialism constitute buffers against marginal extremist parties rather than against an authoritarian movement coming to power with support of the majority or large plurality of the electorate. But one can argue that the fragmentation of the political system and large number of veto points effectively restrains democratically elected authoritarians from spreading control over the entire political system.

More specifically, the institutional design of constitutional review may be made more or less conductive to manipulation and paralysis by the executive. For instance, a system of electing constitutional court judges may be made better or worse, and the Polish/Hungarian system is bad because the parliamentary winner can appoint all the judges to vacancies that become open during the parliamentary term, so that the compromise-oriented election of judges depends largely on the political culture and goodwill of the ruling party/parties rather than being compelled by institutions, as is the case in Germany, for instance. The centralized, Kelsenian review, with a single constitutional court enjoying a monopoly on the constitutional scrutiny of statutes, for all its benefits, has a major weakness: it is much more capable of being captured and disarmed than a decentralized, diffuse system of review where every judge in the nation has a right to set aside a statute s/he considers unconstitutional. Just as it is easier to attack and neutralize a staff composed of ten or fifteen generals than the entire army, so is it easier to disable a small constitutional court and turn it into an ally of an autocrat. Some constitutional courts were set up precisely for that reason: to make them easy to control by the executive (e.g. the case of the 1982 Turkish Constitution which adopted, as dictated by the military, a centralized judicial review). This was not the case of the Polish CT at its inception (it was decidedly not a shrewd trick by an autocratic government, as in Turkey 1982), but it *was* the case of Polish CT at the point of its paralysis in 2015–16. The transformation of the CT by PiS in these years, first by disabling it and then by turning it into an ally of the government, confirms a general observation by Tamir Moustafa and Tom Ginsburg that

> a regime can constrain judges more effectively by imposing a centralised structure of judicial review in place of a decentralised structure. Centralised review yields fewer judges who must be bargained with, co-opted, or contained, resulting in predictable relationships with known individuals.[64]

Nevertheless, no matter how well designed the system is, it will not protect itself against a dishonest president 'appointing' improperly elected 'judges', and the executive refusing to comply with judgments: 'constitutional enforcement requires the kind of intersubjective agreement on violations that is difficult to obtain, especially under mutative and precarious political conditions'.[65] The test for the resilience of institutions is whether powerful officials back down when those institutions issue decisions that officials dislike or even abhor, as was the case of President Nixon having to hand over audiotapes in connection with the Watergate scandal, as ordered by the Supreme Court (SC); or President Trump having to comply with the US District Court in the state of Washington regarding proposed travel bans, and more generally, federal courts having struck down or stayed his administration's immigration policies or 'sanctuary cities'; or when the UK SC told the government of Theresa May that it could not appeal to the Brexit referendum to sidestep parliamentary mechanisms of unwinding Britain's membership in the EU. Often, the effectiveness of enforcement of law towards the top executive is based on the likelihood of legal sanctions for recalcitrance: for instance, in the case of Nixon, it was clear to almost everyone that if he defied the judicial order in the tapes case, 'impeachment and conviction almost surely would have followed'.[66]

In other cases, the sanction may be expressed in terms of political costs. Adrian Vermeule, discussing a hypothetical scenario of a president breaching the (unwritten) norms of the independence of agencies (such as the president's Office of Legal Counsel), says that the professional norms of objectivity and detachment by the lawyers of the Office of Legal Counsel may support the relevant convention 'either by making such lawyers relatively resistant to pressure from the White House, or in the extreme case causing them to resign (or credibly threaten to resign) in a visible and politically damaging fashion'.[67] But the force of such predictions, either of the likelihood of impeachment, or of mass resignation by officials to protest the president's breaches, is a contingent matter. In other cases, such second-guessing is less reliable (as, arguably, is the case of President Trump) and yet the strength of pressure and of public expectations is such that the president complies with the court order. This is of course the most dramatic test for institutional resilience, and often the frontal confrontation between two institutions does not take place: resilience may be measured by whether the (judicial) institution succumbs to political pressure (usually, from the executive) by taking the decisions the executive wants, and whether it succumbs to blackmail, hateful speech and insinuations, threats of a financial or other nature against individual judges, etc. Constitutional review increases the political costs of non-compliance, and in some systems, these costs are viewed as prohibitively high for politicians to bear. But in others, they are low enough for determined executives who view them just as minor irritants that may be set aside for political aims. Politicians such as Viktor Orbán or Jarosław Kaczyński either dismantle or hollow out the institutions that offer resistance to their plans. Legislatures are dissolved or subordinated to the leader's views, courts are dismissed or packed with party loyalists, constitutional rights are interpreted out of existence. Constitutional constraints on the rulers are reduced to 'parchment barriers', to use James Madison's memorable words.[68]

Fragility of Institutions

The restraining effect of strong and resilient political institutions on a would-be populist leader is encapsulated in the colourful if irreverent metaphor regarding President Trump and the US democratic system:

> Having survived for two hundred and forty-two years, American democracy is more like a stoutly built ocean liner, with a maniac at the helm who seems intent on capsizing it ... So far, some members of the ship's crew—judges, public servants, and the odd elected official—have managed to rush in, jag the tiller back, and keep the ship afloat.[69]

But what if the ship is not a 'stoutly built ocean liner' but a small and defective dinghy? With a devoted 'maniac' at the helm, the danger facing the vessel and its passengers will greatly increase. Madison and his fellow Founding Fathers designed a system in which, as they hoped, the 'parchment barriers' would be converted into effective constraints on rulers: federalism and checks and balances were to create, together, a set of mechanisms producing self-enforcement of the constitution, whereby the ambitions of some would counteract the ambitions of others.[70] No doubt, an institutional design may be made smarter or less ingenious in producing this effect. But institutions are not 'robust' or 'resilient' per se, without the actual will and determination of both the people staffing those institutions and stakeholders in society at large to defend and maintain them. There are no failsafe institutional designs to guarantee that constitutional norms and provisions will actually constrain recalcitrant politicians.

Especially in a democracy, the institutional system is often unable to deal with determined efforts to hollow out democratic institutions, and strong instruments of 'militant democracy' are viewed often, and with good reason, as suspect because the cure may be worse than the disease and, in the process, mechanisms may become more militant than democratic. And there may be *occasional* cases of justified executive non-compliance with law, as for instance when, in the run-up to the Civil War in 1861, Abraham Lincoln suspended the capacity of courts to issue writs of habeas corpus and defied the chief justice's decision based on a (reasonable) understanding of the US Constitution that only the Congress, not the president, could suspend habeas corpus in emergencies.[71] If such executive defiance can be judged illegal but morally legitimate,[72] or based on good underlying reasons behind the existing constitutional provisions, the reasons 'which remain, and we sometimes need to consult them to decide whether, in particular circumstances, they are so extraordinarily powerful or important that the law's trump should not prevail',[73] it is because it may be convincingly viewed as aiming at the preservation of the constitutional system as a whole, and as an extremely rare exception to the general norm of executive compliance with the law, as interpreted by courts.

No such justification can be even remotely provided for the cases of executive (and legislative) non-compliance with constitutional law in Poland, as documented earlier in the book (Chapters 3, 4, and 5). Duda is no Lincoln. Rather than disobeying the court on a specific provision in order to save the Republic (as admittedly, Lincoln did), President Duda's unconstitutional actions were aimed at the incremental dismantling of one piece of liberal constitutional democracy after another. None of them—whether the non-swearing-in of judges, or swearing-in of improperly elected judges, or signing one patently unconstitutional law after another—can reasonably be conceptualized as 'a very rare case in which the practical imperatives confronting the President morally justified his violation of constitutional law'.[74] Duda did not respond to, but created himself, the threat to the constitutional system as a whole, and constitutional breaches were not 'very rare' but routine in the first three years of his presidency.

One approach, flagged by David Strauss, would be to treat 'a systematic effort to undermine liberal democracy norms as a kind of emergency, in the way that, say, a natural disaster or a terrorist attack is an emergency'.[75] But as Strauss observes, there are two disanalogies. First, the determined effort at eroding liberal democracy is a 'slow motion emergency', in which the erosion is gradual, with each step being perhaps objectionable, but not alarming. Second, unlike the familiar types of emergency, a slow motion erosion requires not granting *more* power to government officials but rather requires the opposite: limiting their powers. 'Emergency' is therefore an unhelpful metaphor, and it is not useful when all governmental institutions, including courts, have *already* been captured or disabled, as is the case in Poland, with few exceptions (some individual SC judges, the Ombudsman).

When not all institutions have been captured in this way, however, perhaps the notion of 'institutional self-defence' may be more fittingly invoked. This concept was used and interestingly elaborated recently by Nicholas Barber who distinguished between institutions using 'shields' or 'swords' against other state bodies in order to protect themselves from other institutions.[76] Occasionally, Barber notes, an action by an institution 'runs contrary to the constitution', even if an institution (say, the president of the US who refuses to abide by a decision of the SC) can get away with it.[77] But this is the situation underplayed by Barber: his main interest is in a calculated friction between constitutional institutions, which is designed in order to track a certain 'valuable division of moral labour'.[78] Barber connects this idea with the 'invisible hand' theory of constitutionalism, where each institution 'fights for their own bit of the common good and, out of this conflict, the totality of the common good is achieved'.[79]

But, once articulated in this way, 'institutional self-defence' is not easily applicable to situations of existential threat to an institution, as was the case with the CT, National Council of the Judiciary (*Krajowa Rada Sądownictwa* (KRS)) or the SC in Poland. Consider one example of what can be considered as an 'institutional self-defence' undertaken by the CT which was compelled to act in a way that was problematic from a constitutional point of view. Case 34/15, decided on 3 December 2015, was a response to a series of actions undertaken by the new parliamentary majority to pack the tribunal with pro-PiS judges, in particular to the unconstitutional action (by Parliament and by the president) of an ex post invalidation of the election of three judges at the end of the previous parliamentary term—an invalidation made easier by a silly earlier gambit by the PO, which had attempted to elect five rather than three judges. In its judgment, the tribunal upheld the constitutionality of the law under which the three were elected, thus rendering unconstitutional the 'election' of three judges by PiS to the filled positions. At the time, the matter was of utmost existential importance for the CT, for reasons discussed at length in Chapter 3. But the judgment was only handed down because halfway through the deliberation, President of the Tribunal Andrzej Rzepliński decided that the decision would be taken by a five-judge panel, rather than by a full panel, as was initially considered (full panels are convened when the matter is deemed to be 'particularly important'). The 'downgrading' of the panel when the proceedings were already in course was done for a very simple reason: a full panel required nine judges, while at the time, when three judges elected by the end of the previous parliamentary term were not sworn in by the president, and three other judges had to recuse themselves (in an old-fashioned act of honesty and decency) because they had been consulted in the legislative work on the statute on the CT which was under scrutiny in that case, only eight judges were available. The alternative would be to fail to consider the matter altogether, and thus let PiS pack the court irregularly.

The choice by the president of the tribunal may be seen as an (ultimately unsuccessful) attempt at institutional self-defence *à la polonaise*. One institution (the CT) acted at the edges of constitutionality in order to protect itself against an assault by another institution (the legislature, supported by the executive). In this sense, it was existential self-defence, not a sort of constructive friction designed to maximize the common good, as in Barber's description. The latter is designed to describe an inter-institutional tension in *normal* times, not at the times in which the very existence of an independent institution is at stake.

So ultimately it is a matter of culture and ethics, and when they are missing, even the best designed institutions will be rendered hollow; in contrast, when they are strongly engrained in the professional group staffing the institutions, they are likely to prevail over determined populists. Consider this hypothetical by a US legal scholar about a possible attack by President Trump on freedom of speech and the press in order to silence his critics:

> A frontal assault on the [Supreme] Court's First Amendment jurisprudence would fail for the time being. Justices on the left and right are committed to strong protections for political speech; Trump would need to replace at least five of them, securing the Senate's consent in each case, and *it would be hard, perhaps impossible, for him to find even a single qualified, mainstream jurist* who would supply the vote he needs.[80]

The confidence with which Eric Posner makes this assessment seems justified, but no such confident judgment could have been made about Poland when its ruling elite went after the CT and the judiciary: they did find a sufficient number of jurists (though, happily, not a very large one) who were willing to occupy positions in the subjugated CT, KRS, SC, presidencies of common courts, etc. even though unconstitutionality of institutional deformations and of appointments was for everyone to see. On the positive side, there has been a strong sense of opprobrium targeted against those individuals; on the negative side, it was not strong enough to prevent them from volunteering or accepting these positions and, in the process, participating actively in the dismantlement of the rule of law.

Similarly, the ethic and culture of the members of parliament is crucial to determine whether they obey, thoughtlessly, the discipline imposed by their party leaders in the face of unconstitutional proposals, or put up resistance, as was the case of the US Congress, which failed to be convinced by Franklin D. Roosevelt trying to enhance his influence upon the SC by packing it. In contrast, court-packing in Poland was made possible by the unquestioning complicity on the part of the parliamentary majority, government, and president. The weakness of institutions in Poland was a reflection of the moral and political weaknesses of its officials, including the judiciary, and there was very little about the institutional design (except for the model of constitutional review, as discussed in Chapter 3, and perhaps the absence of federalism, which was never considered in any constitutional debates in Poland as a real option)[81] which could have made a difference.

Institutions must be underwritten by norms that are mostly shared, and by common understandings about what counts as a norm violation, even if formal legal rules are silent about it. No institution can survive without a reasonable consensus about norms. Institutions without a degree of consensus about what counts as norms transgressions become hollow, that is, eroded of the potential to serve the purposes for which they were originally set up, because the norms supply the rules of behaviour that cannot be captured by written rules constitutive of these institutions. They oil the wheels of the governing arrangements of any state. They are often taken for granted, but this is just another way of saying that there is a degree of consensus, within a country's governing elite, about their meaning and weight. Such consensus collapsed in Poland.

As Bojan Bugarič convincingly observes:

> Ultimately, democratic political parties and social movements with credible political ideas and programs offer the best hope for the survival of constitutional democracy. The role of law and constitutional checks and balances is less of an essential bulwark against democratic backsliding than is traditionally presumed in the legal literature.[82]

To those who say that the institutions designed by the Polish Constitution turned weak and vulnerable to capture, an answer may be that it took PiS *no less than* two years to complete its colonization of the key institutions rather than saying that it took *only* two years. The proposition belongs to the 'half empty/half full glass' type of arguments. During these two years, which saw a constant conflict, both domestic and international, the arguments about (un-)constitutionality played a main role in the controversies surrounding the capture of institutions. The very fact that the Constitution supplied such argumentative assets to its defenders shows its relative resilience; unfortunately, it proved insufficiently entrenched in the political culture and attitudes to protect itself against enthusiastic colonizers.

Notes

1. Steven Levitsky and Lucan Way, 'The Myth of Democratic Recession' (2015) 26/1 *Journal of Democracy* 45, 54.
2. With apologies to Richard Hofstadter, 'The Paranoid Style in American Politics' (November 1964) *Harper's* 77.
3. Rafał Matyja, 'Wrogowie ludu', *Tygodnik Powszechny* (Cracow, 30 July 2017) 20.
4. Ibid.
5. Hofstadter (n. 2) 77.
6. The most extreme and durable manifestation was a frequently repeated allegation by Kaczyński and his collaborators (especially, by Minister of Defence Antoni Macierewicz) that the former Prime Minister Donald Tusk plotted with Russian leaders to kill Lech Kaczyński in the air crash near Smolensk in 2010, see later in this section of the chapter). Another example: the decision by the (briefly) former Prime Minister Ewa Kopacz (Tusk's successor) to accept a very limited number of refugees was presented as part of a plot to undermine Christianity in Poland, etc.
7. Kaczyński's speech on 10 December 2017, to commemorate the 10 April 2010 air crash (Michał Wilgocki and Kacper Sulowski, '92. miesięcznica katastrofy smoleńskiej. Był Mateusz Morawiecki. Kaczyński: Nasi wrogowie nie spoczną' (*Gazeta Wyborcza*) 11 December 2017, http://wyborcza.pl/7,75398,22764709,92-miesiecznica-katastrofy-smolenskiej-jest-mateusz-morawiecki.html (accessed 11 January 2018)).
8. Hofstadter (n. 2) 77.
9. Kaczyński's speech on 10 December 2017, to commemorate the 10 April 2010 air crash, see 'Kaczyński: Nasi wrogowie nie spoczną', *TVN24* (10 December 2017), on-line edition <https://www.tvn24.pl/wiadomosci-z-kraju,3/jaroslaw-kaczynski-92-miesiecznica-katastrofy-smolenskiej,797515.html> (accessed 6 August 2018).
10. See Komisja Badania Wypadków Lotniczych Lotnictwa Państwowego, 'Raport końcowy z badania zdarzenia lotniczego nr 12/2010/11 samolotu TU 154M nr 101 zaistniałego dnia 10 kwietnia 2010 r. w rejonie lotniska Smolensk Północny' (Warsaw 2011).
11. Speech by Jarosław Kaczyński on 10 April 2011, 'Kaczyński sets fire to Poland', *Gazeta Wyborcza* (Warsaw, 11 April 2011) online edition <http://wyborcza.pl/1,76842,9417172,Kaczynski_podpala_Polske.html> (accessed 2 July 2018).
12. Timothy Snyder, *The Road to Unfreedom* (Penguin Random House 2018) 206.
13. Ellen Lust and David Waldner, 'Unwelcome Change: Understanding, Evaluating and Extending Theories of Democratic Backsliding' (USAID, 2015) [PDF] <http://pdf.usaid.gov/pdf_docs/PBAAD635.pdf> 20 (accessed 9 November 2017).
14. Ibid.
15. For such a warning, see Levitsky and Way (n. 1) 54–5.
16. Lust and Waldner (n. 13) 9.
17. Ibid. 9–10.

18. Bart Bonikowski, 'Ethno-nationalist populism and the mobilization of collective resentment', (2017) 68 Supp 1 *British Journal of Sociology* S181, S192, reference omitted.

19. Ibid. 193, footnote omitted.

20. All data from Sławomir Sierakowski, 'Rachunki krzywd' *Polityka* (Warsaw 7 November 2017), online edition.

21. For an articulation of this thesis, see Milan W. Svolik, 'Which Democracies Will Last? Coups, Incumbent Takeovers, and the Dynamic of Democratic Consolidation' (2014) 45 *British Journal of Political Science* 715, 718.

22. See Ko Maeda, 'Two Modes of Democratic Breakdown: A Competing Risks Analysis of Democratic Durability' (2010) 72 *Journal of Politics* 1129, 1140–1. As Maeda concludes, based on a large statistical basis, 'the analysis shows that the hazard of endogenous breakdown is independent of the levels of economic development and growth', ibid. 1141.

23. All data from Maciej Gdula, *Nowy Autorytaryzm* (Wydawnictwo Krytyki Politycznej 2018) 18–19.

24. See Noam Gidron and Peter A. Hall, 'The Politics of Social Status: Economic and Cultural Roots of the Populist Right' (2017) 68 Suppl. 1 *British Journal of Sociology* S57.

25. Andrzej Balcer, Piotr Buras, Grzegorz Gromadzki, and Eugeniusz Smolar, 'Polish Views of the EU: The Illusion of Consensus' (Stefan Batory Foundation, January 2017) 5.

26. Ibid. 6.

27. Ibid. 2.

28. For emphasis on this factor as decisive for PiS victory, see Jacques Rupnik, 'Surging Illiberalism in the East' (2016) 27/4 *Journal of Democracy* 77, 82.

29. Yascha Mounk, *The People vs. Democracy* (Harvard University Press 2018) 175–6.

30. See eg Cezary Michalski, 'Higienista Kaczyński walczy z zarazkami roznoszonymi przez obcych' (*Newsweek Polska online*, 14 October 2015) <http://www.newsweek.pl/opinie/jaroslaw-kaczynski-o-walce-z-zarazkami-i-uchodzcami,artykuly,372228,1.html> (accessed 17 May 2018).

31. Opinion polls in the late 2015 showed that two-thirds of Poles were against receiving refugees from the Middle East and Africa, and that '[t]his reluctance is linked to the fact that the vast majority of refugees are Muslim and/or non-whites', Andrzej Balcer, Piotr Buras, Grzegorz Gromadzki, and Eugeniusz Smolar, 'Polish Views of the EU: The Illusion of Consensus' (Stefan Batory Foundation, January 2017) 10.

32. Gidron and Hall (n. 24) S63.

33. Balcer, Buras, Gromadzki, and Smolar (n. 31) 10, footnote omitted.

34. Gdula (n. 23) 71.

35. Ibid.

36. Bonikowski (n. 18) S201–2.

37. Joanna Fomina and Jacek Kucharczyk, 'Populism and Protest in Poland' (2016) 27/4 *Journal of Democracy* 58, 60.

38. Stephen Holmes, 'How Democracies Perish' in Cass R Sunstein (ed.), *Can It Happen Here? Authoritarianism in America* (HarperCollins 2018): 387, 412.

39. Ibid. 418, footnote omitted.

40. Ibid. 427 n. 42.

41. See 'Pikieta narodowców w Katowicach. Powiesili zdjęcia posłów na szubieniach' (*Nasze Miasto: Katowice online*, 26 November 2017) <http://katowice.naszemiasto.pl/artykul/pikieta-narodowcow-w-katowicach-zdjecia-powiesili-zdjecia,4324641,artgal,t,id,tm.html> (accessed 2 July 2018).

42. See e.g. 'Hinduski student pobity w Polsce. Sprawę bada szefowa indyjskiego MSZ oraz ambasador' (*Gazeta.pl*, 1 April 2017) <http://wiadomosci.gazeta.pl/wiadomosci/7,114871,21577504,hinduski-student-pobity-w-polsce-sprawe-bada-szefowa-indyjskiego.html> (accessed 2 July 2018).

43. Jerzy Zajadło, 'Pojęcie "imposybilizm prawny" a polityczność prawa i prawoznawstwa' (2017) *3 Państwo i Prawo* 17, 21.

44. Paul Blokker, 'Populist Constitutionalism' (*ResearchGate*, 20 September 2017) <https://www.researchgate.net/publication/319938853_Populist_Constitutionalism> (accessed 1 January 2018) 2

45. See Gráinne de Búrca, 'How British was the Brexit Vote?' in Benjamin Martill and Uta Staiger (eds), *Brexit and Beyond: Rethinking the Futures of Europe* (UCL Press 2018) 46.

46. Matt Taibbi, *Insane Clown President: Dispatching from the 2016 Circus* (Spiegel and Grau 2017) xx.

47. 7.5 per cent went to the United Left Coalition and 3.6 per cent to a newly formed Together Party.

48. See Kim Lane Scheppele, 'Unconstitutional Constituent Power' in Rogers Smith and Richard Beeman, *Constitution-Making* (University of Pennsylvania Press, forthcoming), manuscript on file with the author, 39. As Scheppele characterizes the campaign, it 'did not feature pledges to change the constitutional order and voting did not carry the symbolic weight of choosing between an old and a new system of government', ibid. 39.

49. Snyder (n. 12) 202.

50. There is a more invidious but credible interpretation of the tapes scandal that alleges that Russian interests were behind the scandal, see ibid. 202–3.

51. For an argument that the legitimacy of states, especially of new democracies, depends less on their democratic qualities and more on their ability to deliver good quality governance, see Francis Fukuyama, 'Why Is Democracy Performing So Poorly?' (2015) *26/1 Journal of Democracy* 11. See also Samuel Issacharoff, 'Democracy's Deficits' (2018) 85 *University of Chicago Law Review* 485, 513–16.

52. Pawel Sonczak and Justyna Pawlak, 'Poland's Kaczynski Calls EU Democracy Enquiry "an absolute comedy"' (*Reuters Online*, 23 December 2016) <https://www.reuters.com/article/us-poland-politics-kaczynski-democracy/polands-kaczynski-calls-eu-democracy-inquiry-an-absolute-comedy-idUSKBN14B1U5?utm_campaign=trueAnthem:+Trending+Content&utm_content=585c5c2204d30126992cd8d9&utm_medium=trueAnthem&utm_source=twitter> (accessed 7 November 2017).

53. The last invective refers to the former PO elite's alleged responsibility for the death of 96 passengers (including President Lech Kaczyński and his wife) in an airplane crash near Smolensk on 10 April 2010, mentioned earlier in this chapter.

54. Milan Svolik, 'When Polarization Trumps Civic Virtue: Partisan Conflict and the Subversion of Democracy by Incumbents' (*Semantic Scholar online*, 2017) [PDF] <https://pdfs.semanticscholar.org/4d2c/50628b3333c52e6f0c7488cae125a996b3f3.pdf> (accessed 12 May 2018).

55. Ibid. 1.

56. Ethan B Kapstein and Nathan Converse, 'Why Democracies Fail' (2008) 19/4 *Journal of Democracy* 57, 58.

57. But note that Svolik introduces an important qualification to this generalization: 'Whereas the risk of a coup almost disappears once a democracy survives for two decades, the risk of an incumbent takeover persists. Therefore, we cannot conclude that democracies consolidate against the risk of incumbent takeovers': Milan W. Svolik, 'Which Democracies Will Last? Coups, Incumbent Takeovers, and the Dynamic of Democratic Consolidation' (2014) 45 *British Journal of Political Science* 715, 719.

58. Noah Feldman, 'On "It Can't Happen Here"' in Cass R Sunstein (ed.), *Can It Happen Here? Authoritarianism in America* (HarperCollins 2018) 157, 167.

59. Aziz Huq and Tom Ginsburg, 'How to Lose a Constitutional Democracy' (2018) 65 *UCLA Law Review* 78, 167.

60. This is the upshot of the theory of Linz and Stepan, see Juan J. Linz and Alfred Stepan, 'Toward Consolidated Democracies' (1996) 7/2 *Journal of Democracy* 14.

61. Jeremy Waldron, *Political Theory* (Harvard UP 2016) 109, endnote omitted.

62. Samuel Issacharoff, *Fragile Democracies* (CUP 2015) 22.

63. Ibid. 23–6.

64. Tamir Moustafa and Tom Ginsburg, 'Introduction: The Functions of Courts in Authoritarian Politics' in Tom Ginsburg and Tamir Moustafa (eds), *Rule By Law: The Politics of Courts in Authoritarian Regimes* (CUP 2008) 1, 19.

65. Huq and Ginsburg (n. 59) 168.

66. Richard H. Fallon Jr, 'Executive Power and the Political Constitution' (2007) *Utah Law Review* 1, 22.

67. Adrian Vermeule, 'Conventions of Agency Independence' (2013) 113 *Columbia Law Review* 1163, 1210.

68. *The Federalist* No. 48, 305.

69. John Cassidy, 'Trump's Assault on American Governance just Crossed a Threshold' (*New Yorker online*, 22 May 2018) <https://www.newyorker.com/news/our-columnists/trumps-assault-on-american-governance-just-crossed-a-threshold?mbid=nl_Humor%20052218&CNDID=20968358&spMailingID=1356108 4&spUserID=MTMzMTc5NzU2MTY3S0&spJobID=1402028675&spReportId=MT QwMjAyODY3NQS2> (accessed 23 May 2018).

70. *The Federalist* No. 51, 319.

71. *Ex parte Merryman* 17 F Cas 144 (CCD Md 1861) (No 9487).

72. See Fallon (n. 66) 20.

73. Ronald Dworkin, 'Thirty Years On (Book Review)' (2002) 115 *Harvard Law Review* 1655, 1672.

74. Fallon (n. 66) 21. Fallon's words apply to Lincoln's suspension of habeas corpus.

75. David A. Strauss, 'Law and the Slow-Motion Emergency' in Cass R. Sunstein (ed.), *Can It Happen Here? Authoritarianism in America* (HarperCollins 2018) 365, 367.

76. N.W. Barber, 'Self-Defence for Institutions' (2013) 72 *Cambridge Law Journal* 558.

77. Ibid. 563.

78. Ibid. 572.

79. Ibid. 573.

80. Eric A Posner, 'The Dictator's Handbook, US Edition' in Cass R Sunstein (ed.), *Can It Happen Here? Authoritarianism in America* (HarperCollins 2018)1, 3, emphasis added.

81. This is outside the bounds of this book so I will only flag it in a footnote: one puzzle about Polish constitutionalism is an absolute absence of any discussion about feasibility and advisability of introducing a federal structure. The only exception to this rule of which I know is a recent article by a public intellectual of a younger generation, Mr Wojciech Przybylski, 'Bardziej federalna niż centralna' (*Res Publica Nowa online*, 25 June 2018) <http://publica.pl/teksty/przybylski-bardziej-federalna-niz-centralna-64619.html> (accessed 2 July 2018). Mr Przybylski calls for federalism based on enhanced self-government and autonomy of the current regional level (*voivodships*). But prima facie there are no obvious reasons against it: it is a large country of over 38 million people, with a vast territory four times larger than the federal Austria, with significant differences in traditions, political cultures and economic structures between the different regions. Despite these factors, the idea of federalism is a taboo topic in Poland. Partly, but only partly, it can be explained by a painful collective memory about the dismemberment of Poland during the partitions, which lasted for the last decades of the eighteenth century, the entire nineteenth century, and first decades of the twentieth century.

82. Bojan Bugarič, 'Central Europe's Descent into Autocracy: On Authoritarian Populism', *CES Harvard Open Forum Paper Series* 2018–2019, 6.

8

Europe to the Rescue

No country is an island, to paraphrase John Donne. Well, some actually are, but definitely not Poland, either literally or metaphorically speaking. Poland has particularly strong linkages with the outside world, both bilaterally and through its active participation in the United Nations, North Atlantic Treaty Organization (NATO), Council of Europe (CoE), European Union (EU), etc. And these linkages have played a very important role in the unhappy developments described in this book, both in terms of how the embedding of Poland in the international order affected the dynamic of domestic development, and also how the growth of Polish anti-constitutional populism in power influenced responses by international and supranational organizations. The EU is, of course, of particular significance here. It is symbolic, and also ironic, that on the day when the European Commission (EC) formally announced that it would open an Article 7 procedure against Poland (20 December 2017), President Andrzej Duda signed two laws figuring at the top of the list of reasons for initiating the Article 7 procedure in the first place.

The role of the 'the European factor' in affecting and constraining member states that show signs of illiberal, anti-democratic or rule-of-law constraining changes has lately been the subject of lively debate, both in political fora and in EU-related scholarship, and some of this debate will be reflected in this chapter. Poland and Hungary are two of the most worrying cases that demonstrate the EU's need to grapple with developments that had admittedly not been considered by the founders of European integration in its subsequent iterations, from the European Economic Community (EEC) to the EU. Rather, it was taken for granted that the EEC or the EU would be a grouping of like-minded states with a satisfactory record on human rights, democracy, and the rule of law. As the EU enlarged in successive waves, these constitutional minimum conditions were taken as non-negotiable, and were codified in the Copenhagen criteria and more detailed rules and yardsticks of political conditionality. On the other hand, acceding states perceived accession as, among other things (but for some, most importantly) a guarantee that would solidify democracy and the rule of law against possible post-accession authoritarian and populist temptations within these new member states. Now came the reality check.

It is against this background that the EU factor (and more broadly, European factor, as it also importantly includes the CoE and its agencies) must be considered. In this chapter, I reflect on the question as to whether the EU—with its assortment

Poland's Constitutional Breakdown. © Wojciech Sadurski 2019. Published 2019 by Oxford University Press.

of different measures of 'naming and shaming' (Art. 7.1 Treaty on European Union (TEU)), sanctions (Arts 7.2 and 7.3 TEU) and legal infringement actions, as well as its newly crafted 'rule of law framework' (also known as the pre-Art. 7 procedure)—has been so far, and can be in the near future, effective in cabining and reversing anti-democratic trends in one of its largest member states.[1] But first, I will briefly discuss that *other* pan-European structure, the CoE, including the Venice Commission (VC) and the European Court of Human Rights' (ECtHR's) contributions to policing Polish assaults on the rule of law, and identifying a way out.

The chapter, like the other parts of this book, is partly descriptive, partly analytic, and partly normative. As far as this last dimension is concerned, I will argue that the EU must (both for practical and principled reasons) intervene more decisively in the case of Poland's systemic and ongoing breach of TEU values proclaimed in Article 2—particularly those of democracy, the rule of law, and individual rights— by combining the use of three institutional devices available to the EU, as mentioned in the previous paragraph: infringement actions by the VC before the Court of Justice of the European Union (CJEU), the Article 7 'nuclear option', and 'rule of law framework' procedure, seen as a possible preliminary stage of the Article 7 procedure. But the success of these measures cannot be a function of the EU alone, and largely hinges upon a synergy with other supranational organizations, and in particular the CoE entities, such as the VC and the ECtHR, in monitoring and criticizing the developments in Poland. Their role will be discussed first.

Poland in Venice

By far the most important contribution by a CoE institution was that done by the VC. In just two years (2016 and 2017), the VC produced no fewer than four lengthy Opinions regarding the Polish rule of law crisis, and in earlier chapters I have referred to all these Opinions, whenever relevant. Here, I wish to provide an overall picture, just to show how seriously the VC took its task. The four Opinions were on: (1) the statutory changes regarding the Constitutional Court (CT), including the Polish government's refusal to publish CT judgments, (2) the statutory changes to the law on the police and related limitations on the right to privacy, (3) the new statute on the office of the public prosecutor, (4) the package of laws regarding the judiciary, namely the Supreme Court (SC), the National Council of the Judiciary (*Krajowa Rada Sądownictwa* (KRS)) and the common courts. As one can see, taken together these Opinions covered much of what was most problematic in the 'reforms' undertaken by the Law and Justice (*Prawo i Sprawiedliwość* (PiS)) party after its 2015 twin victories.

The first Opinion on the CT was written, strangely enough, at the invitation of the Polish government itself. It was a blunder by the minister for foreign affairs (who had hoped, naively, that by such a preventive action he would minimize the political costs of the Opinion), for which his deputy-in-charge of legal affairs later lost his job. Before the Opinion was finalized, the government had submitted its own explanation regarding the situation on the CT at the end of 2015.[2] On the presence of 'quasi-judges' on the CT, the government argued that the election of three new judges by the end of a previous parliamentary term was irregular because there was a constitutional custom that Parliament must not elect new judges whose term of office would begin in the last days of the parliamentary term. (No relevant precedent to justify such an opinion was produced. In fact, one may argue that the whole point of *not* making judicial terms correspond to parliamentary terms was to ensure that Parliament would have to live with potentially 'hostile' constitutional judges.) The government also strongly condemned CT judgment K 34/15 of 3 December 2015, which concerned the composition of the tribunal, and also criticized the CT judges who had participated, as experts, in discussions about reforms of the procedure before the CT since 2010.

The VC Opinion did not buy any of the government's views.[3] Beginning with the last point, the VC found nothing objectionable about the CT judges participating in discussions on the law concerning the CT itself, so long as they did not exceed their role as experts: 'While it is not the function of a constitutional court and its members to participate in political debate, ... it is a common feature of European constitutional culture that constitutional courts may comment on reform proposals, which concern the Court itself.'[4] Having said that, the VC very critically scrutinized a number of proposed regulations regarding the CT, including the extraordinary requirement for a two-thirds majority for judgments invalidating a law: 'Such a very strict requirement carries the risk of blocking the decision-making process of the Tribunal and of rendering the Constitutional Tribunal ineffective, making it impossible for the Tribunal to carry out its key task of ensuring the constitutionality of legislation.'[5]

As one can see, the VC very perceptively understood the real point of PiS reforms which, at a time when it still did not have a majority on the tribunal, were aimed mainly at paralysing its decision-making process. Going point by point, the first Opinion of the VC provided scathing views about virtually all of the new important proposals, including the sequence rule, which required the CT to consider cases strictly in the order of challenges submitted, which (with the backlog at the time) would basically immunize any new PiS laws from effective control. The VC also refuted the government's claim about the alleged 'constitutional custom' whereby an outgoing parliamentary majority would not elect new judges,[6] and queried the bizarre 'principle of pluralism' articulated by the government's experts in a meeting with representatives of the VC in Warsaw, by responding:

> This view of the Constitutional Tribunal with judges 'belonging' to one party and other judges 'belonging' to the other party seems to equate the Tribunal with another chamber of Parliament ... The Venice Commission cannot subscribe

to such an approach and it has difficulty understanding the aim of establishing 'pluralism' in the Constitutional Tribunal if this just means appointing a sufficient number of one's own 'representatives' to the Tribunal.[7]

In its conclusions, the VC warned against 'crippling' the CT's effectiveness, which would adversely affect three basic principles of the CoE: democracy, human rights, and the rule of law.[8]

In addition, the VC criticized the government's failure to publish CT judgments: publication, the Opinion urged, was 'a precondition for finding a way out of this constitutional crisis'.[9]

The second Opinion of the VC concerned the law on the police (discussed in Chapter 6),[10] which regulated various methods of secret surveillance employed by law enforcement and intelligence agencies. The main reason why the amendments attracted so much public attention and criticism was the power of such agencies to obtain information by monitoring the means of communication and other tools including computers, telephones, databases, emails, social networks etc. In its Opinion, the VC criticized, among other things, the overly broad range of metadata collection;[11] the possibility of surveillance infringing lawyer-client privilege;[12] the excessively long maximum period of surveillance allowed by the new law;[13] and the weakness of judicial controls, complaints mechanisms, and oversight.[14] In its conclusions, the VC formulated a number of amendments to be made, including strengthening the proportionality principle throughout various instruments covered by the new law, as well as making the oversight and judicial review of surveillance more effective.[15] There is no need to add that the government has never even contemplated such amendments.

In December 2017, at the request of the Monitoring Committee of the Parliamentary Assembly of CoE (PACE), the VC produced its Opinion on the Public Prosecutor's Office (*prokuratura*).[16] The Opinion, at the outset, lamented the extremely fast-tracked procedure of adopting the law, and the absence of any meaningful consultations, thanks to the submission of the proposed law as a private-member bill, even though the government de facto prepared the law.[17] When it came to substance, the VC strongly criticized the merger of the office of public prosecutor general (PG) with that of minister of justice (MJ): 'None of the applicable European standards anticipate a situation in which the Public Prosecutor General is not only subordinated to the Minister of Justice, but the Public Prosecutor General is indeed the Minister of Justice.'[18] As the Opinion shows, the problems arising out of this merger are 'exasperated' by the new law on common courts, according to which the powers of the MJ over court presidents are greatly enhanced.[19] This, combined with the PG's power to intervene in every specific case, creates a 'risk of political manipulation by an active politician of individual cases'.[20] The conclusions are absolutely devastating to the new law, which 'creates a potential for misuse and political manipulation of the prosecutorial service, which is unacceptable in a state governed by the rule of law'.[21] None of the recommendations have been heeded, and all the dire predictions about the effects of the extreme politicization of the public prosecutor's system have been vindicated in practice, as shown in Chapter 4.

The VC adopted its fourth Opinion in December 2017, and it concerned the law on ordinary courts (already signed into law by President Duda at this stage) and draft laws on the SC and the KRS, which at the time of the writing of the VC Opinion were both still in a state of rewriting, under Duda's vetoes. Concerning the law on the KRS, the VC recommended abandoning the new mode of electing judicial members, and returning to the model of electing judges by their peers. Concerning the law on the SC, the VC criticized the establishment of two new chambers, and reserved special criticism for the idea that electoral issues would belong to the competences of one of the newly set up chambers, which were peopled exclusively by new judges. The power of the president of the Republic to decide on the fate of judges aged over sixty-five years old was also criticized. When it came to the new law on common courts, the VC criticized the enhanced powers of the MJ vis-à-vis those courts, and in particular the minister's competence to decide whether to extend the service of judges beyond the newly lowered retirement age, and also his stronger powers over court presidents.[22] Very perceptively, the VC concluded that the combination of the three laws in a judiciary package 'amplifies the negative effect of each of them to the extent that it puts at serious risks the independence of all parts of the judiciary in Poland'.[23]

One good thing about all four Opinions by the VC in 2016–17 was that the it did not mince words, and depicted all the pathologies, risks, and dangers related to PiS's legislative production in that period. The bad thing was that the VC was largely ineffective—if effectiveness is judged by actual changes and amendments introduced by the government as a result of VC advice and recommendations. But it was to be expected: right from the beginning, the government treated the VC as a hostile body, and its first step to invite the VC to produce its first Opinion on the CT was immediately treated by the government as a grave error. The VC became a target of PiS propaganda, joining the EC or international human rights organizations in a club of the enemies of Poland.

It does not follow, however, that the VC interventions had no positive effect. Quite to the contrary: they supplied valuable resources to the government's critics, including the political opposition, media, non-governmental organizations (NGOs), the Ombudsman, academics, etc. The VC, which had been a virtually unknown body in Poland, became a familiar name to a very large number of people, and its visits to Warsaw were treated as front-page news stories. The four Opinions constitute a very important archive of what was wrong about PiS's post-2015 assault on the rule of law.

Poland in Strasbourg

The ECtHR has not had an occasion, so far, to pronounce on the constitutional crisis and assault on the rule of law in Poland, in contrast to the situation in Hungary in which it found a breach of the European Convention on Human Rights (ECHR) in the dismissal of the president of the SC,[24] thus prefiguring the possibility of a similar judgment on the premature dismissals of Polish SC judges. But at least some of its cases originating from Poland have had an important political as well as legal meaning, in depicting the highly objectionable practices of PiS regarding the matters sensitive to the government.

One string of cases concerned the horrific treatment that Polish border guards gave to refugees from countries such as Chechnya and Syria (the matter is briefly described in Chapter 6). In these cases, complaints to the ECtHR were made by refugees who were not allowed into, or were immediately deported from, the territory of Poland, without having an effective opportunity to lodge applications for refugee status, in violation of Article 3 of the ECHR (prohibition of degrading and inhuman treatment), Article 34 (admissibility of individual applications to the ECtHR) and Article 4 of Protocol 4 (prohibition against the collective expulsion of aliens). Representative of the four cases concerning this matter[25] is *M.A. and Others v. Poland*,[26] lodged by a family of refugees from the Chechen war, depicting a truly disturbing story of a man who had been cruelly tortured back in Chechnya and, accompanied by his wife and children, was turned away several times from the border crossing in Terespol (at the border of Poland with Belarus), despite a Polish judge having made an order, as an interim measure, to allow the family to stay in Poland until their asylum requests were properly considered. In its questions communicated to the government, the European Court queried, among other things, whether 'the denial to review the applicants' motion for international protection' was in breach of Article 3 ECHR,[27] whether the applicants were expelled 'as part of a collective measure' in breach of Article 4 of Protocol 4,[28] and whether there had been any 'hindrance by the State … with the effective exercise of the applicants' right of application', in breach of Article 34 of the Convention.[29] The facts summarized earlier by the ECtHR suggest that the answers to these questions are all affirmative, and that the judgment will find Poland in breach of the Convention. The case (as the other cases in this line of cases) is still pending, and at the time of writing, the government's answer is still being awaited.

While the cases relating to the treatment of refugees raised relatively little reaction in Poland, both because the judgments have not been yet handed down and because of the general public's overall insensitivity to the fate of refugees, the judgment in Strasbourg of 20 September 2018 produced a huge wave of reactions from both proponents and critics, as it directly touched an issue of great symbolic and political value to PiS, namely the aftermath of the Smolensk air crash (discussed in Chapter 7). In *Solska and Rybicka v Poland*,[30] the First Section of the ECtHR unanimously found Poland in breach of the Article 8 rights of the relatives of some victims who disagreed with the exhumation of dead bodies of those victims, as ordered by public prosecutors. The exhumation process was part of PiS's paranoia-ridden policy, under which it has continuously maintained a conspiracy theory about the crash, and used it to mobilize its hard-core electorate in its hatred against political opponents. Some relatives—including the complainants in this case—strongly opposed the exhumations, maintaining that they were pointless and contribute to their mental anguish, but their objections were not recognized, and they found themselves with no means of seeking judicial review of the prosecutors' decisions, which were clearly politically motivated.

But the judgment was also very important for reasons exceeding its directly relevant subject matter, specifically having to do with the extreme insensitivity of the actions of public prosecutors employed to carry on a partisan, political campaign, and also concerned, albeit indirectly, with issues regarding the condition of the rule of law in today's Poland. One such matter arose with regard to the status of the CT as allegedly providing a domestic remedy, the exhaustion of which is a prerequisite for taking the matter to Strasbourg. Or so the government argued. The complainants, in turn, pointed to the unconstitutional staffing of the tribunal as a result of which it 'could no longer be regarded as an effective and impartial judicial body able to fulfil its constitutional duties'.[31] The ECtHR opted for a Solomonic solution. On the one hand, it said that in this concrete case, the CT procedure of constitutional complaint was not relevant because of the specificity of the exhumation issue: whatever the CT decided, it would not have stopped the exhumation proceedings. For this reason, there was no need to consider 'the alleged lack of effectiveness and independence of the Constitutional Court'.[32] On the other hand, the ECtHR itself left the door open to reconsider the status of the CT in some future case; it just 'does not consider it necessary to examine' this issue in the present case.[33] In this way, the issue of the Polish CT's disabling made its way to a judgment of the ECtHR for the first time.

But perhaps the most striking aspect of the judgment is that it was based on a categorical statement of illegality (a government action not carried out 'in accordance with the law') rather than being as a result of employing a proportionality analysis, which the ECtHR did not even embark upon. As one knows, in order to proceed to a proportionality analysis, the ECtHR must be first satisfied as to certain early stages of scrutiny, the failure with regard to which pre-empts the need for 'proportionality'. One of these is scrutiny into whether the action was 'in accordance with the law'. Failure under this test is much more invidious than failure under proportionality, on the conduct of which reasonable lawyers may disagree. The ECtHR foreclosed the road to conducting a proportionality test by categorically condemning Poland at an earlier stage. Polish prosecutorial practice based on the Polish code of criminal procedure was found to be lacking in 'adequate legal protection against arbitrariness',[34] and failed 'to ensure that the discretion left to the executive is exercised in accordance with the law and without abuse of powers'.[35] The ECtHR found that *some* prosecutorial decisions are subject to judicial review, but decisions on exhumations are not reviewable.[36] This led the ECtHR to conclude that 'Polish law did not provide sufficient safeguards against arbitrariness with regard to a prosecutorial decision ordering exhumation'.[37] This was a harsh condemnation of the law, but also of the barbaric practice of Polish prosecutors under PiS rule.

In his analysis of the ECtHR's impact upon the observance of the rule of law in the states of Central and Eastern Europe (CEE), Jernej Letnar Černič observed that the ECtHR 'has set out foundational *de iure* principles for the functioning of the rule of law and constitutional democracies in Central and Eastern Europe in a wide range of areas'.[38] While the post-2015 constitutional breakdown in Poland has not yet registered as such in Strasbourg case law, it is just a matter of time before the issues, regarding for instance judicial independence and irrevocability, find their way to the ECtHR (or so one may foresee and hope).

The Constitutional and Democratic Meaning of Accession to the EU

One of the most important reasons that have led many politicians, activists, and commentators in Poland, as elsewhere in CEE, to strongly favour accession to the EU was the conviction that, once in the EU, the state would be more robustly democratic. The view that '[t]he enlargement and the integration into the European Union will provide a stimulus for strengthening the institutional order in the countries of Central and Eastern Europe'[39] was accompanied by an understanding that 'strengthening the institutions' meant first and foremost democratization. The idea was sometimes presented metaphorically as a democratic straitjacket—a set of constraints on the political structure of the state that protects it against authoritarian and populist excesses. Accession, many observers hoped, would render democracy more resilient against crises and potential upheavals, cushioning democratic institutions against threats and challenges, against moral panic and the oppression of minorities. It was, of course, not the only factor that produced broad support for joining the EU within Polish society, but the so-called civilizational arguments, of which the argument for the protection of democracy formed an important part, also played a large role in convincing the people of the benefits of accession. The popular rhetoric of a return to Europe meant, in particular, the reassertion of membership in a community of nations that highly values democracy, human rights, and the rule of law.

This sentiment was underwritten by a sense of frustration with the state of democracy in Poland after the transition, combined with a high esteem for West European democracy (which somehow also applied to EU institutions). On the eve of the 2014 accession, only 12 to 16 per cent of Poles declared that they trusted fundamental democratic institutions in their own country, and only 7 per cent believed that the national institutions functioned effectively. In contrast, over one-half of respondents believed that EU institutions worked well, even if the general level of knowledge of their work and structure was very low.[40] This mix of distrust in the democracy in one's own state with a quasi-mythical trust in Brussels created a favourable socio-psychological context for accepting the accession, with all its costs. It is against this background that one can evaluate the contribution to the consolidation of liberal-democratic rules and practices made by both the *prospect* of accession to the EU, and by the actual accession.

As to the former, political conditionality, based on the Copenhagen criteria and then concretized in the EC's evaluation of Poland's progress in adopting the *acquis*, as evidenced by annual reports since 1997, it actually helped consolidate democratic institutions and the absorption of norms conducive to the rule of law. While there is no consensus among students of the EU about the actual impact of conditionality, and the process has been much maligned by some scholars,[41] my own study does not corroborate such a sceptical approach. In my previous book, I have suggested that, by and large, the process of political conditionality did make a difference, though one has to be careful not to exaggerate the independent contribution of the process, but rather see it in the context of a synergy between EU conditionality and the actions of the domestic actors (including their actions *preceding* the process of accession), and of the synchronization between the EU and other international entities, but also that it differed from one domain to another.[42]

When it comes to the *post-accession* impact of the EU upon a consolidation of democracy in Poland, evaluating the EU factor is a much more difficult task because the scrutiny of membership eligibility has been discontinued, in addition to the absence of the ultimate sanction in the form of the non-acceptance of a candidate state to the club. The pattern of incentives operating on a state is completely different in the pre- and post-accession periods, and the measures that the EU has at its disposal towards its existing members are different (and overall, much less effective) than towards its applicants. Hence, many scholars predicted that there would be a dramatic retreat from democratic standards in the region soon after the 2004–7 wave of accessions to the EU, and that the states who put on their best behaviour in the run-up to accession would degenerate into their bad old forms, as if there was some fatalism in the non-democratic norms displayed in Central Europe. In an article published in October 2007, Ivan Krastev announced: 'The liberal era that began in Central Europe after 1989 has come to an end. Populism and illiberalism are tearing the region apart.'[43] And in April 2008, *The Economist* magazine proclaimed the following sequence observable in CEE: 'The pattern of intensive reform to qualify, followed by a let-up in the process once the membership [in the EU] is achieved, is too common to be happenstance.'[44]

But to simply state that there was inevitable backsliding after the unusual mobilization in the run-up to accession is too offhand, especially regarding Poland. After all, it had taken over ten years for a populist turn in government to take place if one does not count the 2005–7 episode of PiS rule, which did not produce any deep institutional changes. Rather, a combination of institutional deterrents (in the form of Art. 7, to be discussed later in the chapter, section 'Article 7: Adding Bite to a Bark'), 'soft' devices of control and monitoring (e.g. through the Fundamental Rights Agency), the norm-learning connected to the day-to-day participation in EU institutions, as well as financial incentives related to the financial transfers from the EU, combined into a complex mechanism favourable to domestic democracy in Poland. As a result, membership of the EU became a powerful strategic asset and a bargaining tool *inside* Polish politics. The scholars who studied this phenomenon (not only related to Poland, but more broadly regarding the new member states) observed a specific peer pressure 'which means that political elites adjust their behaviour to avoid the embarrassment of being singled out as reform laggards in their interactions with their Western counterparts'.[45]

Alas, accession-based democratization had its limits, as 2015 has shown. Socialization of at least some elite within the democratic culture of the EU turned out to be skin-deep, and the internalization of democratic standards turned out quite shallow and propaganda-oriented. For a number of political actors in Poland, democratic rules and practices had been adopted for instrumental reasons (to help attain the desired EU membership) rather than for the sake of democracy itself. A general hypothesis by a student of democratization was confirmed: 'An important drawback of an incentive-based approach to democratization is that democracy . . . may become devalued in the eyes of both elites and citizens because its tenets are adopted not as an end but as a means to an end'.[46]

In the face of post-2015 developments, the limits and insufficiencies of incentives and soft measures in preventing democratic backsliding have been painfully demonstrated. Poland (as, mutatis mutandis, Hungary before it) became a laboratory for experimenting with tougher measures to police anti-democratic and anti-rule-of-law developments in an EU member state.

The two polar extremes among those measures are infringement actions lodged by the commission with the European Court of Justice, and Article 7 actions. The former is feasible but relatively ineffective: one may argue that you need *political* measures to deal with *political* infractions, and the Article 258 TFEU infringement procedure is basically tailored to specific violations that can be made good for the parties concerned via *legal* remedies. There is a view among scholars, not necessarily a dominant one but nevertheless popular, that 'the Commission is limited in its ability to prosecute member state infringements of vague legal principles'.[47] In turn, the latter action, under Article 7, may be effective yet is not very feasible: the requirement of unanimity for sanctions under Article 7.3 renders its use virtually unthinkable.

Hence, a number of in-between measures have been contemplated and occasionally used. Among the measures being contemplated is the idea of setting up a 'Copenhagen Commission' to apply the eponymous criteria to current member states,[48] and Kim Lane Scheppele's idea of 'systemic infringement' actions.[49]. The rule-of-law framework adopted in 2014 and activated by the Commission with respect to Poland in January 2016 is newly designed, and thought of as a pre-Article 7 procedure, but also as valuable in its own right.[50] All these measures and proposals will be discussed later in this chapter, 'Policing Member States: New Ideas'. As Dimitry Kochenov and Laurent Pech note, the adoption of this new procedure 'showed that the Commission finally understood the serious, if not existential, threat posed by the solidification of authoritarian regimes within the EU'.[51]

Poland before the CJEU: A Call from Dublin

In the Preface to this book, I allude to the preliminary reference by the Irish High Court in the *Celmer* case, regarding a European Arrest Warrant (EAW)[52] issued by Polish judicial authorities for the purposes of conducting a criminal prosecution. As the Irish Court found out, Mr Celmer was objecting to his surrender primarily on the ground that the legislative changes to the judiciary, the courts and the public prosecutor brought about within the last two to three years in Poland undermined the possibility of him having a fair trial. He also opposed his surrender on the basis of prison conditions in Poland, in particular, that his safety could not be guaranteed there.[53]

The High Court of Ireland examined in detail the various actions of the Commission taken under the rule of law framework, the Polish government's statements as well as the most important Polish legislation on the substance and structure of the CT and judiciary branch.[54] In its conclusion, the High Court observed 'that the rule of law in Poland has been systematically damaged by the cumulative impact of all the legislative changes that have taken place over the last two years'. The court emphasized the comprehensiveness and inter-connectedness of Polish legislative changes, many of which, 'when viewed in isolation, may not self-evidently appear to violate the rule of law'. The fact, however, that a particular change might be acceptable in another EU member state (such as Ireland) 'is not conclusive or even necessarily relevant to whether the rule of law has been damaged in Poland' because the constitutionality of those changes within Poland cannot be ascertained due to the actions taken towards the CT, and because they come within a concerted legislative package to politicize the judiciary and to take away its independence. The High Court concluded:

> The totality of changes in Poland, especially as regards the constitutional role in
> safeguarding independence of the judiciary by the National Council for [sic] the

Judiciary, combined with the Polish government persisting with invalid appointments to the Constitutional Tribunal and refusing to publish certain judgments, also amounts to an undermining of the rule of law.[55]

The High Court of Ireland referred to the judgment in the *Aranyosi and Căldăraru*[56] case, which also concerned a refusal to surrender a person within the EAW framework, and where the European Court of Justice held that if the executing judicial authority makes a finding of general or systemic deficiencies in the issuing member state, that authority must make an assessment, specific and precise, of whether there are substantial grounds to believe that the individual concerned will be exposed to a real risk of being subject to inhuman or degrading treatment in that member state. A two-step procedure must then be applied: first, a court must make a finding of systemic deficiencies and, second, seek all necessary supplementary information as to the protections for the individual concerned. Hence the uncertainty expressed by the Irish court: if the common value of the rule of law, as enshrined in Article 2, has been breached by the member state issuing an EAW, which by its nature constitutes a fundamental defect in the system of justice, the second requirement of *Aranyosi* still applies. If the deficiencies of the system are systemic, then 'it appears unrealistic to require a requested person to go further and demonstrate how, in his individual case, these defects will affect his trial'.[57] And further:

A problem with adopting that approach [of *Aranyosi*] in the present case is that the deficiencies identified are to the edifices of a democracy governed by the rule of law. In those circumstances, it is difficult to see how individual guarantees can be given by the issuing judicial authority as to fair trial when it is the system of justice itself that is no longer operating under the rule of law[58].

The Irish court's actions provoked strong reactions, both in Poland and elsewhere in Europe. Polish constitutional scholar Tomasz Koncewicz observed, approvingly, that

the Irish judge acting in her capacity as the EU judge of general jurisdiction, has elevated the discourse about the EU rule of law crisis to another level. We are now moving away from the political arena marred by cynicism and rotten compromises to the courtroom with its own logic and principles.[59]

Some commentators went a step further in linking the preliminary reference to the Article 7 procedure, and thought that the question in *Celmer* should best be framed in rule-of-law terms, and therefore the Irish court 'should ... freeze the case awaiting a resolution of the matter from political actors in accordance with the procedure provided for in Article 7 TEU or the [democracy, the rule of law and fundamental rights] monitoring and enforcement mechanism called for by the European Parliament.'[60] But others took a much more restrained view and claimed that the

> review of the rule of law in Poland by the CJEU would constitute an ultra vires action, as this competence is determined in the TEU solely for the Member States acting through the Council or the European Council in accordance with the procedure provided in Art. 7 TEU. The CJEU ruling should be limited solely to the application of the *Aranyosi-Caldararu* test to assess whether the systemic changes in the judiciary in Poland comprise a violation of the right to a fair trial as defined in Art. 47 of the Charter.[61]

It was against this legally and politically controversial background that the Opinion of Advocate General Evgeni Tanchev was announced on 28 June 2018.[62] Tanchev AG suggested that the legal problem in the case should be framed as a fundamental rights issue and not as a rule-of-law issue. Moreover, in his view, the Court of Justice should follow the path from the *Aranyosi and Căldăraru* case without pronouncing on the legislative changes in the judiciary branch in Poland. The Court should leave the final decision on the possibility of a fair trial in Poland to the Irish High Court. The national court has to decide whether or not to execute an EAW even if an Article 7 TEU procedure is pending. He also agreed that a potential breach of the right to a fair trial *can* be the basis to postpone the execution of the EAW. He pointed out that the executing judicial authority should engage in a two-stage examination to find not only that (1) there are systemic deficiencies in the issuing judicial system, but also (2) that the person concerned is actually exposed to such a risk because she is a political opponent.

So this was an extremely cautious approach, aimed at identifying the strongest possible *limits on exceptions* to the principle of mutual trust, which is the engine of the EAW system. Tanchev AG declined the invitation to rule on the state of the rule of law in Poland in general terms. At the same time, however, he rejected the claims by the Polish government that the Irish Court's question was premature, and emphasized that the Article 7 procedure and a case before the CJEU regarding the EAW have totally different functions and character:

> The former enables the European Union to intervene in the event of serious and persistent breach by a Member State of the values on which the European Union is founded. The latter enables the executing judicial authority to protect the fundamental rights of the person who is the subject of a European arrest warrant.[63]

Hence, there is no need to postpone the decision regarding the fundamental right until the European Council decides on Article 7(1); such a link between two procedures 'would be tantamount to prohibiting th[e executing] authority, *for a period that is at the very least indeterminate*, from postponing the execution of a European arrest warrant'.[64]

One can note a paradoxical convergence between the harshest critics of the government in Poland on the one hand and, on the other hand, the Polish government itself in pleading for a link between the *Celmer* case and the Article 7 procedure, the link being established by the framing of the *Celmer* case in rule-of-law terms. The difference was, of course, that while this link led the critics to conclude that the Irish court should 'freeze' the case, and suspend the extradition until the outcome on Article 7 is known, for the government that link meant that, since the determination regarding the rule of law in Poland is not known and not to be expected any time soon, the surrender of Mr Celmer should go ahead regardless. Ostensibly striking a more prudent line of argument, the moderate solution chosen by Tanchev AG was to re-articulate the matter in terms of the fundamental right to a fair trial. But if the Polish government were tempted to view it as a victory, it was a Pyrrhic one. Later on in his Opinion, Tanchev AG constructed a link with ECtHR case law under Article 6 of the ECHR, and to its doctrine of a 'flagrant denial of justice'. What is required for a flagrant denial is a 'breach of the principles of fair trial guaranteed by Article 6 [of the ECHR] which is so fundamental as to amount to "a nullification, or destruction of the very essence, of the right guaranteed by that Article" '.[65] If it sounds, however, like an excessively high standard to apply, Tanchev AG reassuringly added: 'it cannot, to my mind, be ruled out that lack of independence of the courts of the issuing member state may, in principle, constitute a flagrant denial of justice'.[66] But then, referring to the Court of Justice judgment of 27 February 2018, *Associação Sindical dos Juízes Portugueses*,[67] he stated that 'the lack of independence and impartiality of a tribunal can be regarded as amounting to a flagrant denial of justice only if it is so serious that it destroys the fairness of the trial'.[68] One may note that by construing the test in such a way, he transformed it into something that is impossible to apply in practice: barely any real-life situation would meet such a test.

The meekness of Tanchev AG's Opinion caused some harsh immediate criticism. Petra Bárd and Wouter van Ballegooij pointed out that '[t]he AG Opinion's construction of the case as a potential human rights deficiency renders challenges to rule of law violations hypothetical'. The application of the two-prong *Aranyosi* test is, according to them, 'incoherent and not workable in practice', and is likely to result in 'impunity for Member States violating the rule of law, as well as individual exposure to fundamental rights infringements'.[69] Michał Krajewski, for his part, pleaded for the linkage between the case and Article 7, saying that 'proceedings under Article 7 TEU and proceedings before the Court of Justice in the *Celmer* case indeed do have the same or at least very similar subject-matter, contrary to what AG Tanchev stated'.[70]

The Court of Justice judgment was delivered a month after the AG Opinion, on 27 July 2018.[71] Right from the outset, the Court framed the issue in terms of a fundamental right to a fair trial *and* connected the EAW case with Article 7, by saying that a reasoned proposal of the EC within Article 7(1) may constitute material indicating that there is a real risk of a breach of that fundamental right. In such cases, a court making a decision about a surrender within the EAW must 'determine, specifically and precisely, whether there are substantial grounds for believing that the individual concerned will run such a risk if he is surrendered to that State'.[72] In this way, the groundwork was set for the rest of the judgment.

On that basis, the Court elaborated on the principle of mutual trust, which requires 'each of [the member] States, *save in exceptional circumstances*, to consider all the other Member States to be complying with EU law and particularly with the fundamental rights recognized by EU law'.[73] The exceptionality of departures from the principle has been restated several times, for instance by saying that '*save in exceptional cases*, [other member states] may not check whether that other Member State has actually, in a specific case, observed the fundamental rights'.[74] In itself, the emphasis on a strong presumption of mutual trust is highly questionable: when an Article 7 procedure is underway, one may legitimately argue that the principles of Article 2 gain priority over the principle of mutual trust.[75] *What*, according to the Court, may constitute such 'exceptional circumstances' justifying exceptions to mutual trust, and hence the refusal to surrender a person under the EAW? The Court made it clear that:

> *In that regard* [i.e. in the context of exceptions to mutual trust], it must be pointed out that the requirement of judicial independence forms part of the essence of the fundamental right to a fair trial, a right which is of cardinal importance as a guarantee that all the rights which individuals derive from EU law will be protected and that the values common to the Member States set out in Article 2 TEU, in particular the value of the rule of law, will be safeguarded.[76]

All that led the Court to establish that the independence and impartiality of courts is a condition of the 'high level of trust between Member States on which the European arrest warrant mechanism is based', and so a real risk that a person to be surrendered would suffer a breach of his/her fundamental right to a fair trial may permit the executing judicial authority, by way of exception', to refrain from surrendering that person. It is up to the executing judicial authority—a court in the country from which extradition is requested—to assess whether there is such real risk to that person.[77] The assessment must be 'on the basis of material that is objective, reliable, specific and properly updated concerning the operation of the system of justice in the issuing Member State'.[78] And for this assessment, the information included in the reasoned proposal by the Commission activating the Article 7(1) procedure is 'particularly relevant'.[79] Again, the Court drew a strict connection between the EAW case and Article 7, the latter serving as a source of information necessary to hand down a judgment in the former.

Some general observations are in order. First, the Commission's reasoned proposal on activation Article 7(1) TEU may be considered as 'particularly relevant' information for the Irish court, as well as other courts in the EU, to recognize the risk of a serious breach of values expressed in Article 2 TEU.[80] In this way, the CJEU expanded the catalogue of sources of information to be considered by a judge in making determinations about an EWA. It does not mean, however, that such material will necessarily meet the *Aranyosi* test. There is always a need for a court to assess the impact of such risk for individuals subject to an EAW.[81] In this way, the CJEU simply evaded the issue of the *systemic* nature of threats to the rule of law signalled by the initiation of the Article 7 procedure, which (one may argue) may render time-consuming and convoluted judicial tests unnecessary.[82]

Second, the judgment may be seen as a judicial legitimization of the commission's actions under the rule of law framework. It may also be recognized as grounds for a future ruling in the cases submitted by the Commission or initiated by the Polish SC's preliminary references concerning the 'reform' of the judiciary in Poland. The Court's repeated references to the case of *Associação Sindical dos Juízes Portugueses* suggests such a future line of case law[83]—something that is yet to be verified if and when the Court hands down its judgment on the Polish SC.

Third, the CJEU itself did not conduct the test, and did not directly rule on the systemic risk that would justify a refusal to surrender in the EAW case. Rather, the Court strongly emphasized the huge obligations of the national court submitting the preliminary question. But the CJEU reasserted the test to be used: the national court's decision on the real risk of a breach of the essence of the fundamental right to a fair trial should depend on specific circumstances and facts that are relevant for an accused person. The Court clearly, and regrettably, did not want to depart from the *Aranyosi and Căldăraru* doctrine. At the same time, an important part of justification was based on the *Associação Sindical dos Juízes Portugueses*. In that decision, the Court directly pointed out that a Member State's judicial structure must be seen as an important part of guaranteeing the right to a fair trial regardless of whether such a structure is under the scope or direct protection of EU secondary law or not.

Fourth, the judgment clearly identified some structural aspects of the control of judiciary that may be considered as symptoms of defects in guaranteeing the independence of judges. In particular, it pointed towards the disciplinary measures and procedures established towards judges; such measures must provide for guarantees in order to avoid the risk that the disciplinary system would lead to political control of the substance of judgments.[84] This warning reads like direct reference to what has actually happened in Poland, where the system of disciplining judges has been fully subjected to the political will of the executive, with the politically appointed Disciplinary Chamber of the SC at its apex, and which has been used by the MJ to persecute and harass judges for taking decisions he dislikes.

Fifth, the judgment wisely abstained from the extremely elevated standard of 'flagrant denial of justice' present in the AG's Opinion, the use of which would have rendered a case-by-case suspension of surrender virtually impossible.[85] Still, the repeated emphases on the 'exceptional' circumstances as to when such a suspension of trust is allowed raises a very high bar before a judge who is concerned about the state of a system of justice, and in particular the independence of judiciary in the other member state. This, combined with the need to conduct the second (individualized) tier of *Aranyosi*, virtually assures that suspensions will be extremely rare, if they occur at all. Perhaps this is a good thing. But in a situation in which the executing authority must seek additional information from the issuing judicial authority presupposes that the latter enjoys significant independence. If it does not, the requirement for such action is self-defeating.

After the CJEU judgment, but before the final judicial decisions in Ireland (which have not been handed down at the time of writing), there were two other decisions by domestic European courts in Spain and Madrid, which issued questions to their Polish counterparts under the tests established by the *Celmer* case, to verify whether the conditions for deportations under EAW are met in Poland. The process has been launched, and a ripple effect may be expected.

Saving the Trees, Saving the Courts

After PiS's ascension to power, the government found itself before the CJEU for reasons not directly connected to the rule of law. The matter became a huge embarrassment, and in addition showed that the Court's interim measures can be effective in compelling an intransigent government to act in accordance with EU rules. To some observers in Poland, it was an optimistic instance of the CJEU's impact on a member state; an impact that, one day, may also apply to the dismantlement of rule-of-law mechanisms.

The Commission's challenge to PiS's policy before the CJEU could be partly understood as reflecting its disregard for environmental concerns: care for the natural environment has been seen as part of a leftist, Western-born syndrome, alien to the traditional culture of Poland. This barbarian attitude was reflected in logging in the Białowieża forest in eastern Poland, one of the most precious European natural habitats. In its action of 20 July 2017,[86] the EC asked the Court to declare that Poland had failed to fulfil its obligations under the Habitats and Birds Directives by failing to take the necessary conservation measures corresponding to the ecological requirements of the directives, and by not guaranteeing the protection of species of birds referred to in the directive. According to the order of the vice chairman of the CJEU of 27 July 2017, 'Poland should have ceased, immediately and until delivery of final judgment in Case C-441/17, the active forest management operations the removal of centuries-old dead spruces and the felling of trees as part of increased logging on the Puszcza Białowieska site'.[87] Poland was only exceptionally allowed to take measures where they were strictly necessary, and in so far as they are proportionate, in order to directly and immediately ensure the public safety of persons, on the condition that other, less radical measures are impossible for objective reasons. Having regard to the fact that Poland ignored the ruling and continued logging in Białowieża, the commission supplemented its application for interim measures by requesting the Court impose a periodic penalty payment on Poland.

In response, the Polish Ministry of the Environment filed a motion to dismiss the injunction as unjustified. Moreover, the Polish government decided to interpret the notion of public safety expansively, as public safety was the only exception to the interim injunction allowed by the Court decision of 27 July 2017. The Polish government argued that public safety encompasses not only the risk posed by falling timber close to roads that can become a threat to tourists and conservation workers, but also by trees inside the woodland, as they could accidentally fall on mushroom pickers. It was a typical argument *ad absurdum* meant to show that public safety does not only apply to people but also to nature. [88]

In its decision of 20 November 2017,[89] the Court granted the Commission's application until delivery of the final judgment in the case. Poland was also ordered to send the Commission details of all measures that it had adopted in order to comply fully with it, no later than fifteen days after notification of that order, as well as the active forest management operations that it intended to continue because they were necessary to ensure public safety, provided with reasons. If Poland was found to have infringed this order, the Court could order it to pay the Commission a penalty payment of at least EUR 100,000 per day. In the end, the monetary penalty was not imposed on Poland due to the fact that the Commission accepted, rather naively, the Polish government's explanations submitted in accordance with the decision of the CJEU.

In his Opinion of 20 February 2018, Advocate General Yves Bott proposed that the CJEU should declare that Poland had violated the provisions of the Habitats Directive as well as the Birds Directive.[90] It was not surprising that the Court ruled on 17 April 2018 that by carrying on logging activities in the Białowieża Forest, Poland failed to fulfil its obligations under EU law.[91] By that time, Poland had a new government and a new minister for the environment: the combative, pro-logging Jan Szyszko was replaced by the much more moderate Henryk Kowalczyk. The PiS government realized that the political costs of heavy logging outweighed the losses suffered by the timber lobby, and gave in. By and large, Poland desisted from logging in the Białowieża Forest.

Again, this was not, strictly speaking, a 'rule of law in Poland' issue, but its symbolic value for opponents of the government was enormous: it has shown that Europe may be effective in imposing restraints upon the PiS government, and if it was effective regarding logging, why would it not be effective regarding the dismantlement of the independence of the courts? The intervention by the

Commission and the Court showed that the EU has sufficient legal instruments and the capacity to enforce them in preventing a recalcitrant government from openly disregarding its EU-based obligations.

Did it augur well for the intervention regarding the Polish courts? With an unusual delay (the law was enacted and entered into force by mid-2017), the Commission also decided to bring the case concerning judicial 'reforms' in Poland before the CJEU in its action of 15 March 2018.[92] The Commission had two main complaints. First, the law distinguished between men and women concerning the retirement age for judges: sixty years of age for women, sixty-five for men, thus breaching EU provisions on equal opportunities and the equal treatment of men and women in matters of employment and occupation.[93] This defect in the law was later remedied, and Polish government levelled the retirement age at sixty-five. This change was politically easy and inexpensive for the government to make, as it did not affect the central point of the reforms, namely to subject judges to strong control by the executive, and by the MJ in particular. The latter issue was addressed by the Commission's second objection, namely that the statute on the common courts granted the MJ the right to decide whether to extend the period of active service of judges. This is of course the key provision of the statute in question, and if the CJEU accedes to the point of view of the Commission, namely that the provision breaches Poland's treaty obligation to adopt remedies sufficient to ensure effective legal protection in the fields covered by EU law, this will be a major blow to the reforms. At the time of the writing this book, the case is still pending.

The second infringement procedure launched by the Commission concerned the statute on the SC. The procedure was launched at exactly the last moment: the changes concerning the compulsory retirement of a large number of judges came into force on 3 July, and the Commission's action was announced on 2 July.[94] Again, the Commission's delay was inexplicable as the statute's last version was enacted on 8 December 2017, and since then it was clear that the president of Republic would be empowered to decide, as a discretionary matter, as to whether to accede to the judges' requests to continue in active service beyond the age of sixty-five. As described in detail in Chapter 4, once 3 July came, the KRS, MJ and the president took concerted rapid actions that managed the purge of the Court with deadly efficiency, clearly trying to win the race with the CJEU and create fait accompli, which would make the CJEU judgment, if unfavourable to the new law, virtually ineffective. In the end, the Commission referred Poland to the CJEU on 24 September 2018.

The infringement procedure by the Commission is based on the view that the measures of the statute undermine the principle of judicial independence, including the irremovability of judges and, as such, Poland has failed to fulfil its obligations under Article 19(1) of the TEU read in connection with Article 47 of the Charter of Fundamental Rights of the European Union. Before the infringement action was launched, the commission engaged in a ritual 'dialogue' with the Polish government regarding the law. The government's argument was that the powers of the president are not that dangerous because the law, as amended, introduced the requirement of 'consultation' by the KRS. But the Commission did not buy this argument, pointing out that this consultation 'does not constitute an effective safeguard' for three reasons: it is not binding, it is based on vague criteria, and the KRS itself, under the law of 8 December 2017, is composed of judges-members elected by the parliament, 'which is not in line with European standards on judicial independence'.[95]

When referring Poland to the CJEU, the Commission called on the Polish authorities to halt the implementation of the law on the SC (to no avail), and emphasized the urgent nature of the situation by requesting an expedited procedure and that the CJEU impose interim measures. As of the time of writing, the case is pending.

Polish Judges Appeal to Luxembourg

The most dramatic instance of the interaction between Polish developments and European law so far took place on 2 July 2018 when, in a rare move for Polish judiciary, the Polish SC decided to ask the CJEU for a preliminary reference regarding the new law on the SC.[96] The questions were asked by an enlarged bench of the SC, appointed to examine a particular legal issue presented in the case of EU coordination of social security systems. The Court used this EU law-related case as a platform to query the new law on SC for its consistency with EU law because two of the judges sitting on the panel belonged to the category of judges affected adversely by the new law in that they were over sixty-five years old and therefore threatened with dismissal should the president decline their request to continue their term of office.

In its preliminary reference, the SC asked the CJEU whether the following provisions of the new law, and their consequences, were consistent with EU primary law: (1) the lowering of the retirement age of SC judges from seventy to sixty-five, without leaving them a right to decide whether or not to exercise a lower retirement age entitlement; (2) the obligation imposed upon judges of sixty-five years and over to obtain the consent of the president of the Republic to continue in their office after statutory provisions entered into force. The SC was also uncertain as to whether the situation created by those statutory provisions might be classified as a case of discrimination on the ground of age, which is prohibited by EU secondary law. Moreover, in case of a finding of discrimination and violation of EU law by the national statutory provisions, the CJEU was asked whether the SC may decline to apply the national legislation on the lowering of the age of retirement for judges, and also, whether acting as a European court, the SC had the authority to suspend the application of all national provisions that violate guarantees for the tenure of judges.

The SC suggested that the newly adopted Polish statutory provisions may violate the TEU obligation of the member state to provide sufficient and effective judiciary protection in the fields covered by EU law, the principle of sincere cooperation in the context of the rule of law guarantees, a right to an effective remedy and to a fair trial as well as rules against discrimination. The SC applied for an expedited procedure. While doing so, it also suspended the application of a Polish law forcing the early retirement of SC judges aged sixty-five and over, including the president of the SC, whose term is guaranteed by the Constitution.

It was this last aspect—the suspension of the application of the new law towards the judges of the SC aged sixty-five and over, which caused the greatest outcry. All top authorities, including the president and the MJ, condemned the SC decision on the basis that it arrogated to itself the power of invalidating properly enacted laws. President Duda even went so far as to say that the decision had no legal basis, was of a purely political character, and that he was not bound by it[97] (indeed, he later manifested his disregard for the SC decision by failing to reappoint some of the judges aged sixty-five and over). The SC spokesperson's explanation that the decision was much narrower than was presented by politicians and the media—namely that it only suspended the applicability of some provisions of the law towards a specifically targeted group of SC judges[98]—has not changed the attitudes of critics of the decision.

Once again, this outcry has shown the regime's cavalier approach to the rule of law: it was compelled to say that the judgments of the SC are not binding for them if the ruling politicians dislike them. In itself, an important effect of the SC decision was eliciting such declarations from the government. Legally speaking, the decision, while unusual, had a strong basis and justification in CJEU case law. The reasons for the decision referred, inter alia, to the CJEU ruling in the case of *Commission v Hungary*,[99] in which the Court found that 'by adopting a national scheme requiring compulsory retirement of judges, prosecutors and notaries when they reach the age of 62—which gives rise to a difference in treatment on grounds of age which is not proportionate as regards the objectives pursued', Hungary violated Directive 2000/78/EC.

The unusual character of the decision was that the connection between the main proceedings, which engaged EU law (concerned as it was with coordination of social security systems), and the issue of SC judges' tenure could be seen as somewhat tenuous. So much was conceded by Professor (and ex-Vice President of the CT) Stanisław Biernat who, writing with Monika Kawczyńska, admits that the preliminary reference 'does not have substantial relevance in the traditional sense of the term to the main proceedings'. And yet, the two authors claimed:

The link between the preliminary references and the substance of the main proceedings is about confirming the ability of the national judges to hear the case where EU law shall be (even potentially) applied. Therefore, it is not a connection between the content of the questions referred and the subject of the main proceedings. It is a close relationship of a different kind that can be described as functional.[100]

Perhaps the most important aspect of the preliminary reference by the Polish SC is that, in its reasons, the Court expressly and directly connected the issue at hand with the ongoing procedure under Article 7 of the TEU. The SC referred to the Opinions of the VC as well as to the Commission's reasoned proposal on the activation of Article 7 TEU, and also to the Commission's infringement action of 3 July 2018. All these connections with European procedures regarding Poland made the decision of the Polish SC particularly powerful: it was woven into a thick European tapestry of legal and political concerns about the rule of law in Poland.

By the end of September 2018, seven other questions were sent to the CJEU by Polish courts through the preliminary reference procedure: four by the SC and three by other courts (the Regional Courts in Warsaw, Łódź, and Gorzów Wielkopolski). They all, by and large, replicated the substance of the SC's preliminary questions submitted on 2 August. It is interesting to note that all three Regional Courts focused their questions almost exclusively on the issue of the new model of disciplinary proceedings against judges, and in this context asked the CJEU for interpretation of Article 19 TEU: can it be understood in such a way as to prohibit disciplinary proceedings that do not give any guarantees for the objectivity and independence of disciplinary authorities dependent on the executive? At the time of writing, the cases were registered as cases before the CJEU, and are still pending. But the courage of the judges—especially from the Regional Courts—has to be highlighted: each of the court decisions were strongly condemned by political authorities, and the judges were subjected to various forms of harassment (such as prolonged interrogations by the disciplinary officials). One positive side effect of these court decisions was Polish judiciary's 'discovery' of the preliminary reference mechanism, which had rarely been used until then, and one can presume, was virtually unknown by many judges in Poland.

The Rule of Law Framework Designed

The rule of law framework is a procedure established early in 2014 as a halfway measure between ordinary infringement actions under Article 258 of the Treaty on the Functioning of the European Union (TFEU) and highly politicized and dramatic actions based on Article 7. From the very beginning, there was a certain ambiguity about the rule of law procedure, namely whether it was a 'pre-Article 7' stage or a standalone procedure. This ambiguity has been glossed over in the initial communication by the EC of 11 March 2014, which described it as 'fill[ing] a gap' but exactly what gap there was to fill was never clearly explained. The procedure, the Commission urged, 'seeks to resolve threats to the rule of law in Member States before the conditions foreseen in Article 7 would be met'[101]—thus envisaging a stand-alone role for when the conditions are not ripe (and hopefully, would not ripen) for Article 7. On the other hand, the Commission also characterized the new procedure as one which '*precedes* and complements Article 7 mechanisms',[102] with a top Commission official describing it as a 'pre-Article 7 procedure',[103] thus clearly positioning it as an early sequence in that procedure. The Commission emphasized that the new procedure is 'without prejudice' to the Commission's powers to address specific situations by means of the infringement procedures under Article 258 of the TEU.[104]

As a relatively soft mechanism, the rule of law procedure was criticized soon after it was announced for its likely ineffectiveness.[105] But the defenders believed that, far from being ineffectual, the framework's actual first activation gave grounds for optimism: it 'has shown its potential to mobilize European public opinion and orient public discourses to the current condition of EU values. Major EU newspapers have taken up the issue, informed commentary is being produced, and the EP [European Parliament] had a promising debate on the issue'.[106] Up to this point, Armin von Bogdandy and his collaborators had a point. But they went on to predict: 'We do not believe that engagement in this phased dialogue can easily be ignored by any government, and it will thus have a domestic impact as well as a ripple effect'.[107] As we shall see, in anticipating (hoping for?) such salutary effects upon the government concerned, they were overly optimistic.

At the beginning, there was some uncertainty as to whether the commission had sufficient legal grounds for initiating the framework, and very shortly after the initial announcement, the Legal Service of the Council delivered an eccentric opinion stating that the Commission's new mechanism was unlawful.[108] As one would imagine, the Legal Service's arguments were to be used later on by the Polish government to claim that the Commission was acting ultra vires, and some Polish pro-government lawyers have endorsed and expanded on these arguments. But these arguments were thoroughly criticized by the majority of scholars, and eventually the Commission's competence to adopt the framework was accepted by the European Parliament, the Council, and the CJEU.[109] A quasi-consensus emerged that the rule of law procedure was the legitimate result of the interpretation of several treaty provisions aimed at ensuring efficiency of EU law.

This quasi-consensus followed from a number of arguments. First, according to Article 17 TEU, the commission is a guardian of treaties, and according to Article 292 TEU it may adopt recommendations. There is no need for the commission to indicate a direct or specific legal competence basis to adopt a particular recommendation when its scope generally falls within EU law. Second, once the Commission was given the competence to submit a motion under Article 7 TEU, there should be no doubt that it is also empowered to take all necessary measures to fulfil its obligations in the most effective and transparent way (i.e. collect materials, enter into dialogue with the member state, or adopt recommendations or other soft and non-binding acts). Without the sort of scrutiny provided in the communication, the Commission would not be able to submit a reasonable and comprehensive justification for its motion from Article 7(1). As Dimitry Kochenov and Laurent Pech say,

> a strong and convincing argument can be made that Article 7(1) TEU already implicitly empowers the Commission to investigate any potential risk of a serious breach of the EU's values by giving it the competence to submit a reasoned proposal to the Council should the Commission be of the view that Article 7 TEU ought to be triggered on this basis.[110]

Third, there is a direct link between the rule of law framework and the principle of 'mutual trust' and 'sincere cooperation' of Article 4 TEU: the framework was designed to avoid the escalation of a rule of law crisis and violation of EU law that would be harmful from the perspective of mutual trust. The Commission's recommendations and proper dialogue with a member state under the rule of law framework may help prevent situations like in the *Aranyosi*[111] case, when a threat to the rule of law justified a narrow exception to the mutual recognition principle in EAW proceedings. In the case of the failure of the effectiveness of the Commissions' efforts within the framework (as that which eventually happened with regard to Poland during 2015–18), the recommendations adopted by the Commission may help the courts of other member states to assess the scale of EU law violations and facilitate a decision on the application of an exception similar to the *Aranyosi* case (which in fact occurred in the *Celmer* case initiated by the Irish High Court, discussed earlier in this chapter, 'Poland before the CJEU: A Call from Dublin').

To summarize, the competence to adopt the commission's recommendations before activation of a pre-Article 7 procedure can be seen as an example of implied powers. Carlos Closa summarizes the legal grounds for the framework well:

> The first argument derives from the model of community that the EU stands for: the EU is a community of law which depends on mutual recognition and mutual trust. Secondly, the breach of the principle of the Rule of Law affects all the members of this community. This principle can be labelled the all affected principle. The third argument refers to the consistency between the EU's own proclaimed values and policies.[112]

But most important of all the arguments concerns its instrumental role vis-à-vis the Article 7 procedure: if the Commission has a role reserved for it in the procedure— namely the capacity to submit a 'reasoned proposal' to the Council to enable it to adopt recommendations prior to finding a clear risk of a serious breach of EU values—the task cannot be properly and responsibly fulfilled without a structured, sequenced procedure envisaged in the newly fashioned framework.[113] For all these reasons, it seems unquestionable that the Commission did not violate the principle of conferral, announced in Article 4 of the TEU.

Going beyond a purely legal defence—that is, that the framework's establishment was not ultra vires—perhaps the most important substantive justification for the framework was that the 'Commission finally understood the serious, if not existential, threat posed by the solidification of authoritarian regimes within the EU.'[114] This was a threat that was not anticipated early on in the process of European integration, when the EU (or rather its predecessors) was a small club of like-minded western European democracies. With its enlargement towards the eastern part of the continent, the threat became more than a hypothetical prospect. And it became clear that the EU must have a variety of tools at its disposal, not limited to Article 7 and infringement actions.

But it does not follow that the Rule of Law Framework has been without weaknesses and blind spots, which were depicted even by those who, by and large, endorsed the new instrument. For one thing, it has been argued that there is no clear and uncontroversial definition of the 'rule of law' within the EU: its understanding, it was pointed out, is sensitive to national constitutional systems, with allegedly no substantive definition at EU level.[115] The point is well taken but it may apply to *any* of the values specified by Article 2, which in itself cannot be seen as an argument against proclaiming such values as democracy or human rights in an international treaty for a polity or organization based on values. It may well be that, as Kochenov urges, the rule of law is an 'essentially contested concept',[116] but it does not follow that, at least *at the lower scale of indicia of the rule of law*, there is no consensus about what these indicia are. And while there may be a reasonable disagreement about the implementation of these indicia—for instance, what should count as a violation of judicial independence, or how much corruption constitutes a violation of the rule of law?—*some* breaches are at least beyond contestation, and 'we know them when we see them'. The original communication by the Commission referred to various standards of the rule of law in Court of Justice case law, as well as in the statements of the ECtHR, VC, and other CoE bodies, which should be seen as points of reference to assist in configuring the scope of the principle of the rule of law. Similarly, it is important to keep in mind that, in the process of the accession of CEE member states to the EU, Copenhagen conditionality used, inter alia, the rule of law 'as a standard against which to measure the progress of accession states';[117] and the Commission's annual reports within that process constitute an important acquis for the understanding of the rule of law within the EU.

The point has also been made, by Amichai Magen among others, that since Article 2 lists a number of other values alongside 'the rule of law' ('human dignity, freedom, democracy, equality, ... respect for human rights, including the rights of persons belonging to minorities'), then it is all the more urgent for the EU bodies to precisely define the rule of law, in order to demarcate it from those other values.[118]

This, the argument goes, is made more important by the fact that the Rule of Law Framework procedure is focused only on one of those values, while Article 7 is activated when a breach of *any* of those values is envisaged. But, in my view, there is a non sequitur in the argument: the fact that the rule of law appears in Article 2 in a configuration with other values means that the drawing of its precise conceptual boundaries is *less* rather than *more* urgent. After all, there are significant overlaps between the rule of law, democracy, and human rights, and one of the points of this book is to show how, in Poland, a comprehensive assault on the rule of law produces important negative externalities for democracy and civil rights. All these principles figure in a mutually supportive, interlocking, integrated scheme of political values, where each is understood and appreciated in the light of the other. I have in mind an interrelationship of values (as contrasted with a 'detached' view) corresponding to what Ronald Dworkin eloquently (though in a different context) described as an 'integrated scheme of values': 'we suppose not only that an integrated value's existence depends on some contribution it makes to some other, independently specifiable, kind of value, ... but that the more precise characterization of a [*sic*] integrated value ... depends upon identifying that contribution'.[119] So even if the Rule of Law Framework picks on *one* of the Article 2 values, it would be pedantic or, worse, unfaithful to the nature of complexity and the inter-connectedness of moral principles to insist on a precise delimitation of the rule of law, as if it was an autonomous or 'detached' principle. To be sure, there were good reasons for the new framework not to be called a 'Democracy Framework' or a 'Human Rights Framework', but its focus on the rule of law does not mean that this value orientation renders the argument in terms of other Article 2 values irrelevant, or that they can be clinically separated from each other.

Some misgivings have been also expressed about the concept of 'a systemic threat to the rule of law' used in the foundational document for the framework. As the communication envisaged, 'The main purpose of the Framework is to address threats to the rule of law ... which are of a systemic nature. The Framework will be activated when national "rule of law safeguards" do not seem capable of effectively addressing those threats'.[120] This means that, as some commentators have pointed out, 'Individual breaches of fundamental rights or an isolated miscarriage of justice are not enough to trigger action against a Member State under the Framework. Action is reserved for extreme cases'.[121] Some critics observed that the Commission did not explain what would count as a 'systemic threat', with isolated violations on one end of the scale as opposed to systemic violations on the other end.[122] But the point goes only so far, and if the framework is read in the context of Article 7 (as it should be, considering that it is largely conceived as a pre-Article 7 procedure), then it is plausible to say that the framework's systemic *threats* (as opposed to actual *violations*) may correspond to a clear *risk* of a serious breach of Article 2 values', as articulated in section 1 of Article 7, while actual violations (which are too severe to merely activate the framework) correspond to 'the existence of a serious and persistent breach', as codified in section 2 of the same article. It may be worth noting, in this context, that the language of the communication establishing the framework does not faithfully track the language of Article 7, in that it omits the concept of 'risk', replacing it with 'threats'. While these two concepts are not identical, in real-life situations they play more or less the same role. At the same time, the framework's concept of 'systemic' plays a role equivalent to 'serious' and 'serious and persistent' in Article 7. While theoretically we can think of serious breaches that are not systemic, and vice versa, of systemic breaches that may not be all that serious, in real-life cases of EU member states embarking upon authoritarian paths such distinctions seem to be pedantic in the extreme.

So, read in the light of the language of Article 7, the terminology used in the foundational document for the framework becomes less indeterminate and vague than it may appear at first blush. It is all the more persuasive since the Commission supplied important interpretive guidance as to what threats are considered to be systemic: it happens 'when national "rule of law safeguards" do not seem capable of effectively addressing those threats'.[123] The absence of effective mechanisms of self-correction may be seen as an important symptom and/or cause of a systemic threat. Every legal system is guilty of some errors, miscarriages of justice, failures to provide effective protection to citizens, and instances of corruption and incompetence. What matters is whether there is a by-and-large effective institutional structure for self-correction, for instance through an appellate judicial structure, judicial review, well-functioning freedom of information mechanisms, and proper reactions to media investigations. It is the collapse of such measures of self-correction, usually resulting from the institutional capture of the entire state apparatus by the executive that renders threats to the rule of law truly systemic.

Rule of Law Framework Proceedings Against Poland

On 13 January 2016, for the first time ever, the EC announced that it would carry out a preliminary assessment of the situation of the Polish CT under the Rule of Law Framework. On that day First Vice-President Frans Timmermans said: 'We are taking this step in light of the information currently available to us, in particular the fact that binding rulings of the Constitutional Tribunal are currently not respected—which I believe is a serious matter in any rule of law-dominated state.'[124] But the process from the very beginning was broader than just regarding the CT, and the breadth of the Commission's concern was evidenced several months later, when it announced its first recommendation on 27 July of that year.[125] In the meantime, a complex set of frenzied activities between Brussels and Warsaw went on, including various letters to and from the Commission and the Polish government, visits by Frans Timmermans in Warsaw, and an Opinion by the

Commission on the rule of law in Poland, adopted on 1 June 2016. Apparently, they led to nothing: hence, the July 2016 recommendation.

While ostensibly the five specific demands contained in that Recommendation all concerned the CT, with the VC's Opinions providing the main platform for a critique of the subsequent actions and laws concerning the CT, the European Commission perceptively connected the paralysis of constitutional review with the enactment of several problematic pieces of legislation, such as the new media law, the new Civil Service act, acts on the police and on public prosecutors, etc.[126] The implication was clear: these laws could have been enacted and kept on the books thanks only to the disabling of effective constitutional review. But knowing the revolutionary zeal in Warsaw in mid-2016, when the paralysis of the CT by legislative bombardment and by packing the court with 'quasi judges' was at its peak, it would take a miracle for the government of Poland to comply with the recommendations, and especially with the first one: to make sure that 'the three judges that were lawfully nominated in October 2015 … can take up their judicial functions in the Constitutional Tribunal, and that the three judges nominated by the new legislature without a valid legal basis do not take up the post of judge without being validly elected'.[127]

The miracle has not occurred. Exactly three months later, that is, right on the deadline the commission gave to the Polish government, the government published its response. The response of 2 October 2016 prefigured the responses to all subsequent recommendations: it was heavy-handed, full of self-righteous outrage, and made no concessions whatsoever to any specific criticisms. The tone of the response can be best gleaned from the statement by the minister of foreign affairs on that day, who denounced the 'interferences into Poland's internal affairs' in violation of the principles of 'objectivism, or respect for sovereignty, subsidiarity, and national identity'.[128] The minister of foreign affairs claimed that the 'consolidation of a democratic rule of law in Poland, including the creation of stable foundations for the Constitutional Tribunal to operate, is an overriding objective for the Polish government'. This was followed by a rather disingenuous expression of goodwill: Poland 'welcomes openly any suggestions on how to improve the work of the constitutional court'.[129] But Poland was hurt and its good intentions were not rewarded: 'In our dialogue with the European Commission, we have assumed that our cooperation will be based on such principles as objectivism, or respect for sovereignty, subsidiarity, and national identity. On top of that, such actions are largely based on incorrect assumptions which lead to unwarranted conclusions'.[130] Later noting: 'we regret to note that the Commission Recommendation is an expression of incomplete knowledge about how the legal system and the Constitutional Tribunal operate in Poland'.[131] So Poland was left with no choice: 'we have concluded that we had no choice but to assess the Commission Recommendation of 27 July 2016 as groundless',[132] and so, therefore, is the entire procedure: 'the ongoing political dispute over the rules governing the work of the Constitutional Tribunal cannot form the basis for claiming that there is a systemic threat to the rule of law in Poland'.[133]

Based on this response, some scholars formed a view that enough is enough and the time for activating the Article 7 was ripe. Laurent Pech, for one, suggested that the Commission was left with no other choice:

> The 'name and shame' and reputational costs associated with an unprecedented recourse to Article 7 TEU should not be underestimated, not to mention the significant financial costs on the borrowing front and the negative impact regarding FDI this might entail for Poland ... Not acting would also seriously endanger the whole EU legal framework.[134]

But it was not to happen: not at the time, anyway. The cat-and-mouse between the Commission and Polish government continued, and took three more iterations of the recommendation-and-reply cycle. The second recommendation, of 21 December 2016,[135] again focused on the CT, repeating earlier objections and adding specific operations regarding the election of the president and vice-president of the tribunal. The point was made unequivocally: the 'procedure which led to the appointment of a new President of the Tribunal is fundamentally flawed as regards the rule of law'.[136] And just like in its first recommendation, the commission connected the disabling of the CT with '[a] number of particularly sensitive new legislative acts [that] have been adopted by the Sejm',[137] including a media law, a law on civil service, a law on the police, and on the public prosecutor's office. Reflecting the speedy legislative production by the PiS government throughout 2016, the second recommendation expanded the range of troublesome legislation that was now basically immune to effective judicial review.

While confirming concerns about the CT and the legislation just mentioned, the third recommendation of 26 July 2017[138] expanded its reach to the acts on the judiciary, which had by that time been the order of the day in Poland. Regarding the act on common courts, the Commission particularly criticized 'the power of the Minister of Justice to arbitrarily dismiss court presidents ... which may affect their personal independence when they adjudicate cases'.[139] The Commission also criticized the draft laws on the KRS and the SC, pointing out in particular that the new retirement age would adversely affect the independence of judges.

Finally, the fourth and last recommendation of 20 December 2017 put together and updated all objections and criticisms so far. It was a particularly important document for at least two reasons: first, the full package of 'judicial' laws had already been enacted in Poland, so there was no uncertainty about the fate of the laws initially vetoed by the president. Second, the recommendation accompanied the 'reasoned proposal' by the Commission made within Article 7 (1) TEU, and was in a functional relationship with the proposal, so it is worth summarizing all seven specific recommendations made on 20 December 2017. The first three concerned the judiciary package: in the law on the SC, the president's discretionary power to prolong the judicial term of office was to be removed; regarding the KRS, the judges-members should be elected by their peers and the terms of office of the current members are not to be terminated; actions and public statements that may further undermine the legitimacy of the courts and judges should be discontinued. The second four recommendations referred to the earlier documents by the Commission, but none of the actions recommended in its earlier recommendations was taken. They concerned the CT (the independence and legitimacy of which is to be restored, meaning the removal of the quasi-judges and inclusion of the three judges properly elected); all the CT judgments are to be published and implemented fully, and the laws on common courts and on the National School of Judiciary are to be withdrawn or deeply amended. The final recommendation called on the government to 'ensure that any justice reform upholds the rule of law and complies with EU law and the European standards on judicial independence'.[140]

With each subsequent recommendation, the tone of the Polish government's official replies grew harsher, and its intransigence in asserting that Poland was a land with an exemplary rule of law became firmer. After the second recommendation, which, as we have just seen, was mainly focused on the CT, the government asserted (in its letter of 20 February 2017) that the new laws on the CT of November and December 2016 'comply with European standards regarding the functioning of constitutional courts'.[141] This was, one should remember, after a PiS majority captured the CT (thanks to the inclusion of quasi-judges and the irregular appointment of Ms Przyłębska as the president). And at that time, some critical judgments of the 'old' CT still remained unpublished and unimplemented. In its response of 29 August 2017 to the third recommendation, the government (in the words of the minister for foreign affairs statement) accused the Commission of 'interference with the ongoing legislative process in Poland', of using 'a language of ultimatums', and of a 'lack of understanding of the fundamental, substantive aspects of the reform [of the judiciary]'.[142]

It was clear that the government was not going to make any concessions regarding its legislative package on the judiciary, and claimed, falsely, that the 'intended changes regarding . . . organization of the judiciary are in line with European standards'.[143] The government insisted, above all, that the organization of national judiciaries is a purely internal competence—a point that ignored the fact that national judges are, in an important sense, EU judges because they apply EU law directly and therefore must not be subject to political interference by national governments. In an act of argumentative overkill, however, the government of Poland kept insisting at the same time that its 'reforms' do not restrict judicial independence and that, whether they do or not, is none of the EU's business.

Reversing the trend for ever-hardening language, the Polish government's response to the fourth recommendation was the most conciliatory of all, perhaps because it was at the same time a reply to the activation of the Article 7 procedure, and the new government in Warsaw, headed by Mateusz Morawiecki (represented in Poland as more pragmatic and less dogmatic than his predecessor, Beata Szydło), needed to lay the groundwork for its subsequent performance in the process that was officially initiated. The launching of the Article 7 procedure was characterized by Poland as 'essentially political, not a legal one',[144] and was accompanied by a threat that it will put 'an unnecessary burden on our mutual relations, which may render it difficult to build understanding and mutual trust between Warsaw and Brussels'. As one can see, the government consistently viewed the 'problem' as a bilateral matter between Warsaw and Brussels, rather than a multilateral one between the Polish government and the remaining member states of the EU. The government reconfirmed that it would go ahead with its 'reforms' of the judiciary ('we owe it to our voters'), but at the same time tried to strike a conciliatory note, pointing out some changes to the legislative package made in response to earlier recommendations, such as: introducing the same retirement age for judges of both genders, abandoning the automatic dismissal of all judges of the SC, strengthening of the role of the president in judicial appointments, and changing the required majority for election of judges to the KRS from a simple majority to three-fifths.

Of all these changes, only the equalization of retirement age for men and women was more substantial than cosmetic, but at the same time it was the least politically sensitive and the least costly for PiS. All other changes were cosmetic. The executive branch (fully controlled by PiS) maintained its decisive role in determining which judges of the SC aged over 65 could carry on judging, except that the decision had been transferred from MJ to the president. The three-fifths threshold for electing judges-members of the KRS was inconsequential once PiS was confident as to the support from its parliamentary ally, the Kukiz-15 party, and in view of a proviso that if the use of the three-fifths majority did not result in the filling of all fifteen judicial positions, a simple majority would be applied.

Article 7: Adding Bite to a Bark

The sanctioning mechanism had already been introduced in the Amsterdam Treaty, well before preparations for eastward enlargement of the EU got underway. And yet, at that stage, Article 7 (in its earlier iteration, confined to the sanctioning mechanism only) was already occasionally viewed in the context of the prospect of enlargement.[145] But, especially after the Haider debacle of 2000 when the article was not activated at all (sanctions were undertaken individually by fourteen EU member states, and were followed by a report from 'three wise men'—a mechanism unknown to Article 7), it became clear that the 'nuclear option' of suspending voting rights in the Council was so radical that it was wildly unrealistic.

At this stage, the accession of candidate states from CEE became a realistic prospect. The addition of a second, more moderate and hence realistic, mechanism to Article 7 by the Treaty of Nice, known as the preventive mechanism (for the determination of a clear risk of a serious breach of EU values, not followed by any other sanctions) could therefore be seen, apart from everything else, as an act in which the EU was equipping itself with the means to properly respond to violations of fundamental values of the EU (i.e. those later codified in Art. 2 of the Lisbon Treaty; in its previous, paler version, Art. 6 of the Amsterdam Treaty) in the face of accession of states with low credibility in the areas of democracy, human rights, and the rule of law. And there is indeed some evidence that this is the way the enhancement of Article 7 was actually seen by the EU decision-makers at the time.[146] Soon after the Nice Treaty, the Commission issued an important communication on 'Respect for and promotion of the values on which the Union is based', in which it stated quite unambiguously that 'at a time when the Union is about to enter on a new stage of development, with the forthcoming enlargement and the increased cultural, social and political diversity between Member States that will ensue, the Union institutions must consolidate their common approach to the defence of the Union values'.[147] Article 7, as enhanced in Nice, was explicitly described as a mechanism for such a 'defence'.

But it is one thing to say that the enhancement of Article 7 with a less radical option rendered the use of the mechanism more palatable, and another thing to say that such a use was to be contemplated lightly. In fact, there are at least seven (an appropriate number in this context) important reasons why the EU member states and institutions would be strongly reticent to the use of Article 7, in either of its versions, whether sanctioning or merely 'naming and shaming'. First, it is still a blunt instrument (even in its weaker, 'preventive' version), in a community that avoids harsh language and sanctions directed at its own members. Voting against a fellow, member state (and note that every Article 7 pathway envisages, at a certain point, votes by other member states in the Council) is politically costly and may easily be portrayed as a case of hostility towards the nation concerned, rather than vis-à-vis the government of the breaching state. Second, it is a political instrument par excellence—in a community that is deeply legalized and where legal remedies are privileged vis-à-vis political measures. For example, a paradigmatic procedure favoured by the EU is that the CJEU has the last word on any given dispute, as in infringement actions brought by the Commission.

Third, the treaty requirement for the EU to respect 'national identities inherent in [member states'] fundamental structures, political and constitutional' (Art. 4(2) TEU) *may* be seen to impose some constraints upon a collective call to action to an individual Member State to align itself to a common European constitutional architecture. The consequence of that argument is that Article 4(2) would effectively render Article 2 (in conjunction with Art. 7) meaningless. The argument, while seductive, is weak even as a matter of textual interpretation of the treaty: the Article 2 values are not closely replicated in Article 4(2)'s features of 'national identities'. Democracy, human rights, the rule of law and other values listed in Article 2 are said to be 'common to the Member States' and as such, do not belong to the scope of features covered by separate 'national identities', which might be read as giving effect to some iconoclastic readings of democracy, etc. In addition, in contrast to Article 4, Article 2 is explicitly cross-referenced in Article 7, which supplies an enforcement mechanism.

Fourth, there has been a view popular among EU decision-makers and scholars that Article 7 was never actually intended to be used, and that its role is epitomized by symbolism and deterrence; the popular metaphor of a 'nuclear option' has reinforced this perception (the strategic role of nuclear weapons could be seen not in their use but in their very existence). Fifth, the procedures for bringing an Article 7-based action to fruition are almost grotesquely complicated and excessively demanding; hence, there is a strong disincentive to embark upon a road that is unlikely to lead to its destination. Sixth, there is always a lingering anxiety, in the collective European memory, that something like the 2000 response—now widely discredited—to the Haider affair may be repeated, notwithstanding the fact that the diplomatic response at the time was not an action taken by the EU but by individual member states.

Seventh, and perhaps most importantly, picking on certain member states may be viewed as a case of double standards and hypocrisy. No EU member state is immune from charges of transgressing the values proclaimed in Article 7: consider the human rights violations by the United Kingdom in the Iraq war, and attacks on media freedom and pluralism elsewhere, the removal of EU citizens of Roma background from a national territory, various legislative provisions allowing excessive governmental interference with independent authorities as well as with courts, etc. Almost every single constitutional 'sin' committed by Hungary and Poland has been prefigured, or echoed, by some other EU Member State. But the cumulative effect of all these actions, as documented throughout this book, matters a great deal and renders Poland and Hungary qualitatively different. That is why the activation of the Article 7 procedure (even with uncertain prospects for its completion) towards these two countries, at long last, was badly needed. The EU cannot look the other way when, for the first time in its history, two of its member states are manifestly sliding into illiberal, authoritarian regimes.

Once this fundamental choice is made, there must be a *pragmatic* judgment about the path to be taken. That selection should be informed by considerations of expediency: which of the roadmaps designed in Article 7 is the most realistic, while at the same time maximizes the clout of 'naming and shaming'? Clearly, the 'preventive' pathway of section 1 is much more likely to succeed than the 'sanctioning' mechanism of sections 2 and 3 combined, since the former does not require, at any of its stages, unanimity. And even though 'a clear risk of a serious breach' is a weaker characterization than the existence of 'a serious and persistent breach', the reputational penalty is quite harsh.

Launching of the Article 7 Procedure Regarding Poland

The Commission adopted a reasoned proposal in accordance with Article 7(1) TEU, regarding 'a clear risk of a serious breach' of the rule of law in Poland, on 20 December 2017.[148] Interestingly, the launch of the Article 7 procedure against Hungary occurred much later, on 12 September 2018, and along a different pathway, namely via the European Parliament rather than the Commission. The launch of the procedure against Hungary may have, paradoxically, both strengthened and weakened the case against Poland at the same time. It strengthened it by showing that the Commission is not biased against Poland, as governmental propaganda has claimed, but instead treats similar cases the same. It weakened Poland's case because it solidified a Polish-Hungarian alliance against EU 'interference', and gave these two governments extra incentives to seek supporters for resistance elsewhere in the European political ecosystem.

As a starting point for its proposal, the Commission observed that, within a period of two years, more than thirteen consecutive laws had been adopted affecting the entire structure of the justice system in Poland: the CT, the SC, the ordinary courts, the KRS, the prosecution service and the National School of Judiciary:

> The common pattern of all these legislative changes is that the executive or legislative powers have been systematically enabled to interfere significantly with the composition, the powers, the administration and the functioning of these authorities and bodies.[149]

According to the Commission, these changes and their combined effects put the independence of the judiciary and the separation of powers in Poland at serious risk, which are key components of the rule of law.[150]

The Commission also observed that such intense legislative activity had been conducted without proper consultation of all stakeholders concerned, without the spirit of loyal cooperation required between state authorities, and without consideration for opinions from a wide range of European and international organizations. Most importantly perhaps, certainly from a rule of law perspective, these changes may be incompatible with the Polish Constitution. Effective constitutional review of these laws, however, is no longer possible in Poland.[151] There is a note of exasperation in the passage in which the Commission recalls that '[d]espite the issuing of three Recommendations by the Commission, the situation has deteriorated continuously'.[152] But overall, the tone of the document is matter of fact, measured and rather restrained.

The Commission's decision to activate Article 7(1) TEU was positively received by a number of EU law scholars. Kim Lane Scheppele and Laurent Pech expressed the view that, although it was section 1 of Article 7 that was cited, Poland was already in fact 'far into the territory of Article 7(2)', that is, it is not 'at risk of breach', but rather 'has already breached the basic principles of the EU on multiple fronts'.[153] Those same authors, in another piece co-authored by Dimitry Kochenov, brought a perspective of a multi-speed Europe into the picture, which may 'provide the perfect opportunity to leave behind states that are unwilling to fully adhere to basic principles'.[154] They went on: 'If the EU proves unable to rein in autocrats any other way, the incorporation of conditionality techniques into policing each of the integration's concentric circles is likely to become a necessary element of the edifice.'[155] The actual activation of Article 7 vis-à-vis Poland may be seen as an instrument of such 'policing' and, ironically, it may therefore be seen as 'the most realistic way forward to preserve the EU as a union of value in the long run, while also being sufficiently open towards the states hijacked by autocratic and plutocratic forces'.[156]

Having made the proposal, the Commission placed the task of further proceedings upon the Council: 'The ball is no longer in the Commission's court. It has been formally passed to the Council'.[157] But that, as T.T. Koncewicz pointed out, does not mean the end for the Commission's role, and 'dialoguing' must go on. '[T]he Commission is now bound to act positively, rather than look back, not to mention entertaining any thoughts of backtracking on its reasoned proposal to trigger Art. 7 TEU'.[158]

As part of its counter-attack to the launching of the procedure, the Polish government produced a White Paper that was meant to be a comprehensive (89-page) response to accusations regarding the reforms of the judiciary, submitted to Brussels in March 2018.[159] In response to the response, the Association of Polish Judges (*Iustitia*) prepared, and also submitted in Brussels, its own critical analysis of the governmental document, of equal length and attention to detail.[160]

There have been two Council hearings so far, following the course of the procedure provided by Article 7 in July and September 2018. The hearings proceeded on the same pattern: the commission produced increasingly damning evidence about violations of the rule of law in Poland, and the government responded with exactly the same defensive arguments, reflecting a mix of self-righteousness and indignation.

Just to give a sense of the nature of the 'dialogue': before the hearing of 18 September, both the Commission and Polish government presented their Opinions and arguments in writing. The Commission focused first on the changes to the law on the SC that had by that time entered into force (on 9 August 2018). The Commission emphasized that the April and May 2018 amendments to the law did not allay the Commission's concerns about the newly established, retroactive retirement regime. This applied, in particular, to the position of chief justice, but also to the twelve other judges who were at risk of forced retirement unless the president consented to their requests to continue in their positions. The Commission's Opinion also mentioned that 'the pace of implementation of the retirement regime has so far not been affected by the SC's requests to the Court of Justice of the EU for a preliminary ruling'.[161] The Commission also lamented the quick process of appointing new judges, as well as the procedure of electing the judges-members of the KRS. The new judges appointed to the SC 'appear to be closely linked to the executive and the ruling party',[162] which in the eyes of the Commission 'confirms the risk of politicisation'.[163]

Further, the Commission depicted the situation of the common courts under the new law of 20 July 2018, which does 'not address the key concern which is that the current ordinary court judges still have no right to serve their full term as originally established'.[164] The Commission also expressed its concern about the mass dismissal of presidents and vice-presidents of courts by the MJ,[165] and criticized the new disciplinary regime for judges.[166] At the end of the document, the Commission reminded Poland that the situation with the CT has not changed since Ms Przyłębska became its president.

For its part, the government maintained that everything is in good order: that under Polish law the president has always enjoyed 'the sole competence to appoint judges' (forgetting, conveniently, that in this competence the president is bound by recommendations of the KRS, so the composition of the KRS is of critical importance); that Chief Justice Gersdorf actually retired as of 4 July because she failed to ask the president for consent to her continued service, while a number of other SC judges did ask for such consent; and that the lowering of the retirement age for SC judges did not interrupt their term of office because no such term exists and judges are appointed for an indefinite period.[167] As far as the charge of the politicization of the KRS is concerned, the government retorted that the members of that council enjoy 'very wide guarantees of independence, insulating them from political influence'.[168] The KRS is still predominantly composed of judges; though the fact that the ruling party elects them was not mentioned. When it came to the common courts, the government's document defended the MJ's right 'to change the structure of ordinary courts',[169] while when it came to the disciplinary regime for judges, the government reminded the commission that 'all disciplinary verdicts remain at the hands of the judiciary'[170]. This is true, but ignores the fact that the MJ determines all the central positions in the disciplinary structure. And judging by established patterns, this sort of *dialogue de sourds* is to continue.

Policing Member States: New Ideas

As the overview provided in this chapter shows, the EU is not quite toothless when it comes to violations of the rule of law and democratic standards in its member states, and its actions taken towards Poland indicate that there is a range of tools that can be applied. Their efficiency is another matter, and in the Polish case it is simply too early to tell, but the Commission's infringement actions before the CJEU, the preliminary reference addressed to the EU either by Polish courts or by courts from the other countries (such as Ireland), the rule of law framework, and the Article 7 procedure between them present a rich toolkit with which to address the problems arising out of a member state openly flouting common values and standards. And it is not a full list: there have been a number of debates within the European Parliament (beginning with a debate as early as 19 January 2016, a few days before the launching of the rule of law framework by the Commission), with all the main parliamentary groupings except for the European Conservatives and Reformists taking the Commission's side against the Polish government. These debates, with resolutions criticizing the Polish government, were repeated on 12 April and 14 September 2016, 15 November 2017 and 1 March 2018.[171]

The Polish, and earlier the Hungarian, cases of a slide towards authoritarianism by a Member State, have stimulated a rich scholarly debate, and many observers have put forward some inventive, often ingenious, proposals going beyond the triad of regular infringement actions, the rule of law framework, and Article 7. One of the best known proposals put forward by Kim Lane Scheppele was the 'systemic infringement action'. Such an action would allow the Commission to 'bundle together a set of infringing practices of an offending Member State'.[172] As a consequence, the CJEU would be able to impose a fine, as provided for in Article 260 TFEU, and it may justify the cancellation of the payment of EU funds. In Scheppele's view, no treaty change is necessary for such an instrument and a mechanism of sanctions may be established through secondary law.

The innovative aspect of the proposal is that the infringement procedure can have both a systemic element and may be used along the lines of conventional infringement actions. As the author of the proposal says:

> Unlike the usual infringement procedure in which narrowly focused elements of Member State action are singled out for attention one at a time, a systemic infringement procedure would identify a pattern of state practice that, when the individual elements are added up, constitute an even more serious violation of a Member State's fundamental EU obligations than the individual elements, taken separately ... By using the common infringement procedure in new ways, the Commission would be deploying a tried and true instrument but using this familiar method to achieve a more ambitious purpose.[173]

As Scheppele added, 'Ordinary infringement actions are important, but they are often too narrow to address the structural problems which persistently noncompliant states pose.'[174]

Some scholars expressed a sceptical view that, given the current attitude of the Commission, it is unlikely that it will bring actions to the CJEU based on broad Article 2 values. Dimitry Kochenov believes that Scheppele's 'proposal, although legally sound, is unlikely to be employed in practice unless the Commission changes its counterproductive and artificially narrow approach to the scope of Article 258

TFEU and the enforcement of values more generally'.[175] Kaarlo Tuori expresses his doubts as to whether 'the generic values enshrined in Article 2 TEU could give rise to justiciable Member State obligations, the breach of which could lead to an infringement action by the Commission'.[176]

One may indeed discern a degree of fuzziness and vagueness in values, such as those proclaimed in Article 2, which do not lend them to enforcement through a standard infraction mechanism before the CJEU.[177] On the other hand, there has been a critical mass of opinions expressing how the Commission and the CJEU should provide effective enforcement based directly (and perhaps exclusively) on Article 2. As an editorial comment of the respected *Common Market Law Review* put it, 'the Treaties neither restrain nor exclude the Court of Justice's jurisdiction in relation to Article 2 TEU'.[178] Christophe Hillion expressed the same view, pointing out that '[t]he only express limitation to the Commission's enforcement powers concerns the Common Foreign and Security Policy (CFSP), as set out in Article 24(1) TEU'.[179] And one may add that a welcome by-product of the direct enforcement of Article 2 through a classic infraction mechanism would be to provide the CJEU with the opportunity to clarify the values proclaimed by Article 2, thus contributing to the development of EU law.[180]

Another doctrinal innovation, proposed by Armin von Bogdandy and his collaborators, was the so-called Reverse *Solange* doctrine.[181] The doctrine 'aims to empower individuals to challenge domestic exercises of public authority which deprive him or her of the substance of a fundamental right in cases of systemic deficiency'.[182] According to its authors, a *serious* violation of a fundamental right of a citizen by a member state can be considered as constituting an infringement of the substance of EU citizenship. Hence, 'beyond the scope of Article 51(1) CFR, Member States should remain autonomous with respect to fundamental rights protection as long as (*"solange"*) it can be presumed that they secure the essence of the fundamental rights enshrined in Article 2 TEU'. This presumption is rebutted, however, in the event 'of a violation which is considered systemic', and in such cases 'individuals may rely on their status as Union citizens to seek redress before national courts'.[183]

The proposal prompted some criticism. One particularly sharp critique was raised by Kaarlo Tuori who expressed his scepticism about 'such a significant constitutional change as an extension of Union fundamental rights jurisdiction to autonomous Member State activity'. As Tuori recalled, 'The German Constitutional Court ... as the most important national interlocutor of the ECJ, has been quick to react to what it has considered threatening signs of the ECJ expanding its fundamental rights jurisdiction and to issue a reminder of the potential use of its ultra vires review'.[184] Kochenov raised a different objection by pointing out that, correctly in my view, some serious and systemic defects in the rule of law in a member state need not necessarily register in the sphere of fundamental rights. In Kochenov's words, 'a well-executed dismantlement of the Rule of Law and the constitutional checks and balances can happen—or at least go through crucial initial stages—without bald violations of human rights'.[185] This, one may add, is precisely the case of Poland, as this book attempts to show. If such a combination of systemic breaches of the rule of law with relatively minor violations of fundamental rights occurs, the Reverse *Solange* doctrine is unhelpful, and the use of systemic infringement actions combined with the Article 7 (and with the rule of law framework as a pre-Article 7) is preferable. This of course does not detract from the fact that *if* serious violations of fundamental rights occur, measured for instance by the standards elaborated by the ECtHR, something like a 'reverse *Solange*' may be one of a number of appropriate doctrinal instruments to be employed.

Another innovative institutional idea came from political scientist Jan-Werner Müller, who proposed 'to create an entirely new institution that could credibly act as a guardian of Europe's *acquis normative*'.[186] The institution was to be called a 'Copenhagen Commission', with an allusion to the Copenhagen criteria, and is conceived as analogous to the VC—a body with a mandate and competence to offer comprehensive and consistent political evaluations. Müller imagined the institution to be composed of legal experts and statespersons with a proven track record of political judgment, and who would be empowered to 'trigger a mechanism that sends a clear signal (not just words), but far short of the measures envisaged in Article 7'.[187] Based on the advice of the Copenhagen Commission, the EC could then impose significant financial penalties. According to Müller, the Copenhagen Commission would constitute an entirely new institution established through treaty revision and equipped with sanctioning powers.

In the subsequent paper, Müller developed the project further, and considered some possible objections, including that of duplicating the institutions already in place, especially the CoE institutions such as the VC and possibly the ECtHR. But 'the EU has reached a depth and density of integration that has no parallel in the Council of Europe', Müller observed, and added:

> the Council [of Europe] also contains members who would probably have had a hard time meeting even the fuzziest or most consciously relaxed Copenhagen criteria. This fact does not impugn the work of the ECtHR or the Venice Commission, but the problem of double standards ... would be exacerbated even further.[188]

When it comes to the CoE's judicial body, 'the European Court of Human Rights can only properly address individual rights violations, whereas the Copenhagen Commission should take a more holistic view; the Venice Commission cannot be proactive, whereas the Copenhagen Commission could routinely monitor the situation in Member States and raise an alarm without having to be prompted'.[189]

The proposal raised mixed reactions. While Kochenov applauded it as potentially an important step towards establishing an independent monitoring mechanism and an early warning system, he expressed doubts as to whether the member states already 'experiencing problems with Article 2 TEU compliance' would agree to it. He also had qualms about 'further complicating the institutional structure of the Union, as well as, fundamentally, the mechanics of the actual *enforcement* of the decisions of the Copenhagen Commission'.[190] Kaarlo Tuori, a leading member of the VC himself, raised the issue of duplication with the VC, and notwithstanding Müller's protests. Tuori reminded Müller that 'The Venice Commission is ... completely capable of assisting the EU within the new Framework. There are no formal obstacles to supporting the Framework, either: the Statute of the Venice Commission permits the Union to request opinions'.[191]

Tuori's criticisms do not, however, seem to be well founded. As much as the VC has played an invaluable role, including in Poland, and with due regard to Tuori's reminder that the VC can be activated by the EC as well, an EU-embedded institution may be able to better establish when rule of law deficiencies acquire a systemic character. On this basis, Armin von Bogdandy and his collaborators put forward a variation on the Copenhagen Commission theme, namely the idea of a Systemic Deficiency Committee. Behind this rather unattractively named institution, is a body that, in the vision of its proponents, would not require a treaty change, in contrast to Müller's Copenhagen Commission.[192] The body would be strictly aligned with the Rule of Law Framework, and be 'composed of eminent figures appointed by the EP and the Council. As foreseen in the Rule of Law Framework, the Systemic Deficiency Committee should build on the already existing expertise of the FRA, the Venice Commission, and the ECtHR in particular'.[193] According to von Bogdandy, Antpöhler, and Ioannidis, the new Systemic Deficiency Committee 'should supervise the compliance of Member States with all the values of Article 2 TEU and issue a public report in case of a threat as part of its supervisory jurisdiction. This report would trigger the activation of the Framework by the Commission'.[194]

As one can see, there has not been a scarcity of innovative institutional and doctrinal proposals sparked by the descent of some EU Member States into authoritarianism, populism, or 'illiberal democracy'. They are all a matter for the future, but for now there is one other obvious means which the EU institutions have at their disposal in policing the state of the rule of law in member states: financial sanctions. A number of politicians and scholars, including the EU Commissioner for Justice Vera Jourová, have proposed strengthening the rule of law conditionality attached to funding. These proposals have been made in the context of preparation for the next multi-annual EU budget 2021–7 and, predictably, provoked strong criticism from the governments of Poland and Hungary. As Commissioner Jourova said, 'We need to make better use of EU funds for upholding the rule of law … In my personal view we should consider creating stronger conditionality between the rule of law and the cohesion funds.'[195]

These voices gained in frequency and prominence, and further authoritarian steps in Poland and Hungary have raised more concerns in other EU states. For instance, French Foreign Minister Jean Yves Le Drian named Poland and Hungary as the EU states that do not respect fundamental principles, and added: 'We are not ready to continue paying for this Europe, this must be said clearly.'[196] The cuts would be a significant cost to the PiS government: Poland is now a recipient of huge transfer funds. As R. Daniel Kelemen and Kim Lane Scheppele noted, 'the EU finds itself in the perverse situation of providing some of the largest transfers of funds to those governments which most prominently thumb their nose at its democratic and rule-of-law norms.'[197] They also point out that, even without rolling out a new conditionality policy, the EU already has a number of mechanisms to use financial penalties at its disposal, for instance by using the Common Provision Regulations in dispensing structural and investment funds. Of course, for the Polish opposition (NGOs and independent officials such as the Ombudsman) to support such sanctions is a very delicate and uncomfortable situation, and most of them do not. But it is quite probable that a financial stick will be used against Poland if the carrot does not turn out to be an effective incentive for respecting the rule of law.

Conclusion

Some years ago Gráinne de Búrca said that, by including Article 7 in the Amsterdam Treaty, 'the EU was asserting its own virtue and the virtue of its existing members, while simultaneously sending a note of warning to the new and future candidate States to the east'.[198] De Búrca's references to virtue are perfectly appropriate: if we take the values that underlie European political integration seriously, then we must also be committed to the virtues displayed by people espousing democracy, human rights, and the rule of law. And, one may add, if the EU puts highly demanding conditions regarding the rule of law and democracy before candidate states, it should apply the same conditions to its member states. If we see Article 7 (as I just argued we should) as an important aspect of the EU's constitutional structure, in conjunction with all the other procedures, instruments, and institutions discussed in this chapter, we must be committed to invoking it whenever there is reasonable suspicion that those values are seriously endangered. This time is now, and we find ourselves faced with an important test: either we take constitutional virtues seriously (to use Professor de Búrca's language), or we fall back into the cynical, nihilist view that a constitution really does not matter. If *this* is to be the case, the (imperfectly codified) constitution of Europe would be bereft of all value. Do we want to belong to *such a* union? A famous maxim by Groucho Marx applies: 'I don't care to belong to a club that accepts people like me as members'.

Notes

1. I have recently sketched my opinion in Wojciech Sadurski, 'That *Other* Anniversary (Guest Editorial)' (2017) 13 *European Constitutional Law Review* 417. For a more extended analysis of Art. 7 and its potential use in policing democratic practices in EU member states, see Wojciech Sadurski, 'Adding Bite to a Bark: The Story of Article 7, E.U. Enlargement, and Jörg Haider' (2010) 16 *Columbia Journal of European Law* 385.
2. 'Position of the Government of Poland on matters related to the amendments to the law on the constitutional court and judgments of the constitutional tribunal of Poland of 3 and 9 December 2015 (cases no. 34/15 and 35/15)' Strasbourg, 22 February 2016, cdl-ref(2016)015.
3. Opinion on amendments to the act of 25 June 2015 on the Constitutional Tribunal of Poland adopted by the Venice Commission at its 106th plenary session, Venice, 11 March 2016, Opinion no. 833/2015, cdl-ad(2016)001.
4. Ibid. para. 45.
5. Ibid. para. 79.
6. Ibid. paras 111–14.
7. Ibid. para. 118.
8. Ibid. para. 138.
9. Ibid. para. 13.
10. Opinion on the act of 15 January 2016 amending the police act and certain other acts adopted by the Venice Commission at its 107th plenary session (Venice, 10–11 June 2016), Strasbourg, 13 June 2016, Opinion no. 839/ 2016, cdl-ad(2016)012.
11. Ibid. paras 66–74.
12. Ibid. paras 77–9.
13. Ibid. para. 88.
14. Ibid. paras 94–7.
15. Ibid. para. 133.
16. Opinion on the act on the public prosecutor's office as amended adopted by the Venice Commission at its 113th plenary session (Venice, 8–9 December 2017), Strasbourg, 11 December 2017, Opinion no. 892/2017, cdl-ad(2017)028.
17. Ibid. para. 24.
18. Ibid. para. 93.
19. Ibid. para. 95.
20. Ibid. para. 99.
21. Ibid. para. 112.
22. Ibid. para. 130.
23. Opinion on the draft act amending the act on the National Council of the Judiciary, on the draft act amending the act on the Supreme Court, proposed by the President of Poland, and on the act on the organization of ordinary courts adopted by the Venice Commission at its 113th plenary session (8–9 December 2017), Strasbourg, 11 December 2017, Opinion no. 904 / 2017, cdl-ad(2017)031, para. 131.
24. *Baka v. Hungary* App No. 20261/12 (ECHR Grand Chamber, 23 June 2012).
25. *MA v. Poland* (App. No. 42902/17), *MK v. Poland* (App no. 40503/17), and *DA v. Poland* (App no. 51246/17).

26. App No. 42902/17, lodged on 16 June 2017, communicated on 3 August 2017.
27. Communication of 3 August 2017, Question 1.
28. Ibid. Question 4.
29. Ibid. Question 6.
30. App No. 30491/17 and 31083/17 (ECHR 20 September 2018).
31. Ibid. para. 61.
32. Ibid. para. 70.
33. Ibid. para. 70.
34. Ibid. para. 112.
35. Ibid. para. 113.
36. Ibid. paras 123–5.
37. Ibid. para. 126.
38. Jernej Letnar Černič, 'Impact of the European Court of Human Rights on the Rule of Law in Central and Eastern Europe' (2018) 10 *Hague J Rule Law* 111, 130.
39. Lena Kolarska-Bobińska, 'The EU Accession and Strengthening of Institutions in East Central Europe: The Case of Poland' (2003) 17 EEPS 91, 95.
40. These figures were provided by Professor Lena Kolarska-Bobińska in an interview 'Unia—szanse na reformę państwa' *Gazeta Wyborcza* (Warsaw, 3 August 2003) 5.
41. See in particular Dimitry Kochenov, *EU Enlargement and the Failure of Conditionality* (Kluwer Law International 2008).
42. See Wojciech Sadurski, *Constitutionalism and the Enlargement of Europe* (OUP 2012) 148–55.
43. Ivan Krastev, 'The Strange Death of the Liberal Consensus' (2007) 18 *Journal of Democracy* 56, 56.
44. Charlemagne, 'Europe's Marxist Dilemma' *The Economist* (London, 26 April 2008) 46.
45. Philip Levitz and Grigore Pop-Echeles, 'Why No Backsliding? The European Union's Impact on Democracy and Governance before and after Accession' (2010) 43 *Comparative Political Studies* 457, 462.
46. Grigore Pop-Echeles, 'Between Historical Legacies and the Promise of Western Integration: Democratic Conditionality after Communism' (2007) 21 *EEPS* 142, 150.
47. Michael Blauberger and R. Daniel Kelemen, 'Can Courts Rescue National Democracy? Judicial Safeguards against Democratic Backsliding in the EU' (2017) 24 *Journal of European Public Policy* 321, 325.
48. Judith Sargentini and Aleksejs Dimitrovs, 'The European Parliament's Role: Towards New Copenhagen Criteria for Existing Member States?' (2016) 54 *Journal of Common Market Studies* 1085, 1088.
49. See Kim Lane Scheppele, 'Making Infringement Procedures More Effective: A Comment on Commission v. Hungary Case C-288/12 (8 April 2014) (Grand Chamber)' (*EUtopia Law*, 29 April 2014) <eutopialaw.com/2014/04/29/making-infringement-procedures-more-effective-a-comment-on- commission-v-hungary-case-c-28812-8-april-2014-grand-chamber/> (accessed 10 July 2017).
50. See Dimitry Kochenov and Laurent Pech, 'Better Late than Never? On the European Commission's Rule of Law Framework and its First Activation' (2016) 54 *Journal of Common Market Studies* 1062.
51. Ibid. 1066.

52. Judgment of Ms Justice Donnelly delivered on 12 March 2018, *The Minister for Justice and Equality and Artur Celmer*, [2018] IEHC 119, High Court Record No. 2013 EXT 295, Record No. 2014 EXT 8, Record No. 2017 EXT 291.

53. Ibid. para. 1.

54. Ibid. paras 50–97.

55. Ibid. para. 127.

56. C404/15 and C659/15 PPU, EU:C:2016:198.

57. Judgment (n. 52), para. 141.

58. Ibid. para. 142.

59. Tomasz Tadeusz Koncewicz, 'The Consensus Fights Back: European First Principles Against the Rule of Law Crisis (part 1)' (*VerfBlog*, 5 April 2018) <https://verfassungsblog.de/the-consensus-fights-back-european-first-principles-against-the-rule-of-law-crisis-part-1/> (accessed 20 April 2018).

60. Petra Bárd and Wouter van Ballegooij, 'Judicial Independence as a Precondition for Mutual Trust' (*VerfBlog*, 10 April 2018) <https://verfassungsblog.de/judicial-independence-as-a-precondition-for-mutual-trust> (accessed 25 April 2018).

61. Michal Dorociak and Wojciech Lewandowski, 'A Check Move for the Principle of Mutual Trust from Dublin: The Celmer Case' (*European Forum*, 25 July 2018) <http://europeanpapers.eu/en/europeanforum/check-move-for-principle-mutual-trust-celmer-case> (accessed 11 September 2018).

62. Opinion of 28 June 2018 of the Advocate General, Case C-216/18 PPU, ECLI:EU:C:2018:517.

63. Ibid. para. 44.

64. Ibid. para. 45, emphasis in original.

65. Ibid. para. 81.

66. Opinion of 28 June 2018 of the Advocate General (n. 62) para. 90.

67. C-64/16.

68. Opinion of 28 June 2018 of the Advocate General (n. 62) para. 91.

69. Petra Bárd and Wouter van Ballegooij, 'The AG Opinion in the Celmer Case: Why Lack of Judicial Independence Should Have Been Framed as a Rule of Law Issue' (*VerfBlog*, 2 July 2018) <https://verfassungsblog.de/the-ag-opinion-in-the-celmer-case-why-lack-of-judicial-independence-should-have-been-framed-as-a-rule-of-law-issue/> (accessed 26 July 2018).

70. Michal Krajewski, 'The AG Opinion in the Celmer Case: Why the Test for the Appearance of Independence is Needed' (*VerfBlog*, 5 July 2018) <https://verfassungsblog.de/the-ag-opinion-in-the-celmer-case-why-the-test-for-the-appearance-of-independence-is-needed/> (accessed 20 August 2018).

71. Judgment of the Court of Justice of 25 July 2018, C-216/18 PPU, ECLI:EU:C:2018:586.

72. Ibid. para. 34.

73. Ibid. para. 36, emphasis added.

74. Ibid. para. 37, emphasis added.

75. I owe this observation to Laurent Pech.

76. Judgment (n. 71) para. 48, emphasis added.

77. Ibid. para. 60.

78. Ibid. para. 61.

79. Ibid. para. 61.

80. Ibid. para. 60.
81. Ibid. para. 68.
82. I owe this observation to Laurent Pech.
83. Judgment (n. 71) paras 49–54, 63–4.
84. Ibid. para. 67.
85. This point is made by Petra Bárd and Wouter van Ballegooij, 'The CJEU in the Celmer case: One Step Forward, Two Steps Back for Upholding the Rule of Law Within the EU' (*VerfBlog,* 29 July 2018) <https://verfassungsblog.de/the-cjeu-in-the-celmer-case-one-step-forward-two-steps-back-for-upholding-the-rule-of-law-within-the-eu/> accessed 20 August 2018.
86. *European Commission v. Republic of Poland,* Action brought on 20 July 2017, *European Commission v. Republic of Poland,* Case 441/17.
87. L'ordonnance du Vice-Président de la Cour, 27 juillet 2017, dans l'affaire 441/17 [The order of the Vice-President of the Court in the Case 441/17 of 27 July 2017].
88. See Robert Grzeszczak and Ireneusz Pawel Karolewski, 'Bialowieza Forest, the Spruce Bark Beetle and the EU Law Controversy in Poland' (*VerfBlog,* 27 November 2017), <https://verfassungsblog.de/bialowieza-forest-the-spruce-bark-beetle-and-the-eu-law-controversy-in-poland/> (accessed 10 December 2017).
89. Order of the Court of Justice of 20 November 2017, C441/17, *Commission v. Republic of Poland,* ECLI:EU:C:2017:877.
90. Opinion of Advocate General Bot of 20 February 2018, C441/17, *European Commission v. Republic of Poland,* ECLI:EU:C:2018:80.
91. Judgment of the Court of Justice of 17April 2018, C441/17, *European Commission v. Republic of Poland,* ECLI:EU:C:2018:255.
92. Action of the European Commission of 15 March 2018, Case C-192/18, *European Commission v. Republic of Poland.*
93. Directive 2006/54/EC of the European Parliament and of the Council of 5 July 2006 on the implementation of the principle of equal opportunities and equal treatment of men and women in matters of employment and occupation, OJ 2006 L204, 23.
94. See European Commission, Press Release: 'Rule of Law: Commission launches infringement procedure to protect the independence of the Polish Supreme Court', Brussels 2 July 2018.
95. Ibid.
96. The Ruling of the Supreme Court of Poland of 2 August 2018, Case III UZP 4/18.
97. The Office of the President of the Republic Communication of 2 August 2018.
98. The Communication of the Spokesman of the Supreme Court of 3 August 2018.
99. Judgment of the Court of Justice of 6 November 2012, C-286/12, *European Commission v. Hungary,* ECLI:EU:C:2012:687.
100. Stanisław Biernat and Monika Kawczyńska, 'Why the Polish Supreme Court's Reference on Judicial Independence to the CJEU is Admissible after all' (*VerfBlog,* 23 August 2018) <https://verfassungsblog.de/why-the-polish-supreme-courts-reference-on-judicial-independence-to-the-cjeu-is-admissible-after-all/> (accessed 1 September 2018).
101. Communication from the Commission to the European Parliament and the Council. A New EU Framework to Strengthen the Rule of Law, Brussels, 11.3.2014, COM(2014) 158 final.

102. Ibid. emphasis added.
103. Viviane Reding, 'A New Rule of Law Initiative', Speech 14/202, Strasbourg, 11 March 2014.
104. Communication (n. 101), para. 1.
105. Dimitry Kochenov and Laurent Pech, 'Monitoring and Enforcement of the Rule of Law in the EU: Rhetoric and Reality' (2015) 11 *European Constitutional Law Review* 512, 532–3.
106. Armin von Bogdandy, Carlino Antpöhler, and Michael Ioannidis, 'Protecting EU values: Reverse Solange and the Rule of Law Framework' in András Jakab and Dimitry Kochenov (eds), *The Enforcement of EU Law and Values Ensuring Member States' Compliance* (OUP 2017) 218, 228.
107. Ibid. 228, footnote omitted.
108. Council of the EU, Opinion of the Legal Service 1026/14 of 2 May 2014.
109. See e.g. European Parliament resolution on the situation in Poland (2015/3031(RSP)) of 13 April 2014 (European Parliament); press release 3362 Council meeting General Affairs Brussels, 16 December 2014 (the Council); judgment of the Court of 25 July 2018, C-216/18, PPU—*Minister for Justice and Equality*, ECLI:EU:C:2018:586 (the Court).
110. Kochenov and Pech, 'Monitoring and Enforcement' (n. 105) 529, footnote omitted.
111. Judgment of the Court of 5 April 2016, C-404/15, *Aranyosi and Căldăraru*, ECLI:EU:C:2016:198.
112. Carlos Closa, 'Reinforcing EU Monitoring of the Rule of Law Normative Arguments, Institutional Proposals and the Procedural Limitations' in Carlos Closa and Dimitry Kochenov (eds), *Reinforcing Rule of Law Oversight in the European Union* (CUP 2016) 15, 15–16.
113. Kochenov and Pech, 'Monitoring and Enforcement' (n. 105) 529–32.
114. Kochenov and Pech, 'Better Late than Never' (n. 50) 1066.
115. Dimitry Kochenov, 'The Missing EU Rule of Law?' in Carlos Closa and Dimitry Kochenov (eds), *Reinforcing Rule of Law Oversight in the European Union* (CUP 2016) 290, 296.
116. Ibid.
117. Kim Lane Scheppele and Laurent Pech, 'Is the Rule of Law Too Vague a Notion?' (*VerfBlog*, 1 March 2018) https://verfassungsblog.de/the-eus-responsibility-to-defend-the-rule-of-law-in-10-questions-answers/.
118. Amichai Magen, 'Cracks in the Foundations: Understanding the Great Rule of Law Debate in the EU' (2016) 54 *Journal of Common Market Studies* 1050, 1054.
119. Ronald Dworkin, 'Hart's Postscript and the Character of Political Philosophy' (2004) 34 *Oxford Journal of Legal Studies* 1, 16.
120. Communication from the Commission to the European Parliament and the Council. A New EU Framework to Strengthen the Rule of Law, Brussels, 11.3.2014, COM(2014) 158 final, para. 4.1.
121. von Bogdandy, Antpöhler and Ioannidis, 'Protecting EU values' (n. 106) 225.
122. Kochenov and Pech, 'Monitoring and Enforcement' (n. 105) 532–3.
123. Communication of 11.3.2014 (n. 120) para. 4.1.
124. Readout by First Vice-President Timmermans of the College Meeting of 13 January 2016, Brussels, 13 January 2016.

125. Recommendation regarding the rule of law in Poland No 2016/1374, Official Journal of the European Union L 217/53.
126. Ibid. para. 65.
127. Ibid. para. 74.
128. Minister of Foreign Affairs (Poland): A statement on the Polish government's response to Commission Recommendation, 27 July 2016.
129. Ibid.
130. Ibid.
131. Ibid.
132. Ibid.
133. Ibid.
134. Laurent Pech, 'Systemic Threat to the Rule of Law in Poland: What Should the Commission do Next?' (*VerfBlog*, 31 October 2016) <https://verfassungsblog.de/systemic-threat-to-the-rule-of-law-in-poland-what-should-the-commission-do-next/> accessed 1 November 2017.
135. Recommendation regarding the rule of law in Poland No 2017/146 complementary to Commission Recommendation (EU) 2016/1374, Official Journal of the European Union L 22/65.
136. Ibid. para. 59.
137. Ibid. para. 34.
138. Recommendation regarding the rule of law in Poland No 2017/1520 complementary to Commission Recommendations (EU) 2016/1374 and (EU) 2017/146, Official Journal of the European Union L 228/19 https://eur-lex.europa.eu/legal-content/EN/TXT/?uri=CELEX%3A32017H1520 (accessed 11 September 2018).
139. Ibid. para. 20.
140. Ibid. para. 47 (g).
141. Minister of Foreign Affairs (Poland) statement on Poland's response to European Commission's complementary Recommendation of 21 December 2016.
142. Minister of Foreign Affairs (Poland) statement following the European Commission's Recommendation of 26 July 2017 regarding the rule of law in Poland.
143. Ibid.
144. Minister of Foreign Affairs (Poland) statement on the European Commission's decision to launch the disciplinary process against Poland laid out in Article 7 of the TEU, 20 December 2017.
145. For examples of statements to this effect, and discussion, see Sadurski, *Constitutionalism* (n. 42) 81–4.
146. See ibid. 84–6.
147. Communication from the Commission to the Council and the European Parliament on Article 7 of the TEU, 'Respect for and promotion of the values on which the Union is based', 15 October 2003, COM(2003) 606, 4.
148. Proposal for a Council Decision on the determination of a clear risk of a serious breach by the Republic of Poland of the rule of law, COM/2017/0835 final—2017/0360 (NLE).
149. Ibid. para. 173.
150. Ibid. para. 173.
151. Ibid. para. 175.
152. Ibid. para. 175.

153. Kim Lane Scheppele and Laurent Pech, 'Was the Commission Right to Activate pre-Article 7 and Article 7(1) Procedures Against Poland?' (*VerfBlog*, 7 March 2018) <https://verfassungsblog.de/was-the-commission-right-to-activate-pre-article-7-and-art-71-procedures-against-poland/> (accessed 30 October 2018).

154. Dimitry Kochenov, Laurent Pech, and Kim Lane Scheppele, 'The European Commission's Activation of Article 7: Better Late than Never?' (*VerfBlog*, 23 December 2017) <https://verfassungsblog.de/the-european-commissions-activation-of-article-7-better-late-than-never/> (accessed 30 January 2018).

155. Ibid.

156. Ibid.

157. Tomasz Tadeusz Koncewicz, 'Dusting off the Old Precedent—Why the Commission Must Stick to the Art. 7 Procedure Against Poland' (*VerfBlog*, 12 June 2018) <https://verfassungsblog.de/dusting-off-the-old-precedent-why-the-commission-must-stick-to-the-art-7-procedure-against-poland/> (accessed 30 August 2018).

158. Ibid.

159. The Chancellery of the Prime Minister (Poland), 'White Paper on the Reform of the Polish Judiciary', Warsaw, 7 March 2018.

160. *Iustitia*, Polish Judges Association, 'The Response of the Polish Judges Association "Iustitia" to the White Paper on the Reform of the Polish Judiciary, Presented to the European Commission by the Government of the Republic of Poland', Warsaw 2018. A personal declaration: I was one of the experts involved in preparing the Response.

161. The European Commission Contribution of 18 September 2018 (Rule of Law in Poland/Article 7 Reasoned Proposal Hearing of Poland). Note that, as of the time of writing this book, neither the Commission's document nor Polish government's observations have been officially published, but were disclosed by journalists on the day of the hearing.

162. Ibid. para. 2.

163. Ibid.

164. Ibid. para. 3.

165. Ibid. para. 6.

166. Ibid. para. 4.

167. 'Poland's Remarks on European Commission Contribution, Hearing of Poland' 18 September 2018, 1.

168. Ibid. 3.

169. Ibid.

170. Ibid.

171. There was also a debate on Poland in the European Parliament on 14 December 2016 but without a resolution adopted. The debate was solely on changes to the CT.

172. Kim Lane Scheppele, 'Enforcing the Basic Principles of EU Law through Systemic Infringement Actions' in Carlos Closa and Dimitry Kochenov (eds), *Reinforcing Rule of Law Oversight in the European Union* (CUP 2016) 105.

173. Ibid. 107–8.

174. Ibid. 109.

175. Dimitry Kochenov, 'The Acquis and Its Principles The Enforcement of the "Law" versus the Enforcement of "Values" in the EU' in András Jakab and Dimitry Kochenov

(eds), *The Enforcement of EU Law and Values Ensuring Member States' Compliance* (OUP 2017) 9, 19.

176. Kaarlo Tuori, 'From Copenhagen to Venice' in Carlos Closa and Dimitry Kochenov (eds), *Reinforcing Rule of Law Oversight in the European Union* (CUP 2016) 225, 235.

177. Laurence W. Gormley, 'Infringement Proceedings' in András Jakab and Dimitry Kochenov (eds), *The Enforcement of EU Law and Values Ensuring Member States' Compliance* (OUP 2017) 65, 77.

178. 'Editorial Comments: Safeguarding EU Values in the Member States – Is Something Finally Happening?' (2015) 52 *Common Market Law Review* 619, 622.

179. Christophe Hillion, 'Overseeing the Rule of Law in the EU Legal Mandate and Means' in Carlos Closa and Dimitry Kochenov (eds), *Reinforcing Rule of Law Oversight in the European Union* (CUP 2016) 5, 66.

180. See similarly ibid. 69.

181. Originally developed by Armin von Bogdandy et al., 'Reverse Solange – Protecting the Essence of Fundamental Rights against EU Member States' (2012) 49 *Common Market Law Review* 489; A. von Bogdandy et al., 'Reverse Solange – A European Response to Domestic Constitutional Crisis: Advancing the Reverse-Solange Doctrine' in Armin von Bogdandy and Pál Sonnevend (eds), *Constitutional Crisis in the European Constitutional Area* (Hart 2015) 248.

182. Armin von Bogdandy, Carlino Antpöhler, and Michael Ioannidis, 'Protecting EU Values: Reverse Solange and the Rule of Law Framework in The Enforcement of EU Law and Values Ensuring Member States' Compliance' in András Jakab and Dimitry Kochenov (eds), *The Enforcement of EU Law and Values Ensuring Member States' Compliance* (OUP 2017) 219.

183. Ibid. 220.

184. Tuori (n. 176) 230.

185. Kochenov, 'The Acquis and Its Principles' (n. 175) 22.

186. Jan-Werner Müeller, 'Should the EU Protect Democracy and the Rule of Law inside Member States?' (2015) 21 *European Law Journal* 141, 150.

187. Ibid. 151.

188. Jan-Werner Müeller, 'Protecting the Rule of Law (and Democracy!) in the EU. The Idea of a Copenhagen Commission' in Carlos Closa and Dimitry Kochenov (eds), *Reinforcing Rule of Law Oversight in the European Union* (CUP 2016) 206, 220.

189. Ibid. 220.

190. Kochenov, 'The Acquis and Its Principles' (n. 175) 23 (emphasis in original).

191. Tuori (n. 176) 241–2.

192. Von Bogdandy et al., 'Protecting EU Values' (n. 106) 229.

193. Ibid. 232.

194. Ibid. 229.

195. Eszter Zalan, 'Justice Commissioner links EU funds to "rule of law"' (*EU Observer*, 31 October 2017) <https://euobserver.com/political/139720> (accessed 15 September 2018).

196. See 'French foreign minister: We no longer want to pay for Poland and Hungary' (*Euractiv*, 5 September 2018 <https://www.euractiv.com/section/future-eu/news/french-foreign-minister-we-no-longer-want-to-pay-for-poland-and-hungary> (accessed 15 September 2018).

197. R. Daniel Kelemen and Kim Lane Scheppele, 'How to Stop Funding Autocrats in the EU' (*Verfblog*, 10 September 2018) <https://verfassungsblog.de/how-to-stop-funding-autocracy-in-the-eu/> (accessed 15 September 2018).

198. Gráinne de Búrca, 'Beyond the Charter: How Enlargement Has Enlarged the Human Rights Policy of the European Union' (2004) 27 *Fordham International Law Journal* 679, 696.

9

Illiberal Democracy or Populist Authoritarianism?

Over twenty years ago, Guillermo A. O'Donnell published an influential article that put forward the concept of 'delegative democracy' (DD): a post-authoritarian system under which 'whoever wins election to the presidency is thereby entitled to govern as he or she sees fit, constrained only by the hard facts of existing power relations and by a constitutionally limited term of office'.[1] While O'Donnell's discussion is modelled on Latin American post-authoritarian presidential systems, it can be adapted, mutatis mutandis, to Polish semi-presidentialism, with the leader of the winning party performing a function similar to that of the Latin American president in O'Donnell's account.

O'Donnell does not use the concept of populism (the word is only mentioned once throughout the article, and without any great significance attached to the concept),[2] and yet many of his observations are apposite to describe Polish constitutionalism under the Law and Justice (*Prawo i Sprawiedliwość* (PiS)) party. DD—just like the PiS version of democracy—is strongly majoritarian: 'It consists in constituting, through clean elections, a majority that empowers someone to become, for a given number of years, the embodiment of the high interests of the nation.'[3] PiS uses majority-based legitimacy as the basis of its claim to represent the 'high interests of the nation' as a whole, and those who are not captured by the interests represented by PiS do not count. Further, under DD, '[t]his majority must be created to support the myth of legitimate delegation'.[4] The legitimacy claimed by PiS is merely a 'myth'—if one considers the fact that power was delegated to it by 18 per cent of eligible voters—but a myth that is constantly reasserted and renewed. DD 'is strongly individualistic ... The leader has to heal the nation by uniting its dispersed fragments into a harmonious whole'.[5] Accordingly, the leader of PiS Jarosław Kaczyński has been referred to as the nation's saviour by his hardest proponents,[6] and the dominant post-victory narrative was full of references to the re-established 'community'.

What is absent in DD, in contrast to a true *representative* democracy, is accountability during the term of office. Specifically, 'horizontal accountability' is missing, which is described by O'Donnell as being exercised through

> a network of relatively autonomous powers (i.e., other institutions) that can call into question, and eventually punish, improper ways of discharging the

Poland's Constitutional Breakdown. © Wojciech Sadurski 2019. Published 2019 by Oxford University Press.

responsibilities of a given official … since the institutions that make horizontal accountability effective are seen by delegative presidents as unnecessary encumbrances to their 'mission,' they make strenuous efforts to hamper the development of such institutions.[7]

Again, if we replace 'delegative presidents' with 'leader of the ruling party', this is a good account of Poland under PiS. As this book documents, the force of the parliamentary majority, the government, and the president—all coordinated skilfully by the leader of the ruling party—was addressed against various institutions of 'horizontal accountability' in Poland, including the constitutional court, ordinary courts, parliamentary opposition, non-governmental organizations (NGOs), and the media.

The point of divergence between Polish anti-constitutional populist backlash and DD concerns, quite simply, how 'democratic' it is. As O'Donnell put it: 'Delegative democracy … is more democratic, but less liberal, than representative democracy.'[8] Whether Poland under PiS will remain democratic at its core—in the moment when the electoral 'delegation' is being decided by the electorate—remains to be seen at the next elections in late 2019 (parliamentary) and 2020 (presidential). As David Landau observes, the notion of DD 'at least assumes a fair shot at periodically ousting incumbents from office'[9]—and we simply do not know whether the opposition parties in the forthcoming elections in Poland will have such a fair shot. What we do know, though, is that PiS's assaults on some par excellence democratic rights and procedures implies that illiberal democracy, Polish style, has a strong anti-democratic tendency built into it.

Samuel Issacharoff considers elections to be 'the shorthand for other factors that we think characterize democratic life'[10]—and these 'other factors' stand for a broad range of rights, practices, and institutions, which, together, structure, facilitate, and render fairer political competition for the hearts and minds of voters.[11] 'Democracy' minus the equal rights to free assembly, free media, constitutional courts, independent electoral commissions, and other checks on arbitrary power degenerates into autocracy. While illiberal democracy may carry some genuine meaning in the first electoral cycle (where free and fair elections give the illiberal leaders of the winning party a mandate to act within their electoral promises even if we dislike them), in the longer term, 'illiberal democracy' becomes an oxymoron. The very liberal rights that are part of the irreducible guarantees of democracy are eroded of substance and dispensed with. More specifically, the institutions charged with the task of protecting democracy against distortions by a current majority—such as constitutional courts and regular courts—become disabled and then are enlisted in service of the majority.

As a result, democracy loses some important guarantees of self-protection and self-correction. To use a popular vernacular, democracy becomes 'merely formal', in that it lacks substance while maintaining the forms resembling or identical to those in truly democratic states. David Landau put it well by characterizing it as 'abusive constitutionalism': 'it is fairly easy to construct a regime that looks democratic, but in actuality is not fully democratic, at least along two important dimensions: vertical and horizontal checks on elected leaders and rights protection for disempowered groups'.[12] Again, this sounds like a good, concise description of Poland post-2015, even if Landau did not have Poland in mind when writing these words.

Populism and Democracy

As two veteran political scientists put it, for a political order to be democratic, it is not sufficient that the authorities emerge from free and fair elections, that is, that they are democratic in their pedigree. Authorities must also actually behave within the bounds of the democratic rules of the game as defined by the constitution and other laws:

> [N]o regime should be called a democracy unless its rulers govern democratically. If freely elected executives (no matter what the magnitude of their majority) infringe the constitution, violate the rights of individuals and minorities, impinge upon the legitimate functions of the legislature, and thus fail to rule within the bounds of a state of law, their regimes are not democracies.[13]

All three instances of 'failing to rule within the bounds of law' listed by Juan Linz and Alfred Stepan have occurred in Poland: the script was followed to the letter. As evidenced throughout this book, the authorities—both formal and informal, including the de facto leader—have infringed the Constitution on several occasions; the rights of individuals and minorities have been trampled on (for instance, through a politically discriminatory law on assemblies and through the law on police infringing privacy rights, both facts occurring in the situation of disabling constitutional review of these laws); and the 'legitimate functions of the legislature' have been breached by the political capture of Parliament by a political majority which, for all practical purposes, has gagged the opposition and prevented a normal deliberation on the proposed bills.

For this reason, at least with regard to Poland, it is difficult to adopt Cas Mudde's formula that, '[i]n essence, the populist surge is an illiberal democratic response to decades of undemocratic liberal policies'.[14] For one thing, Mudde traces the populist appeal to a reaction against transfers of authority to supranational entities (such as the European Union (EU) and International Monetary Fund) and also unelected national bodies such as central banks and courts—but neglects the fact that these transfers themselves often had democratic support. So rather than viewing populism as prompted by *excesses* of liberal democracy, it is closer to the truth to see it as responding to democratic *deficits*: there was not too much but too little of it. This led to a victory by a grouping that paid lip service to democracy and legality (Jarosław Kaczyński had never promised the destruction of the court system, the hollowing out of the rule of law, limiting the right of assembly, etc.) while at the same time persuading its electorate that it is more sensitive to traditional values and societal concerns, including fears, anxieties, and paranoias. The darker self in the people is retrieved and rehabilitated, and being attuned to it is presented as an ultimate victory of true democracy over the liberal, cosmopolitan elite.

Another point is that the democratic ingredient of populist movements has always been thin.[15] A statement that populism 'is both democratic and illiberal'[16] is simple but misleading because illiberal themes in populism—in particular, the dismantling of minority rights and constitutional checks and balances— undermine democracy. Often, populists target instruments of the electoral process, including its institutions (electoral commissions, courts in charge of electoral disputes) and electoral rules (the boundaries of districts, limits on terms of office, etc.) to make it more difficult for the opposition to dislodge populist in- cumbents. This undermines democracy, even in its thinnest meaning of securing an alternation in power. Some scholars distinguish between populism's *nature* and its likely *effects*; the former, we are told, is democratic, but the latter render it difficult for democracy to survive.[17] But this is unconvincing: populism's na- ture (for instance, viewed through the populists' motivations), insofar as we can second-guess the populist's true intentions, often reveals impatience with democratic procedures and a desire to construct a centralized, monolithic power structure, as evidenced, for instance, by Kaczyński's fascination with a single, extra-constitutional centre of politically strategic decisions (*centralny osrodek dyspozycji politycznej*). We need not credit populists *en bloc* with good demo- cratic motivations.

More generally, by rejecting effective checks and balances, populists under- mine the subjection of democratic politics to the constitutional rules of the game. Furthermore, by denying equal moral status to members of groups they despise, whether recent migrants, Islamists, Latinos, atheists, or political rivals, they strike at the value of political equality, which is at the core of democracy. Majority rule de- rives its weight precisely from the value of political equality it serves, and insofar as it is inconsistent with that value, it loses its normative bearings.[18] The widespread tendency to characterize contemporary populisms as fundamentally democratic, or at least as not non-democratic,[19] is therefore highly questionable, and assumes an arithmetical, purely majoritarian concept of democracy. It ignores the fact that the liberal pillars of democracy—protection of individual rights, maintenance of checks and balances, and constitutional restrictions on politics—are indispensable to the democratic process itself. It also ignores the right-wing populists' distaste for *representative* democracy, and their claim to communicate directly with the people as a whole, over the heads of representative institutions.

This is partly due to the fact that various established institutions of representation are seen and dismissed as serving the interests of the elite rather than of ordinary men and women. More importantly, for populists it is the mechanism of representation that distorts the formation of the true will of the people and introduces an irritating intermediation between the rulers and the people, which detracts from true democracy. As Nadia Urbinati puts it:

> Populism aims at a more direct identification of the represented with the representatives than free elections allow because it sees representation primarily as a strategy for embodying the whole people under a leader, rather than regulating the political dialectics among citizens' plural claims and advocacies.[20]

Populists favour *simple* solutions, where alternatives are reduced to black-and-white stories, and *quick* solutions, as the frenzied pace of pushing through the main pieces of legislation in Poland under PiS exemplifies; but, as Waldron observes, 'simplicity and haste are the obverse of responsible legislative decision-making, precluding, as they do, the time and space for thought and speech—and, within the realm of speech, for successive rounds of proposal, reply, amendment, and reconsideration that genuine engagement with legislative issues requires'.[21] Representative democracy, at its best, offers scope and opportunities for representatives of the people to listen carefully to each other, and allow them to be convinced by an argument employed by their adversaries. This must mean at least a relative freedom from a strict party discipline.

Reflection and careful deliberation are the cornerstones of the representative model; as Cass Sunstein puts it, reconstructing the views expounded in the Federalist Papers: 'Representatives would have the time and temperament to engage in a process of reflection. ... [They] would be free to engage in the process of discussion and debate from which the common good would emerge'.[22] None of this is even remotely approximated in legislatures dominated by a populist executive. To the contrary, populism leads to the centralization of power because the executive 'is seen as the most direct embodiment of the political will of a homogeneous polity'.[23] Hence the distaste to the separation and dispersion of powers, so characteristic of Kaczyński's ideas about the state.

Another strikingly non-democratic characteristic of right-wing populism is its inherently exclusionary nature: exclusionary not only vis-à-vis the non-citizens (potential immigrants), but also those citizens who are not seen as 'real' Poles (Hungarians etc. or, in a memorable phrase used by Jarosław Kaczyński, those who make an 'inferior sort' of citizen), and who do not deserve to belong to the nation by virtue of their identity, views or conduct.[24] PiS's tendency towards delegitimizing the opposition, as evidenced here, is a case in point. The exclusionary character of populism is not something merely contingent, but is inherent to populism as such: if it claims to speak for the entire nation (as it often does), it must resolve the necessary clash between this claim and the visible presence of those who do not identify with the populists' programme, by relegating them beyond the pale of the community. As political scientist Robert Mayer observe: 'It is here that the politics of identity becomes important in authoritarian ideology, for the dimension of standing is the domain of authenticity and inauthenticity, in which "real" members are distinguished from "false" ones on the basis of ascriptive status.'[25]

Consequently, populists are anti-pluralist not just in their political philosophy but also in their approach to institutions, which must distinguish between 'real' and 'false' Poles (Hungarians, Czechs, etc.). Only the interests, preferences, and identities of the 'real' ones matter (or, under a weaker version of the 'unequal standing' theory, they matter more). As Roberto Foa and Yascha Mounk observe: 'The core of the populist appeal ... sets populists in opposition to a pluralist vision of democracy in which groups holding disparate views and opinions must resolve their differences through channels of democratic dialogue and compromise.'[26] In an anti-pluralist paradigm, 'dialogue' and 'compromise' are replaced by a winner who 'takes all' because the winner better personifies the unitary interest of the people.

Illiberal, anti-representative, exclusionary, anti-egalitarian, and anti-pluralist... One wonders how much and what sort of 'democracy', compatible with the circumstances of the modern world (marked as it is by important pluralism and diversity, and by growing claims for inclusion), is left after all of populism's characteristics are taken into account. To be blunt, what is democratic about an illiberal, exclusionary, and anti-pluralist democracy? One may recall that Fareed Zakaria, in his influential article, when drawing a difference between democracy *tout court* and liberal democracy, attached a caveat to a description of classical, merely electoral, democracy: 'Of course elections must be open and fair, and this requires *some* protections for freedom of speech and assembly.'[27] A lot of work is undertaken by the word 'some'. Protections for freedom of speech and assembly extend to some other freedoms, also indispensable in the democratic process, such as freedom of religion and the rights of privacy. Degrees in the protection of those freedoms matter, and so do the independence of courts and robustness of constitutional review in maintaining the implementation of those rights consistent with established constitutional meanings.

To be sure, and as emphasized in Chapter 1, we need a language to preserve a distinction between an autocracy that cares about and pursues popular support, and an autocracy that relies on naked power and oppression. The term 'populism' does the job of striking this difference. But it is not as if we had two equally legitimate conceptions of democracy: a liberal and an illiberal one. Illiberal democracy cannot survive over time as democratic because the democratic process simpliciter presupposes protection of liberal rights. Without them, it is all too easy for an originally democratically elected majority to distort the process to an extent that future majorities will not be capable of acquiring a political status that will carry them to the government. In this sense at least, 'majority rule without liberty rights is unlikely to persist'.[28] Liberal democracy is not one of a number of interpretations of democracy, but a composite concept, in which both the adjective and the noun describe two interconnected preconditions of each other (rather like in 'free will' where the adjective 'free' does not restrict the scope of the noun, but rather amplifies its meaning). The best philosophical articulation of this interconnectedness that I have found is offered by Jürgen Habermas who refers to

> the intuition that, on the one hand, citizens can make adequate use of their public autonomy only if, on the basis of their equally protected private autonomy, they are sufficiently independent; but that, on the other hand, they arrive as a consensual regulation of their private autonomy only if they make adequate use of their political autonomy as enfranchised citizens.[29]

The intuition of which Habermas speaks explains why democracy (the citizens' use of public autonomy, or the 'freedom of the ancients') is impossible without strong protection of individual rights ('freedom of the moderns'), and why the interconnection is 'internal' to both. Just as there cannot be a truly democratic process without liberal safeguards, liberal rights only acquire a socially legitimate meaning in the context of democratic deliberation, including judicial interpretation conducted against the backdrop of a larger democratic system of government.

I am not claiming that all populism is *by definition* non-democratic. It need not be. Many movements dubbed in the literature as populist (such as Southern European left-wing populisms) are not necessarily authoritarian in their aspirations or effects. Bart Bonikowski is right that 'populist claims need not lead to authoritarian governance' and that 'authoritarianism can rely on a variety of other legitimating discourses besides populism'.[30] Rather, I am making a narrower and more limited claim: the sort of populism of which the Polish variant is an example leads inevitably to authoritarian, non-democratic consequences. We must be careful not to make this link as a matter of definitional fiat.

Perhaps the concept of 'plebiscitary autocracy' is more adequate to describe a state such as the one likely to emerge from the PiS rule: there are, by and large, free and regular elections, though they are not necessarily fair, due to some restraints on democratic rights, such as restrictions on assembly and the media, various ways of delegitimizing the opposition, unabashed pro-government propaganda in public media, and the politicization of the institutions that manage the electoral process.[31] With the government controlling all the levers of government, and suffocating the opposition and pluralism in the media, election days are a plebiscite in favour or against the ruling elite. As Samuel Issacharoff says: 'Elections under a completely controlling party, even if untainted by rampant fraud or violence, are in substance no different from the plebiscite.'[32] There is, however, no accountability and no subjection of the government to effective constitutional constraints *between* elections (which renders the system non-democratic, except for the brief electoral episodes).

The plebiscites are about whether the electorate approves of the governmental disregard for the Constitution in the period between elections. By providing generous welfare provisions, as well as an elaborate system of patronage and spoils, and a sense of pride based on restrictive-nationalistic rhetoric and a sense of protection based on fear of immigrants,[33] the government posits to the voters a Faustian bargain for the net benefit of confirming the government's place in power despite its constitutional non-compliance. Part of the bargain is about dispensing with strong and independent courts, because such courts are not vital for a party that confidently controls all of the branches of government and that does not anticipate an imminent defeat (in which case such courts would be helpful to it). This confirms Samuel Issacharoff's observation that '[c]ourts are at their strongest when there is uncertainty among rivals for political power, and at their most precarious when all the other institutional levers are under the unitary control of a single dominant party'.[34] This is the direction in which the Polish system is quickly evolving—one may say, degenerating—these days.[35]

Such a diagnosis, though, is made more difficult by the fact that, as noted in Chapter 1, the Polish transformation occurs without any revolutionary rhetoric and without an outright destruction of the institutions.[36] There is no revolutionary rhetoric employed by the winners—no overarching Utopia—but instead a systematic capturing of one institution after another by cadres loyal to PiS and, in particular, to its leader. We do not know what the *finalité* of this movement is, or at least we are not being told. Perhaps there is none; perhaps all that matters is the mere fact of unrestrained power; or perhaps there are many *finalités* pursued by different factions within the ruling elite. The trajectory of PiS's 'reforms' is a relentless movement towards the colonization of the state. But other than some banalities about restoring dignity to hard-working people, there is no grand design that would alert us to the revolutionary (or counter-revolutionary, if you prefer) zeal of PiS. Polish democratic backsliding does not have an ideological blueprint. What it has, and what is odious about it, is an *attitude*, a particular *sensibility*. Literally speaking, Polish institutions are not being dismantled or destroyed or demolished, but are instead being *hollowed out*, eroded, and emptied: their sense and meaning, which confer value on them, are all but lost, but their shells remain. For a spectator, this creates the illusion of business as usual, while in fact the institutions have been thoroughly colonized by the governing party.

Consider again, as just one example, a sequence of actions regarding the reform of the judiciary, and in particular of the National Council of the Judiciary (*Krajowa Rada Sądownictwa* (KRS)), as described in Chapter 4 in this book. A stylized but correct account may go like this:

The Parliament—the Sejm and the Senate—debates on the presidential bills in December 2017. No matter that the opposition is given only one or two minutes for their speeches; formally speaking, it is permissible. And the

opposition's input is dispensable anyway because the parliamentary arith-
metic renders any discussion pointless. The same applies to the legislature's
obligation to subject important bills to public consultation: no such consult-
ation was organized, but the duty is not imperative. In any event, the 'old'
KRS representatives were allowed to attend the parliamentary committee's
meeting (even though the chairman switched off the KRS spokesman's micro-
phone now and again; but what difference would he make anyway were he
allowed to speak at his leisure?). The president eventually signed the amended
bills that were, after all, the result of a compromise, but only a compromise
between a PiS President and the PiS parliamentary majority. The issue of
the constitutionality of the signed statutes does not arise as a problem be-
cause the newly reconstituted Constitutional Tribunal (CT) will not invali-
date these laws. In any event, it was the same new CT which had, back in
June 2017, found the previous KRS statute to be unconstitutional and thus
opened up the pathway for a new KRS law. So, strictly speaking, the legisla-
ture had no choice but to change the law on the KRS, and so it just used this
occasion to replace the entire judicial composition of the KRS. Going back to
the CT's June 2017 judgment regarding the KRS, it was handed down by a
five-judge panel that included, inter alia, Ms Przyłębska (as chairperson of
the panel, as her elevated position dictated) and two quasi-judges (including
one serving as judge-rapporteur). Ms Przyłębska became the president of the
CT, notwithstanding irregularities of her election, only thanks to the gen-
erosity of the president, who looked the other way when the objections to
her election were raised. The quasi-judges made it to the CT only thanks
to a choice by President Duda, who had sworn them in instead of the three
judges who were properly elected under a previous political dispensation. In
this way, he had aided and abetted the creation of the CT as an institution
laundering unconstitutional laws enacted by PiS and invalidating old laws
adopted in pre-PiS times. So what would be the point now for him or anyone
else to send a motion to such a CT to review the constitutionality of the laws
adopted by PiS? Especially since Ms Przyłębska, prior to the adoption of the
judiciary laws in their first (more radical) version in July 2017, had declared
on governmental TV that they were perfectly compatible with constitutional
separation of powers.

This account demands a lot from an external observer: a lot of knowledge and a lot
of understanding. The approach must be, as Renata Uitz pleas, 'comprehensive and
context-sensitive', otherwise 'a routine comparative constitutional law analysis is
likely to overlook symptoms of gradual constitutional decline'.[37] The account must
be attentive to small details, often hidden under the surface, often of uncertain
relevance, which jointly render the picture diametrically different from that man-
dated by the Constitution, or from that which appears at first blush.

We have seen the same sequence of events in the Supreme Court (SC) and regular courts, in the prosecutor's office, electoral institutions, media regulatory boards, and in the government's dealings with civil society. Old procedures and institutions are complied with, with some notable exceptions (such as the Constitution itself). But the overall system has been radically transformed from within, without the language of radicalism and without many formal changes of institutions. If the system is evil (and admittedly to many Poles it is *not*), it is, with apologies to Hannah Arendt, the evil of banality: a façade of 'normal' democracy hides a set of interconnecting arrangements converging into an overall pattern of authoritarianism (even if it is a plebiscitary one), radically contrary to democratic values.

Populist and Political Constitutionalism

There is an unfortunate tendency, among some scholars,[38] to treat Polish anti-constitutional populism as an instance of so-called political constitutionalism as contrasted with the legal brand of constitutionalism. Political constitutionalism, as advanced by John Griffith,[39] Paul Blokker,[40] and Richard Bellamy,[41] expresses dissatisfaction with court-oriented constitutionalism, and especially with strong judicial review, emphasizing its anti-democratic character. In contrast to legal constitutionalism as a negative frame for democratic politics, Paul Blokker makes a plea for constitutionalism as 'a vehicle for inclusive, democratic political interaction and ... a continuous deliberative process on the fundamental values of a political community'.[42] In opposition to the narrowing of space for democratic politics, Blokker argues for a restoration of the balance between democracy and constitutionalism by 'shifting constitutional politics towards the legislative'.[43]

The temptation to associate Polish developments post-2015 with political constitutionalism may be understandable. Both the PiS assault on the separation of powers and the theory of political constitutionalism diminish the role of constitutional courts, both are impatient with the judges' 'last word' on constitutionality of statutes, and both applaud majoritarian virtues of constitutional democracy. But it is a mistake to believe that Poland seriously gives effect to political constitutionalism.

For one thing, the critique by political constitutionalism is addressed not against *any* constraints on arbitrary exercises of political power, but, in contrast to legal constitutionalism, it views political mechanisms, especially those found in the separation of powers, as a superior form of constraining politics. In post-2015 Poland no such constraints have been meaningful, and all branches of power have become subordinated to unconstrained control by the supreme party leader. It is interesting to note that in his classic article, Griffith urged that solutions to problems such as limits to freedom of speech 'should not lie with the imprecisions of

Bills of Rights *or the illiberal instincts of judges*';[44] it is the potential illiberalism of judges rather than their lack of electoral mandate that he feared most. His ideal of liberal democracy is that based on limited government, not unrestrained parliamentarianism. Similarly, Bellamy compared 'the "thin" constitution of rights as determined by judicial review' to 'the "thick" constitutional processes of democratic law-making'.[45] The 'thickness' of political constitutionalism implies strong constitutional constraints placed on a democratic process, aimed at affording equal respect and concern for various rights and interests, at providing citizens with roughly equal political resources, and at assuring fair competition in elections, among other things.[46]

Second, a critique of robust judicial review as articulated by adherents to political constitutionalism assumes certain facts about a well-functioning political democracy, including the existence of fair and well-ordered democratic institutions, and in particular a legislature in which its members

> deliberate and vote on public issues, and the procedures for lawmaking are elaborate and responsible, and incorporate various safeguards ... and multiple levels of consideration, debate, and voting'; whereby 'these processes connect both formally (through public hearings and consultation procedures) and informally with wider debates in the society'.[47]

Further, 'these debates are informed by a culture of democracy, valuing responsible deliberation and political equality'.[48] No such conditions are even remotely met in today's Poland.

Third, under an attractive conception of 'political constitutionalism', constitutional meanings are reasonably determinate and binding, and this conception does not recommend disregarding constitutional meanings whenever the executive (or the parliamentary majority) finds it opportune. Without that, the noun in the composite term 'political constitutionalism' would become devoured by the adjective. If the executive—or the majority of people, for that matter—can give whatever meanings to constitutional provisions they wish, the constitutional constraints on political action become hollow. This is precisely what is going on in Poland: the Constitution is treated as a set of non-binding recommendations, which can be twisted around and used against its original purposes when the political leadership considers it convenient. A democracy-based critique of legal constitutionalism launched by advocates of political constitutionalism is not something that can be seen as vindicated by Poland post-2015; to the contrary, democracy is as much a victim of unrestrained political rulers there as is the rule of law and indeed constitutionalism *tout court*. So when Adam Czarnota says: 'I interpret the present constitutional crisis in Poland and some other countries in Central-Eastern Europe as an attempt to take the constitution seriously and return it to the citizens',[49] he may be accused of taking the assurances of Kaczyński and his legal advisers at face value, and not inquiring into what they actually *do*. One may of course adopt a purely majoritarian view of political legitimacy, but as a critic of the US version of political constitutionalism puts it simply: 'this overlooks the possibility that majorities may support unconstitutional positions'.[50]

Fourth, under political constitutionalism constitutional courts exercise a less robust and less final judicial scrutiny than under a Kelsenian, legal constitutional model: they are invited to exercise self-restraint, and various forms of 'weak' judicial review are recommended. But some critics of legal constitutionalism actually urge a broadening of access to constitutional courts, for instance viewing *actio populari* as a sort of 'civic access' to constitutional review, and thus in fact acknowledging the importance of constitutional review by those courts.[51] Nevertheless even under 'weak review' courts still exist as independent and robust quasi-judicial bodies, though with various constitutional devices (parliamentary override; the power of finding incompatibility only, without setting the law aside, etc.) aimed at rebalancing constitutional compliance with parliamentary supremacy. But this is *not* the fate of the CT in Poland: it has simply been captured by the hegemonic party, and used to legitimize laws brought about by the political hegemon and to delegitimize the laws enacted earlier by its present opponents. To describe its role in post-2015 Poland in the terms in which 'political constitutionalists' write and talk about constitutional courts is to dignify it in a way that it does not deserve.

Unwritten Rules and the Rule of Law

What about respect for the rule of law? As documented in this book, Jarosław Kaczyński and his collaborators alternated between breaching certain express rules and working largely within the letter of the law while at the same time violating unwritten norms without which those rules lose meaning—because so neutered, the deeper reasons for adoption of these rules in the first place are undermined. Examples of breaches of outright rules are numerous: a parliamentary resolution to cancel the election of new CT judges by the Parliament of the previous term, or the government's refusal to publish the judgments of the CT that it does not like, are just two of the many instances of blatant illegality. More importantly, however, PiS violated the (unwritten) norms that are essential for democracy. When President Duda granted a pardon to the politicians who had been sentenced in a non-final judgment for abuse of office (including an ex-minister Mariusz Kamiński, anointed by PiS leader to be minister again, with the same ministerial portfolio of supervision of secret services), while he may have used his constitutional power of pardon correctly, he breached the norm that states that a pardon is a means of last resort, which can be applied only to those sentenced in *final* judgments. To think otherwise—that is, to allow presidential pardon at *any* stage of the judicial trial—would bring the chief executive right into the centre of judicial proceedings and make him or her a super-judge, thus fundamentally breaching the very essence of the separation of powers. It also seems incoherent: if a person not punished by a final judgment is supposed to be considered innocent, how can you 'pardon' an innocent person? By breaching the unwritten norm, Duda helped Kaczyński appoint his trusted aide to the new government, which again seems to contradict rational presuppositions about the proper *rationale* for a presidential pardon: even if the president does not have to produce any reasons for it, it does not follow that *any* reason is good enough.

When PiS brought about a law on KRS which transferred the power to elect KRS judicial members from the judges to Parliament, it may have been legally correct— the Constitution does not say explicitly that they are elected *by* judges—but the law breached a customary norm taken for granted from the beginning of the post-communist history of Poland up to now. It had been ordained in a founding constitutive document of post-communist Poland, that is, in the agreements of the Round Table. It is also a generally recognized European standard with which Poland, as member of the Council of Europe and of the EU, has an obligation to comply, whether it is textually stated in its Constitution or not.

When PiS adopted the law on electoral commission, which replaced the key figures in the electoral machine from judges to administrators subordinate to the minister for interior, it acted within a lacuna left by the Constitution but against a norm that the apparatus of electoral commissions should be independent of politicians. Similarly, when the new law on the SC conferred on a newly created chamber, inter alia, the power to determine the correctness of election results and at the same time constructed the election of judges to the new chamber in such a way as to give the majority party in Parliament control over the identity of all the new judges (via the newly designed KRS), it breached an unwritten but nonetheless stringent norm that elected politicians do not control the judges who control the elections.

To move to less momentous but still significant events: in June 2018, the Speaker of the Sejm, Mr Marek Kuchciński, denied the opposition a right to ask the prime minister a question on the weakened position of Poland within the EU, although it was their turn to have a voice in parliamentary question time. In doing so, Kuchciński breached an unwritten convention, which had up to that point been respected in the Sejm, irrespective of which party had the majority at the time, according to which there is a certain customary sequence for each party to have its turn in interrogating ministers. Instead, he used a provision of the new regulation on the functioning of the Sejm, which gives the parliamentary majority a right to decide whom to give a right to ask a question if more than one question is foreshadowed, even though it was clear that the last-minute announcement of a question by the majority party was a trick to silence the opposition.

All these norms were unwritten but considered clear and peremptory, until PiS took power and breached them, one by one, pretending they did not exist. This uses the law against itself: acting within the literal meaning of the rules or within an apparent legal gap, but disregarding the norms of conduct necessary to accomplish the original purposes for specific legal provisions. In other words, even when a particular PiS action was not a breach of the law, textually speaking, it was corroding the norms that are a necessary support for the law if it is to perform its functions. The situation has been well encapsulated in a recent op-ed article by an ex-member of the KRS, Mr Łukasz Bojarski:

> Everything [in Poland, with regard to the judiciary] seems to happen on the basis of some legal provision or other, and in case any are missing PiS will enact something overnight, in a trice. And yet we sense that in fact it is happening by force, contrary to the constitution and to the spirit of the laws, to the principles accepted by civilized people.[52]

Indeed, PiS tries as much as it can to subject its coercive actions to legal rules it hastily enacts or changes: its modus operandi is to cloak its actions in legality. But the ideal of the rule of law is not satisfied by a mere fact of subjecting political action to 'some legal provision or other' (to use Mr Bojarski's words).[53] As Martin Krygier lucidly says in a recent essay,

> when populists make over legal institutions with cadres and legal ruses and purposes designed to lubricate their arbitrary sway over power, the ideal of the rule of law is being violated, even while forms familiar in rule of law institutional 'laundry lists' are being perpetuated; honoured, so to say, in the breach.[54]

'Unwritten rules' are not exactly the same thing as 'norms', though the boundaries between the two may seem blurred. Unwritten rules are usually at the same level of specificity as written provisions; for instance, 'judicial members of the KRS shall be elected by judges, not by politicians'. This is not the text of the Polish Constitution but a constitutional convention, based on a proper reading of the rationale for having the KRS in the first place. Norms are more general: 'respect your opponents in politics, and abstain from undermining their legitimacy' is an example; it may be articulated more generally as 'treat your political opponents as adversaries, not as enemies'. Further, norms can be distinguished from constitutional conventions, in that the latter may be thought to regulate relationships within and among governmental institutions while the former may be broader,[55] though it is a rather pedantic distinction and not much hinges on it. Both unwritten rules and norms/conventions are essential for the health of democracy and the rule of law. Both types of commands are peremptory and binding.

Populists manipulate public opinion to believe that if a norm is unwritten then it is not binding, and not really a norm, so that unwritten norms are usually the victim of populist actions that often observe the written norms to the letter. But the unwritten norms are equally, or more, important: consider the catalogue of examples of unwritten norms necessary for a democracy provided by Anna Grzymala-Busse: 'conflict of interest laws, financial transparency, respect for the opposition access and accountability to the media, and preventing party loyalty from becoming the basis for the awarding of tenders, contracts, and government responsibilities'.[56] Yascha Mounk adds norms such as: the government does not change electoral rules shortly before the election in order to maximize its output, the incumbents losing in the elections do not restrict the powers of office gained by their adversaries in the last moment of their rule, or '[t]he opposition confirms a competent judge whose ideology it dislikes rather than leaving a seat on the highest court in the land vacant'.[57] Regardless of whether it is written into a law or not, there is obviously a norm that the top executive does not intervene in individual criminal investigations, especially those that involve him/her or his/her family.

As one can see, some of these norms are articulated only in consequence of their breach; they become evident because of specific conduct which strikes us intuitively as highly improper. Unwritten norms prevent interpreting legal rules in ways which would be contrary to their original and/or best rationales, so that written provisions are read and interpreted in accordance with the spirit, not always à la lettre. Articulating these norms may be controversial and some proposed meanings may be contested, but in a healthy democracy there is a degree of consensus on unwritten norms. What is required is not just knowledge of the norms, but also knowing that others know them, and that they will abide by them, and, if they do not, they will know that they have violated them. For often the norms become salient only when broken; as with health or good plumbing, we know its importance in its absence.

Akhil Reed Amar's book on 'America's Unwritten Constitution' provides a good example of how to read unwritten norms into the Constitution, or, in his words, how to detect 'rules and principles residing between the lines'.[58] One example is taken from the experience of America's first ever impeachment trial in which the participation of Ohio's Senator Benjamin Wade—who was serving as Senate President *pro tempore* and was therefore next in line to the presidency—was called into question. Amar then asks whether it would be constitutionally permissible, in contemporary times, to allow the vice-president to sit as a judge at the president's impeachment trial. No, he says, for this situation would give rise to an 'intolerable conflict of interest'.[59] Even though the textual Constitution does not prohibit it, no judge would tolerate such a 'gross impropriety'.[60] Among Amar's sources in reaching this conclusion is Blackstone's *Commentaries on the Laws of England*, in which the great jurist posits that, as paraphrased by Amar, 'unless the supreme legislature made crystal clear its specific intent to command an absurd or unjust result, the supreme law was to be interpreted so as to avoid patent absurdity or gross injustice'.[61] According to Amar, the reason for the text's silence is precisely that '[i]n the case of a man literally presiding over his own case, it obviously went without saying that such a thing was impermissible'.[62]

Often, unwritten norms have a decisively moderating effect on written rules, and supplement them in ways that render written rules much more constraining on public officials than the mere reading of the textual rule would suggest. Mark Tushnet gives an example of the Canadian system of choosing SC justices.[63] The formal rule gives the prime minister complete discretion in making appointments, subject only to the proviso that three out of nine justices come from Quebec. However, Tushnet adds: 'That formal system ... is supplemented by extremely strong norms of deference to professional judgments about potential appointees' ability. The prime minister would act inappropriately, and suffer politically, by departing from these norms'.[64] The same textual rule, Tushnet continues, adopted in another country but without the accompanying unwritten norm (which of course cannot be 'enacted'), would be disastrous because, for instance in the US, 'there is little reason to think that, at least in the short to medium run, informal norms would constrain the president's choices'.[65] This example shows that the force that informal norms confer on the same written norms in different systems may produce different outcomes.

Consider, from this point of view, some examples of PiS's violation of un-written rules and norms, when the constitutional text was (or was alleged to be) silent on the matter. One is the presidential pardon (as discussed in Chapter 3 and in this chapter), for reasons of political expediency (the need to quickly render Kaczyński's close collaborator eligible for a sensitive ministerial post) President Duda pardoned Mariusz Kamiński even though the criminal appellate procedure regarding a serious felony while in office was still underway, in order for Kamiński to be able to re-occupy the office. The Constitution does not spell out explicitly that a presidential pardon applies only to final, binding judgments, but isn't it the case that (to repeat Amar's words) 'it [goes] without saying that such a thing [is] imper-missible'?[66] After all, you can pardon only a person found guilty, while before the final sentence a defendant must be deemed innocent; how can you 'pardon' an in-nocent person without running into absurdity? And would not a generalization of the practice of pardoning before the process is exhausted include the top executive into the routine operation of the justice system: an intolerable violation of separ-ation of judicial and executive branches?

The second example is that of the composition of the KRS. As also already men-tioned, the Constitution is indeed silent on the mode of electing the judicial mem-bers of the KRS. But doesn't a 'holistic' reading of the Constitution, advocated by Amar,[67] suggest that if the remaining (i.e. non-judicial) members of the KRS are in a strong sense *representatives* of the president, the Senate, and the Sejm (be-cause they are elected/appointed by these bodies),[68] then the judicial ingredient of the KRS *represents* the judiciary and, by analogy to presidential or parliamen-tary representatives, should be elected by those whom the judges-members of the

KRS are said to represent? So, to use Amar's words again, does it not 'go without saying' that the election of judges by Parliament (who already has its representatives on the KRS) is constitutionally 'impermissible'? Amar urges: 'we must read the Constitution as a whole—between the lines, so to speak'.[69] If we do so, the (unwritten) rule that the judicial members of the KRS should be elected by judges themselves, and that the silence of the Constitution is due to the fact that it was so *obvious* to the Constitution drafters that they even did not bother to spell it out explicitly, becomes compelling. In addition, it is a European norm, in the statistical sense that the election by peer judges is adopted in a majority of European legal systems that possess a national judiciary council, and also in a normative sense in that it is viewed as a prudent safeguard against the political control of the judiciary.[70]

The third example is that of the president who signs a bill into law and then sends it to the CT for an ex post review, as he did with regard to the statute on the 'attribution of guilt to the Polish Nation' for the crimes of Holocaust and other war crimes. But isn't it 'patent absurdity or gross injustice' that the president *at the same time* attests to the law's constitutionality (otherwise, he would have no right to sign it rather than send it to the CT for preliminary control) and expresses constitutional doubts in his motion to the CT for an ex post review? Even if the Constitution is silent on such a combination of signing and sending for ex post review, the implicit presupposition of both acts suggests the 'patent absurdity' of the president's conduct.

The fourth example resonates with a specific example used by Amar, regarding the ineligibility of the US vice-president to sit as a judge at the president's impeachment trial, even if the US Constitution is silent on the matter. Impermissibility of such an outcome is based on a principle *nemo iudex in causa sua*: not a written principle but a paradigmatic rule to be read 'between the lines', so much so that 'we should place no weight on the omission of an explicit recusal clause for vice presidential impeachments'.[71] On 24 October 2017 the 'new' Polish CT considered the case (discussed in Chapter 3) directly concerning the status of judges alleged to have been elected improperly in 2015 (as their critics say, 'quasi-judges').[72] The panel of five included two judges who belong to that category, including Mr Mariusz Muszyński who was presiding over the panel. Neither the Constitution nor the statute on the CT states explicitly that a judge whose status on the tribunal is affected by the outcome of the case shall not sit on a panel considering this case. But, as Amar says with regard to US constitutionalism, the reason for the text's silence is that it goes without saying that such a thing is impermissible.[73]

The fifth example concerns changes in the rules regarding the composition of a top court. The US Constitution does not provide for the number of SC justices, but the court-packing attempt by President Franklin Delano Roosevelt, exploiting this gap, was generally considered to be violating a constitutional norm. As Richard Primus observes:

Congress seems strongly disinclined to change the size of the Court even when doing so would be to the manifest advantage of the party in power. That disinclination stems from legitimacy concerns, derived perhaps partly from the historical meaning of President Franklin Roosevelt's court-packing plan and partly from a more abstract sense that the nine-justice Court should not be manipulated.[74]

But a 'manipulation' of the court numbers is precisely what PiS did: in order to guarantee the ruling party control of the majority of SC judges, it increased the number of judges (from 93 to 120) which, in combination with new retirement rules, and the creation of two new chambers (to be filled only by new judges, twenty in the Chamber of Extraordinary Control and Public Affairs, and sixteen in the Disciplinary Chamber), gave the party the capacity to appoint a majority of SC judges by a newly constituted KRS. This amounted to a legislative flaunting of the norm against manipulating the composition of a court for party-political advantage.

As Josh Chafetz and David Pozen show, the breakdown of constitutional norms may have any of three forms: destruction, decomposition or displacement by law. Destruction occurs when a norm is openly flouted, and ceases to exist; decomposition, when through interpretation or application the norm is gradually altered and its force reduced; and displacement by law takes place when norms are converted into legally binding directives.[75] Putting the third category aside (after all, a conversion of a norm into a legally binding instrument may be seen as a triumph rather than a breakdown of the norm), both these categories are discernible in Poland, but with the preponderance falling under the first category. When the president grants pardon to a person unpunished by a final sentence, or when the legislators decide to ignore a norm regarding the election of judicial members of the KRS, the pre-existing constitutional norms vanish overnight, so to speak. But the incremental isolation and sidelining of the opposition—for instance by departing from conventions regarding the participation in parliamentary question time—reflects more a decomposition than a destruction. In both cases, the norm ceases to be respected but the trajectory is different. In the case of the latter, the final disappearance of the norm is usually preceded by a period of persuasion and propaganda, paving the way to an argument by norm-breaking office holders that the old norm is obsolete or counter-productive. In Poland the denial of parliamentary entitlements to the opposition was preceded and accompanied by a demonization of the opposition depicted as uncommitted to democratic rules of the game.

Democratic unwritten norms are often pre-constitutional, not to be discerned even from a 'holistic' reading of the Constitution 'between the lines', but from the democratic culture underlying the system. There is, for example, a norm in a democracy that you do not question the integrity of electoral process, and do not contest the electoral results unless you have strong grounds for such claims, in which case you go to court or any institution competent to hear your claim. But prior to

2015, PiS (and its friendly NGOs) continuously and systematically challenged the legitimacy of elections, without any grounds, and with no legal vindication of such claims. False charges of electoral fraud undermine public trust in democratically elected institutions, and ultimately weaken the legitimacy of democracy.

When you are in power, there is a norm that you do not push your legal competences to their limits, by, for example, testing their outer boundaries or constantly being on the verge of overreaching. Steven Levitsky and Daniel Ziblatt define this as a norm of 'forbearance' which is 'the idea that politicians should exercise restraint in deploying their institutional prerogatives'.[76] Another way of articulating this norm can be: as a politician, do not go all the way, expanding your power as far as the literal reading of a legal text permits, and in particular insofar as there are gaps in the text. There is also a norm that, no matter how harsh the words said during the electoral campaign, there is a sort of reconciliation after the election, which allows the governing majority and the opposition to work towards a public good. The opposite happened after Duda's and PiS's victories in 2015: the chasm between the winners and the losers grew larger, and the accusations against the opposition only became harsher. Public insults devastated the public sphere and contributed to a growing public cynicism about politics: a toxic element in a democracy.

The alarming level of norm-breaking caused a phenomenon in public opinion of 'defining political pathology down', to paraphrase Daniel Patrick Moynihan's observation about 'defining deviancy down'. As Moynihan wrote (in the context of attitudes toward crime), 'there are circumstances in which society will choose *not* to notice behavior that would be otherwise controlled, or disapproved, or even punished'.[77] Some such circumstances lead to what Moynihan called 'normalizing'. This is largely what has happened in Poland: political aberrations have become 'normalized' because people have a limited ability to grasp and face continuous breaches of norms, so the conduct once considered pathological becomes part of the mainstream. It is more than citizens can consciously absorb, but is typical of the PiS assault *tous azimuts* on democracy and the rule of law.

There may be a temptation to characterize the actions by PiS as 'constitutional hardball', to use a concept coined by Mark Tushnet to describe political actions that are 'in tension with existing pre-constitutional understandings',[78] and that 'alter the previously taken-for-granted institutional arrangements'.[79] Levitsky and Ziblatt used Tushnet's concept to describe, for instance, 'unrestrained' presidential (e.g. ruling by decree) and congressional (e.g. refusing to fund the government) actions in the US, or actions by President Juan Péron in Argentina in the 1940s (taking a maximum advantage of vaguely defined constitutional clauses in order to impeach supreme court justices), and they helpfully characterize constitutional hardball as 'playing by the rules but pushing against their bounds and "playing for keeps"'. They also add: 'It is a form of institutional combat aimed at permanently defeating one's partisan rivals—and not caring whether the democratic game continues'.[80] Tushnet's own examples of constitutional hardball taken from the American legal history are *Marbury v. Madison*, Nixon's attempt to impound money that Congress appropriated for other purposes, or President Roosevelt's court-packing plan in 1937.[81]

All these instances exemplify constitutional hardball: actions that politicians take 'when they try to displace settled processes with ones that would make it easier for them to put in place the new institutional arrangements they favor'.[82] The last characterization applies well to PiS. But there is a difference: Tushnet's constitutional hardball is in tension with past and existing *pre-political* constitutional understandings and yet is 'without question within the bounds of existing constitutional doctrine and practice'.[83] This is not the case with PiS assault on constitutionalism. For instance, neither the changing of the way judges-members of the KRS are elected, nor refusing to swear in properly elected judges of the CT, were within the bounds of established 'constitutional doctrine and practice'. They had never happened before.

Perhaps another sport-based metaphor included in Tushnet's article may be more appropriate: that of 'brushback'.[84] This is a pitch in baseball, thrown near a batter's head, usually for the purposes of intimidation. This is, in Tushnet's interpretation, a good metaphor for Roosevelt's court-packing plan: while the plan itself failed it nonetheless intimidated his political opposition into accepting his substantive plans.[85] Some actions by PiS have a brushback quality in that they were clearly meant to intimidate the opposition into compliance with the ruling party's wishes (e.g. when in mid-2018 PiS enacted a law, eventually vetoed by President Duda, to amend the rules of election to the European Parliament, as a result of which most small parties in the opposition would lose any chances to elect their representatives). If so, they hardly achieved the aim; the compliance with non-constitutional actions, thankfully, has, by and large, not materialized.

Three Strategies

By way of summary, one may borrow a simple but useful taxonomy of three main strategies—as described by Levitsky and Ziblatt in their recent book under the ominous title *How Democracies Die*—that elected authoritarians use in order to consolidate their power: capturing the referees, sidelining the key players, and rewriting the rules 'to tilt the playing field against opponents'.[86] PiS attempted, with varying success, all three of these strategies. First, it 'captured the referees' by turning the CT into an active aide and enabler of the government, subordinating all other judges, and in particular in the SC, to the will of parliamentary majority and of the minister of justice, thoroughly merging law enforcement with the administration of the ministry of justice, etc. Second, it sidelined key players in the political system, using government resources against unfriendly media, denying them advertising for state-owned enterprises and threatening with penalties for unfavourable coverage, while dispensing benefits and privileges on pro-government media. It continuously demonized and insulted the parliamentary opposition, delegitimizing its position in the political system by representing it as aides to foreign, anti-Polish interests. Third, it rewrote the rules of the political game by tilting the playing field: it created a new Electoral Commission, packed with loyalists, thoroughly 'dejudicialized' and vulnerable to political pressure from the government; it created a brand-new chamber of the SC tasked, among other things, with hearing electoral complaints and staffed entirely by new judges elected by a politically partisan KRS; it changed the law of assembly by giving privileges to governmental or church-sponsored assemblies; and it gave the police and secret services expanded means of surveillance and supervision not subjected to any meaningful judicial control.

Those actions, which follow the usual script of elected authoritarians, have not yet led to drastic outcomes. No national elections have been held yet so we do not know whether the new electoral law will serve as a mechanism for massive rigging of the electoral results. No journalists or public commentators were charged under the new law, which forbids inculpating Poland for co-responsibility for crimes during 2nd World War, during the five months of the operation of this scandalous law. Even though many counter-demonstrators have been prosecuted for intruding on the governmental 'cyclical' events, no one was sentenced to jail for manifesting disagreement with the ruling party and its leaders.

But the institutional infrastructure for these actions *is* there, and the sliding all occurs incrementally in one direction. There is nothing unusual, nothing puzzling in an authoritarian degradation brought about by a party that originally won in free and fair elections; if anything, it would be a replication of a pattern worldwide whereby '[d]emocratic backsliding today begins at the ballot box'.[87] Venezuela, the Philippines, Turkey, and Russia are just a few examples illustrating this trend. This is what Leszek Balcerowicz calls 'bad political transitions', meaning developments 'whereby an individual and his (her) group win genuinely free elections and then—by reducing the civil liberties and the level of the rule of law—lower the level of the legal political competition (democracy)'.[88] That is why the electoral contests in Poland in the coming years (especially at a national level) will not be about competition between different policy alternatives, but about the rivalry of competing political regimes. PiS often dismisses its rivals by claiming that their only programme is 'anti-PiS' but, even putting to one side the question of whether it is an accurate characterization, 'anti-PiS' refers to a huge agenda of the fundamentals of constitutional democracy.

Notes

1. Guillermo O'Donnell, 'Delegative Democracy' (1994) 5/1 *Journal of Democracy* 55, 59.
2. Ibid. 62.

3. Ibid. 60.

4. Ibid. 60.

5. Ibid. 60.

6. See 'Jarosław Polskę Zbaw! Dziś imieniny Jarosława!' [Jarosław, save Poland! Today is the name day of Jarosław] (*Fronda.pl*, 18 June 2016) <http://www.fronda.pl/a/jaroslaw-polske-zbaw-dzis-imieniny-jaroslawa,70492.html> (accessed 1 September 2018).

7. O'Donnell (n. 1) 61–2.

8. Ibid. 60.

9. David Landau, 'Abusive Constitutionalism' (2013) 47 *UC Davis Law Review* 189, 199 n. 23.

10. Samuel Issacharoff, *Fragile Democracies* (CUP 2015) 5.

11. Issacharoff puts it well elsewhere in his book: 'In reality, democracy is a more complex form of political organization than simply a fact of holding periodic elections for government. Behind the image of the voter at the polls stands a conception of civil liberties that allows political organization and speech, and a series of institutional actors who provide the structure for political competition, most notably political parties', ibid. 243.

12. Landau, 'Abusive Constitutionalism' (n. 9) 200.

13. Juan J. Linz and Alfred Stepan, 'Toward Consolidated Democracies' (1996) 7/2 *Journal of Democracy* 14, 15.

14. Cas Mudde, 'Europe's Populist Surge' (Nov/Dec 2016) 95 *Foreign Affairs* 25, 30.

15. For an analysis of parties such as Front National in France, Golden Dawn in Greece, Jobbik in Hungary, and the Vlaams Blok in Belgium as fundamentally anti-democratic, see Takis Pappas, 'Distinguishing Liberal Democracy's Challengers' (2016) 27/4 *Journal of Democracy* 22, 25–6. But note that Pappas himself defines populism as illiberal but democratic, hence he does not classify those parties as populist, see ibid. 29. To Pappas, PiS is populist in his sense of the word, see ibid. 30.

16. Yascha Mounk, *The People vs Democracy* (Harvard University Press 2018) 35.

17. Ibid. 35.

18. See Wojciech Sadurski, 'Legitimacy, Political Equality, and Majority Rule' (2008) 21 *Ratio Juris* 39; Ronald Dworkin, *Sovereign Virtue* (Harvard University Press 2000) 363; Jeremy Waldron, *Political Theory* (Harvard University Press 2016) 164; Jeremy Waldron, *God, Locke, and Equality* (CUP 2002) 130–1.

19. See eg Sheri Berman, 'Populism Is Not Fascism' (Nov/Dec 2016) 95 *Foreign Affairs* 39, 43 (stating that current right-wing extremisms, which she dubs populisms, 'are certainly illiberal, but they are not antidemocratic').

20. Nadia Urbinati, 'Populism and the Principle of Majority' in Cristóbal Rovira Kaltwasser, Paul Taggart, Paulina Ochoa-Espejo, and Pierre Ostiguy (eds), *The Oxford Handbook of Populism* (OUP 2017) 571, 577.

21. Waldron, *Political* (n. 18) 141, endnote omitted.

22. Cass R. Sunstein, 'Lessons from the American Founding' in Cass R. Sunstein (ed.), *Can It Happen Here? Authoritarianism in America* (HarperCollins 2018) 57, 69.

23. Bart Bonikowski, 'Ethno-nationalist populism and the mobilization of collective resentment', 68 (2017, Suppl. 1) *British Journal of Sociology* S181, S185.

24. A recent express statement of this exclusionary approach was made by a sociologist Andrzej Zybertowicz who is well placed in the PiS establishment (currently a

presidential advisor on security issues, formerly a PiS candidate in the elections to the European Parliament). As he said at a public forum organized by the TVN24 channel on 12 November 2017, the Polish nation consists of all those who meet 'a patriotic minimum' made up of three conditions: first, one must believe that 'Poland and Poles need their own, independent and effective state'; second, 'regardless of whether one is a religious believer or not, one must not neglect the role of Catholic Church'; and third, 'Polish history may be criticized but one must not turn one's back on it or falsify it'. Whoever fails to meet any of these threshold conditions, Dr Zybertowicz added, 'signs off on Polishness'. See 'Plemię to za łagodne określenie. Plemiona mogą współistnieć' (*TVN24*, 12 November 2017) <https://www.tvn24.pl/wiadomosci-z-kraju,3/arena-idei-czy-polacy-to-jeden-narod-a-dwa-plemiona,789533.html> (accessed 29 December 2017).

25. Robert Mayer, 'Strategies of Justification in Authoritarian Ideology' (2001) 61 *Journal of Political Ideologies* 147, 158.

26. Roberto Stefan Foa and Yascha Mounk, 'The Signs of Deconsolidation' (2017) 28/1 *Journal of Democracy* 5, 13.

27. Fareed Zakaria, 'The Rise of Illiberal Democracy' (1997) November/December *Foreign Affairs* 22, 25, emphasis added.

28. Stefan Rummens, 'Populism as a Threat to Liberal Democracy' in Cristóbal Rovira Kaltwasser, Paul Taggart, Paulina Ochoa-Espejo, and Pierre Ostiguy (eds), *The Oxford Handbook of Populism* (OUP 2017) 554, 557.

29. Jürgen Habermas, 'On the Internal relation between the Rule of Law and Democracy' (1995) 3 *European Journal of Philosophy* 12, 18.

30. Bart Bonikowski, 'Ethno-nationalist populism and the mobilization of collective resentment' (2017) 68 (Suppl. 1) *The British Journal of Sociology* S181, S190.

31. As a result, this account by Larry Diamond who referred to 'electoral authoritarianism' in hybrid regimes, may soon apply to Poland: 'While an opposition victory is not impossible . . ., it requires a level of opposition mobilization, unity, skill, and heroism far beyond what would normally be required for victory in a democracy'. See Larry Diamond, 'Thinking about Hybrid Regimes' (2002) 13/2 *Journal of Democracy* 21, 24. It also resonates with a well-known characterization by Levitsky and Way of 'competitive authoritarianism': 'Such regimes are competitive in that opposition parties use democratic institutions to contest seriously for power, but they are not democratic because the playing field is heavily skewed in favor of incumbents'. See Steven Levitsky and Lucan A. Way, 'The Rise of Competitive Authoritarianism' (2002) 13/2 *Journal of Democracy* 51, 52.

32. Issacharoff, *Fragile* (n. 10) 272.

33. Not every nationalism can be so characterized; one may, following Bonikowski, distinguish 'restrictive nationalism' from a milder, 'creedal nationalism' which merely 'displays moderate pride in all aspects of the nation-state', see Bonikowski (n. 23) S189.

34. Issacharoff, *Fragile* (n. 10) 273.

35. Some democracy scholars classify Poland under PiS as a case of 'electoral democracy': lower in the rank than a 'liberal democracy' (because it is deficient in the field of the rights-securing rule of law and effective judicial constraints on executive power) but better than 'electoral autocracy' (which displays significant irregularities regarding democratic standards concerning party competition etc). See Valeriya Mechkova,

Anna Lührmann, and Staffan I Lindberg, 'How Much Democratic Backsliding?' (2017) 28/4 *Journal of Democracy* 162, 165.

36. For a similar observation, see also Rafał Kalukin, 'Wielka normalizacja', *Polityka* (Warsaw, 26 December 2017), online edition.

37. Renáta Uitz, 'Can You Tell when an Illiberal Democracy is in the Making? An Appeal to Comparative Constitutional Scholarship from Hungary' (2015) 13 *International Journal of Constitutional Law* 279, 300.

38. See eg Adam Czarnota, 'The Constitutional Tribunal' (*VerfBlog*, 3 June 2017) <https://verfassungsblog.de/the-constitutional-tribunal/> (accessed 21 February 2018).

39. John A.G. Griffith, 'The Political Constitution' (1979) 42 *Modern Law Review* 1.

40. Paul Blokker, *New Democracies in Crisis?* (Routledge 2014). Note that Blokker describes his own conception as 'civic' rather than 'political' constitutionalism; I place him here in the category of endorsers of political constitutionalism because on the main point in the legal/political divide, i.e. rejection of a strong constraining function vis-à-vis legislatures performed by constitutional courts, Blokker is clearly on the side of political constitutionalism, ibid. 41–2.

41. Richard Bellamy, *Political Constitutionalism: A Republican Defence of the Constitutionality of Democracy* (CUP 2007).

42. Blokker, *New Democracies* (n. 40) 41.

43. Ibid. 32.

44. Griffith (n. 39) 14, emphasis added.

45. Bellamy (n. 41) 6.

46. Ibid. 4–5.

47. Jeremy Waldron, 'The Core of the Case against Judicial Review' (2006) 115 *Yale Law Journal* 1346, 1361, footnotes omitted.

48. Ibid. 1361.

49. Czarnota (n. 38).

50. Corey Brettschneider, 'Popular Constitutionalism contra Populism' (2015) 30 *Constitutional Commentary* 81, 82.

51. See Blokker, *New Democracies* (n. 40) 167–8.

52. Łukasz Bojarski, 'Bez żadnego trybu', *Dziennik Gazeta Prawna* (Warsaw, 15 May 2018) 2. Mr Bojarski was member of the KRS (appointed to this position by President) in 2010–15, and currently is President of the Institute of Law and Society (INPRIS).

53. Ibid.

54. Martin Krygier, 'Democracy and the Rule of Law' in Jens Meierhenrich and Martin Loughlin (eds), *Cambridge Companion on the Rule of Law* (forthcoming 2019), manuscript 20, footnote omitted.

55. See Josh Chafetz and David E. Pozen, 'How Constitutional Norms Break Down' (2018) 65 *UCLA Law Review* 1430, 1434 n. 14.

56. Anna Grzymala-Busse, 'Global Populisms and Their Impact' (2017) 76 (Suppl. S1) *Slavic Review* S3, S6.

57. Yascha Mounk, *The People vs Democracy* (Harvard University Press 2018) 12.

58. Akhil Reed Amar, *America's Unwritten Constitution: The Precedents and Principles We Live By* (Basic Books 2012) 6.

59. Ibid. 12.

60. Ibid. 12.

61. Ibid. 10.
62. Ibid. 13.
63. Mark Tushnet, 'Comparing Right-Wing and Left-Wing Populism' in Mark Graber, Sanford Levinson, and Mark Tushnet (eds) *Constitutional Democracy in Crisis?* (OUP 2018): 639, 642.
64. Ibid. 642.
65. Ibid. 641.
66. Amar (n. 58) 13.
67. Ibid. 47.
68. By a 'strong' representation I mean not only that *A* represents *B*'s interests (preferences, concerns, identity), but also that *A* has *B*'s actual mandate to do so (paradigmatic cases are those of an arbitrator or of an MP).
69. Amar (n. 58) 47.
70. See the statement by the European Network of Councils for the Judiciary (ENCJ) to the effect that the election of judges-members of a judicial council should be 'solely by their peers': ENCJ Project Team, 'Councils for the Judiciary 2010–2011' (ENCJ, 2011) [PDF] <https://www.encj.eu/images/stories/pdf/workinggroups/report_project_team_councils_for_the_judiciary_2010_2011.pdf> para. 2.3, at 5 (accessed 20 June 2018).
71. Amar (n. 58) 13.
72. Case no. K 1/17.
73. Amar (n. 58) 13.
74. Richard Primus, 'Unbundling Constitutionality' (2013) 80 *University of Chicago Law Review* 1079, 1123.
75. Chafetz and Pozen (n. 55) 1435–8.
76. Steven Levitsky and Daniel Ziblatt, *How Democracies Die* (Crown Publishing 2018) 8–9.
77. Daniel Patrick Moynihan, 'Defining Deviancy Down' (1993) 62(1) *The American Scholar* 17, 19, emphasis in original.
78. Mark Tushnet, 'Constitutional Hardball' (2004) 37 *John Marshall Law Review* 523, 523, footnote omitted.
79. Ibid. at 532.
80. Levitsky and Ziblatt (n. 55) 109.
81. Tushnet, 'Constitutional Hardball' (n.78) 538–46.
82. Ibid. 533.
83. Ibid. 523.
84. Ibid. 544–5.
85. Ibid. 544–5.
86. Levitsky and Ziblatt (n. 76) 177.
87. Ibid. 5.
88. Leszek Balcerowicz, 'Institutional Systems and Their Dynamics, Including Good and Bad Transitions' (September 2017), unpublished manuscript on file with the author, 23.

Afterword

The picture drawn in this book is gloomy: the hegemonic party in Poland controls much of the media, courts, law enforcement, agencies such as the electoral commission, media boards, national bank, the military, and civil society grant-dispensing institution, and deploys the machinery of government in its favour. The ruling elite has a firm stranglehold on nearly all public institutions with its effective capacity to suppress dissent, to enrich itself, and to further consolidate its power. The Law and Justice Party (PiS) circumvents democratic norms and the rule of law, and relies on a centralized authority which can be traced to decisions by one man and a narrow group of his closest collaborators, in a way invisible to the constitutional design. All senior positions are occupied by party loyalists whose main pattern of accountability is to the party leader, not to the Parliament or the electorate. The main concerns regarding any public decision within the sphere of discretion left by the party leader is not about its rationality, effectiveness or legality, but about how it will be viewed and assessed by the leader. Second-guessing by all political decision-makers about the leader's response (which may come with a delay, or be ambiguous and capricious) distorts the reasonableness calculus but further consolidates the centralized, personal control of the state. Stephen Holmes observes, pessimistically: 'When a politically adroit counter-elite has gained sufficient power to control the country's media, neutralize the courts, and undermine the capacity of the opposition to contest the next election, as it has in Hungary and Poland, liberal democracy will need some kind of miracle to help it back to life.'[1]

But there is no inevitability in further backsliding for Polish democracy, and perhaps even in maintaining populist authoritarianism as is the case now: as at the time of writing, no political movement in the history of human society has carried inevitable outcomes with it. PiS is hopefully no exception. Poland has the strong societal and political resources necessary to arrest and reverse the trends described here, and then unravel all the nefarious institutional changes brought about by PiS rule, difficult though it will be. There is still a vibrant and resilient civil society (with notable examples including the demonstrations held in more than two hundred Polish towns in July 2017 to protest against the law on the judiciary); there are strong even if rather ephemeral social protest movements; there is an independent body of commercial media, both electronic and print; and there are passionate debates in social media. Universities are politically free, and the only censorship, when it occurs in academia, is self-imposed. Cultural institutions—theatres, film industry, museums—articulate a rich diversity of political views, and although

Poland's Constitutional Breakdown. © Wojciech Sadurski 2019. Published 2019 by Oxford University Press.

the state makes occasional and rather awkward attempts at censorship, Polish culture maintains an independent spirit. The opposition parties, while divided along many lines, have a combined electorate, equal to, or exceeding, the electorate of PiS. There are a number of iconic personalities with great historical credentials and impeccable liberal-democratic outlooks who constitute a symbolic asset that PiS lacks: Lech Wałęsa, Adam Michnik, and Władysław Frasyniuk have the moral authority that Kaczyński and his cronies may only dream about. There is a courageous, tenacious, and intelligent Commissioner for Human Rights (Ombudsman) Dr Adam Bodnar, who enjoys a degree of constitutional protection against dismissal, even though PiS media and individual politicians (as well as a comically aggressive quasi-judge of the Constitutional Tribunal, Mariusz Muszyński) occasionally suggest terminating his tenure prior to the end of his term.

Populisms, such as PiS's, often carry a seed of self-destruction: they are, in the long run, ineffective and counterproductive, relying on the knowledge (imperfect) and charisma (doubtful) of a single person. With its paranoid excesses and narrow epistemic base, populism has a low capacity for effective governance. By disconnecting the real centre of political power from constitutionally established institutions and procedures, the regime reduces the likelihood of self-correction facilitated by inter-institutional accountability. There may be some grounds for optimism in Stephen Holmes's observations (not formulated specifically with regard to Poland) about populist leaders' propensities: 'populist leaders almost always prefer a personally loyal to a professionally competent staff. This makes it somewhat less likely that a cornered populist president will be able to design and implement a truly shrewd and effective survival strategy'.[2] The main legitimating ground of populism, that it effectively delivers the goods to its electorate, seems to have a long-term tendency to decline. A major instrument by which PiS maintains its popularity—mass clientelism—may become increasingly costly, especially if the externally driven economic boom ends. But even a dramatic worsening of the economic situation (something that should not be wished for, even by PiS critics) may not lead to a political reversal. As Leszek Balcerowicz observes, 'the worsening economy may not be sufficient to stop and reverse a bad transition if forces of intimidation are already strong'.[3] And yet, a traditional 'remedy' used by elected authoritarians in such circumstances, namely strengthening of intimidation against political opponents (as in Russia after the economic situation deteriorated due to lowered oil prices), may be counterproductive in Poland: compliance with authoritarians and acceptance of an apodictic strongman goes hand in hand, in a strange way, with a spirit of freedom in the Polish collective psyche.

Furthermore, populism in power runs into a universal paradox: how to reconcile *being* the establishment with the anti-establishmentarian appeal that fuels populism's popularity? As Ben Stanley notes, populist parties 'often fell victim to the same public scepticism they had sought to cultivate when attacking established parties'.[4] There is no reason to believe that, in the longer term, PiS will escape the force of this 'scepticism' espoused by its most faithful electorate, which is, at the same time, the most conducive to anti-establishment attitudes. Finally, splits within the ruling elite cannot be excluded, especially due to Kaczyński's eventual departure from politics for age or health reasons. In such circumstances, PiS may simply lose elections: contemporary authoritarianism has some examples in store where a ruling group with autocratic tendencies has conceded loss in elections (as in Macedonia in 2016 or in Sri Lanka in 2015). Whether PiS will try to avoid such a result by resorting to electoral fraud, remains to be seen. What we know is that, with the capture of the electoral apparatus, it has given itself effective means for such fraud on a massive scale.

***

One way of reading this book, admittedly somewhat perverse, would be to treat it as a 'playbook' for would-be authoritarian leaders: a set of guidelines about how to move a system that democratically brought you to power into a system in which all institutions are fully subordinate to your will, while formally speaking, their design may be mistaken for a 'normal' democracy. Looking at the sequence of PiS actions in Poland after it won the double elections in 2015, the following steps can be taken:

(1) depicting the opposition as disloyal and demonizing critics as illegitimate, unpatriotic, and out of touch with 'real people'

(2) attacking courts' independence (forcing the removal of many existing judges, for instance through changes in the retirement age, and creation of new methods of appointing new judges), with special emphasis on dismantling the constitutional court and reinventing it as the executive's faithful ally

(3) weakening and demonizing the independent media; mobilizing public opinion against an independent press as expressing the old elite's interests and views; discouraging advertising in independent media to weaken their economic base; supporting 'friendly' private media

(4) capturing and politicizing public media; turning them into government's propaganda machine; providing them regularly with fake or true 'compromising' materials on the government's critics, gained by secret services

(5) intimidating civil society and support for government-friendly non-governmental organizations

(6) politicizing the civil service, law enforcement, and security apparatus

(7) engaging in a generous policy of spoils and patronage for party faithfuls and supporters

(8) gaining control of the electoral administration, packing the electoral institutions with party loyalists or persons dependent on the executive branch

(9) redesigning the contours of the right of freedom of assembly (with privileges for government-supported assemblies and disfavouring opposition's counter-assemblies) and freedom of speech (penalizing speech that undermines the nationalistic propaganda)

(10) playing a game of 'cat and mouse' with supranational attempts at monitoring, criticizing, and policing transgressions of the rule of law and democracy by the ruling elite: at times depicting these attempts as illegitimate interference, at times giving in by allowing cosmetic changes parading as compliance.

This playbook is deliberately and self-consciously based on Larry Diamond's catalogue of actions characteristic of anti-democratic versions of populism compiled in his moving lecture delivered at Stanford University in November 2017.[5] Diamond argued that 'because populism is intrinsically majoritarian and plebiscitary, it poses some intrinsic dangers for democracy, even when it is not peddling prejudice against cultural minorities. These can be exacerbated by populism's suspicion of established institutions and its tendency to want to work around them or blow them up'.[6] He followed this statement with his playbook, which I used as a template for the Poland-based playbook just suggested.[7] There are just a few local variants. Items (7), (9), and (10) are absent from Diamond's catalogue, but are an important part of the Polish assault on liberal democracy. In turn, Diamond included items that so far (thankfully) have been missing from the Polish toolkit: imposition of restrictions on Internet communication,[8] unleashing of crony capitalist forces,[9] and gerrymandering.[10] Item (9) on my list is a Polish contribution to the universal authoritarian playbook; *ditto* for the politics of spoils and patronage, which replaces Diamond's crony capitalism in Poland.

But knowing this playbook is useful not only to would-be and actual autocrats: it is also empowering and illuminating to those who advocate, strategize or are involved in resistance to today's enemies of democracy.

Notes

1. Stephen Holmes, 'How Democracies Perish' in Cass R. Sunstein (ed.), *Can It Happen Here? Authoritarianism in America* (HarperCollins 2018) 387, 420.
2. Ibid. 422–3.
3. Leszek Balcerowicz, 'Recent attacks against freedom' (April 2015) 2, unpublished manuscript on file with the author.
4. Ben Stanley, 'Populism in Central and Eastern Europe' in Cristóbal Rovira Kaltwasser, Paul Taggart, Paulina Ochoa-Espejo, and Pierre Ostiguy (eds), *The Oxford Handbook of Populism* (OUP 2017) 140, 157–8.
5. Larry Diamond, 'When Does Populism Become a Threat to Democracy?' Lecture presented at the FSI Conference on Global Populisms, Stanford University (3–4 November

2017) [PDF] <https://fsi.stanford.edu/sites/default/files/when_does_populism_become_a_threat_to_democracy.pdf> (accessed 10 May 2018).

6. Ibid. 6.
7. Ibid. 7–8.
8. Item (5) in Diamond's list.
9. Item (7) in Diamond's list.
10. Item (9) in Diamond's list.

Bibliography

Ackerman, B., *The Future of Liberal Revolution* (Yale University Press 1992).

Ackerman, B., *Revolutionary Constitutions: Charismatic Leadership and the Rule of Law* (Harvard University Press forthcoming 2019).

Alston, P., 'The Populist Challenge to Human Rights' (2017) 9 *Journal of Human Rights Practice* 1.

Amar, A.R., *America's Unwritten Constitution: The Precedents and Principles We Live By* (Basic Books 2012).

Anon, 'Editorial Comments: Safeguarding EU Values in the Member States – Is Something Finally Happening?' (2015) 52 *Common Market Law Review* 619.

Bałaban, A., 'Odpowiedź na ankietę konstytucyjną' in B. Banaszak and J. Zbieranek (eds) *Ankieta konstytucyjna* (Instytut Spraw Publicznych 2011).

Balcerowicz, L., 'Recent Attacks against Freedom' (April 2015) unpublished manuscript.

Balcerowicz, L., 'Institutional Systems and Their Dynamics, Including Good and Bad Transitions' (September 2017) unpublished manuscript.

Balkin, J.M., 'Constitutional Rot' in C.R. Sunstein (ed.), *Can It Happen Here? Authoritarianism in America* (HarpersCollins 2018).

Barber, N.W., 'Self-Defence for Institutions' (2013) 72 *Cambridge Law Journal* 558.

Berman, S., 'Populism Is Not Fascism' (2016) 95 *Foreign Affairs* 39.

Bermeo, N., 'On Democratic Backsliding' (2016) 27/1 *Journal of Democracy* 5.

Blauberger, M. and Kelemen, R.D., 'Can Courts Rescue National Democracy? Judicial Safeguards Against Democratic Backsliding in the EU' (2017) 24 *Journal of European Public Policy* 321.

Bellamy, R., *Political Constitutionalism: A Republican Defence of the Constitutionality of Democracy* (CUP 2007).

Bodnar, A., 'Protection of Human Rights after the Constitutional Crisis in Poland' (2018) 66 *Jahrbuch des öffentlichen Rechts der Gegenwart* 639.

Blokker, P., *New Democracies in Crisis?* (Routledge 2014).

Bonikowski, B., 'Ethno-Nationalist Populism and The Mobilization of Collective Resentment' (2017) 68 (Suppl 1) *British Journal of Sociology* S181.

Brettschneider, C., 'Popular Constitutionalism contra Populism' (2015) 30 *Constitutional Commentary* 81.

Brzezinski, M. and Garlicki, L., 'Polish Constitutional Law' in S. Frankowski and Stephan P.B. III (eds), *Legal Reform in Post-Communist Europe* (Martinus Nijhoff 1995).

Bugarič, B., *Central Europe's Descent into Autocracy: On Authoritarian Populism*, 2018–2019 CES Harvard Open Forum Paper Series 5.

Bugarič, B. and Ginsburg, T., 'Assault on Postcommunist Courts' (2016) 27/3 *Journal of Democracy* 69.

Carothers, T., 'The End of the Transition Paradigm' (2002) 13/1 *Journal of Democracy* 5.

Černič, J.L., 'Impact of the European Court of Human Rights on the Rule of Law in Central and Eastern Europe' (2018) 10 *Hague Journal on the Rule of Law* 111.

Chafetz, J. and Pozen, D.E., 'How Constitutional Norms Break Down' (2018) 65 *UCLA Law Review* 1430.

Chmaj, M., 'Odpowiedź na ankietę konstytucyjną' in B. Banaszak and J. Zbieranek (eds), *Ankieta konstytucyjna* (Instytut Spraw Publicznych 2011).

Cholewinski, R., 'The Protection of Human Rights in the New Polish Constitution' (1998) 22 *Fordham International Law Journal* 236.

Chruściak, R. and Osiatyński, W., *Tworzenie konstytucji w Polsce w latach 1989–1997* (Instytut Spraw Publicznych 2001).

Closa, C., 'Reinforcing EU Monitoring of the Rule of Law: Normative Arguments, Institutional Proposals and the Procedural Limitations' in C. Closa and D. Kochenov (eds), *Reinforcing Rule of Law Oversight in the European Union* (CUP 2016).

Czarnota, A., 'The Constitutional Tribunal' (*VerfBlog*, 3 June 2017) <https://verfassungsblog.de/the-constitutional-tribunal/> (accessed 21 February 2018).

Dawson, J. and Hanley, S., 'The Fading Mirage of the "Liberal Consensus"' (2016) 27/1 *Journal of Democracy* 20.

De Búrca, G., 'Beyond the Charter: How Enlargement Has Enlarged the Human Rights Policy of the European Union' (2004) 27 *Fordham International Law Journal* 679.

De Búrca, G., 'How British was the Brexit Vote?' in B. Martill and U. Staiger (eds), *Brexit and Beyond: Rethinking the Futures of Europe* (UCL Press 2018).

Diamond, L., 'Thinking about Hybrid Regimes' (2002) 13/2 *Journal of Democracy* 21.

Diamond, L., 'When Does Populism Become a Threat to Democracy?' Lecture presented at the FSI Conference on Global Populisms, Stanford University (3–4 November 2017) [PDF]   <https://fsi.stanford.edu/sites/default/files/when_does_populism_become_a_threat_to_democracy.pdf> (accessed 10 May 2018).

Dixon, R. and Ginsburg, T., 'Deciding Not to Decide: Deferral in Constitutional Design' (2011) *International Journal of Constitutional Law* 636.

Dworkin, R., *Sovereign Virtue* (Harvard University Press 2000).

Dworkin, R., 'Thirty Years On (Book Review)' (2002) 115 *Harvard Law Review* 1655.

Dworkin, R., 'Hart's Postscript and the Character of Political Philosophy' (2004) 34 *Oxford Journal of Legal Studies* 1.

Eisler, J., *Czterdzieści pięć lat, które wstrząsnęły Polską* (Czerwone i Czarne 2018).

Enyedi, Z., 'Populist Polarization and Party System Institutionalization: The Role of Party Politics in De-Democratization' (2016) 63 *Problems of Post-Communism* 210.

Fallon, R.H., 'Executive Power and the Political Constitution' (2007) *Utah Law Review* 1.

Feldman, N., 'On "It Can't Happen Here"' in C.R. Sunstein (ed.), *Can It Happen Here? Authoritarianism in America* (HarperCollins 2018).

Florczak-Wątor, M., Radziewicz, P., and Wiszowaty, M.W., 'Ankieta o Konstytucji Rzeczypospolitej Polskiej. Wyniki badań przeprowadzonych wśród przedstawicieli nauki prawa konstytucyjnego w 2017 r.' (2018) 73/6 *Państwo i Prawo* 3.

Foa, R.S. and Mounk, Y., 'The Signs of Deconsolidation' (2017) 28/1 *Journal of Democracy* 5.

Fomina, J. and Kucharczyk, J., 'Populism and Protest in Poland' (2016) 27/4 *Journal of Democracy* 58.

Fukuyama, F., 'Why Is Democracy Performing So Poorly?' (2015) 26 *Journal of Democracy* 11.

Gardbaum, S., *The New Commonwealth Model of Constitutionalism* (CUP 2013).

Gardbaum, S., 'Are Strong Constitutional Courts Always a Good Thing for New Democracies?' (2015) 53 *Columbia Journal of Transnational Law* 285.

Garlicki, L., 'The Experience of the Polish Constitutional Court' in W. Sadurski (ed.), *Constitutional Justice, East and West* (Kluwer Law International 2002).

Gdula, M., *Nowy Autorytaryzm* (Wydawnictwo Krytyki Politycznej 2018).

Gibler, D.M. and Randazzo, K.A., 'Testing the Effects of Independent Judiciaries on the Likelihood of Democratic Backsliding' (2011) 55 *American Journal of Political Science* 696.

Gidron, N. and Hall, P.A., 'The Politics of Social Status: Economic and Cultural Roots of the Populist Right' (2017) 68 (Suppl. 1) *British Journal of Sociology* S57.

Ginsburg, T., *Judicial Review in New Democracies* (CUP 2003).

Ginsburg, T. and Moustafa, T. (eds), *Rule By Law: The Politics of Courts in Authoritarian Regimes* (CUP 2008).

Ginsburg, T. and Simpser, A. (eds), *Constitutions in Authoritarian Regimes* (CUP 2014).

Góralczyk, B., 'Axiological Disintegration of the EU? The Case of Hungary' (2015) 18 *Yearbook of Polish European Studies* 81.

Gormley, L.W., 'Infringement Proceedings' in A. Jakab and D. Kochenov (eds), *The Enforcement of EU Law and Values: Ensuring Member States' Compliance* (OUP 2017).

Griffith, J.A.G., 'The Political Constitution' (1979) 42 *Modern Law Review* 1.

Grzymala-Busse, A., 'Global Populisms and Their Impact' 76 (2017) Suppl. S1 *Slavic Review* S3.

Habermas, J., 'On the Internal Relation between the Rule of Law and Democracy' (1995) 3 *European Journal of Philosophy* 12.

Harding, A., Leyland, P., and Groppi, T., 'Constitutional Courts: Forms, Functions and Practice in Comparative Perspective' (2008) 3/2 *Journal of Comparative Law* 1.

Hillion, C., 'Overseeing the Rule of Law in the EU: Legal Mandate and Means' in C. Closa and D. Kochenov (eds), *Reinforcing Rule of Law Oversight in the European Union* (CUP 2016).

Hofstadter, R., 'The Paranoid Style in American Politics' (1964) November *Harper's* 77.

Holmes, S., 'How Democracies Perish' in C.R. Sunstein (ed.), *Can It Happen Here? Authoritarianism in America* (HarperCollins 2018).

Huq, A. and Ginsburg, T., 'How to Lose a Constitutional Democracy' (2018) 65 *UCLA Law Review* 78.

Issacharoff, S., *Fragile Democracies* (CUP 2015).

Issacharoff, S., 'Democracy's Deficits' (2018) 85 *University of Chicago Law Review* 485.

Judis, J.B., *The Populist Explosion* (Columbia Global Reports 2016).

Kaltwasser, C.R., 'Populism and the Question of How to Respond to It' in C.R. Kaltwasser, P. Taggart, P. Ochoa-Espejo, and P. Ostiguy (eds), *The Oxford Handbook of Populism* (OUP 2017).

Kapstein, E.B. and Converse, N., 'Why Democracies Fail' (2008) 19/4 *Journal of Democracy* 57.

Kiš, J., 'Introduction: From the 1989 Constitution to the 2011 Fundamental Law' in G.A. Tóth (ed.), *Constitution for a Disunited Nation: On Hungary's 2011 Fundamental Law* (CEU Press 2012).

Kochenov, D., '*EU Enlargement and the Failure of Conditionality* (Kluwer Law International 2008).

Kochenov, D., 'The Missing EU Rule of Law?' in C. Closa and D. Kochenov (eds), *Reinforcing Rule of Law Oversight in the European Union* (CUP 2016).

Kochenov, D., 'The Acquis and Its Principles: The Enforcement of the "Law" versus the Enforcement of "Values" in the EU' in A. Jakab and D. Kochenov (eds), *The Enforcement of EU Law and Values Ensuring Member States' Compliance* (OUP 2017).

Kochenov, D. and Pech, L., 'Monitoring and Enforcement of the Rule of Law in the EU: Rhetoric and Reality' (2015) 11 *European Constitutional Law Review* 5.

Kochenov, D. and Pech, L., 'Better Late than Never? On the European Commission's Rule of Law Framework and its First Activation' (2016) 54 *Journal of Common Market Studies* 1062.

Kolarska-Bobińska, L., 'The EU Accession and Strengthening of Institutions in East Central Europe: The Case of Poland' (2003) 17 *East European Politics and Society* 91.

Koncewicz, T.T., 'On the Politics of Resentment, Mis-memory, and Constitutional Fidelity: The Demise of the Polish Overlapping Consensus?' in U. Belavusau and A. Gliszczyńska-Grabias (eds), *Law and Memory: Towards Legal Governance of History* (CUP 2017).

Kotkin, S., *Stalin*, vol. 2 (Allen Lane 2017).

Krastev, I., 'The Strange Death of the Liberal Consensus' (2007) 18 *Journal of Democracy* 56.

Krygier, M., 'The Rule of Law: An Abuser's Guide' in A. Sajó (ed.), *Abuse: The Dark Side of Fundamental Rights* (Eleven 2006).

Krygier, M., 'Institutionalisation and Its Discontents: Constitutionalism versus (Anti-) Constitutional Populism in East Central Europe', lecture delivered to Transnational Legal Institute, King's College, London, Signature Lecture Series (17 November 2017).

Krygier, M., 'Democracy and the Rule of Law' in J. Meierhenrich and M. Loughlin (eds), *Cambridge Companion on the Rule of Law* (forthcoming 2019).

Landau, D., 'Populist Constitutions' (2018) 85 *University of Chicago Law Review* 521.

Landau, D., 'Abusive Constitutionalism' (2013) 47 *UC Davis Law Review* 189.

Law, D.S. and Versteeg, M., 'Sham Constitutions' (2013) 101 *California Law Review* 863.

Levitsky, S. and Way, L., 'The Myth of Democratic Recession' (2015) 26/1 *Journal of Democracy* 45.

Levitsky, S. and Ziblatt, D., *How Democracies Die* (Crown Publishing 2018).

Levitz, P. and Pop-Echeles, G., 'Why No Backsliding? The European Union's Impact on Democracy and Governance before and after Accession' (2010) 43 *Comparative Political Studies* 457.

Linz, J.J. and Stepan, A., 'Toward Consolidated Democracies' (1996) 7/2 *Journal of Democracy* 14.

Ludwikowski, R., *Constitution-Making in the Region of Former Soviet Dominance* (Duke University Press 1996).

Łętowska, E., 'Zmierzch liberalnego państwa prawa w Polsce' (2017) 1-2 *Kwartalnik o prawach człowieka* 5.

Łukaszczuk, A., *Kształtowanie się modelu ustrojowego służby cywilnej w Polsce* (Wydawnictwo Sejmowe 2014).

Maeda, K., 'Two Modes of Democratic Breakdown: A Competing Risks Analysis of Democratic Durability' (2010) 72 *Journal of Politics* 1129.

Magen, A., 'Cracks in the Foundations: Understanding the Great Rule of Law Debate in the EU' (2016) 54 *Journal of Common Market Studies* 1050.

Magyar, B., *Post-Communist Mafia State: The Case of Hungary* (CEU Press 2016).

Mayer, R., 'Strategies of Justification in Authoritarian Ideology' (2001) 61 *Journal of Political Ideologies* 147.

Mechkova, V. Lührmann, A., and Lindberg, S.I., 'How Much Democratic Backsliding?' (2017) 28/4 *Journal of Democracy* 162.

Mounk, Y., *The People vs Democracy* (Harvard University Press 2018).

Moustafa, T. and Ginsburg, T., 'Introduction: The Functions of Courts in Authoritarian Politics' in T. Ginsburg and T. Moustafa (eds), *Rule By Law: The Politics of Courts in Authoritarian Regimes* (CUP 2008).

Moynihan, D.P., 'Defining Deviancy Down' (Winter 1993) 62/1 *The American Scholar* 17.

Mudde, C., 'Europe's Populist Surge' (2016) 95 *Foreign Affairs* 25.

Mudde, C., 'Populism: An Ideational Approach' in C.R. Kaltwasser, P. Taggart, P. Ochoa-Espejo, and P. Ostiguy (eds), *The Oxford Handbook of Populism* (OUP 2017).

Müller, J.-W., 'Should the EU Protect Democracy and the Rule of Law inside Member States?' (2015) 21 *European Law Journal* 141.

Müller, J.-W., 'Protecting the Rule of Law (and Democracy!) in the EU: The Idea of a Copenhagen Commission' in C. Closa and D. Kochenov (eds), *Reinforcing Rule of Law Oversight in the European Union* (CUP 2016).

Müller, J.-W., 'Populism and Constitutionalism' in C.R. Kaltwasser, P. Taggart, P. Ochoa-Espejo, and P. Ostiguy (eds) *The Oxford Handbook of Populism* (OUP 2017).

O'Donnell, G., 'Delegative Democracy' (1994) 5/1 *Journal of Democracy* 55.

Ogien, A. and Laugier, S., *Antidémocratie* (La Découverte 2017).

Pappas, T., 'Distinguishing Liberal Democracy's Challengers' (2016) 27/4 *Journal of Democracy* 22.

Piątek, T., *Macierewicz i jego tajemnice* (Arbitror 2017).

Pop-Echeles, G., 'Between Historical Legacies and the Promise of Western Integration: Democratic Conditionality after Communism' (2007) 21 *East European Politics and Society* 142.

Posner, E.A., 'The Dictator's Handbook, US Edition' in C.R. Sunstein (ed.) *Can It Happen Here? Authoritarianism in America* (HarperCollins 2018).

Primus, R., 'Unbundling Constitutionality' (2013) 80 *University of Chicago Law Review* 1079.

Przeworski, A., 'Ruling Against Rules' in T. Ginsburg and A. Simpser (eds), *Constitutions in Authoritarian Regimes* (CUP 2014).

Puddington, A. and Roylance, T., 'The Dual Threat of Populists and Autocrats' (2017) 28/2 *Journal of Democracy* 105.

Rapaczynski, A., 'Constitutional Politics in Poland: A Report on the Constitutional Committee of the Polish Parliament' (1991) 58 *University of Chicago Law Review* 595.

Rose-Ackerman, S., *From Elections to Democracy* (CUP 2005).

Rummens, S., 'Populism as a Threat to Liberal Democracy' in C.R. Kaltwasser, P. Taggart, P. Ochoa-Espejo, and P. Ostiguy (eds), *The Oxford Handbook of Populism* (OUP 2017).

Rupnik, J., 'Is East-Central Europe Backsliding? From Democracy Fatigue to Populist Backlash' (2007) 18/4 *Journal of Democracy* 17.

Rupnik, J., 'Surging Illiberalism in the East' (2016) 27/4 *Journal of Democracy* 77.

Rzepliński, A., *Sędzia gorszego sortu* (Prószyński 2018).

Sadurski, W., 'Porządek konstytucyjny' in L. Kolarska-Bobińska, J. Kucharczyk, and J. Zbieranek (eds), *Demokracja w Polsce 2005–2007* (Instytut Spraw Publicznych 2007).

Sadurski, W., 'Legitimacy, Political Equality, and Majority Rule' (2008) 21 *Ratio Juris* 39.

Sadurski, W., 'Adding Bite to a Bark: The Story of Article 7, E.U. Enlargement, and Jörg Haider' (2010) 16 *Columbia Journal of European Law* 385.

Sadurski, W., *Rights before Courts: A Study of Constitutional Courts in Postcommunist States of Central and Eastern Europe,* 2nd edn (Springer 2014).

Sadurski, W., *Constitutionalism and the Enlargement of Europe* (OUP 2012).

Sadurski, W., 'That *Other* Anniversary (Guest Editorial)' (2017) 13 *European Constitutional Law Review* 417.

Sargentini, J. and Dimitrovs, A., 'The European Parliament's Role: Towards New Copenhagen Criteria for Existing Member States?' (2016) 54 *Journal of Common Market Studies* 1085.

Scheppele, K.L., 'Constitutional Coups and Judicial Review: How Transnational Institutions Can Strengthen Peak Courts at Times of Crisis (with Special Reference to Hungary' (2014) 23 *Transnational Law & Contemporary Problems* 51.

Scheppele, K.L., 'Enforcing the Basic Principles of EU Law through Systemic Infringement Actions' in C. Closa and D. Kochenov (eds), *Reinforcing Rule of Law Oversight in the European Union* (CUP 2016).

Scheppele, K.L., 'Unconstitutional Constituent Power' in R. Smith and R. Beeman (eds), *Constitution-Making* (University of Pennsylvania Press, forthcoming).

Schwartz, H., 'The New East European Constitutional Courts' in A.E.D. Howard (ed.), *Constitution Making in Eastern Europe* (Woodrow Wilson Center 1993).

Skąpska, G., 'The Decline of Liberal Constitutionalism in East Central Europe' in P. Vihalemm, A. Masso, and S. Opermann (eds), *The Routledge International Handbook of European Social Transformations* (Routledge 2017).

Snyder, T., *The Road to Unfreedom* (Penguin Random House 2018).

Stanley, B., 'Populism in Central and Eastern Europe' in C.R. Kaltwasser, P. Taggart, P. Ochoa-Espejo, and P. Ostiguy (eds), *The Oxford Handbook of Populism* (OUP 2017).

Strauss, D.A., 'Law and the Slow-Motion Emergency' in C.R. Sunstein (ed.), *Can It Happen Here? Authoritarianism in America* (HarperCollins 2018).

Suchocka, H., 'Checks and Balances under the New Constitution of Poland' in M. Wyrzykowski (ed.), *Constitutional Essays* (Institute of Public Affairs 1999).

Sunstein, C.R., 'Lessons from the American Founding' in C.R. Sunstein (ed.), *Can It Happen Here? Authoritarianism in America* (HarperCollins 2018).

Svolik, M.W., 'Which Democracies Will Last? Coups, Incumbent Takeovers, and the Dynamic of Democratic Consolidation' (2014) 45 *British Journal of Political Science* 715.

Taibbi, M., *Insane Clown President: Dispatching from the 2016 Circus* (Spiegel and Grau 2017).

Tuori, K., 'From Copenhagen to Venice' in C. Closa and D. Kochenov (eds), *Reinforcing Rule of Law Oversight in the European Union* (CUP 2016).

Tushnet, M., 'Constitutional Hardball' (2004) 37 *John Marshall Law Review* 523.

Tushnet, M., 'Authoritarian Constitutionalism: Some Conceptual Issues' in T. Ginsburg and A. Simpser (eds), *Constitutions in Authoritarian Regimes* (CUP 2014).

Tushnet, M., 'Authoritarian Constitutionalism' (2015) 100 *Cornell Law Review* 391.

Tushnet, M., 'Comparing Right-Wing and Left-Wing Populism' in M.A. Graber, S. Levinson, and M. Tushnet (eds), *Constitutional Democracy in Crisis?* (OUP 2018).

Uitz, R., 'Can You Tell when an Illiberal Democracy is in the Making? An Appeal to Comparative Constitutional Scholarship from Hungary' (2015) 13 *International Journal of Constitutional Law* 279.

Urbinati, N., 'Populism and the Principle of Majority' in C.R. Kaltwasser, P. Taggart, P. Ochoa-Espejo, and P. Ostiguy (eds), *The Oxford Handbook of Populism* (OUP 2017).

Varol, O.O., 'Stealth Authoritarianism' (2015) 100 *Iowa Law Review* 1673.

Vermeule, A., 'Conventions of Agency Independence' (2013) 113 *Columbia Law Review* 1163.

Von Bogdandy, A., Kottmann, M., Antpöhler, C., Dickschen, J., Hentrel, S., and Smrkolj, M., 'Reverse Solange – Protecting the Essence of Fundamental Rights Against EU Member States' (2012) 49 *Common Market Law Review* 489.

Von Bogdandy, A., Antpöhler, C., Dickschen, J., Hentrel, S., Kottmann, M., and Smrkolj, M., 'Reverse Solange – A European Response to Domestic Constitutional Crisis: Advancing the Reverse-Solange Doctrine' in A. von Bogdandy and P. Sonnevend (eds), *Constitutional Crisis in the European Constitutional Area* (Hart 2015).

Von Bogdandy, A., Antpöhler, C., and Ioannidis, M., 'Protecting EU values: Reverse Solange and the Rule of Law Framework' in A. Jakab and D. Kochenov (eds), *The Enforcement of EU Law and Values Ensuring Member States' Compliance* (OUP 2017).

Waldron, J., *God, Locke, and Equality* (CUP 2002).

Waldron, J., 'The Core of the Case against Judicial Review' (2006) 115 *Yale Law Journal* 1346.

Waldron, J., *Political Political Theory* (Harvard University Press 2016).

Weyland, K., 'Populism: A Political-Strategic Approach' in C.R. Kaltwasser, P. Taggart, P. Ochoa-Espejo, and P. Ostiguy (eds), *The Oxford Handbook of Populism* (OUP 2017).

Winczorek, P., 'The Political Circumstances of the Drafting of the Republic of Poland's Constitution of 2 April 1997' in M. Wyrzykowski (ed.), *Constitutional Essays* (Institute of Public Affairs 1999).

Winczorek, P., 'The Polish Constitutional System and The Law Making Process' in J. Kucharczyk and J. Zbieranek (eds), *Democracy in Poland 1989–2009: Challenges for the Future* (Institute of Public Affairs 2010).

Wyrzykowski, M., 'Legitimacy: The Price of a Delayed Constitution in Poland' in J. Zielonka (ed.) *Democratic Consolidation in Europe*, vol. 1 (OUP 2001).

Wyrzykowski, M., 'Antigone in Warsaw' in M. Zubik (ed.) *Human Rights in Contemporary World: Essays in Honour of Professor Leszek Garlicki* (Wydawnictwo Sejmowe 2017).

Zajadło, J., 'Pojęcie „imposybilizm prawny" a polityczność prawa i prawoznawstwa' (2017) 3 *Państwo i Prawo* 17.

Zakaria, F., 'The Rise of Illiberal Democracy' (1997) 76 *Foreign Affairs* 22.

Index

abortion 49, 58–59
'abusive constitutionalism' 13, 243–44
accession to the EU 199–202
  political conditionality 200
ABW (Internal Security Agency) 157–58
Ackerman, Bruce 38, 44–45
actio popularis 84–85
Agencja Bezpieczeństwa Wewnętrznego (Internal
  Security Agency) 157–58
agentic theories 163, 166–67
amendments, constitutional 16–18, 52–53
Amar, Akhil Reed 256–58
Anders, Anna Maria 117–18
anti-constitutional populist backsliding vi, 1–2,
  14, 58
  'anti-constitutional' 14–20
  'backsliding' vii, 27–29, 200–1
  incremental change 5–6
  invisible changes 6–8
  'populist' 20–27, 246–47
anti-establishment sentiments 168, 171–72,
  173, 175
anti-globalism 168, 170
anti-Islamism 173
anti-modernism 10
anti-pluralism 20–21, 22, 23–24, 247
anti-Semitism 157
anti-Western orientation 11–12
Antpöhler, C 231–32
Aranyosi and Căldăraru case (CJEU) 203, 204,
  205, 207
Arendt, Hannah 251
Arndt, Wojciech, 135
Article 7 procedure 134–35, 172, 192–93, 201, 203–7,
  213–18, 220–22, 227–28, 229–30, 232
  procedure regarding Poland 225–27
  sanctions 222–24
assembly *see* freedom of assembly
Associação Sindical dos Juízes Portugueses case
  (CJEU) 205, 207
asylum-seekers 145, 159 (*see also* refugees)
Aviation Law 59–60
authoritarianism 13, 227–28, 232
  Hungary 2, 4, 26–27, 227–28, 232
  playbook 269–70
  Singapore 4
  stealth authoritarianism 7–8

strategies to consolidate power 261–62
uses of constitutions 18–19
vs populism 20, 26

backlash 12–13
backsliding *see* anti-constitutional populist
  backsliding
Balcerowicz, Leszek 40–41, 138, 268
Balkin, Jack 8–9
Barber, Nicholas 184, 185
Bárd, Petra 205
Bellamy, Richard 251–52
Bermeo, Nancy 5–6
Białowieża forest case (CJEU) 208–10
bicameralism 38, 179, 180
Biernat, Stanisław 16–17, 68, 74, 79
Blokker, Paul 172–73, 251
Bodnar, Adam 82–84, 86, 150, 153, 267–68, *see*
  also Ombudsman
Bojarski, Łukasz 254–55
Bonikowski, Bart 22, 167, 171, 248
Bott Yves 209
Brexit 25, 172–73, 181
Broadcasting Council *see* National Broadcasting
  Council
Brudziński, Joachim 142
'brushback' 261
Bugarič, Bojan 26–27, 86, 186

Canada 257
Catholic Church 10, 11–12, 46–47, 138, 139
  (*see also* Christian values; church-state
  relationship)
CBA (Central Anti-Corruption Bureau) 118–19
CEE *see* Central and Eastern Europe
Celmer, Artur v, 202–5
Celmer case (CJEU) 202–8
censorship 267–68
Central and Eastern Europe (CEE)
  populism 1–2, 24
  post-transitional democracies 27, 86–88, 180
Central Anti-Corruption Bureau (CBA) 118–19
centralization 179
Centralne Biuro Antykorupcyjne (Central
  Anti-Corruption Bureau) 118–19
Chafetz, Josh 259
Chavez, Hugo 178–79

checks and balances vi–vii, 2, 8, 15–16, 26–27, 38–39, 58, 88, 123, 132, 144, 159, 164, 168, 172–73, 175, 177, 178–79, 183, 186, 229–30, 245
Chief Justice *see* Gersdorf, Małgorzata
Christian values 4, 11, 46, 58–59, 144–45, 171
church–state relationship
    Constitution of 1997 46
    pre-2015 58–59
Cioch, Henryk 64–66, 75
Citizens of the Republic of Poland 154
Civic Legislative Forum 134
Civic Platform party *see* PO
civil liberties 26–27
civil service 136–38
civil society 144–46, 267–68, *see also* NGOs
civility of discourse 8–9
Closa, Carlos 215
clientelism 138, *see also* spoils and patronage
collection of money 145–46
Committee for Public Benefit 144–45
Committee of Defence of Democracy (KOD) 117–18
comparative constitutional law 250
comprehensiveness of change 5
concentration camps 155
Confederation of Independent Poland (KPN) 49
consensus vi–vii, 3, 6–7, 19–20, 22, 53, 86, 102, 170, 186
Constitution
    amendments 16–19
    Constitution of 1952 35–36, 41
    Constitution of 1997
        legitimacy and durability 52–54
        process 43–45
        substance 45–50
    direct application 83–84, 86, 97
    Round Table (RT) agreements 36–39, 42
    'Small Constitution' 36, 39–42, 47–48
    violations 15–16, 19–20
constitutional breakdown 2–12 (*see also* anti-constitutional populist backsliding)
    agentic theories 163, 166–67
    causes 162
    paranoia 162–64, 166–67
        post-Smolensk 164–66
    populism *see* populism
constitutional consensus vi–vii, 3, 6–7, 19–20, 22, 53, 86, 102, 170, 186
constitutional coup 14
'constitutional hardball' 260–61
'constitutional moment' 36, 53–54
constitutional referendum 50, 53
constitutional review 86, 87–88, 244, 247
    decentralized review 96–97
    institutional design 180–81, 182

constitutional rights *see* human rights; individual rights; political rights
constitutional rot 12–13
constitutional scrutiny 83–84
Constitutional Tribunal (CT) v, 35
    appointment of president 74
    church–state relations 58–59
    conservatism 58–59
    Constitution of 1997 49–50
    contest of competencies 80–81
    election of judges 180–81
    European Court of Human Rights and 86
    human rights record 59–60
    incapacitation by PiS 3, 5, 7, 15–16, 19, 58, 61, 150, 180–81, 185–86
        blame games 85
        comparison with Hungary 84–85
        court-packing 61–70, 75, 184–85, 186
        fall in number of judgments 84
        legislative bombardment 2015–16 70–75
        refusal to publish judgments 75–79
        Rule of Law Framework recommendations 220, 221
        transformation of the CT into government's enabler 79–84
    institutional self-defence 184–85
    legal culture 86
        linguistic minorities 58–59
        media freedom 58–59
    non-published judgments 75–79, 126
    PiS legislative initiatives blocked by 60–61
    politically sensitive cases 69
    powers of the executive and legislative 73–74
    pre-1997 42–43
    pre-2015 58–61
    quasi-judges 62, 64–66, 69–70, 75, 82–84, 152–53, 220–21, 258
    separate opinions 82–83
    Venice Commission Opinions on 193–95, 196
Consultative Council of European Judges (CCJE) 100
contest of competencies 80–81
Copenhagen Commission (proposed) 230–31
Copenhagen criteria 192, 200, 202, 230
Council of Europe (CoE) 100, 192–93
Council of Ministers 35
Council of National Media 16–18
Council of State 35
counter-revolution 10–11
counter-terrorist measures 157–59
Court of Justice of the European Union (CJEU) 106, 193
    case law
        Celmer case v, 202–8, 215
        environmental protection 208–10

judicial independence and retirement
    age 210–12
    preliminary references 211–13, 227–28
court-packing 61–70, 75, 184–85, 186, 258–59,
    260–61
court presidents 115–19
criminal defendants 150
    judges 119
cultural counter-revolution 10–11
cultural norms 179, 186
cumulative effect 5, 58, 123–24
cynicism 260
Czabański, Krzysztof 15
Czarnota, Adam 252–53
Czerwińska, Małgorzata 119
Czeszkiewicz, Dominik 117–18

De Búrca, Gráinne 232
death threats 172
decentralization 96–97, 179
decentralized judicial review, *see* diffuse judicial review
democracy *see also* illiberal democracy,
    representative democracy
    delegative democracy (DD) 242, 243
    direct democracy 50
    liberal democracy 247–48, 251–52
    populism and 244–53
    representative democracy 245–46
democratic backlash 12–13
democratic decay 12–13
democratic deficits 244–45
Democratic Left Alliance (SLD) 43–44, 50–51
deportation 159
diffuse judicial review 83–84, 96–98
direct democracy 50
disabilities 176
disciplinary system for judiciary, 112–13, 118–21,
    227
distrust 8–10, 260
Dobrowolski, Tomasz 78
Donnelly, Aileen v
Duda, Andrzej 1, 10, 11, 15, 19, 62–63, 64–66,
    81–82, 98–99, 175
    judicial appointments 101, 102, 107,
        108–10, 111–12, 196, 212
    new law on statements violating the
        reputation of Poland 156
    presidential pardons 80–81, 253–54, 257
    support for freedom of assembly 152–53
    unconstitutional actions 183–84
Dunin, Artur 78
Dworkin, Ronald 216–17

economic growth 2, 169
economic insecurity 168, 169

Ehrlich, Stanisław 14–15
electoral system 112–13, 140–43, 159, 173–74,
    261–62
    Hungary 140, 143
elites 20–22, 97–98, 168, 169, 171–72, 175, 177–78,
    201, 244–45, 246
emergency 184
environmental protection 208–10
Equality Parade 60–61, 152
EU *see* European Union
European Arrest Warrant (EAW) v, 50–51, 59–60,
    202, 203, 204–5
European Commission 72, 78–79, 192, 218–21,
    225–27
European Court of Human Rights (ECtHR) 86,
    150, 152–53, 192–93, 197–202, 230
European Court of Justice (ECJ) *see* Court of
    Justice of the European Union
European Network of Councils for the
    Judiciary 106
European Parliament 227–28, 261
European Union 52–53, 59–60, 134–35, 192
    ambivalence towards 170
    Article 7 procedure 134–35, 172,
        192–93, 201, 203–7, 213–18,
        220–22, 227–28, 229–30, 232
        procedure regarding Poland 225–27
        sanctions 222–24
    constitutional and democratic meaning
        of accession 199–202
    enlargement 192
    policing member states 227–32
    Rule of Law Framework 213–18,
        227–28, 229–30, 231
        proceedings against Poland 218–22
    subsidies 169
exhumation case 197–99
extraordinary review 114
extradition v

fair trial 204, 205
federalism 180
Feldman, Noah 179
Fidesz party 3, 143, 174
Foa, Roberto 247
foreign policy 11–12
foreign pressure 82 (*see also* European Commission;
    European Court of Human Rights; Venice
    Commission)
Frasyniuk, Władysław 267–68
freedom of assembly 59–61, 82, 151–54, 247
    anti-government rallies 154
    'cyclical assemblies' 82, 151, 152–53
    Equality Parade 60–61, 152
Freedom of Information requests 76–77

freedom of speech 139, 154–59, 185, 247
Freedom Union (UW) 49, 50–51
Fronczyk, Alicja 119

Gardbaum, Stephn 86–88
Garlicki, Leszek 43
gay pride parades 60–61, 152
Gazeta Wyborcza 39
Gdula, Maciej 9, 171
Geremek, Bronisław 11–12, 38
Germany 11–12
   German Basic Law 38–39
Gersdorf, Małgorzata 16–17, 81–82, 96, 104,
   105, 107, 108–11, 227
Gidron, Noam 169, 171
Ginsburg, Tom 5–6, 61, 85, 180–81
globalization 168, 170
Gowin, Jarosław 174
Granat, Mirosław 65
Greece 24–25
Griffith, John 251–52
Gross, Jan T. 155
Grzymala-Busse, Anna 255–56

habeas corpus 183
Habermas, Jürgen 247–48
Haider, Jörg 222, 224
Hall, Peter 169, 171
Hauser, Roman 62, 65
Herbert, Zbigniew 162
Hermeliński, Wojciech 143
High Court of Ireland 202–5
Hillion, Christophe 229
historical policy 137
   heroism and victimhood 155
   Holocaust 85, 155, 156
   Institute of National Remembrance
      137, 154–55
   Second World War 11–12, 154–55, 157
Hofstadter, Richard 163–64
Holmes, Stephen 172, 267, 268
Holocaust 85, 155, 156, 258
horizontal accountability 243
human rights 59–60, 150, 159 (*see also*
   individual rights)
Hungary
   Article 7 procedure 225
   as the model 3–4
   authoritarianism 2, 4, 26–27, 227–28, 232
   constitutional changes 17, 18, 26–27
   different than Poland 4–5, 17–18, 84–85
   ECtHR case law 197
   electoral system 140, 143
   Fidesz party 3, 143, 174
   populism 2, 3

right-wing 'reforms' 3–4
   incapacitation of the constitutional
      court 84–85, 106
Huq, Aziz 5–6, 180
hybrid regimes 14

identity politics 8–9, 177–78, 246–47
illiberal democracy 11, 13, 243, 244–45,
   247–48
illiberal impatience 168, 172–73
immigration 169, 170–72, 177–78
'impossibilism' 172–73
incrementalism 5–6
independent media 267–68
individual rights 48, 58–60, 159, 248 (*see also*
   human rights; political rights)
   freedom of assembly 59–61, 82, 151–54
   freedom of speech 139, 154–59
   privacy rights vs counter-terrorism
      measures and Police Act 157–59
infringement actions 192–93, 208–11, 227–28
   systemic infringement action 202, 228–30
Institute of National Remembrance (Instytut
   Pamięci Narodowej) 137, 154–55
institutional design 179, 180–82, 186
institutional fragility 179, 182–87
institutional resilience 181–82
institutional self-defence 184
insurance theory of judicial review 61
Internal Security Agency (ABW) 157–58
Internet 139
Invocatio Dei 46
Ioannidis, M. 231
Islam 177–78
Issacharoff, Samuel 180, 243, 248, 249
Iustitia 102, 113, 116
Iwulski, Józef 108–10

Jaki, Patryk 119
Jakubecki, Andrzej 62, 65
Jaruzelski, Wojciech 37, 38, 39, 42–43, 45–46
Jaskulski, Marek 103
Jedwabne massacre 155–56
Jędrejek, Grzegorz 75
Jędrzejewski, Zbigniew 75
Johann, Wiesław 111–12
journalists 154
Jourova, Vera 231–32
judges
   allocation of cases 122
   appointment of court presidents 115–19
   career progression 122–23
   court-packing 61–70, 75, 184–85, 186, 258–59,
      260–61
   direct application of the Constitution 83–84, 97

harassment, persecution, and disciplinary
     proceedings 118–21
independence v, 86–87, 123–24, 207, 210–11, 220
legal culture 86
'midnight judges' 64
National Council of the Judiciary see KRS
PiS 'reforms' 8, 98–99, 106–15
     Law on the KRS 99–106
     Law on the Organization of Common
          Courts 115–24
     Law on the Public Prosecutor's Office
          (prokuratura) 124–26
     Law on the Supreme Court 106–15
     political control of 123, 162–63
     powers of the Minister of Justice (MJ) 115–17,
          118, 120–21, 122, 227
     merger with the Public Prosecutor's
          Office 124–26
     propaganda campaigns against judges 98, 99
     public perceptions 99, 123
     quasi-judges 62, 64–66, 69–70, 75,
          82–84, 152–53, 220–21, 258
     removal by Sejm 73–74
judicial independence 86–85, 100, 123–24
judicial review 7, 19, 83–84, 179, 252, 253
     insurance theory 61
     legislative override 49–50, 86–87
     'weak review' 86–87
Judis, John 24–25

Kaczyński, Jarosław 1, 2–3, 4, 6–7, 11–12, 19, 58,
     80–81, 83, 140
     anti-constitutional centre of power 14–15,
          51–52, 125, 245
     assault on institutions 182
     breaching unwritten norms 253–54
     commemorations of Smoleńsk air
          crash 82, 151–52, 165–66
     continuing popularity 177
     exclusionary populism 246–47
     paranoia 163–64, 167
          post-Smoleńsk 164–66
     sources of success 168, 170, 171, 172–73,
          174–75
     vote maximization 25
Kaczyński, Lech 1, 2–3, 51–52, 60–61, 99–100
     death in Smolensk air crash 82, 151–52, 164
Kaltwasser, Cristóbal Rovira 22
Kaminski, Mariusz 80–81, 97–98, 253–54, 257
Karp, Hanna 139
Katyń massacre 164
Kelemen, R. Daniel 232
Kis, János 8
Kiszczak, Czesław 38
Kluziak, Małgorzata 118

Kochenov, Dimitry 159, 202, 214–15, 216,
     229–30, 231
KOD (Committee of Defence of Democracy)
     117–18
Kołodziej, Magdalena 126
Komitet Obrony Demokracji (Committee of
     Defense of Democracy) 117–18
Komorowski, Bronisław 1, 52–53, 81–82,
     171–72, 175
Koncewicz, Tomasz Tadeusz 58, 156, 203, 226
Konfederacja Polski Niepodległej 49
Kowalczyk, Henryk 209
Kozlovska, Lyudmyla 159
KPN (Confederation of Independent Poland) 49
Krajewski, Michał 205
Krajowa Rada Sądownictwa (National Council of
     the Judiciary) see KRS
Krastev, Ivan 200
KRS (National Council of the Judiciary) 16–17,
     98–99, 142, 249–50
     changes to manner of election of members 79–80
     law on the KRS 79–80, 99–106, 254
     control over appointment of court
          presidents 116–17
     executive control of 121, 123–24
     judicial component 100–1, 227, 257–58
     Venice Commission Opinion on 193, 196
Krygier, Martin 6–7, 79, 87–88, 255
Kuchciński, Marek 134–35, 254
Kukiz-15 party 103, 132, 157, 222
Kurski, Jacek 15
Kwaśniewski, Aleksander 43–45

Labour Union (UP) 49
Landau, David 13, 18, 243–44
Law, David 19
Law and Justice party (PiS) see PiS
Le Drian, Jean Yves 232
Le Pen, Marine 167–68
League of Polish Families 2–3, 50–51
Legal Service of the European Council 214
legal culture 86
legal norms see norms
legal constitutionalism 251, 252–53
'legal scepticism' 172–73
legalism 19–20
legislative bombardment 70–75
legislative fast-tracking 133–34
legislative override 49–50
legitimacy 242, 259–60
Levitsky, Steven 162, 260–62
liberal constitutionalism 86
liberal elite 169, 177–78, 244–45
liberal rights 48, 58–60, 247–48, see also human
     rights; political rights

Liga Polskich Rodzin see League of Polish Families
Lincoln, Abraham 168
linguistic minorities 58–59
Linz, Juan 244
Lithuania 24
logging 208–10
Lust, Ellen 28–29, 166, 167
lustration 60–61
Łączewski, Wojciech 104
Łętowska, Ewa 43

Maciejewska, Ewa 119–20
Macierewicz, Antoni 154, 165–66, 174
Madison, James 182, 183
Magen, Amichai 216–17
Mainwaring, Scott 166
majoritarianism 2, 3, 6–7, 8, 58–59, 61, 84, 86,
    172–74, 242, 252–53
'Martian's test' 7
Matczak, Marcin 104
Matyja, Rafal 162–64
May, Theresa 181
Mayer, Robert 246–47
Mazowiecki, Tadeusz 11–12, 39, 46
Mazur, Leszek 104
Mazur, Witold 104
media 16–17, 26–27
    'deconcentration' 139, 140
    foreign ownership 139
    independent media 267–68
    KRRiTV 139
    monopolization by PiS 138–40
    'repolonization' 139, 140
    TVP 21
Michnik, Adam 39, 267–68
'midnight judges' 64
migrants 168, 170, 171–72
militant democracy 183
Miller, Jerzy 164–65
Miłosz, Czesław x
Minister of Justice (MJ) 115–17, 118, 120–21,
    122, 227
    merger with Public Prosecutor's
        Office 124–26
misogyny 150
Mitera, Maciej 3, 104
Morawiecki, Mateusz 10, 11, 78–79, 134–35, 221–22
Morawski, Lech 64–66, 75
Mounk, Yascha 247
Moustafa, Tamir 85, 180–81
Moynihan, Daniel Patrick 260
Mudde, Cas 244–45
Müller, Jan-Werner 21–24, 230, 231
multiculturalism 169
Muslims 171, 173

Muszyński, Mateusz 63–66, 69–70, 75, 81–83,
    152–53, 258, 267–68

naming and shaming 192–93, 220, 224
National Broadcasting Council 16–17, 43, 51–52,
    60–61
National Council of the Judiciary *see* KRS
National Electoral Commission (PKW) 141–43, 144
National Electoral Bureau 141
National Institute of Freedom 144–45
national media *see* media
National School for Judiciary and Public
    Prosecution 121
nationalism 10, 150, 168, 170
NATO 2, 27
neo-Nazis 10, 157
newspapers 140
NGOs 3, 4, 10, 144–46, 150, 154, 159, 197
Nitras, Sławomir 135
Nixon, Richard 181, 260–61
norms 179, 186
    unwritten norms 253–61
North Atlantic Treaty Organization (NATO) 192
Nowoczesna party 132
Nowogrodzka street 15

Obóz Narodowo-Radykalny (ONR) 10
Obywatele RP (Citizens of the Republic of
    Poland) 154
O'Donnell, Guillermo A. 242–43
Ombudsman 19–20, 35, 50–51, 82–84, 144, 152,
    153, 158, 196, 267–68
Open Dialogue Foundation 159
opposition parties 132–35, 254, 260
Orbán, Victor 3, 4, 6–7, *see also* Hungary
    assault on institutions 182
    constitutional changes 17

Państwowa Komisja Wyborcza (National
    Electoral Commission) 141–43, 144
paranoia 162–64, 166–67, 268
    post-Smolensk 164–66
pardons, presidential 80–81, 253–54, 257
Parliament *see* Sejm
parliamentary override 49–50
Paruch, Waldemar 135
Pawełczyk-Woicka, Dagmara 102, 117
Pech, Laurent 202, 214–15, 220
Pérez-Liñan, Annibal 166
Péron, Juan 260–61
Piątek, Tomasz 154
Piebiak, Łukasz 121
Pietrzak, Magdalena 141
Pilarczyk, Agnieszka 119
PiS (Law and Justice party) vi–vii, 15, 242

assault on individual rights 150–51, 159
  freedom of assembly 59–61, 82, 151–54
  freedom of speech 139, 154–59
  privacy rights vs counter-terrorism
    measures and Police Act 157–59
constitutional violations 19–20, 96
continuing popularity 175–79
electoral victory 2015 2–3, 269–70
Hungarian parallels and differences 4–5
incapacitation of Constitutional Tribunal
    (CT) 3, 5, 7, 15–16, 19, 58, 61, 150, 180–81
  blame games 85
  comparison with Hungary 84–85
  court-packing 61–70, 75, 184–85, 186
  fall in number of judgments 84
  legislative bombardment 70–75
  refusal to publish judgments 75–79
  Rule of Law Framework
    recommendations 220, 221
  transformation of the CT into
    government's enabler 79–84
  Venice Commission Opinions on 193–95, 196
legislative initiatives blocked by
    Constitutional Tribunal 60–61
manipulation of distrust 9–10
paranoia 163, 166
  post-Smolensk 165–66
'reform' of the judiciary 8, 98–99, 115, 249–50
  Law on the KRS 99–106, 254
  Law on the Organization of
    Common Courts 115–24
  Law on the Public Prosecutor's Office
    (prokuratura) 124–26
ruling in 2005–7 50–52, 53–54
sources of success 168, 169, 170, 172–73, 174–75
strategies to consolidate power 261–62
undoing institutions of the democratic
    state 132, 146, 243, 249, 267
  civil society 144–46
  dismantling neutral and professional
    civil service 136–38
  electoral system 140–43, 159
  Parliament: silencing and delegitimation
    of the opposition 132–35
  public media 138–40, 154
voter profiles 168
Piskorski, Justyn 75
PKW (National Electoral Commission) 141–43, 144
Platforma Obywatelska (Civic Platform) see PO
'plebiscitary autocracy' 248–49
pluralism 139, 144–45
PO (Civic Platform party) 1, 44, 62, 78, 83, 132,
  134–35, 165
  election failure in 2015 171–72, 173–77, 178–79
  voter profiles 168

polarization 178
police powers 158–59
  Venice Commission Opinion on 193, 195
Polish Peasants' Party (PSL) 1, 44, 49, 62, 132, 135
Polish United Workers' Party (PZPR) 35, 37,
  40–41
political constitutionalism 251–53
political culture 186–87
political distrust 8–10, 260
political polarization 178
political rights 150, 159
political values 216–17
politics of identity 8–9, 177–78, 246–47
Polska Zjednoczona Robotnicza (Polish United
  Workers Party) 35, 37, 40–41
Polskie Stronnictwo Ludowe (Polish Peasants'
  Party 1, 44, 49, 62, 132, 135
populism vi, 1–2, 13, 20–27 (see also
  anti-constitutional populist backsliding)
  anti-pluralism 20–21, 22, 23–24, 247
  assault on individual rights 150–51
  Brexit 25
  CEE 1–2, 24
  democracy and vi–vii, 244–53
  effective populism 167–68
  emergence 1–2, 167–75
  exclusionary nature 246–47
  forms of law 6–7
  Hungary 2, 3
  institutional 23–24
  left-wing populism 24, 25, 248
  loss of trust and 8–10
  persistence 175–79
  political constitutionalism and 251–53
  right-wing populism 2–3, 25
  self-destruction 268–69
  vote maximization 25
  vs authoritarianism 20, 26
  welfare policies 20, 25
populist democracy vi–vii
Posner, Eric 185–86
post-communist transformations 1989–2015 27
  Constitution of 1952 35–36, 41
  Constitution of 1997
    challenge of 2005–7 50–52, 53–54
    legitimacy and durability 52–54
    process 43–45
    substance 45–50
  Constitutional Tribunal
    Constitution of 1997 49–50
    pre-1997 42–43
  Round Table (RT) agreements 36–39, 42
  'Small Constitution' 36, 39–42, 47–48
Poświata, Agnieszka 119
Pozen, David 259

Prawo i Sprawiedliwość (Law and Justice party) *see* PiS
preliminary references *see* Court of Justice of the
    European Union
President of Poland *see* Duda, Andrzej
presidential pardons 80–81, 253–54, 257
presidential portfolios 41
presidential vetoes 98–99, 101, 106
press 139, 140
Primus, Richard 258–59
privacy rights 157–59, 247
    Venice Commission Opinion on 193, 195
prokuratura see Public Prosecutor's Office
propaganda 4, 21–22, 122–23, 140–41, 177
    against judges 98, 99
    national media 138, 154
Przeworski, Adam 35–36
Przyłębska, Julia 63–67, 68–70, 75, 78–79, 82–83,
    157–58
PSL (Polish Peasants' Party) 1, 44, 49, 62, 132, 135
Pszczółkowski, Piotr 70, 75
public administration 136–38
public assemblies *see* freedom of assembly
public discourse *see* civility of discourse
public media *see* media
public morality 59–60, 152
Public Prosecutor's Office 124–26
    Venice Commission Opinion on 193, 195–96
purges 98, 112, 116–17, 126, 137, 138, 141
PZPR (Polish United Workers' Party) 35, 37, 40–41

Quasi-judges 62, 64–66, 69–70, 75, 82–84,
    152–53, 220–21, 258

racism 10, 157, 172, 173
radio 139
Radio Maryja 10, 138
Rapaczynski, Andrzej 39
Rechtsstaat 38–39, 42–43
redistributive policy 25
referenda 50, 53
refugees 145, 168, 170, 177–78, 197–98, *see also*
    immigration
'repolonization' 139, 140
representative democracy 242, 246
retirement age 176–77
    judges 4, 16–17, 26–27, 81–82, 96, 106–10,
        121, 123–24, 210, 211–12, 220, 222
Reverse *Solange* doctrine 229–30
right to life 49
Roosevelt, Franklin D. 186, 258–59, 260–61
Round Table (RT) agreements 36–39, 42
rule of law v, 82, 86, 105, 159, 192, 195, 212,
    216–17, 232
    ECtHR impact 198, 199
    unwritten norms and 253–61

Rule of Law Framework (EU) 213–18, 227–28,
    229–30, 231
    proceedings against Poland 218–22
Rummens, Stefan 22–23
Russia 11–12
Rydzyk, Tadeusz 138, 139
Rymar, Stanisław 67
Rzepliński, Andrzej 64–65, 75–76, 79, 98–99,
    101–2, 184–85

Safjan, Marek 77
Samoobrona (Self-Defence party) 2–3, 24, 50–51
sanctions 192–93, 222–24
Schengen Information System 159
Scheppele, Kim Lane 225–26, 228–29, 232
Second World War 11–12, 154–55, 157
Sejm (Parliament)
    Constitutional Tribunal and 42–43
    election of judges 62, 63–64, 75, 100–1, 102
    institutional fragility 186
    legislative fast-tracking 133–34
    opposition parties 132–35, 254
    parliamentary question time 134–35
    post-communist transformations 1989–2015 35
        Constitution of 1997 44–46,
            47–48, 50, 52–53
        Round Table (RT) agreements 37–39
        'Small Constitution' 39–40, 41, 47–48
    removal of judges 73–74
Self-Defence party (*Samoobrona*) 2–3, 24, 50–51
semi-presidentialism 38, 42, 45–46, 47–48, 179, 242
Senate 37, 133–34, 179
    post-communist transformations 1989–2015
        37–40, 45–46, 50, 52–53
    senators sitting on the KRS 100–1
separation of powers 41, 49–50, 82
'sham constitutions' 19
Singapore 5
single-issue protests 9
Skąpska, Grażyna 17
SLD (Democratic Left Alliance) 43–44, 50–51
Ślebzak, Krzysztof 62, 65
Slovakia 24
'Small Constitution' 36, 39–42, 47–48
Smoleńsk air crash 82, 151–52, 164–66
    aftermath and ECtHR ruling 197–99
Snyder, Timothy 165–66, 174–75
social cohesion 168
social media 267–68
social protest movements 267–68
social psyche 177–78 (*see also* historical policy)
social security systems 211, 212
socio-economic rights 48–49, 53
Sojusz Lewicy Demokratycznej (Democratic Left
    Alliance) 43–44, 50–51

Solidarność 36–37, 38, 39, 40–41, 44–45
Solska and Rybicka v Poland (ECtHR) 197–99
sovereignty 12
Sowul, Jacek 117–18
Spain 24–25
spoils and patronage 138, 270
Stanley, Ben 24, 268–69
state administration 136–38
stealth authoritarianism 7–8
Stepan, Alfred 244
Strauss, David 184
Strzembosz, Adam 102
Styrna, Paweł 103
Suchocka, Hanna 49–50
Sunstein, Cass 246
Supreme Administrative Court (SAC) 35, 105
Supreme Court
   Disciplinary Chamber 112–13, 259
   election of chief justice 81–82
   Extraordinary Review and Public Affairs
      Chamber 112–13, 139, 259
   lay judges 113
   PiS 'reform': Law on the Supreme Court
      106–15
   preliminary reference 211–13
   Venice Commission Opinion on 193, 196
surveillance 82–84, 195
Svolik, Milan 178–79
systemic infringement actions 228–30
Szarek, Jarosław 155–56
Szydło, Beata 76–77, 78, 98, 122–23, 135, 174,
      221–22
Szyszko, Jan 209

Tanchev, Evgeni 204–5
Terlecki, Ryszard 135
Themis 113
Timmermans, Frans 218–19
Tóth, Gábor Attila 6–7
transitional democracies 86–88, 180
Trump, Donald 8–9, 11–12, 173, 181, 182, 185
trust 8–10
Tuleja, Piotr 67
Tuleya, Igor 119–20
Tuori, Kaarlo 228–30, 231
Turkey vii, 180–81
Tushnet, Mark 5, 15–16, 257, 260–61
Tusk, Donald 164, 174–75, 176–77
TV Trwam 138

Uitz, Renata 28, 250
Unia Pracy (Labour Union) 49

United Nations 192
unwritten norms 253–61
UP (Labour Union) 49
Urbinati, Nadia 246
US Congress 186
UW (Freedom Union) 49, 50–51

vacatio legis 72–73
van Ballegooij, Wouter 205
Varol, Ozan 7
Venezuela 178–79
Venice Commission (VC) v, 72–73, 75, 100–2,
      158, 192–96, 213, 230–31
Vermeule, Adrian 182
Versteeg, Mila 19
veto points 179
vetoes *see* presidential vetoes
von Bogdandy, Armin 214, 229, 231
vote maximization 25
voting rights 140–43, 159

Wade, Benjamin 256–57
Waldner, David 28–29, 166, 167
Waldron, Jeremy 180
Wałęsa, Lech 38, 39, 40–41, 45–46, 267–68
Warchoł, Michał vi
Warciński, Michał 75
Waszczykowski, Witold 11
Watergate scandal 181
Way, Lucan 162
welfare policies 20, 25, 175–76
White Paper (Polish government) 226
Wilders, Geert 167–68
Winczorek, Piotr 53–54
Women's Rights Centre 145
Wronkowska-Jaśkiewicz, Sławomira 68–69
Wyrembak, Jarosław 68–69, 75
Wyrzykowski, Mirosław 16–17, 42, 45, 74–75, 77

xenophobia 10, 150, 168, 170, 173, 175

Zabłocki, Stanisław 107
Zajadło, Jerzy 172–73
Zakaria, Fareed 13, 247
Zakrzewska, Janina 43
Ziblatt, Daniel 260–62
Zielonacki, Andrzej 75
Ziobro, Zbigniew 51–52, 67, 103, 104, 105, 111–12,
      116, 117–18, 119, 124–25, 126
Zoll, Andrzej 102
Zubik, Marek 67
Żurek, Waldemar 117–19